UNQUIET

THE LIFE & TIMES OF
MAKHAN SINGH

UNQUIET

THE LIFE & TIMES OF
MAKHAN SINGH

ZARINA PATEL

ZAND GRAPHICS
NAIROBI

ISBN 9966-7123-0-5

Printed and bound in Kenya by
Colourprint Ltd., Nairobi

PUBLISHER
Zand Graphics Ltd.
PO Box 32843 00600, Nairobi, Kenya

CONCEPT, DESIGN & LAYOUT
Lakhvir Singh
www.scorpiusink.com

Contents

FOREWORD

Makhan Singh is among a select pantheon of Indian settlers who not only made Africa home but also became leading anti-colonial freedom fighters. But what distinguished Singh from many legendary leaders – including even the great Mahatma Gandhi – was the conscious multiracialism of his politics. He refused to accept a trade union movement segregated by race and poisoned by the colonial apartheid that classified black Africans and Asians in a humiliating hierarchy. He demonstrated for the first time in colonized Kenya that Asians and black Africans were bound in the same fate and that their liberation was inextricably linked. In this powerful example, he properly argued that both colonialism and imperialism were the enemies of the people. That is why Singh's enduring legacy to Kenya must continue to be the basis for construction of a society free of exploitation and racial animus.

Singh's political work in the trade union movement was a response to the repressive colonial state generally, and the labor law regime in particular. Under the colonial state – and its post-colonial successor – Kenya was imprisoned in labor laws that were designed to cheapen and exploit so-called native labor. This was the trend worldwide in the relationship between labor and capital. No wonder workers have been at the forefront of the human rights struggle over the centuries. This epic biography of Singh demonstrates how the struggle for the rights of workers was planted in Kenya. In it, Zarina Patel, an indefatigable Kenyan freedom fighter herself, has comprehensively analyzed how Singh created the building blocks and pillars of the trade union movement in Kenya.

The life of Makhan Singh is an object lesson on how class formation developed in Kenya. It is a powerful example of worker solidarity based on both racial and class-consciousness. Even though Asians were economically stratified, the colonial state still considered them a single class. Realizing that the trade union by 1937 was still an exclusive Asian affair, Singh set out to involve African workers in the labor movement. The African workers had organized isolated strikes in the past but Singh managed to convince them that a united non-racial approach was essential if the workers were to succeed in their demands. Class-consciousness was crucial in galvanizing and consolidating the struggle by labor against capital. In fact, Singh made trade unions so formidable that the colonial administration devised ways to undermine and curtail their influence and power. For example, Ordinance No. 35 of 1939 required that all craft organizations apply for registration that could be denied unless their dealings were considered "legitimate" by the state. Cancellation of registration under the ordinance was not subject to judicial review or appeal in a court of law.

Singh led workers to assert their right to strike, a key achievement in the struggle for labor and human rights. By organizing and mobilizing workers to strike, Singh not only ensured the implementation of a cardinal right but also legitimized the right of workers to withdraw their labor as a bargaining tool. This effort contributed to ensuring full and universal respect for trade union rights in their broadest sense. This struggle and legacy reaffirmed that strike action is the most important and fundamental tool that the workers have against capital. Even so, the rigid control of trade unions that was maintained by the colonial government persists to this day. Industrial confrontation arose not merely from traditional trade union activities, but also from the movement's political role in the struggle for freedom from colonial domination, particularly after individual political leaders had been arrested and detained. This notwithstanding, the movement was able to grow both in numerical strength and power. That is how workers became the lone African voice in the colonial wilderness, challenging white supremacy, demanding independence, and defending the interests of the workers.

The legacy of Makhan Singh points to the centrality of trade unions as one of the major epicenters of democracy. Singh wanted workers to get organized on both practical and strategic issues. The practical issues varied from housing, wages, working conditions, health, and safety, among others. Strategically, he was conscious of the fact that colonialism and crude capitalism were the key foundations for the privation of workers. That is why in 1950, Singh proposed a resolution urging complete independence and sovereignty of the East African territories as the only viable solution to suffering of the people. This biography challenges the trade unions in Kenya today. It reminds workers that they must control and be central to the trade union movement if it is to succeed. Indeed one of the major problems in the trade union movement today is the chasm between the leadership of the trade union movement and the workers. Most unions are lead by individuals and oligarchic groups which do not share the interests or the vision of the workers. This augurs very poorly for the future of democracy in Kenya. Kenyan workers must overthrow bumbling, corrupt, and compromised leaders if the legacy of Singh is to be kept alive.

Finally, we would like to congratulate Zarina Patel for her illuminating work on this towering Kenyan patriot. We know that writing a good book is a daunting task. But we believe that Patel has risen to this enormous challenge and written an account for the ages. This wonderful account also reminds us why it is critically important for Asians and Africans to tell their own stories. This is a book that every Kenyan – and particularly those still in school – must read.

MR. STEVE OUMA
DEPUTY EXECUTIVE DIRECTOR
Kenya Human Rights Commission

PROFESSOR MAKAU MUTUA
STATE UNIVERSITY OF NEW YORK
BUFFALO LAW SCHOOL
Chair, Kenya Human Rights Commission

January 2006

PREFACE

I was aware of Makhan Singh's reputation as a renowned Kenyan patriot and as a founding father of trade unionism in our country but, residing as I did in Mombasa, I had unfortunately never made the necessary effort to go to Nairobi to meet him. And then in May 1973, came the news of his death. As so often happens, I dearly wished I had made that effort.

I had then just moved to Nairobi to set up a community and race relations project within the National Christian Council of Kenya. Together with Rasik Shah, an advocate, we interviewed Makhan Singh's family and wrote an obituary which appeared in the *Sunday Post* on 3rd June, 1973.

A decade later, I embarked on a project of portraying events in Kenyan history in the form of social art. My first oil painting depicted

the exploitation of women's labour; the subject of the second one was Makhan Singh leading a demonstration of workers under the banner of the 'Labour Trade Union of East Africa'. It was based on an actual photograph taken of the event on 25th May, 1937. I placed it within the context of the anti-colonial struggle being waged at the time. I also produced a poster with drawings and writings about the early Kenyan South Asian patriots. The writing was in Kiswahili, with a view to communicating this history to ordinary Kenyans. Makhan Singh featured as one of the *wazalendo* (patriots) and I talked with his widow, Satwant Kaur, in the family home in Park Road, Nairobi, to get the story.

A decade later, the saga of the attempted land-grabbing of the Jeevanjee Gardens in Nairobi catapulted me into researching and writing about Alibhai Mulla Jeevanjee, my maternal grandfather. What was envisaged as a booklet grew into a 290-page book and involved research in three different continents. In the process I discovered the tremendous impact that the South Asians had made in Kenya's history in the colonial period. One name stood out conspicuously, that was the name of Makhan Singh.

I began to speak with political leaders, trade unionists, journalists and others who had known Makhan Singh in one capacity or another. I interviewed his sons, Hindpal Singh and Swarajpal Singh Jabbal. The history of the trade union movement in colonial Kenya, and Makhan Singh's involvement in it, is well documented in the two books authored by him. I wanted to learn more – about his childhood in India, his life outside his concerns in the labour movement, the evolution of his ideology, his experiences while in detention both in India and in Kenya and the circumstances of his 'retirement' after his release in 1961.

I searched in vain. Most of those who had known him admired him greatly, but even his closest associates, including family members, could not offer much more information than what was already generally known. Makhan Singh was an intensely private person and, added to this, was his incredible humility and the discipline of his ideological persuasion. He never wrote about himself unless it had a direct bearing on some national or social event, and he is not known to have ever expressed, or confided to anyone, his innermost thoughts or feelings. Makhan Singh's entire adult life was devoted solely to developing the trade union movement in Kenya within the context of anti-imperialism.

I began to consider abandoning the project but, as a last resort, consulted a labour historian based at the University of Nairobi. It was Dr George Gona who directed me to the Makhan Singh collection in the university's archives. There I found 25 large boxes of meticulously documented material, chronologically arranged dating back to 1927. It ranged from correspondence, poetry, press cuttings, statements, election campaign posters, photographs, membership and invitation cards and reams and reams of Makhan Singh's own handwritten notes. I did not need to look any further. Makhan Singh had collected and secured for posterity an 'autobiography' of his life in the expectation that future historians would someday make it available for general reading.

I feel privileged and fortunate to be one of those historians. I am deeply indebted to Dr Gona for enabling me to write this book. That someone like him, a scholar of organised labour, should have played such a crucial role in the writing of Makhan Singh's biography is, I think, very appropriate.

The collection was by no means the end of the road – it opened up many pathways leading to different directions. Makhan Singh's poetry and writings of his high school days in Nairobi, and soon after, had many references to the history of the Indian subcontinent and were almost entirely in Punjabi, in the Gurumukhi script. The poet, Mehram Yaar, then a resident of Kenya, was actively involved in the Communist Party in the Punjab both before and after the attainment of independence in India and Pakistan. As he translated the writings of Makhan Singh, he opened up for me a world of peasant-and worker-led revolution and nationalist fervour. I knew then that I had to visit India to experience the region where Makhan Singh grew up.

I travelled to India in May 2003 and even the searing summer heat could not contain my excitement. Makhan Singh's birthplace, the village of Gharjak in Gujranwalla district is now, across from India's northern border, in Pakistan which I was unable to visit. But I travelled in the Punjab countryside and spent time in Delhi, Jalhandar and Amritsar.

The gallery of the Golden Temple in Amritsar was an inspiring lesson in noble ideals, and the militant defence of them, in Sikh history. Adjoining the temple was the Jalianwala Bagh or Garden where, in 1918, when Makhan Singh was five years old, hundreds of

Punjabis were massacred by a British army regiment. In Jalhandar I met Jagjit Singh Anand, the editor of a Punjabi newspaper printed in the Gurumukhi script. He had been a co-editor with Makhan Singh in the 1940s when they published *Jang-e-azadi*, the organ of the Communist Party of India. He told me how, a few years previous to that time, a handwritten manuscript had landed on his editorial desk. It was a translation into Punjabi of 'Historical and Dialectical Materialism' from *Das Kapital*. He was struck by the competence of the translation, the ideological understanding and the beautiful hand-writing and immediately looked for the author. That is how he had first met Makhan Singh.

In Jalhandar I spent time at the Desh Bhagat Yaadgar – a complex built and maintained by the followers of the Ghadr Party. This party was established in 1913 in San Francisco, USA, by immigrants from India and had branches all over the world. Its most active militants were based in the Punjab. The majority of the Ghadrites joined the Communist Party of India in the 1950s and a group of them, known fondly as 'Babas,' developed the complex in Jalhandar. Bilga Singh, who is in his nineties, is chairman of Desh Bhagat Yadgaar. The complex consists of a hall, offices, a well-stocked library and a gallery of portraits. I met Ghadrites who had known and worked with Makhan Singh. The library had a short biography of him but it was the gallery which fascinated me most. It had over 200 large-sized portrait paintings of the Ghadrites, men and women, who had fought against the British colonialists in India. The display included five Ghadrites who had lived and worked in Kenya. Many of these guerrillas had been trained internationally and served in different countries. At least a dozen of them had been based in Kenya, others had passed through it on their way between India and the then Soviet Union. Some of these Ghadrites, I was to discover later, had worked with Makhan Singh to build the trade union movement in Kenya.

Just north-east of Jalhandar was the village of Khatkarh Kala (changed to Shaheed Bhagat Singh Nagar in 2005), the birthplace of Bhagat Singh who was executed by the British in 1931, at the age of 24 years. Makhan Singh seems to have shaped his revolutionary path on that taken by this freedom fighter and was in fact nick-named 'Bhagat Singh' in his home village. Bhagat Singh was a political activist with a socialist ideology, committed to the liberation of the poor, Hindu-Muslim unity and the establishment of a just and democratic society. He demanded total independence for India when the Indian National Congress was still negotiating for dominion status and when he was jailed, he remonstrated with his father for pleading with the British authorities for his release. These events were mirrored in Makhan Singh's life.

In Jalhandar and Delhi I visited the offices of the Communist Party (Marxist Leninist) of India. Harkishan Surjeet, the General Secretary of the party was imprisoned in the 1940s and briefly shared a cell with Makhan Singh. Repeated efforts, made then and later, to interview Surjeet have not been successful. Over ninety years old, at the time of this writing, he was leading his party as a member of India's ruling coalition government. The visit to India gave me a tangible insight into Makhan Singh's childhood and the background to his philosophical growth and also further confirmed to me the integral role that had been played by the Indian sub-continent in Kenya's anti-colonial struggle.

Back in Kenya, Mehram Yaar put me in touch with Amarjit Chandan, son of Gopal Singh Chandan to whom Makhan Singh had entrusted the Labour Trade Union when he sailed to India in 1939. Gopal Singh died in 1969 in India, Amarjit lives in the UK. Himself once a member of the Naxalite movement in independent India, Amarjit has been a wealth of information regarding the Ghadrites in Kenya and in Jalhandar, as well as regarding other colleagues of Makhan Singh.

With all this additional information I began documenting the life history of Makhan Singh. My primary concern was to present his story as he himself had so painstakingly assembled it over the years. Hence, the book is based on the Makhan Singh private collection in the University of Nairobi archives and references to it can be made easily as the papers are arranged chronologically and according to subject. It did become necessary to add background information or supportive details; much of this is extracted from Makhan Singh's two books on the history of trade unionism in Kenya. Additional references are documented in the endnotes and the bibliography. Chapters 1, 3 and 10 give brief overviews of the socio-political dynamics of the relevant periods in Kenya and India.

I would like to state here my own particular bias as a Kenyan South Asian who, while appreciating the many positive contributions of colonialism, is firmly opposed to all forms of imperialism and neo-colonialism. I do believe that the struggle which Makhan Singh and his comrades waged for freedom for the majority of the world's peoples and a better world, continues. I offer this book in the hope that these role models will inspire today's freedom fighters and enhance their understanding of the significance of patriotism and commitment as well as of ethical and principled struggle. A luta continua!

ZARINA PATEL,
March 2006

WAESIA MASHUJAA — WAZALENDO WA KENYA

ACKNOWLEDGEMENTS

My first and foremost acknowledgement is to Makhan Singh himself. The research and writing for this biography took place at a not-so-easy period in my own life as illness and new responsibilities impinged on my writing space. However as I continued to delve into Makhan Singh's life I was constantly strengthened and inspired by his indomitable spirit, his commitment and his ability to cope with all odds.

To the Ford Foundation I am deeply indepted for their support, both financial and moral. Dr Tade Aina and Dr Willy Mutunga have been trusted friends of my work and a pillar of support. I thank them for helping to facilitate a great part of the research and publication of this book. The Kenya Human Rights Commission agreed to part sponsor the book, I felt this to be most appropriate knowing the Commission's special interest in the labour movement and I'm grateful for it's support. Hindpal Singh Jabbal, oldest son of Makhan Singh, has not only been a munificent source of information but has also provided financial support in the publication of the book. I am indeed privileged to have this close connection to Makhan Singh as a friend.

To my editor and friend, Cynthia Salvadori, I once again owe a debt of gratitude for her meticulous corrections and suggestions and for her prompt responses whether from Ethiopia, the USA or in Kenya itself.

Dr George Gona, Lecturer in History at the University of Nairobi, led me to the Makhan Singh Papers in the University of Nairobi archives and in doing so introduced me to a treasure of information. He has continued to take a keen interest in my writing as it progressed and his insistence on elucidation has brought me to a better understanding on several issues.

Most of the writings of the earlier period in Makhan Singh's papers are in the Punjabi language and in Gurumukhi script. The late Mehram Yaar spent many hours with me translating them and in the process put me in touch with the revolutionary history of the Punjab. Having been a political activist himself, I got a frontal view of the unfolding scenes. Being a poet himself, I could not have found a more apt translator for Makhan Singh's poetry.

Amarjit Chandan, whom I have never met but with whom I have corresponded at length, is based in the UK. He made known to me the names and histories of the persons, especially of Sikhs, who had interacted with Makhan Singh and helped him to set up the trade union movement. As many of them belonged to the revolutionary Ghadr Party Makhan Singh, in order to protect them, did not disclose their true identities in his writings. Amarjit's own father, Gopal Singh Chandan, was vice-president of the Labour Trade Union of East Africa and a Ghadarite. This information helped me to piece together Makhan Singh's early years in Kenya and the beginnings of the Labour Trade Union.

Terry Hirst, Abdulquadir Nassir, Francis Atwoli, Secretary-General of the Central Organisation of Trade Unions and his team which included his assistant, Rajab Omondi, the veteran trade unionist Maina Macharia and the staff of Desh Bhagat Yadgar in Jalhandar, are among those who assisted me with their advice and guidance. The encouragement, support and technical help given to me by my comrade, Zahid Rajan, and the joy I derive from one of my added responsibilities, our son Raahat, are all interwoven into this biography.

PHOTOGRAPHS
& ILLUSTRATIONS

❋xxiii❋

CHAPTER ONE

COLONIAL INDIA
(THE RAJ)

Makhan Singh grew up in the era when India was still 'the jewel in the Crown.' In the 1600s, Britain's East India Company had begun to establish trading posts and settlements on Indian soil. The company faced competition from the Portuguese and the French who were similarly establishing themselves on the eastern and western sea boards of India, and also encountered resistance from local rulers and communities. The resistance was especially intense from the great Mughal Empire, which ruled over most of northern India. Nevertheless, by the mid-eighteenth century, the British were able to create a powerful army consisting of Indian soldiers officered by Englishmen. Using the vast resources of the country, they embarked on a series of wars and were able to consolidate their territorial expansion. By the mid-nineteenth century they had conquered the whole of India. Although Queen Victoria passed away in 1901, the British were still in firm control, albeit facing an increasingly restless population.

In 1913, the year of Makhan Singh's birth, the struggle for independence was advancing in India. British colonialism, while introducing the technological and sociological advances of a capitalist society, did not give much thought to the rights of the colonised people, much less to their welfare and future. But the people were not dormant; they rose in their different capacities to oppose the oppression and injustice to which they were being subjected. From their midst, in Asia, Africa and elsewhere, arose leaders who understood the concepts of democracy and civil liberty; they had been inspired by the earlier French and English revolutions as well as by the teachings of Marx and Lenin and developments in the Soviet Union.

These brilliant intellectuals were able to mobilise the creative genius and energies of the people into mass nationalist movements. In India, the precursor to the liberation movement was the Mutiny of 1857. The revolt of the soldiers soon spread into a revolutionary war that cut across northern India. It was strengthened by Hindu-Muslim unity and was supported by the civilian population. However outmoded Indian customs, traditions and institutions of the time were obstacles to success. The heroes of the revolt nevertheless became a source of inspiration to the country. Although the rebels were defeated, it was the first great struggle of the Indian people for freedom from British imperialism and paved the way for the rise of a modern national movement, led by Lokmanya Tilak, Mahatma Gandhi and Jawaharlal Nehru.

THE SIKHS

Some of the fiercest resistance to British rule was centred in the Punjab where Sikh warriors had a centuries-long history of militant confrontation, first with the Mughals and then with the British. The term *sikh* means 'disciple'. Sikhs are followers of Guru Nanak who had been born in the Punjab in 1469, in a village close to Makhan Singh's birthplace. At that time the followers of the Hindu Maharajas and the Muslim Mughal emperors lived in close proximity in northern and central India. Guru Nanak founded a new religion, started a new pattern of living and an agrarian movement. He reconciled the noblest aspects of the Hindu and Muslim faiths, preaching unity, equality

Guru Nanak, founder of the Sikh faith

and simplicity, discouraging ritualism, idol-worship and casteism. He preached both the oneness of God and the oneness of humanity – the name *Nanak* means 'in whom duality is not'. The Sikh greeting is *Sat Sri Akaal*, Immortal is God.

Guru Nanak died in 1539 and was followed by nine gurus, the last of whom was Guru Gobind Singh who organised the spiritually awakened society into a socio-political unit and transformed it into a militant force. Arnold Toynbee, the 20th century historian, has stated that Guru Gobind Singh had predated Lenin by two centuries. He baptised his followers *khalsa*, meaning pure, and said 'From now on you are casteless; you must abandon all rituals and superstitions, Hindu or Muslim, and believe in one God. The lowest rank will be equal to the highest, and women to men, in every way.' He decreed that all Sikh males should be called *singh* (lion), an appellation taken from the Rajput Hindus. Some Sikhs added the term *sardar* (chief). For the women he chose *kaur*, a typically Punjabi word meaning prince. He chose the masculine gender term deliberately as he wanted to give women the dignity of men.

To the Rajput traditions of wearing a beard (*kesh*) and turban and carrying a dagger (*kirpan*), he added a comb (*kangha*), knee-length cotton drawers (*kaccha*) and steel bracelet (*kara*). These came to be known as the 5 Ks. He emphasised the importance of community service and communal kitchens. To counter caste consciousness and inter-religious (in this case Hindu-Muslim) hostility, to practise equality, the Sikhs require that people eat together and so their communal dining halls and rest rooms are open to everyone regardless of caste, race, religion or gender. In Kenya the Sikh temple at Makindu is a popular stop for those journeying on the road between Nairobi and Mombasa with its glittering white dome and yellow flag with three swords a welcoming sight, it is open to weary travellers of any race or religion.

While Guru Gobind Singh clarified that the *deg* (kitchen) was as important as the *teg* (sword), he also declared that 'When no other remedy is of any avail, it is but righteous to

Gurdwara Makindu Sahib, one of the landmark temples of the Sikhs in Kenya

unsheathe the sword' and urged magnanimity in victory and defiance in defeat.

Ranjit Singh, a great warrior, took the sword to new heights when he conquered and consolidated the state of Punjab for the Sikhs. He was born in 1780 in Gujranwalla, the town where Makhan Singh, several centuries later, went for his schooling. Ranjit Singh captured Lahore and became Maharajah of the Punjab. The Sikhs fought valiantly against both the Mughals and the British and the sword became predominant. This shift led to the decline of Sikhism as a social and political force. Religious principles gave way to meaningless rituals; the *Guru Granth Sahib* (Holy Book) was worshipped as an idol and not studied for its philosophy, while the Sikhs themselves became divided into upper and lower castes.

These reactionary tendencies further galvanised the progressive movements and in 1885, Indian nationalists formed the Indian National Congress to spearhead the freedom movement. Mainstream nationalists tended to support the British in the mistaken belief that a grateful Britain would reward India by granting it greater autonomy. The revolutionaries, however, charted their own course.

THE GHADR PARTY

At the turn of the nineteenth century, driven by the harsh economic conditions in their home province, some Sikh peasants and soldiers migrated to North America and settled in California and British Columbia. But by 1906 they faced a wave of anti-Indian racism in their new home. The following poem, which appeared in a Canadian newspaper, describes it well:

> We welcome as brothers all white men still
> But the shifty yellow race
> Whose word is vain, who oppress the weak
> Must find another place.[1]

The North American *gurdwaras* (Sikh temples) became centres of political activity and in San Francisco in 1913 the Sikhs, together with some educated Hindus and Muslims, formed the *Ghadr* (Revolutionary) Party, the main aim of which was the overthrow of British rule in India through armed revolution. The party published a weekly journal called *Ghadr*; one of its issues proclaimed:

> No pundits or mullahs do we need
> No prayers or litanies we need recite
> These will only scuttle our boat
> Draw the sword; 'tis time to fight'.[2]

The Ghadr Party established branches in India, China, Hongkong, Singapore, Iran, Thailand, the Phillipines, Borneo and Japan, and had propaganda centres in Britain, France and Germany. The *Ghadr* was distributed widely, with readers in South America and the West Indies as well as in East and South Africa.

By 1914 the Ghadr Party had 10,000 active members and was cooperating with the Germans. When World War I broke out large numbers of Ghadrites from various countries returned to India to launch an uprising. The rebellion, however, was crushed and the leaders arrested. Hangings and imprisonment for life were punishments meted out on a mass scale, especially in the Punjab. In British East Africa the Ghadrites were charged with sedition – 3 were shot, 2 hanged, 8 imprisoned and about twenty were deported to India.

The Ghadrites' leader in British East Africa was Sita Ram Acharia who was employed as a telegrapher on the Uganda Railway and served in the military branch of the East African Pay Corps at the beginning of World War I.[3] He was deported to India late in 1915. One of the group was a Punjabi named Lal Chand Jawahir Ram who worked as a fuel contractor in Voi. He was convicted of conspiring to dynamite the Uganda Railway, and was sentenced to death. The sentence was subsequently commuted to ten years' imprisonment with rigorous labour; he was released about March, 1919, and sent back to India. He returned to Nairobi in August, 1921, settled there and worked for a firm of lawyers, Stevens and Kindall. He was described as 'politically minded' by the authorities in Nairobi.[4]

Another of the group was Tirath Ram Bali, also a Punjabi. Employed by the Uganda Railway, he was twice dismissed for seditious utterances. He regularly received the *Ghadr* from the USA and was a distributing agent for such literature. In July, 1914, he was involved in a strike by railway and public works department workers against the introduction of the poll tax and poor working conditions and was deported to India in February, 1915, and interned there. Two other leaders of the strike, L W Ritch and Mehrchand Puri were also deported. Tirath Ram's brother, Ganesh Das, worked as a fuel contractor in Voi and was executed for treason in November, 1915. Tirath Ram returned to Kenya in 1926 but was prosecuted for being a prohibited emigrant, imprisoned for two months and then sent back to India. He sailed from Mombasa on the S S Karapara on 29th December, 1926. In 1932, he was imprisoned in India for his political activities[5]. L M Savle and Keshavlal Dwivedi, who with A M Jeevanjee founded the East African Indian[6] National Congress (EAINC), were accused of being Ghadrites.

After the War the Ghadr Party moved from nationalism to communism. Punjabis were attracted to the ideology, minus its atheism, as it shared ideals with Sikhism, namely humanitarianism, equality and freedom. A group of Ghadrites in the United States and Canada, with the support of two Americans, Agnes Smedley and Jack London, travelled to Moscow to meet Lenin and study Marxism. Several of them passed through Kenya. (A more detailed account is given below). They later linked up with the Ghadrites who were being released from jail in India and started a paper there which they called *Kirti* (Worker). In 1926, the Ghadr Party itself was renamed Kirti Kisan Sabha (Party of Workers and Peasants). Teja Singh Sutantra was its leader and at one time he passed through Kenya.

In 1915, hundreds of Ghadrites were hung in the Lahore central jail, others were imprisoned for life, exiled or had their property confiscated. This large-scale purge and the increased injustice and lawlessness of the British at the end of the war resulted in widespread disillusionment amongst the Indian populace. That same year, Mahatma Gandhi had returned from South Africa and taken command of the nationalist movement. He had developed a new method of struggle, *satyagraha*, a form of passive resistance based on the principles of truth and non-violence. Hence, he did not subscribe to the ideals of the Ghadrites.

On 30th March, 1919, Gandhi declared satyagraha and a

complete *hartal* (suspension of business) in Amritsar, the holy city of the Sikhs. On 13th April, the anniversary of the founding of the Khalsa, a large crowd from far and wide assembled in the holy city as they did every year. A large section of fifteen to twenty thousand unarmed people including women and children gathered to celebrate the occasion in an enclosed wasteland called Jallianwala Bagh, next to the Golden Temple. In keeping with the mass agitation prevalent in the city, the essentially religious gathering included political protests.

The Jallianwala Bagh massacre, 1912

A British regiment armed with machine guns and led by General Dyer arrived. He had his troops block the only avenue of exit and fire on the crowd until all their ammunition was exhausted. 1,650 rounds were fired, 379 persons lay dead or dying and 1,500 wounded. A mighty wave against everything British swept the land and the demand for 'complete independence' was raised.

The Indian National Congress held its annual December session in Amritsar with Gandhi and Nehru leading it. The Congress now adopted Gandhi's plan for non-cooperation with the government and asked the Indian people to boycott the textiles being imported from Britain, and instead practise hand-spinning and hand-weaving. The great poet and humanist, Rabindranath Tagore, renounced the knighthood the British had conferred on him. The British tried and exonerated Dyer but many years later, in 1940, Udham Singh shot Sir Michael O'Dwyer dead in a London street. (O'Dwyer, as governor of the Punjab, had authorised the massacre at Jallianwala Bagh). Udham Singh was arrested, tried and hanged in London but, in 1976, the government of the Punjab brought his ashes to India and proclaimed him a national hero. Interestingly, Udham Singh had lived for some years in Nairobi and worked in Lockett Moore Co. as a fitter.[7]

THE COMMUNIST PARTY

Reformist movements accompanied the revolutionary upsurge. In the Punjab, in 1921, the Akali Movement arose to wrest control of the gurdwaras from the corrupt priesthood. Many of its members were Ghadrites; they cooperated with the Communists and politicised the entire Sikh community right down to its cultural roots; drawing it into the national struggle for freedom. In 1925, the Communist Party was launched in India, as well as the All-India Trades Union Congress. The relationship between the Kirtis (previously known as Ghadrites) and the Communist Party was a stormy one until 1941, when the Kirtis merged with the Communist Party. Teja Singh Sutantra was the chief negotiator of the merger.

The first quarter of the twentieth century was a period of

great ferment in India as revolutionary activity affected the whole structure of Indian society – political, social and religious. This was the environment of Makhan Singh's early childhood and the cultural legacy he inherited.

CHAPTER TWO
EARLY LIFE IN INDIA
1913-1927

Makhan Singh was born on 27th December, 1913, in a village called Gharjakh, in the district of Gujranwalla in the Punjab province of India. The Panj-ab, the 'land of five waters', lies geographically on the northern border of present-day India and has historically been the country's gateway. Greeks, Persians, Pathans, Arabs and Turks; invading races that brought with them their languages and customs, have passed through it. New religions, Buddhism, Jainism and Islam, were added to the Hindu Vedas.

The weather in the Punjab is extreme, going from bracing cold in the winter (November to January) to scorching heat in the summer (April to June). February is springtime, when the countryside blossoms into an expanse of yellow mustard flowers interspersed with solid squares of green sugar cane.

In the summer temperatures rise to fever heat, the parched earth becomes an unending stretch of khaki dust. Camels and bullocks turn the water wheels to irrigate the fields with water from the canals. There is hardly any greenery; the thorny acacia is the commonest tree of the Punjab. And then in July the monsoon descends in torrents. Two months of incessant downpour turn the land into a vast swamp. Frogs croak and peacocks cry with joy. The pied crested cuckoo takes advantage of the monsoon winds and flies from the East African coast to reach India a day or two before the monsoon breaks.

New leaves sprout on the trees and grass covers the barren ground. Mangoes ripen and rice, wheat, maize, barley and millet, indigo and tobacco, oil seeds and pulses of many kinds are sown. *Jaggery* (sugar) and flour mills churn away. October to early November is harvest time when *Diwali* – the Festival of Lamps – is celebrated. The peasants don their best, brightly coloured clothes and dance the spirited *bhangra* to the beat of the drum.

The Punjab is essentially a rural state made up of innumerable brick villages built on the ruins of older villages. Indian villages are not like those in Kenya. Here, a village consists of a shopping and administrative centre while the

Punjab State

homesteads are scattered on the land around it. In India, villagers live close together in a cluster of houses, shops and work places and vast fields and a network of irrigation canals surround this core. The land is privately owned, never communally. Though in each village some majority community is dominant, villagers of different classes, castes and religions co-exist and share many folk and religious practices.

The village of Gharjak is situated about a kilometre away from the district's main town, Gujranwalla – both places are now in Pakistan, the new country created when India got its independence from Britain in 1947. The villagers in Gharjakh at the time of our story were mainly Sikh.[1] The community in Gharjakh consisted of two main classes, the rich landowners (*zemindars*), on the one hand, and the workers and peasants on the other. It was further divided into castes based on occupations; jats did the farming, *kshatriyas* the trading and administration and *ramgharias* the skilled work. A group of elderly men elected by the villagers looked after the village welfare and helped to resolve disputes.

Gharjakh was a well-planned village. It had a wide main road, with several lanes crossing it. At one entrance, on the right, was a Hindu temple, on the left a primary school. Next to the school was a wheat mill owned by a Muslim called Malik. It was run with electricity that was available to the rich, mostly the zemindars. Farm workers were largely poor Muslims. They were almost a third of the population and lived in mud houses in a congested area near the temple and school. The Hindus and Sikhs had bigger and better houses. The jats and zemindars lived at end of road; in the centre were the ramgharia artisans and their small workshops. Class and caste separated the gurdwaras although there were no differences in religious practice.

In the village was a large hand-dug *talao* (pond) more than a

Village scene, Punjab

kilometre square. During the
monsoon when it filled with
water, the villagers used it to
wash their animals, their
clothes and utensils. In
summer it dried up and then
the villagers scooped out
mud from it to plaster their
houses.

Almost every family had
cows or buffaloes but
Makhan Singh's family had
none. They were the middle
level artisans in the village.
They lived near the edge of
the *talao* in a small double-
story brick dwelling that they

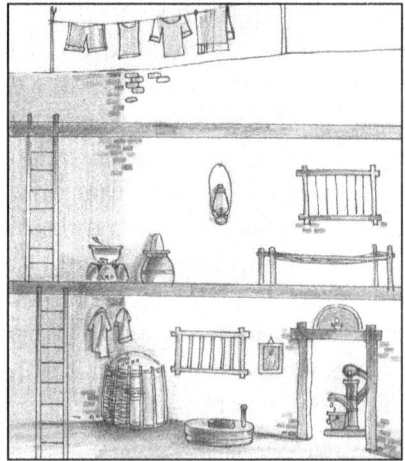

A sketch of the kind of home young Makhan Singh grew up in

had inherited from Makhan Singh's grandfather, Sant Singh
Jabbal. The surface of the ground floor was the bare earth
levelled down and it contained a borehole with a hand pump,
the water table being some 40 feet below the surface. A room
built for stacking hay held the carpentry tools; the grains were
stored in an adjoining room. A staircase led to the second floor
where there were two rooms, and a kitchen which opened out
on to a veranda where the family slept during the hot summer
months. There was, typically, no electricity and no furniture so
Makhan Singh studied by lamplight, seated on the mud floor.
Most of the houses, even those of the well-to-do, did not have
latrines, the custom being for villagers to relieve themselves in
the fields.[2]

Makhan Singh's family belonged to the ramgharia caste that
consists mainly of carpenters, masons and blacksmiths. The
Sikhs, who came to Kenya at the turn of the twentieth century
to work on the railway being built by the British, were mostly
ramgharias. Makhan Singh's ancestors were carpenters. His
father, Sudh Singh Jabbal, was a direct descendant of Baba

FAMILY TREE

```
Baba Sadhana,            Sant Singh Jabbal
Baba Buta,               (Mata Jinda)
Gurmukh Singh (1833)
(became Sikhs)           Sudh Singh
                         (Isher Kaur)

   Kulwant Kaur          Makhan Singh
   (Shivcharan Singh)    (Satwant Kaur)

   Gurdev Singh          Hindpal Singh Jabbal
   Trilochan             (Joginder Kaur)
   Surinder Kaur
   Amrit Kaur            Swarajpal Singh Jabbal
                         (Amarjeet Kaur)

                         Inderjeet Kaur
                         (Sardul Gill)
```

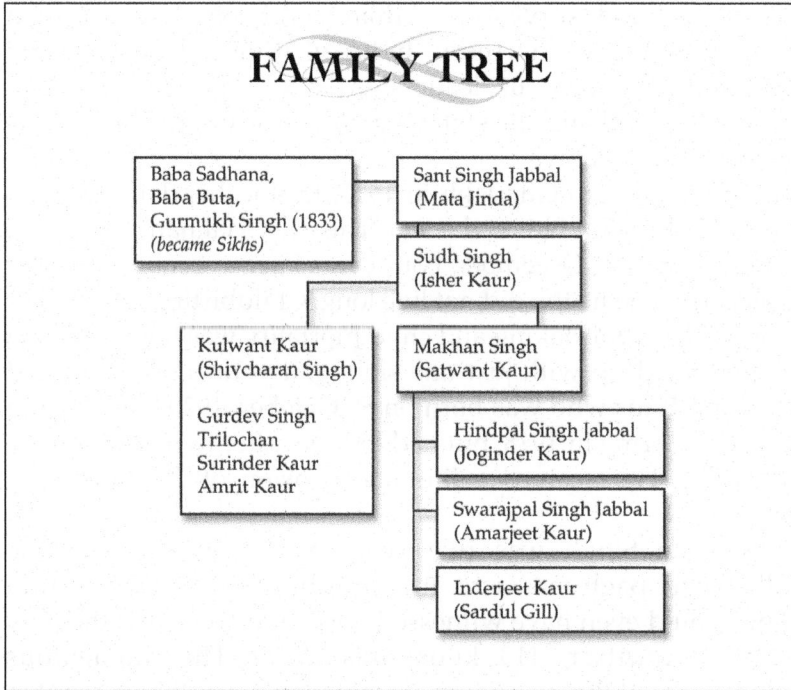

Family tree, Makhan Singh

Sidhana who had settled in Gharjakh in the early nineteenth century. His surname was Jabbal and his family occupation was carpentry. Sudh Singh was born in 1893; his father was Sant Singh and his mother, Mata Jinda.

In 1903, a deadly epidemic of plague swept through the region and in a period of five days, Sudh Singh lost his parents, his two brothers and his grandfather. At the tender age of ten he was left with no family. An uncle and aunt took care of Sudh Singh and his elder brother's widow, Isher Kaur, who was fifteen years old. Sudh Singh worked as a herd's boy and studied the Sikh religious texts, later on he learnt carpentry.

In 1909, breaking off an earlier engagement, he was married to Isher Kaur. A baby girl was born the following year. Soon after, Sudh Singh left home without informing anyone. He had no money and survived by doing odd jobs. He travelled through most of northern India visiting gurdwaras and meeting Sikh religious leaders. At one place he helped to publish a novel and the skill he gained was of great assistance to him later in Kenya.

He returned to Gharjakh in 1913, to find his daughter had died. But he soon fathered a son. This was Makhan Singh who was born on 27th December. Four years later a second daughter was born, but she too did not live long. Childbirth in those days was a risky undertaking and child mortality was high. Makhan Singh ended up with just one sibling, a younger sister called Kulwant Kaur who was born on 8th October, 1920. Sudh Singh joined the army in 1918, but had to leave after two years due to ill health. He received a life-time pension of 20 rupees per month.[3]

Makhan Singh was five years old at the time of the Jallianwala Bagh massacre. It is possible that his father, Sudh Singh could even have witnessed it as he often visited the holy city of Amritsar, 113 kilometres away. The momentous happenings of that period, as explained in the previous chapter, must have left a deep impression on the family and the young Makhan Singh. He grew up in a period of great social and political upheaval in a pluralistic religious and cultural setting. Too young to understand the whys and wherefores of this historical background, the religious inspiration and his first-hand experience of injustice undoubtedly were the building blocks of his later life, a life dedicated to the struggle for freedom and to the rights of the working class.

From 1920 to 1924 Makhan Singh attended the District Board Primary School in Gharjakh. He then joined Class V at the Khalsa High School in Gujranwala walking the two kilometres from and to his home daily. Little is known of his life as a young student but we do know that he attended school regularly and was a diligent learner.[4] One imagines that he preferred reading to playing *guli-danda* (a game using a stick and piece of wood). He dressed in tight *churidar* pyjamas and a long, buttoned up coat over a high-necked kurta and tied his hair in a turban.

His father was often away from home looking for work, or visiting the gurdwaras, so young Makhan Singh spent much of his time with his mother and sister. He had uncles whom he helped with the washing and feeding of their buffaloes. His mother was extremely protective of him, the only son.

The Jallianwala Bagh massacre affected Sudh Singh deeply and was for him a climax to the worsening colonial situation. Not surprisingly, a year later, he decided to leave the country. Even before Kulwant was born, Sudh Singh had sailed on the S S Toroba for East Africa.

Towards the end of the nineteenth century many Sikhs from the Punjab, mostly ramgharias, went to Kenya to work as artisans on the railway the British were constructing. The building of the Uganda Railway was completed in six years but some of the Sikhs stayed on and settled in Kenya. Some of these were relatives of Sudh Singh and it was only natural that in 1920, when he sought to escape from the misery of colonial India, he sailed westwards across the Indian Ocean to

Makhan Singh as a young student

East Africa. He settled in Nairobi where he signed a three-year contract as a carpenter for work on the Uganda Railway. His monthly salary was 55 rupees with a 50 rupee bonus, rations and travelling expenses both ways.

Sudh Singh was tall and well built with an erect posture and a long flowing beard. He was literate in Punjabi and could write in the Gurumukhi script. Deeply religious, he was well known in the Sikh community. Always dressed in traditional kurta and pyjama, he was very abstemious, never touched alcohol and lived frugally. Although he took no active part in any political movement he used to attend meetings in Nairobi addressed by speakers such as Manilal Desai, Shams-ud-Deen, B S Varma and Mohamed Hussain Malik, and Charles Andrews and Srinivasa Shastri from India. His lonely childhood and his many travails in India and East Africa had turned him into a stoic with an understanding and sympathy for those who had to struggle for survival.

Manilal Desai

Of course colonialism was little different in East Africa and soon Sudh Singh, together with his fellow artisans, who were all Indian, started to agitate for better wages and working conditions and formed the Railway Artisans Union. The founder members were Ujaggar Singh, Gurbux, Khuda Bux,

Kishan Singh, Bhagwan Singh, Mohamed Hussain, Gurbux Singh, Sher Mohamed, Kaiser Singh, Mehraj Din and Birdi Chand. Sudh Singh was its secretary and he was dismissed from the Railways in 1923, three months prior to the termination of his contract, when the authorities closed down the Union. Six of the artisans were deported to India.

The members being mostly Sikh relied on communal organising; they did not see class differences as one of the problems. They appealed to the EAINC whose members were largely of a higher class. Manilal Desai, its very dynamic secretary, did intervene but did not succeed in getting the deportation order rescinded[5]. The colonial government at this time was getting very nervous as it was faced by demands being made by the workers, by Harry Thuku's East Africa Association and by the EAINC.

After his dismissal, Sudh Singh went back to India and bought a plot of land in Chandigarh. Then he returned to Kenya in October 1924, and worked on various jobs including one with the army for the supply of wooden boxes for ammunition shells, another with the government's Supply and Transport Department in the Northern Frontier Province, and one with the Kilimanjaro Saw Mills in Tanganyika. In 1926, he decided to settle in Nairobi and got a job making furniture for the Hutchings Biemer furniture shop, at a salary of KShs 210 per month.

CHAPTER THREE
COLONIAL KENYA

The development of capitalism in Europe was made possible by a global division of labour whereby one part of the globe produced the resources to feed the industrial machines of the other. Africa was consigned to be the producer of the raw materials for the metropolis. By the 1870s, the inflow of information from explorers and missionaries and the opening of the Suez Canal in 1869 had begun to interest investors in Britain. The first step was a serious campaign to abolish the East African slave trade, established by the Arabs in the first half of the nineteenth century. Other major European powers were also surveying Africa and to minimise confrontation, the Berlin Conference of 1884-85 dissected the continent into spheres of influence, an exercise better known as the 'Scramble for Africa.' Britain's first official claim was made in 1890, when she declared a protectorate over Zanzibar.

British imperialism had spread its tentacles across the globe. Its conquests had enslaved nations in the continents of Asia, Australia and the Americas. In East Africa, as in India, it was a trading company, the Imperial British East Africa Company (IBEAC) that first established contact with the area that then came to be known as British East Africa.

The IBEAC overextended itself and hence, in 1895, the British Government intervened directly. British political hegemony was formalised by the declaration of the East African Protectorate and construction commenced on the building of the Uganda Railway extending from Mombasa to Kisumu with a ferry link to Entebbe. The goal was to penetrate, open and administer East Africa from the coast inland through to Uganda and thus also maintain control of the Suez Canal via the Nile waters and Egypt.

Indian artisans and labourers were recruited from India to build the railway. They came mainly from the Punjab and Gujerat provinces in the north-west of the subcontinent. Of the 37,747 indentured labourers imported from India about 7,000 remained behind by choice. Their immediate and extended families joined them. The British encouraged Indian immigration as they needed the Indians to develop the country, provide services for the administration and *dukas* (shops) for supplying the white settlers. In the early 1900s, many British government officials were seconded from India, laws and regulations were based on Indian statutes and even the currency was the Indian rupee.

Using their overwhelmingly superior military and administrative force the British used the Railway to effectively occupy the country and subdue its people. It totally transformed the economy of the region to serve the economic interests of the metropolis. Britain, France, Germany, Russia, Japan and the USA continued in their attempts to extend their control over different areas of the world. World War 1 was fought from 1914 to 1918 to redraw boundaries and give the victors a greater share of the land seized.

From the very beginning, the African people resisted and struggled against foreign rule and its consequences – land grabbing, forced labour, long working hours, compulsory registration for males (*kipande*), racial segregation and generally oppressive laws. Though occupying a higher status than Africans and Arabs in the colonial structure, Indians were nevertheless also discriminated against and suffered injustices in housing, trade, land ownership and services such as health and education. They too began to agitate for their rights.

The first trade union or workers' organisation in Kenya was formed by the Africans working for the C M S Mission at Frere Town near Mombasa for protecting and promoting their interests as employees of the mission. It was called the African Workers Council. Its members were freed slaves both young and old. In 1900, in the Railways, European subordinate staff initiated a strike and were joined by some Asian and African workers. Secret and informal workers' groups got organised on settler farms. These were the early beginnings of the trade union movement that Makhan Singh later developed.

In the same year Alibhai Mulla Jeevanjee and Allidina Visram founded the Indian Association in Mombasa and

Nairobi to assert Indian rights. In 1902, twenty-two European settlers got together to discourage Indian immigration and foster white settlement. This was the start of a long and bitter rivalry that was fuelled by an influx of near-illiterate white settlers from South Africa, the Boers. While in 1901 there were only thirteen European settlers in Kenya, during the next half-century, the number had increased to 29,660. European settlement and the alienation (or theft) of African lands grew rapidly.[1]

In 1914, A M Jeevanjee founded the East Africa Indian National Congress, the first political body organised on a national platform. In 1918, Harry Thuku, a Kikuyu, followed suit with his East Africa Association and worked closely with the Indian leaders. World War I was a turning point as the colonial office, with the aim of maximising the war effort, tipped the balance of power in favour of the settlers. The next few years were marked by tense confrontations between the white settlers and the colonial government on the one hand and the Indians on the other and came to be known as 'the Indian Question.'

The protectorate was renamed 'Kenya Colony' in 1920, and the following year the colonial government arrested and sent Harry Thuku to restriction in Kismayu.

The Devonshire Declaration of 1923 was another landmark as Britain declared that in Kenya, African interests were paramount. This was in response to the rising African protests, the severe economic crisis and the vexed Indian Question. The settlers were rushing headlong towards their goal of white supremacy but the colonial office had regained some of the control it had lost. Though the paramountcy clause did not translate into much meaningful benefit for the Africans, the declaration did put a stop to the creation of a settler-controlled state with dominion status, as in South Africa. Kenya had become a 'white man's paradise' with economic conditions of serfdom and physical conditions scarcely less than those of slavery.[2]

Thuku's East African Association was renamed the Kikuyu Central Association and African nationalist leaders accelerated mobilisation of the masses against the repressive colonial practices. On the other hand, the economic distress and their sidelining by the Devonshire Declaration had mitigated the political fervour of the Indians. They became polarised into religious and ideological camps – Hindu vs. Muslim vs. Sikh, and radicals vs. moderates.

In 1927, the year young Makhan Singh arrived in Kenya, two individuals of note had entered public life. One was Jomo Kenyatta (then Johnstone Kamau) who had been working in Nairobi municipality while secretly supporting the Kikuyu Central Association. In the same year, he officially became the secretary general of the Association and the editor of the newspaper, *Muigwithania*, (Liberator). The Kikuyu Central Association played a significant role as a political organisation and as a forum to articulate workers' grievances. By 1930 it had 10,000 members. The other person was Isher Dass, a fiery Marxist originally from the Punjab. He was brought to Kenya by A M Jeevanjee in 1928, ostensibly as his personal secretary but actually to replace the late Manilal Desai as secretary of the EAINC. Amongst the Indian community were many Sikhs from the Punjab, some were from Gujranwalla and Lahore and were known to Makhan Singh. A few of the Sikhs were Ghadrites who kept their ideological convictions a well-guarded secret.

CHAPTER FOUR

KENYA
1927-1939

In May 1927, Sudh Singh brought his wife and two children from India to live with him in Kenya. This meant interrupting Makhan Singh's schooling; he was in class seven at the time. But he was quickly admitted to a new school in Nairobi. Makhan Singh was fourteen years old. He was therefore at a very impressionable age when he started life in this new country, in a new colonial setting. His first home was in Nairobi's Mincing Lane, now Wakulima Lane. He was immediately enrolled in the Government Indian Senior Secondary School (later called the Duke of Gloucester School and now known as Jamhuri High School) to continue his education.

Duke of Gloucester School

The late Chief Justice Chunilal Madan was one of his classmates and in later years was to assist him with legal services.

Makhan Singh and I grew up together in school. We were pupils in the same class and we completed our secondary education in the Government Indian High school, now Jamhuri School, Ngara Road, Nairobi in the year 1931. In those days we both passed the Matriculation examination of University of London. I remember distinctly that while we were in school Makhan Singh had a magic brain and he used to leave most of his class mates behind in the subject of maths - arithmetic, geometry, algebra.[1]

The principal, J R Maxwell, was British, but the teachers were almost all Indian[2]. Makhan Singh, even at the age of fourteen, was already an unusually socially conscious young man. This is evident from his poetic writings, which he often recited at Sikh poetry readings at the time. Though he studied English and later communicated in it, all his poems are in Punjabi, written in the Gurumukhi script. The earliest poem he wrote after moving to Kenya is dated 27th November, 1928, and signed 'Makhan Singh Gharjakia'. It is a poem in praise of Guru Nanak and illustrates both Makhan Singh's awareness of his religious foundations and also his concern for justice, truth and suffering. A

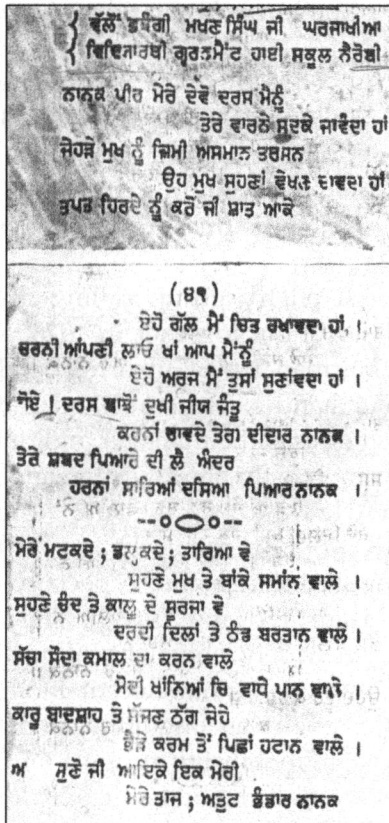

Original poem in Gurumukhi

translation of some of the stanzas reads:

Oh the shining star of my life's firmament
Oh you the beautiful and the sublime One
Oh you the moon of your mother
And the sun of your father Kalu[3]

You are the One who can bring solace
To the troubled hearts
Because you stand for Truth
Amid the sordid business of this world
You have shown the right way

Even to the most deceitful ones
Like Sajan Thug and Karu Badshah
Come and listen once to me
Oh the bountiful who holds the key
To all the treasures of the world.

A poetry group calling itself *Kaviya Phulwari* (Garden of Poetry) got together in 1928. Ragi Labh Singh was elected as chairman, Kavi Gursarn Singh Mit as secretary, Hermane Singh Parchand as treasurer and Kavi Prem Singh as master. Sudh Singh was the manager and publisher in the group. The poems were mostly hand-written and Makhan Singh participated.

He was by far the youngest member of the group. The poets would meet regularly and recite their compositions at various public places and especially at festivals such as Vaisakhi, Basant, Eid and Diwali. They would follow a literary norm, then widely prevalent, of writing on an agreed theme with a common refrain. Recent literary discussions tend to dismiss this poetry as 'one-dimensional patriotic' but it played a major role in mobilising support for the mass movements.[4]

Not all the Sikhs in Kenya shared a homogeneous view of social politics. At one time, the Kaviya Phulwari wrote a play titled *Mera Punjab* (My Punjab). Its theme was the caste system

Makhan Singh (standing left), Gopal Singh Chandan (third right), Vasudev Singh (seated first left)

and it was an expose of the prejudices inherent in the Sikh community. In it, a carpenter comes looking for a job and the employer tells his servant not to let him in because he cannot stand ramgharias. 'They have no culture, they don't know how to dress, and they are illiterate and inexperienced,' the employer asserts. The East African Ramgharia Board itself was a caste-centred institution and it was not surprising that the Ramgharia Committee stopped the play's production in December, 1930, terming it 'too controversial'.

At this time printing in the Gurumukhi script was done by the Ramgharia Press in Nairobi and Sudh Singh decided to try his hand at it too. In April, 1929, he started operating a printing press at home, under the name of 'Khalsa Press'.

He had only one room in which the whole family of four was living; he kept his boxes of printing material under the

	The Khalsa Printing Press,	*Printing done in:*
Bankers: THE STANDARD BANK of South Africa Ltd., Nairobi. *Tele:* "KHALSA PRESS"	*(Prop:-* S. S. GHARJAKHIA.*)* Printers, Book-binders & Rubber Stamp Makers.	ENGLISH, GUJARATI, GURUMUKHI, HINDI, URDU & SWAHILI,

Our *ref.* _____   RIVER ROAD,

Your *ref.* _____   P. O. Box 1183.

$\mathcal{N}airobi,$ _____ *193*

Letterhead of Khalsa Printing Press, which was founded by Sudh Singh in 1929

---

beds. In June, 1931, he acquired a shop in River Road and began printing in Gurumukhi, Gujerati, Urdu, Hindi, English and various African languages.

Makhan Singh now joined him and a year later they moved the press to more spacious premises in the Alibhai Shariff Building on Latema Road.[5]

Khalsa Press had a letterpress machine and used hand setting, whereby each letter was imposed manually. It printed invitation cards, letterheads and later even pamphlets. It was advertised in a magazine called *Phulwari* (Garden) using Gurumukhi script and published in the Punjab. In addition to booklets of Punjabi poetry, the press printed religious texts and other literature for the members of the Siri Guru Singh Sabha and the Bazaar Gurdwara, two Sikh temple associations. It printed a tribute to Lal Singh[6] who was an Akali fighter and most probably a Ghadrite too. And as we shall see later, the Sabha leadership acted as a front organisation for the Ghadrites.

To begin with there was not much of a demand for printing and it is said that Sudh Singh would run his press empty to impress his neighbours.

Khalsa Printing Press printed a tribute, in Gurumukhi, to Lal Singh, an Akali fighter

INTRODUCTION
TO MARXISM

Makhan Singh passed his London Matriculation examination in 1930. He had a burning desire to go abroad for further studies but his father's poor financial condition did not allow for this. Instead he started working full time in the press from June, 1931. Now he had more opportunities to learn about political events in Nairobi and Kenya generally. He made friends with the African workers in the press and began to learn about their lives, their problems and their experiences with colonialism. In his hand-written biographical notes written in 1963, he states that at that time he began a serious study of political literature of all types. He was influenced by the workers' and peasants' movements (both communist and socialist) and trade union struggles going on throughout the world, as well as by freedom movements.

In 1931, Makhan Singh wrote to someone, either an old classmate or teacher of his school, who had moved to the UK. He bemoaned the deterioration in the school's standards and made some queries regarding printing. The correspondent wrote back that 'one who advocates a theory must give it his practical help and so must you.' He went on to say he found London 'depressing . . . people are starving, business is dull. The socialists resent the manufacturers' cry for protection and tariffs.' He requested Makhan Singh to 'write me something more in detail about Nairobi, about politics and the Congress.'

Clearly by this time Makhan Singh had been introduced to left-leaning ideology. An emotional letter, written by one Sardar Rawal Singh in 1931, begged Makhan Singh to return to Gharjakh. 'All our student friends have left, Gharjakh is now desolate, barren and dull . . . we had such happy times, political enthusiasms are less now . . .' Obviously even before he left India the young teenager had delved into the realm of politics. And this is not surprising given the context of colonial injustices, the valiant fight for freedom by the Ghadrites, the Akalis and the Communists, the freedom struggle led by Gandhi and the background of a revolutionary Sikh history.

THE 'LEFT' IN KENYA IN THE 20'S & 30'S

In Kenya he met various Sikh Ghadrites who had arrived from abroad. As mentioned earlier, several of them passed through East Africa on their way to or from Moscow. A few stayed and worked in EA, activists such as Harbans Lal Sarda who formed a branch of the Ghadr Party in Tanganyika. There was another Ghadrite, Waryamu Singh, in the Kisumu area. Makhan Singh certainly knew Kabul Singh, who had first come to East Africa in 1899 and worked as a sub-overseer on the Uganda Railway for three years, before returning to India. Disaffected and pro-German, he regularly received issues of the *Ghadr*. After visiting several countries, he returned to settle in Kenya in 1933, and carried on a correspondence with Makhan Singh.

In 1928, Devinder Singh, alias Teja Singh, was the honorary secretary of the Siri Guru Singh Sabha in Nairobi and in 1931, was employed as a clerk in Barclay's Bank. He was a great agitator and a staunch communist with a large following. He claimed that he had organised a branch of the Ghadr party and requested that copies of its organ, *Mazdoor Kisan* (Worker Peasant), be sent to some twenty addresses in Kenya. He was last heard of in Zanzibar in 1932. He was one of the most active members of the Ghadr Party in East Africa and was highly thought of by party officials.[7]

Another left-wing Sikh activist, Kalyan Singh Dhillon of India, applied for a passport in 1928 to visit Kenya, but was refused. Suba Singh, (alias Kato) from Amritsar, who worked as a mechanic in the Nairobi Electric Light Company, was selected and sent for revolutionary training to Moscow in 1932. He was able to acquire passport No A 21423 in Nairobi. (The issuance of passports to the Ghadrites is evidence that their revolutionary activities were highly secretive and remained largely unknown not only to the colonial authorities but also in Kenya's historical records.) After completing his training in

Ujagar Singh, 1930

Moscow and being briefly imprisoned in India, Dhillon settled in Kenya. Ujagar Singh (alias Maroj), mentioned earlier as one of the founder members of the Railway Artisans Union, hailed from Jalhandar. He returned to Kenya in 1929, worked here as a mason and painter, and then as a salaried priest in a Nairobi gurdwara and joined the labour movement. He travelled together with Suba Singh in 1932 to Moscow, allegedly as a nominee of the Ghadr Party, Kenya. His passport, No A21538, was issued in Nairobi. They stayed with Gopal Singh who was then doing a temporary job at Mombasa's railway station. Ujagar Singh returned to India in 1935, via Nairobi. Another Ghadrite, Iqbal Singh Hundal, had been to Moscow and used to give study lectures in Nairobi.[8]

Vasudev Singh was from Sheikhupura in India. He worked as a watchmaker in Nairobi and is mentioned in the *Ghadr Directory* as an 'accommodation address for the Ghadr Party in British East Africa.' He was in contact with George Padmore, Chairman of the International Trade Union Committee of Negro Workers and a founder member of the Labour Trade Union, which was identified as a 'Communist-Ghadr organisation,' in the East Africa Directory. His address was PO Box 300, Nairobi. Rattan Singh, who was the conduit in Paris for Ghadrites on their way to and from Moscow, stopped briefly in Mombasa on his way to Madagascar in 1944.[9]

Devindar Singh hailed from Jalhandar, India. He was a sympathiser of the Akali Movement and a matriculate. In 1926, he travelled to Kenya. He was then between 25 and 30 years old. In 1928, he was working as honorary secretary of the Siri Guru Singh Sabha, one of Nairobi's Sikh gurdwara associations, and in 1931 was employed as a clerk in Barclay's Bank in Nairobi. Notes on him say that 'he was said to have a sizeable following there

Vasudev Singh

and to be a great agitator and a rank Communist. Was said to have been receiving financial help from Moscow through Ishar Das for his communist propaganda .

In the latter half of 1931, he wrote a letter to Bhag Singh in Canada, requesting that copies of the *Masdoor Kisan* (Worker Peasant) be sent to some 20 addresses in Kenya and asked for a letter of introduction to assist those of its members whom he hoped to send to Moscow for training. He also contributed an article to the *Hindustan Ghadr* for February, 1932, in which he exhorted the youths to strive hard to free their country.' He was issued with Kenya passport No A 18994 valid for the British Empire and endorsed for Panama. In his application he stated that he had lost his previous passport. He returned to India in 1932 and was later executed by his party, the Communist Party of India, on a charge of betrayal.[10]

Teja Singh Sutantra passed through Kenya in the early 1940s on his way from Moscow to India where he reorganised the Ghadrites into a Kirti Party and later merged it with the Communist Party of India. The Ghadrites in Kenya were a close-knit group that maintained their solidarity during their return visits to India to do revolutionary work there.[11]

Isher Dass, unlike Manilal Desai, was a self-avowed Marxist who did not believe in hiding his light under a bushel. Both men, however, were committed political activists and shared a liking for fashionable western suits, complete with waistcoat and tie. Dass had a European wife, an English Jewish woman who shared his ideology. Desai never married.

Thus there was a sizeable group of Indian leftists in Kenya during the 20s, 30s and early 40s. In his introduction to Makhan Singh's second volume, *1952-56 Crucial years of KENYA TRADE UNIONS*, Bethwell Ogot affirms that 'it was during this period that Makhan Singh seems to have been introduced to Marxist literature. Throughout his life he remained a non-violent Marxist, who sought to improve the position of the workers not through violent revolution, but through trade unionism, democratically organised. And trade unionism in Kenya from 1935 to 1950 owes its success to the vision, dedication and selflessness of one person: Makhan Singh.'

Makhan Singh's notes (which he jotted down in his own handwriting in January, 1962) contain an interesting list of names and happenings.

The list has the date 1915-1916 but no other heading or title. The names are Mr B R Sharma, Mr Lal Chand Sharma and Mr Mangal Dass, all from Nairobi. Mr Narain Singh from Nakuru and 'Singer' from the USA, previously in Zanzibar. Narain Singh was hanged at the site of the Mombasa Market; his beard had been 'snatched' and was bleeding. A 'brother Bishen Watchendu' was asked to go away to India where he remained for two years. B R Sharma, Lal Chand Sharma, Mangal Dass and 'Singer' were all sentenced to death. Chief Justice Hamilton intervened at the request of Mrs Damyanti Sharma,

1915 - 1916

- Mr. B. R. (Balu) Sharma - Advocate also
  Parkland,
- Mr. Lal Chand -
  Nairobi. South. Sharma &
  Bali Advat
- Mr. Mangal Das,
  Nairobi South.
- Mr. Narain Singh -
  Nakuru.
- Singh, who was hanged at the
  - site of Manhara Market.
  - Beard matched — Bleeding.
- Chief Justice Hamilton
  intervened at the request of
- Mrs. Damyanti Sharma, - Prevented
  hanging.
  Bishen Singh Watchman was
  asked to go away to India where
  he remained for two years.
  arrested. Sharma, Mangal Das,
  Lal Chand were sentenced to
  death.
  "Singer" from U.S.A. - Parmanand
  at Langilata, —
  Three were hanged at Manchest.

A list in Makhan Singh's handwriting

Lal Chand's mother so his sentence was commuted to a prison term – the other three were hanged in Mombasa.

In his memoirs, Lal Chand Sharma describes his imprisonment in Mombasa's Fort Jesus, then the town's jail, where he learnt to read and write. At the onset of World War I, the British became extremely wary of any pro-German tendencies. Supporters of the Ghadr Party used to clandestinely distribute party literature that originated from their headquarters in the USA. It was defiantly anti-British and anti-imperialist and hence, understandably, considered 'subversive' by the colonial government. A crackdown on the organisation had occurred in 1915-16 when hundreds of Ghadrites in India were hanged, expelled, imprisoned and banned by the British Raj.

Dr Vishva Sharma, son of Lal Chand Sharma, maintains that this group of Indians in Kenya, including those who were executed, deported or imprisoned, was in fact innocent.[12] Robert G Gregory in *India and East Africa* also surmises that they had not committed any crime but that the authorities were conveniently getting rid of agitators. However considering the anti-British feelings being expressed in both Kenya and India in that period, it would have been only natural for some of these men to have held pro-Ghadr and pro-German sympathies.[13]

The Ghadhr Party later regrouped and several Ghadrites visited Kenya, a few even settled here and became involved in the trade union movement. Gopal Singh Chandan and Vasudev Singh were the leading Ghadrites in Kenya. Makhan Singh had close relations with them though he himself has left no records of this.[14] The Ghadr connection in Kenya and East Africa needs to be more thoroughly researched.

POETIC WRITINGS

During this period, Makhan Singh put many of his thoughts into poetry.[15] The bulk of his writings were on the Sikh religion and the martyrdom of its gurus and he stressed the qualities of truthfulness, honesty, dedication and commitment and the need for Hindu-Muslim-Sikh unity. There were, however, variations as his concerns subsequently broadened into wider socio-political issues. With the gurus as his role models he urged:

Strive and struggle
For a just society
Where there will be
Neither rich nor poor.

No cruelty to mankind
No exploiter of any kind
We have to throw off
The yoke of slavery forever
We have to defeat the enemy
With all our might
Our cause is ever right.

The following poem captures much of the organisational strategy he developed in his later years:

To liberate India is not so difficult
If we all get together
And struggle against the common enemy
We must not have any personal needs
We must be ready to sacrifice all
Wealth, belongings, your body
Be ready to face the gallows

Like Bhagat Singh and Sarabha[16]
To save the life of India
We have to face the
Capitalists, exploiters, blood-suckers
Only then can we say
We have saved the motherland.

Makhan Singh was most probably the author of a letter addressed to the EAINC dated 14th December, 1932, and written in Punjabi by a 'Suffering Sikh'. It refers to the betrayal by Abdul Wahid and Hukam Singh who were nominated by the EAINC as candidates for the Legislative Council (Legco) elections, on a pledge that they would not take the oath of loyalty and would boycott the Legco. They later called off the boycott. 'How can we pledge loyalty to a government which has destroyed and demeaned India and Kenya?' the letter asks.

In 1933, he composed a poem in memory of Manilal Desai, the dynamic secretary of the EAINC who had died in 1927.

My fellow Kenyan brothers
Let me tell how we can celebrate
The spirit of patriotism
Of our dear brother Desai
I place these few flowers of devotion and respect
Under the feet of the one
Who has sacrificed everything.
Who has quoted the love of the Goddess called Sacrifice
With everything he had.
For this love he did not spare anything
Setting the example of how one can
Serve one's mother land
The beloved Desai
Was the true son of India
That is how my pen is letting out the truth
Of these words
He was the man of words

And the master of action
He didn't spare his personal well-being
His money or his belongings
For this great cause.
He was a learned man, a brave man
A humble man
He was great in every way
I am at a loss of how to explain
The total goodness
That was Desai.

Many other Indians shared Makhan Singh's sentiments, for in 1934, the Desai Memorial Hall and Library were built in his honour.

MARRIAGE TO SATWANT KAUR

In November, 1933, Makhan Singh and his parents travelled to India by ship. Many years earlier Sudh Singh had accepted a marriage proposal for his son from a close friend, Tara Singh Mahal. The Mahal family lived in Lahore, a large city about 64 kilometres from Gharjakh. Mahal had pledged his daughter, Satwant Kaur, as a wife for Makhan Singh. Such marriage arrangements were the custom and now Makhan Singh, aged twenty-one, agreed to fulfil the pledge his father had made to the father of Satwant Kaur, now eighteen. The two young people had never met so he was pleased when his friend Sohan Singh in Gujranwala, who was a close relative of the Mahals, informed him that Satwant Kaur could 'read Gurumukhi and was very respectful to elders. She is interested in politics and knows the country's problems. Her nephew is a member of the Indian Congress.'

The Mahals were an upper class family. Satwant Kaur's brothers all had professional qualifications and they raised doubts as to whether Makhan Singh could take adequate care of their sister. 'He does not even have a job; he lives and works with his father. And he will be taking her so far away,' they grumbled. But the father sternly put a stop to the family disagreements. 'I made a promise to Sudh Singh and it must be kept,' he pronounced.

The wedding was held on 20th January, in a gurdwara in Lahore. Sudh Singh and the Mahals issued the invitations and informed invitees that the baraat (the bridegroom's procession) would assemble one mile outside Gharjakh and travel from there. The wedding was a short and simple ceremony but Makhan Singh lamented the unnecessary expenditure and in December Sohan Singh wrote to Makhan Singh agreeing that, 'We spent far too much on the wedding.'

Following tradition, Satwant Kaur returned to her parents' home after the wedding while Makhan Singh returned to Kenya with his father. They sailed from Porbandar, a port on the west coast of Gujerat, travelling by deck class. It was March, the hot weather had set in, and Makhan Singh suffered from sea-sickness, whiling away most of his time playing cards and engaging in idle talk. The ship stopped in Bombay and there he met with a few political activists and trade unionists who were working with Mahatma Gandhi in the freedom struggle.

During this period in India it was common for poets, especially those writing in Urdu, to clothe their political messages in a romantic genre. Thus Makhan Singh wrote to his abandoned bride.

Oh my love
Do not cry too much
Like the *papiha* bird
Which waits for the moon
Throughout the night.

Your plaintive cries
Have touched my heart
They have struck my chest
Like poisoned arrows

Oh God – listen to our prayer
Papiha needs water
Bring us rain
Her pain is like
The pangs of separation
It needs to be pacified
Like the troubled heart
Of humanity.

No doubt, Makhan Singh's longing for his bride was intertwined with his longing for a more just and fair society. He was convinced of the importance of education and often quoted the gurus' dictum that 'education is emancipation'. In 1934, he noted the aims of state education and private schools. Such schools should 'a) present a model of character and natural qualifications, b) mould the character and national qualifications in the shape of patriotism, and c) infuse in the youth the spirit of truth and honesty to lead his career in the best possible and honest way.' He admonished the British for closing down the

Makhan Singh's poem to Satwant Kaur

100,000 indigenous village schools in Bengal in order to create a class of subordinate officials.

If you raise the pen
In front of the sword
It will make the tyrants run . . . .

If you have it in your heart
You can put an end to this slavery
Therefore brothers I am telling you
Education is the one to serve humanity.

Once back in Kenya, father and son were busy with their Khalsa Press. In May, 1934, Kartar Singh, Makhan Singh's brother-in-law, wrote to him with advice about printing processes. He explained that the quality of the gum used affected brilliance when embossing and that the ink should not be very thick or wet. He went on to decry the lack of co-operation among the Sikhs in Kenya. He said he was pleased that Makhan Singh was keen to improve his English as 'a sound knowledge of English is essential for every walk of life'. Apparently Makhan Singh was considering returning to India for Kartar Singh added that there was 'no scope for any line including banking in India at present.' Later, in August, he wrote to Makhan Singh urging him not to make any investments in Kenya as 'the British Government was not sincere about the settlement of Indians in Kenya.'

In the same month Harbajan Singh, Makhan Singh's other brother-in-law who was a medical doctor in Delhi, sent Makhan Singh a prescription for the treatment of malaria and told him that he would be regularly posting to him copies of the *Illustrated Weekly*, a feature magazine published in India.

Makhan Singh must have been a good learner. By August Kartar Singh was congratulating him on his excellent embossed printing. He also commented that Makhan Singh was too conservative for the twentieth century as he had objected to a

The fiery revolutionary – Makhan Singh

lottery and equated it to gambling. (This was in connection with a Sikh Social Fund lottery launched by the Siri Gurdwara Bazaar, another of Nairobi's gurdwara associations).

Printing, however, was not displacing Makhan Singh's other interests. His handwritten notes of this period touched on a variety of socio-political issues.

The colonial government was considering forming a closer economic union between the three British East African territories, uniting the customs, fiscal and administrative services of Kenya, Uganda and Tanganyika. Makhan Singh was in support of this and bringing them under the control of the imperial government because

> this would put the economy on a sound, progressive basis, create better understanding between the three sister territories. They will be able to present a united front to any question concerning it.

He was bothered by the caste system which labelled lower grade menial workers as 'untouchables' and wrote that 'it was the primary cause of India's decline.' He was also concerned about injustice to women in Indian society. He listed the injustices as:

a) she has to remain under the influence of her father, husband and sons from birth to death, b) no joy is ever shown when a mother gives birth to a girl child and c) *haya*, purda, modesty, shame. These were like shackles in her life.

In marriage he criticised the custom that boys and girls were not allowed to choose their marriage partners, as well as 'child marriage . . . marriage of a young girl with an old man . . . widows not permitted to marry again . . . expense of dowries.'

On religion he noted 'wrong interpretation, communal hatred and superstition.' Education was too much on Western lines and resulted in 'looking down on elders, hating the uneducated, hating Indian culture and becoming admirers of the British Government.' This led to a loss of self-respect and

Wishing Gopal Singh Chandan farewell

dignity and became a major obstacle in the struggle against imperialism. His assessment of village life in India was 'narrow streets, dark rooms, no ventilation, dirt, drains and sewerage.' In a letter to Nairobi's *Colonial Times* he praised the Indian-run Social Service League for starting a dispensary and stressed the need for preventive medicine. He himself used the League for his own and his family's medical needs. In later years his father, Sudh Singh, was quite active in the League.

He ascribed the causes of all these negative factors to capitalism, foreign rule, negligence of the intelligentsia, blind belief and misdirection of the people. His prescription was 'True education, united propaganda, true sense in religion and removal of foreign rule and capitalist system'. In 1933, he had compared a Sikh guru to 'today's Bolshevik'. He participated in youth fora and corresponded with the *Navyug* (New Youth), a tabloid published in Nairobi[17]. In a four-page article he decried the widespread unemployment and poverty, and the corruption and infighting in Kenya's Sikh community. He attributed it to the fact that 90% of Sikh men were addicted to alcohol and was living contrary to the basic tenets of Sikhism. (While Makhan Singh did eat meat, he refrained from drinking alcohol or smoking). Colonialism had emasculated them and the leaders were fighting each other. 'We the workers have appointed these leaders but lack of proper education is destroying us.'

Among the many poems Makhan Singh wrote at this time, was one he composed for his close friend Sardar Gopal Singh Dhukia, a leading Ghadrite and poet who was departing for a short visit to India. 'If there were more persons like you, the mother land would not be so troubled . . .' he wrote. Another poem dated 10th October, 1933, was a tribute to Teja Singh Sutantra, also a Ghadrite, who at the time was imprisoned in India.

> Moghul Raj is ending
> Light is coming from the West
> With it come poisonous gases
> Communalism and divide and rule
> Sikhs have lost their integrity.
> Babu Teja Singh stood up and fought
> He carried a basket of rubbish on his head
> To end untouchability
> He made mistakes, he was not perfect
> But that does not lower
> Our respect for him.

To Swami Dayanand, a Hindu reformist in India, he said:

Dayanand you saved us
From slavery and oppression
We were suffering
You have shown us the way.

Other national leaders of India, Hindu-Muslim-Sikh unity, the Punjabi language and spirit and Lord Krishna were the subjects of several poems. In one he lamented:

If our only motive is to fight against our own brothers
Then what is the meaning of this fight for freedom
If you want to put an end to slavery my brother
You have to follow the path of truth unflinchingly.

Sudh Singh's press did a lively business printing election campaign leaflets in Gujerati, Gurumukhi and English script.

Two campaign posters printed by Sudh Singh's press in support of Shams-ud-Deen, one in Gurumukhi script and the other in Gujerati script

One leaflet supported Shams-ud-Deen, Isher Dass, K Nemchand, Dr A C L de Sousa and Dhanwant Singh for election to the Legco on an EAINC platform. Another leaflet written in March, 1934, by Vasudev Singh was a polemic against Isher Dass, accusing him of having quarrelled with Phadke, T M Jeevanjee, Mohamed Malik, Shams-ud-Deen, H S Verjee, J B Pandya, N S Mangat and A C L de Sousa.

In May, Sudh Singh printed a notice disassociating himself from an abusive article about Ramgharias printed by his press.

Vasudev Singh was one of the leaders of the Ghadrites in Kenya and he may have supported collaboration with the Germans. As mentioned above, the Ghadr Party had supported Germany in World War 1 and though many Ghadrites went on to become communists, a handful of leaders maintained an uneasy relationship of double-dealing with the Germans and Italians on the one hand and the Russians on the other.[18] Vasudev was antagonistic to the strict Stalinist line taken by Isher Dass, whose loud and flamboyant manner must have further aggravated him.

Makhan Singh noted Gandhi's speech to workers in Madhura, India. In an article in the *Kenya Daily Mail* of 30th May, 1934, he quotes Gandhi as having said

> I am a worker too. . . you have a right to demand your rights but you must produce too . . . you should save a little of your salary and buy shares so you can become owners . . . work with diligence . . . do not strike.

Makhan Singh felt nostalgic and homesick and that same month he wrote to Kartar Singh, a childhood friend of his in Gharjakh:

> When as friends we got together
> To play the games of life
> Under the stars at midnight
> Telling sweet stories to each other

In the open we would play
Guli danda, kabadi and hockey
And lovingly compete with each other
Even engage in mock fist fights
Yet next day
Be bosom friends again
What a beautiful world it was
What halcyon days we had
Where, oh where is that world
Now instead of love and friendship
There is only hatred and deceit.

In November one Charanjit Suri in Mombasa wrote to Makhan Singh requesting him to print posters for a Sikh Conference.

I have sent you a copy of the poster, please make the necessary corrections, you are the only person who can do this. Prepare the final and print it - we will send you details of who will be coming and when.

Harbans Singh (most probably from India) was to chair the conference, as he had chaired a similar one in 1917.
Makhan Singh by now had printed his own letterhead and was maintaining a regular correspondence with friends and relatives, political and trade union colleagues. He asked for books and magazines and one time even applied to a Writers' Society in India for a correspondence course related to Sikhism.

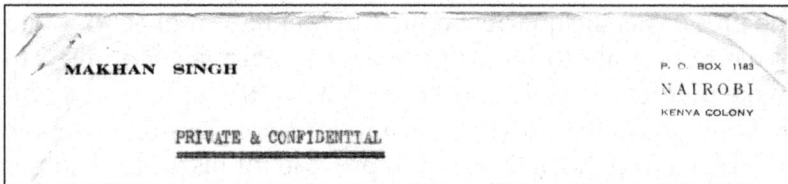

MAKHAN SINGH

P. O. BOX 1183
NAIROBI
KENYA COLONY

PRIVATE & CONFIDENTIAL

Makhan Singh's letterhead

He seems to have had a close and much respected relationship with a like-minded compatriot, Jagjit Singh. Two excerpts from their correspondence throws light on the close links Makhan Singh maintained with India and the kind of guidance he benefited from.

On 12th October, Jagjit wrote,

You have gone far but have not forgotten us. When we see the whites here in their uniforms, it hurts us. At one time there was Sikh Raj here – today we are not allowed even to carry a knife. I will send you the book [on Sikh history] but do not pressure me.

And then on 15th December, he advised,

Whatever steps you take, you must take carefully. If the horse does not move well, the rider has to lead it. If the person you gave the work does not do so, you have to do it. We have read the Mangat case; someone must have wished him badly.[19]

Clearly Makhan Singh had begun to broaden his vision. He was looking beyond the scope of his job as a printer and focussing more on his concerns regarding the injustices of colonialism and the distortions of religious ethics. He had started to explore the dynamics of organisation and social activism.

In December, there was a disagreement between Makhan Singh and his father regarding Sudh Singh's proposal to sell off the press. Was the quarrel because of Makhan Singh's refusal to agree to relocate to India? Or was it because he continued to make politics his main concern instead of trying to get gainful employment to raise his standard of living, become independent of his father and to provide for his wife? Another bone of contention could have been that Makhan Singh had begun to involve himself in trade union organisation.

INVOLVEMENT IN TRADE UNIONISM

In 1933, the railway authorities had reduced the position of most of the Indian artisans from 'permanent grade' to 'temporary grade'.

The railway artisans sent petitions but to no avail, so in December, 1934, they decided to form a union. Early trade unions included the Indian Trade Union (Mombasa and Nairobi, 1914), Workers Federation of British East Africa (for European workers) which was formed in 1919 with Lee Mellor as the president, and the Indian Employees Association formed in 1919 under Hassanali Amershi's presidency. The first strike was organised in the year 1900. The colonial administration tried to divide the working class by preventing the formation of non-racial trade unions. Being well aware of the 1923 experience when Sudh Singh and his group were victimised, the railway artisans recruited non-railway workers to join them and to take the leadership positions.

On 16ᵗʰ December, six prominent artisans, Shah Mohamed, Rambhai Gopalji, Daulat Singh, Jagjiwan Kalidas, Gulam Mohamed and Partap

Indian Workmen's TRADE UNION.

The lot of Indian Workmen in this country is becoming from bad to worse every day. Workmen's Trade Union ought to have been formed in this country thirty years ago, and we could have been saved from this evil day to-day. It is never too late, however. Better late than never.

A Mass MEETING of all Indian artisans and workmen will be held in the Desai Memorial Hall at 10 a.m. on Sunday, the 16th instant to lay the foundation of "Kenya Indian Workmen's Trade Union."

Every Indian workman is expected to attend.

Shah Mohamed, Rambhai Gopalji, Daulat Singh, Jagjivan Kalidas, Gulam Mohamed, Partap Singh.

NAIROBI.

Indian Workmen's Trade Union poster

Shah Mohamed

Singh, called a mass meeting of workers 'to lay the foundation of an organisation of Indian artisans and workmen.'

Five hundred working class people attended, a temporary managing committee was formed and the Indian Labour Trade Union established. The Hon. Shams-ud - Deen opened the meeting; regional, racial and religious distinctions were completely absent among the participants. However, due mainly to the migratory nature of the workers, the hostility of employers and the colonial rulers and the absence of labour legislation, the earlier difficulty of sustaining the activities of a union persisted.

'Employees form groups, even go on strike and have had some successes,' explained Pardhan Gujjar Singh, president of the Workers' Protective Society of Kenya.

But these groups never last for long. We face opposition both from the Government and the employers. And then on our side, because industry is so undeveloped, workers move from job to job.

In February, 1935, the artisans requested the 23-year old Makhan Singh to help the union. Makhan Singh recognised the need for consistent and systematic organisation and agreed to help the fledgling union. In March he was elected honorary secretary of the Indian Trade Union, a post without any remuneration. At a meeting on the 20th Makhan Singh, described the plight of Indian workers in Kenya since 1895, stating that the main cause was the absence of an organised labour union. He pointed out that the EAINC and its Indian Associations and the Indian religious societies had never done anything in the interest of workers. Hence, the total failure of the strikes held in 1931, and between 1933 and 1935.

Management committee meetings began to be held regularly. Five weeks later new officials were appointed with Gulam Mohamed as president and Makhan Singh again as honorary secretary. The membership fee was fixed at 50 cents per month. A decision was also made to open the membership to all workers irrespective of race, religion, caste, creed, colour or tribe. The renamed non-racial Labour Trade Union of Kenya (LTU) (renamed LTUEA the following year to include Tanganyika and Uganda) was launched at the Alexandra Cinema Nairobi, on Sunday, 21st April 1935.

Its main objectives were to organise the workers in Kenya to defend their rights and struggle for anything in their interests.[20] Makhan Singh began to write to the *Colonial Times*, the *East African Standard* and the *Kenya Daily Mail* on trade union matters, signing himself as 'Acting Secretary, Labour Trade Union of Kenya.'

One of the LTU's first acts was to purchase a typewriter and a rotary cyclostyle machine. This brought the relevant technology within the reach of the working class thus enabling communication between the workers and their organisation through handbills. Their issues could now be addressed without having to contend with the colonial-controlled press and exorbitant printing charges. It also gave them a measure of independence and ensured that their communication lines were not disrupted by the employers or the colonial authorities. A whole new set of worker-related activities developed around the production and distribution of handbills.[21]

A Press Workers' Union was formed in July, 1936, and registered as a branch of the LTUEA in 1937. It served eleven presses in Nairobi having a total of 229 employees. Makhan Singh compiled a list of the staff of the various printing presses. They were almost all Asian as they were run as family concerns. The Union had Mangal Dass as its president, Douglas Kamau as vice-president and Makhan Singh as secretary.

The second annual general meeting of the Labour Trade Union of Kenya was held on 6th and 13th September, 1936. Almost all correspondence, minutes and notices were in Punjabi but Makhan Singh made short summaries of the main items in English.

The first item on the agenda was 'Condolence on the death of Maxim Gorky.' A major decision taken was the setting of 1st October, 1936, as the target date for the implementation of the eight-hour day. Letters were dispatched to the main employers of Nairobi (mostly building contractors, vehicle body builders and furniture makers) informing them of the demand. Handbills in Urdu, Gujerati, Punjabi, Kiswahili and English were distributed. In spite of their initial hesitation, by mid-October all the 40 employers approached had agreed to the demand.

This success motivated the African workers who now supported the campaign for an eight-hour working day. A circular in Kiswahili was issued which began: *Hii ni kuwapa habari ya kuwa tangu mwezi wa 1st October, 1936, mafanyaji-wa-kazi wowote asifanzi kazi zaidi ya saa nane, na wala asipunguziwe mshahara wake.* (This is to inform you that starting from 1st October, 1936, all workers should not work more that eight hours a day, and there should be no reduction in their wages.)

Thus the groundwork was prepared for bringing African workers into the union. Strikes organised by African workers were becoming better coordinated and more effective. Pardhan Gujjar Singh explained that 'the biggest drawback is that we are racially divided. Our problems are common – low wages, forced labour, poor conditions of work – but the Government has organised teachers, civil servants and railway staff into European, Asian and African associations so the workers follow the same pattern. The Workers' Protective Society is open to all but the members are still only Indian.'

The effect of the success was felt all over Kenya and in Uganda and Tanganyika too. The membership of the Union went up to more than 1,000. The campaign clearly demonstrated how the unity and solidarity of workers could be built up for a common cause. The success created a tremendous enthusiasm and encouragement amongst members of the Union and other workers for the coming struggle for increase in wages and recognition of the Union.

The handbills, printed by the Khalsa Press became a regular way for the Union to announce its meetings, to organise workers for strikes, and to educate workers on their rights. An example of the issues addressed can be seen in one inviting workers to a meeting on Sunday, September 6th, 1936. It was issued in several languages; twelve points were itemised some of which were:

+ Do not work for low salary, work 8 hours a day, and be paid monthly, not by hours.
+ Railway and PWD [Public Works Department] workers are temporary, and should be made permanent.
+ Congratulate press workers for establishing their own Union.
+ Reduce school fees.
+ Compensation should be paid by Government on injury at work.
+ Appeal to all Kenyan workers to unite.

The handbill dated 31st October, 1936, had a distinctly ideological content:

Struggle between capitalists and workers has started in earnest

Our worker comrades! Come forward! March ahead! If you do not march ahead today, then remember that you will be crushed under the heels of capitalists tomorrow. Workers should have a united stand and should stand up strongly against the capitalists so that they should not ever have the courage to attempt to exploit workers again, nor to take away workers' rights from them.
Note: The workers of M/s Karsan Ladha have gone on strike for higher wages. It has been reported that the strike situation is becoming serious.
This has now become a question of life or death for workers.

- LABOUR TRADE UNION OF KENYA
November 29, 1936

The employers were not slow in following the lead of the Union in its mass communication tactics, so successful were the handbills in publicising Union activities. But the employers did not achieve much success, as the workers just ignored such propaganda. The Union was successful in the strike because of good organisation and solidarity which could only be achieved with a good communication system.

Makhan Singh was the main person behind the consolidation of the trade unions at that time and he brought with him working class experience from India which he creatively applied to the Kenyan situation. Not only was he a good organiser and trade unionist, he was also an excellent communicator and understood well the needs of ensuring effective communications between trade unions and workers. It was largely his influence that shaped the successful strikes and publishing policies of the trade union movement in Kenya.[22]

The subject of taxes was the next matter of concern. A handbill calling workers for a meeting on 18th October 1936, stated: 'Taxes should be reduced. No taxes should be imposed on the poor.' The government was planning to introduce new taxes in the New Year and the unionists wanted to ensure that the poor would be exempted from these. Throughout the 1930s and 40s lengthy lists of grievances were a feature of Makhan Singh's strategy – but wages and hours were the main issues workers were interested in.

In November, 1936, the union took the decision to express international solidarity when it passed a resolution condemning the execution by the Nazi government in Germany of Comrade Edgar Andre, a German trade union leader, for his anti-Hitler activities. In the same month, the union published a handwritten monthly called *Kenyan Worker*. After three issues, two in Punjabi and one in Urdu, it was replaced by a weekly Punjabi newspaper called *Kirti* (Worker) which was launched in Nairobi. Makhan Singh was its editor. A few months later it was renamed *East African Kirti* and Mota Singh, president of the union, took over as editor. Stockily built and of medium height, Mota Singh walked with a slight limp. The papers contained articles about

East African Kirti

the Union's policies and news about workers' struggles and national and international news of general interest.

Publication was stopped after three issues as the government prosecuted Mota Singh for not registering the paper and it ceased publication for a while. Mota Singh was fined for the 'offence'.[23] Makhan Singh later revived the *East African Kirti* and circulated cyclostyled copies handwritten by him in the Gurumukhi script. The proprietor was named as "Mota Singh, occupation mason". The annual return made under the Newspaper Registration Ordinance in 1938 stated the *East African Kirti* was published weekly and that its average circulation was 1,000 copies per week.[24] He continued to write the Kirti pamphlets by hand in Gurumukhi under a masthead of the Sikh emblem and initially cyclostyled them for distribution. Later they were printed.

His concerns were mainly around class issues and the need for unity. He maintained that only 5% of the population was rich but the 95% were weak because of lack of unity. He explained how the 5% threatened workers with loss of jobs and other strategies and, at any sign of unity, penetrated and disrupted their organisation and brought fictitious cases against the leaders.

Makhan Singh distributed a circular stating that 'capitalists do not desire the good of workers and never give a concession on their own. They have generally no mercy, and any capitalist who shows mercy is considered a bad one by the others. They do not like unity of the workers.' On Sunday, 29th November, a meeting of workers was held on the Ramgharia plot, the subject which Makhan Singh addressed was 'Life and Death Struggle with the Capitalists.'

The Arya Samaj invited Makhan Singh to a poetry session and interestingly, the subject matter of his poems had now changed to worker and human rights issues. Other matters that particularly interested him in 1936 were the Kenya Budget Speech by Hon. Dr A C L de Sousa; Immigration; the Hindu Marriage and Divorce Bill, and the Constitution of the EAINC.

In March, 1936, the *Kenya Daily Mail* had printed a flurry of protest letters in response to a supplement on '*Indians in East Africa*' by U K Oza, a journalist who had just then been appointed special organising secretary of the EAINC. In the supplement, published by the *Indian Social Reformer* of Bombay, he claimed that 'our women are greater slaves in the colonies, and are to a far greater extent objects of men's lust and tyranny than in India.' The same paper also published a Gujerati translation of a speech by Stalin addressing issues of imperialism, fascism, capitalist wars and the contest for business and markets abroad, the China-Japan war and the Spanish civil war.

A letter to Makhan Singh dated 6th July, 1936, from a Harjinder Singh in Kampala explained that if one worked hard for four months one can earn enough for the whole year, everybody was able to get work, literate or illiterate. 'The workers spend a lot of money on drinks, donate some to the gurdwara and send some to India.' He complained about Kampala having a bad climate, mosquitoes, mud and dust and went on to the topic of women. 'Sikhs have their own wives but also keep native mistresses. Many African prostitutes loiter in the streets even though the police do arrest them. An Englishman said that prostitutes are necessary to deal with stress.' He then asked, 'Is your wife 'good' or just so-so?' Makhan Singh appears to have terminated the correspondence there.

At a mass meeting on 20th December, 1936, the union decided to demand a 25% increase in wages as of 1st April, 1937. Notices were sent out in January, 1937. The LTU's strategy was to secure concessions from the smaller firms and then pressure the larger European and Asian contractors.[25] The Indian Contractors and Builders Association rejected the LTU demand as 'false propaganda' but a week later, in April, announced that they accepted the new wage terms. Many employers agreed to the new terms – but not all. 'We request you to refrain from sending threatening letters to us otherwise we shall resort to legal action,' wrote one.

The Motor Service Co. Ltd complained of 'unreasonable demands' and that its Asiatic staff had been forced to join the union. However it conceded that 'your union is recognised by a large number of workmen and we are prepared to recognise its constitutional actions.' Later it rejected the wage increases.

The previous year the LTU had initiated a campaign to induce the Railway authorities to restore to their previous permanent status all those artisans who had been changed to 'temporary'. (In 1933, owing to the prevailing economic depression, they had agreed to this change.) Railway workers now drew up a petition which was signed by 90 workers in the Locomotive and Carriage Section, 45 in the Shed, 38 in Maintenance, 14 in Nakuru and 43 in Eldoret. The Mombasa Indian Association and the Indian Youth League supported them. The Railways' response was: 'No change can be made in the service conditions'. This campaign continued to be waged for some years until most of the artisans were able to regain their permanent status.

LABOUR TRADE UNION OF EAST AFRICA

In March, the LTU supported a successful general strike by the Asiatic Labour Union in Dar es Salaam for an 8-hour working day and a wage increase. With trade unionism becoming active in Kenya's neighbouring countries, on 6th March, 1937, the LTU changed its name to 'Labour Trade Union of East Africa (LTUEA)'.

Owing to the resistance of many employers to the demand for a wage increase, a strike was planned and started on 1st April, at six firms. The *East African Standard* of 11th May, publicised 'The Strike of Asian Artisans.' The editorial was headed 'Trade Unionism in Kenya' and described the use of phrases such as 'class consciousness, robbery, capitalism and unending poverty' as 'crude propaganda.' It stated that the conditions of work in Kenya were better than in India for artisans and that the future of trade unionism should be properly visualised and regulated.

S G Amin, U K Oza, A R Cockar and Vasudev Singh called a mass meeting of Indian citizens in Nairobi in support of the LTUEA and the Indian Association approached

The Labour Trade Union
of East Africa.

NOTICE.

For the information of the general public and those concerned it is hereby announced that as Messrs. W. H Lewis & Sons have declared a lockout of their Indian artizans in order to fail the workers' strike at the works of some other employers, the Strike Committee has decided that unless and until the above firm agrees to the demands of the workers, advanced by the Labour Trade Union of East Africa, the Union shall have the right to declare strike at the works of those employers, who have entered or will enter into any sort of agreement or contract with the above firm.

MAKHAN SINGH,
Secretary,

Nairobi,   The Labour Trade Union
12th May, 1937.   of East Africa.

LTU Strike Notice

the town clerk to set up a conciliation committee from an impartial agency to settle the dispute between the building contractors and the LTUEA.

The employers tried to divide the workers along religious and communal lines and divisions arose in the ramgharia community.[26] The officials of the East Africa Ramgharia Board and the Siri Gurdwara Bazaar were landlords and employers while the general membership consisted of workers. The officials, using the ramgharia name, formed the Ramgharia Artisans Union but the workers did not support this move and they formed the Ramgharia Labour Union.

The E A Ramgharia Board and the Siri Gurdwara Bazaar were built in the vicinity of Nairobi's Racecourse Road in 1934 and 1939 respectively. In 1972, the Ramgharia Board was moved to a larger and more modern structure on Muranga

Road; the original hall now houses a school but the façade has been retained. In 1963, an imposingly domed gurdwara was added to the Gurdwara Bazaar and the complex is still fully functional and under the control of the jats, originally of the farming community in India.[27]

In the Siri Gurdwara Bazaar, a new management committee was elected with most of the new members belonging to the LTUEA. A fracas outside the temple in August resulted in some Sikhs being arrested and court cases followed. Daly & Figgis were the lawyers for the plaintiffs, S G Amin for the defendants. Makhan Singh was also accused and protested.

> I am secretary of the LTUEA. The contractors are against me. I have been opposing them during the strike and the Trade Union has defeated them. In the gurdwaras, the contractors and their agents had a majority. Now their team has been overthrown, in order to take revenge they have included me in this case.

There followed a period of repression and the strike picketers, including Mota Singh, the president of LTUEA, were arrested and prosecuted. Finally the government intervened and a settlement was reached on 2nd June. The employers agreed to a wage increase ranging from 15% to 22%, an eight-hour day and reinstatement of all the strikers. The strike had lasted 62 days. At a mass meeting the LTUEA announced that 'Victory in the strike was won by the unity and sacrifice of the workers.'

The first annual conference of the LTUEA was held on 18th July, 1937 and, for the first time, the notices advertising it included Kiswahili. In August Makhan Singh circulated the following in Hindustani: 'Not tolerating the increasing power of the workers and the LTU, a few contractors in Nairobi organised a separate union, the Ramgharia Artisans Union. But the Ramgharia Labour Union, a branch of the LTU, was able to defeat it. Gains from the strike are that workers have learnt

Workers' procession in 1937, Government Road, Nairobi

how to unite, how to fight for their rights and have imbibed the spirit of self-sacrifice. The greatest gain has been the 8-hour working day and the wage increase. The lesson to be learnt was that capitalists don't desire the good of the workers and are happy in their disunity.'

In July a Trade Unions Bill was moved in the Legco, with Honourable Shams-ud-Deen and Amar Nath Maini presenting LTUEA's position. The Trades Union Ordinance came into force on 24th September, and a Registrar of Trade Unions was appointed. The LTUEA then formalised its constitution, rules and regulations and was registered on 30th September. Makhan Singh noted that 'trade unionism in Kenya had come to stay'[28].

Early in 1937, Makhan Singh had drafted a list of resolutions that he presented to Siri Guru Singh Sabha in Nairobi. The key points were that the EAINC must unite, Indian education policies must be revised, India's independence struggle must be supported and 'we must demand the release of Baba Gurumukh Singh and Teja Singh Sutantra who had been arrested by the Government of India'. His memorandum did not get very far as he received a communication stating: 'The committee thanks you for your paper. It was decided not to allow your resolution to be presented to the Sabha'.

In the midst of his reading, writing and organising, Makhan Singh found time to assist fellow workers. In May, 1937, Walji Premji Purshottam sent him an urgent plea to get him and another man, who had been jailed for non-payment of taxes, out on bail. 'You are the only one who can help us,' the letter concluded.

All the while Makhan Singh continued to write poems in Punjabi to express his strong feelings about imperialism and its exploitation of labour and capital.

On Workers:
Let us face the fact
The capitalists of this world are drinking
The blood of the workers and peasants.
Imagine! A large container
Constructed and owned by them
And when they take a sip of it
They find it very intoxicating
The big vehicles they drive
Run not on petrol
But the blood of the toiling masses.

With utmost cruelty and repression
This monster of an exploiter
Has broken the pot of our patience
He has stripped us to the bone
And left us with not a drop of blood.

The fruit of your sweat is lustily coveted
By the exploiting money bags
After appropriating whatever we have produced
These cunning, conniving thieves
Are strutting like proud cockerels.

They are enjoying to the hilt
Yet they know it very well
That workers are left with nothing.
They have no pity, no compassion
No shame. They move in the open.

There is nothing to eat
Or to drink or to sleep on
They have looted us so badly
There is nothing left
For we the destitute.

They have not only sucked our blood
They have crunched our bones
Between their steely jaws
And we are completely
Forsaken and abandoned.

My fellow workers
Let us be united as one man
With utmost determination
We must unite and organise
Like a clenched fist

Resolute and determined
We should strive and struggle.
Our unity is the affirmation of our faith
To achieve the lasting victory
We must fight unto the last.

We have to uproot
This mighty baobab of capitalism
From the very roots.
We will cut, burn and destroy
All the toady toadstools cluttering around.

We know who, why and when
Has sucked our blood
And stripped our flesh from the bone
You think we will spare him?
Not at all.

We have not trampled on anybody's rights
Likewise we will not allow
Our rights to be trampled on
We will not tolerate
The parasites and the bloodsuckers

We will not budge
We will not move an inch
Until we settle our score
With those
Who live on our sweat and blood.

Our demands are fair
Our cause is just
That is the reason
We will not retreat
Until we get what we deserve.

On Racism:
Tell me
What is wrong with me
If you are a human being
So am I
If we both are educated
You are as good a learned person
As I am
If we get good food to eat
I will be equally strong as you
If we both get good clothes

You will be fashionable
So will I
Your colour is dark
So is mine
Neither you are different
Nor I
Pluck this idea from your heart completely
Neither you are different
Nor I.

On Untouchability:
What has happened
That in such a burning heat
My child has taken a cup of water
This would not have caused
A shortage of water in the pool
Or hurt anyone
Even dogs and cats drink from this pool
But the water does not get contaminated
Then why are you so agitated
As if you have been stung by a snake?
Why have you beaten my son?
You may be high class in your home
But we are not different

The poems give us an insight into the very strong feelings Makhan Singh had regarding the exploitation of workers, the inhumanity of racism and the absurdity of the caste system. Writing poetry, no doubt, helped to relieve some of the pain and frustration he felt so acutely.

November appears to have been the month for renewing subscriptions to journals. Mota Singh, president of LTUEA, sent five shillings to the *Congress Socialist*, published in Bombay, and the same amount to Agra for *Nayi Duniya* (New World). These were annual subscriptions and must have included postage to East Africa. Makhan Singh remitted six shillings to Lahore for the newsletter *Akali Patrika*. From a list of 35 left-wing periodicals available in London, Makhan Singh subscribed to the weekly *International Press Correspondence*. He also received the foreign newsletters of the All India Congress Socialist Party which dealt mainly with the international situation, socialist unity and trade union organisation.

Early in 1939, Makhan Singh wrote to the secretary of a Labour organisation in Johannesburg thanking him for his Christmas and New Year greetings and for two copies of the *Cape Federation Journal*. He sent information regarding a strike taking place in Mombasa in the building trade and requested help with the registration of unions in Tanganyika. The LTUEA had already submitted a memorandum on the labour situation in Uganda to it.

A pamphlet titled 'Victims of *Shikar* (Hunting) Lust' narrated how H H the *Maharao* (Prince) of Cutch, a state in Gujerat, India, was importing cheetahs from Africa for hunting. The animals were attacking and killing villagers who were banned from defending themselves, and the British rulers supported this venture. The writers encouraged readers to voice opposition to it. The Africa-India connection seems to have interested Makhan Singh and, no doubt, the subjugation of the villagers' rights to the interest of the hunting elite. (The conflict between wildlife and subsistence farmers in present-day Kenya bears similarities to that situation.)

Ambu Patel, a very earnest young man, arrived in Nairobi from India in 1933 with his wife Lila, and started a book binding and publishing business. Prior to immigrating to East Africa, he had participated in the movement for independence in India and his nationalist concerns continued to be the focus of his life in Kenya. Soon after his arrival he met Makhan Singh and in his autobiographical notes written many years later, in the 1970s, he wrote, 'In 1933 I came from India and met Makhan Singh. During this first meeting I found Makhan Singh interested in Indian affairs. After a short personal talk he asked me about the freedom movement, political institutions and communal harmony in India. We met frequently after that and always discussed these subjects.

'The following year, by chance, an acquaintance of mine from San Francisco was my guest for a few days. When he heard me talking on labour conditions in Kenya, he suggested that I should organise workers and establish a trade union. I discussed the suggestion with Makhan Singh. He was already studying socialism and Marxism. He began to study trade unionism deeply. After a few months study, Makhan Singh told me to find some more people to join us, to start propaganda. We found

WORLD'S
COMING POLITICAL STRUGGLE
AND
YOUR DUTY
COME AND HEAR
AT THE
PUBLIC MEETING
IN THE
PLAYHOUSE
(OPPOSITE MUNICIPAL MARKET)
ON
SUNDAY October 3rd at 11-15 a.m.
NAIROBI.
1st Oct. 1937.   *Isher Dass.*

Notice of Public Meeting

two or three people and started the propaganda work. Under the leadership of Makhan Singh, the group identified several people and recruited members. When our membership exceeded twenty we formed a committee. Makhan Singh drafted a constitution and got the East African Trade Union registered.

'Makhan Singh approached workers in up country areas and suggested that they should establish local committees [branches] of the trade union to look after the interests of the workers and forward their grievances to the head office at Nairobi for action. Through Makhan Singh's untiring efforts, four or five branches were established in East Africa.

'When the EATU[C] was in full swing Makhan Singh had to work day and night for the union. He approached higher authorities to put before them the grievances of the workers. His language was very good, his arguments based on facts and figures.'[29]

EAST AFRICA INDIAN NATIONAL CONGRESS

Makhan Singh had by now become actively involved in the affairs of the EAINC and the Nairobi Indian Association. He became a member of the executive and standing committees of the EAINC in 1938 and attended many public forums. A public meeting was held by the association to hear Sheth Govind Das, a member of the Viceroy's Legislative Assembly in India, who was touring Africa to study the Indian problem. In October, Isher Dass organised a public meeting in the Playhouse Theatre in Playhouse Lane, opposite the municipal market, to discuss the 'World's Coming Political Struggle.'

In the same month, Makhan Singh held a General Meeting of the LTUEA to elect the Union's Nairobi Local Committee. Later he himself paid a fee of two shillings to the Union, one shilling as entrance fee and one shilling as membership for the month of December.

In December, he participated in the meeting called to organise the next session of the EAINC. His position was that the Congress needed to be revived. His suggestions were that it must resolve to eliminate unfair practices and disunity in the electoral process, the candidates must sign a loyalty pledge and that resolutions must not remain as scraps of paper. Most importantly, the EAINC should be driven by the ideas and decisions of the masses. He underscored the restrictive aspects of the Trade Unions Ordinance, the need to urge unity and mass action, to keep in touch with events in India and further the struggle for freedom being waged there and to condemn the attacks by Japan on China and by Germany and Italy on Spain. An extract from the *Congress Socialist* in his collection was headed 'Honesty in Controversy'. It dealt with the struggle between left and right viewpoints pitting 'Socialists against True Congressmen' and looked at India's Trade Union Congress and its ideological affiliations.[30]

A correspondent, a Mr. Batlivala, had discussed the ideological merits of a 'True Congressman.' 'Even right wingers are anti-imperialist who have sacrificed in [the] national cause for freedom, who have the good of the country at heart and once convinced of the correctness of our attitude, will willingly go as far as any Socialist dare go in the anti-imperialist front,' he wrote.

Makhan Singh sent the article to the *Kenya Daily Mail* which published it on 22nd December, 1937, just prior to the fourteenth session of the EAINC, held in Nairobi in January, 1938. The paper also printed an 'Open Letter to M. D. Gautama.' Gautama was the acting president of the Nairobi Hindu Union and the letter was from an organisation called the League Against Communalism. It challenged the concept of Hinduism and advocated the closure of the Hindu Union. To Makhan Singh, religious and communal chauvinism were major obstacles in building a united front against colonialism, a front comprised of nationalistic Asians and Africans. His major concern was to ensure that the trade union movement was at all times non-racial, non-communal and non-religious because he was convinced that the workers were the backbone of the anti-colonial struggle.

The EAINC held its fourteenth session on 1st and 2nd January, 1938. Congress sessions were customarily opened with the singing of *Vande Mataram*, the national anthem of India. For communication, both English and Gujerati were used interchangeably. Makhan Singh took an active part – he was

Delegate No 9, paid ten shillings as an entrance fee and was a member of the reception committee. The president was Sheth Alibhai Hajee, the president-elect Sheth Kaderbhai from Mombasa. The main subjects were the need for greater unity and the ill effects of rumour-mongering.

At the fourteenth session of the EAINC, resolutions were passed bemoaning the demise of pioneer leaders A M Jeevanjee and B S Varma. M H Ismail was welcomed as the first Indian Trade Commissioner for East Africa. Most of the resolutions concerned grievances against colonial policies. One expressed sympathy for the struggle of the Indian community in Zanzibar against the discriminatory colonial legislation imposed on the clove industry. Another, while appreciating the support received from the National Congress of India, expressed regret at the lack of understanding and support shown by some members in the Indian Legislature, towards overseas Indians. Isher Dass proposed the demand for a common electoral roll and was seconded by A B Patel. Shams-ud-Deen challenged the European monopoly on the sale of wheat, while K K Pradhan called for greater encouragement of native cash crops and urged increased settlement of Indian agriculturalists.

Makhan Singh's participation in the Congress was geared to a larger vision, that of organised workers

SHOP-ASSISTANTS!

Dear Shop-Assistants,

I would sound a note of warning to you in exercising your two votes in the forthcoming election. Give none to a person for whom there is the slightest possibility of working against your interest. You should vote for those and those only who can take up your cause as their own in the event of it being necessary to do so by tightening up the means for effectual operation of Shop Hours Ordinance etc.

Who will side with you in case of a conflict between interests of your employers and yourselves?

Do not be misguided. Vote for those two who, you think, will stand shoulder to shoulder with you in case of need without being afraid of opposition.

Yours Sincerely,
Nairobi,
24.3.38.
SECRETARY,
Indian Youth, League.

નોકરીયાત બંધુઓ!

વ્હાલા નોકરીયાત બંધુઓ,

Khalsa Press, Nairobi.

An election leaflet in English and Gujerati

mobilising the anti-colonial movement. He constantly sought to sensitise EAINC members regarding the plight of workers and their rights, and proposed resolutions demanding a repeal of the 1937 Trade Union Ordinance. He also urged employers to agree to give workers an 8-hour day and 45-hour week. Mota Singh, president of the LTUEA, drew attention to the poor condition of Indian workers in Kenya.

Makhan Singh was elected to serve on the Executive and Standing Committees of the EAINC. To realise his goal of organising African and Indian workers, he cooperated with all organisations that could further that goal. A receipt of six shillings, as annual membership for 1939, confirms that he was also a member of the Nairobi Indian Association. In the Indian Youth League in 1939, he was elected as secretary.

The League had earlier played an important role in shortening the working hours of shop-assistants through out Kenya. The League's letterhead bore the slogan 'Non Religious and Non Political' and as its motto it had 'Faith and Sympathy Our Sinews.'

Makhan Singh worked closely with Hon. Shams-ud-Deen and Hon. Isher Dass who took the lead in promoting African political interests. On the 24th, he attended a farewell party held in their honour. They, together with P A Mehta and S G Amin, were part of an EAINC deputation leaving for India. Their objective was

DEEN & DASS

The Indian Community is in need of guidance at this critical stage when it is about to choose its two representatives for the Central Electoral Area.

The East African Indian National Congress called for volunteers to go out to India to make representations there on our behalf. The Congress sounded the bugle. The cry went far and wide, to all corners in Kenya. It was a strongly beseeching cry of war which humbly requested the Indian community to produce a few brave, unselfish, gallant warriors to make up the Deputation. The Congress knew its material. It also knew where it could draw upon. All the prominent people in the Colony were approached individually to answer the call of the nation. Only four rallied round – Shams-ud-Deen, Isher Dass, S. G. Amin and P. A. Mehta. The first two are now seeking election in the Central Area.

These two warriors are now fighting out our battles in India. Not easy battles ! They are fighting at their own expense, at considerable personal inconvenience and at the great risk of losing an election victory which their personal attendance would have easily ensured for both. Will the Indian community renounce its own ambassadors ? Shall we stab them in the back ?

There was only one course for us all to follow on the nomination day. Shams-ud-Deen and Isher Dass should have been the only two candidates for nomination. They should have been allowed to walk into the Council freely and unopposed. This would have been the expression on our part of merely a scintilla of the great debt of gratitude which we owe to these gentlemen. We owe them this much and a great deal more.

These two gentlemen answered the war cry of the Indian National Congress. This institution should have taken meticulous care to see that no one else offered himself as a candidate in the Central Area. This area should have become forbidden land, sacrosanct on the nomination day. This Area should have been made a sanctuary of prestige and dignity for both Dass and Deen.

There are some gentlemen who would like to discuss this proposition on the merits of the men candidates. Although both are as capable as any other, I do not wish to make a detour in order to be shown that the remaining four candidates are equally deserving of our support. I have never doubted the capacity of some of the remaining candidates. But the situation at the present moment is odd. On the one side are Deen and Dass who are away from the base of all election operations, who placed their trust in us simply in order to fill the vacancies in the Deputation. On the other side are people who were unable to leave the Colony. Shall we betray Deen and Dass ? But all is not lost yet. I talk about what faith, trust and confidence demand of us, all of us. Our slogan should be "DEEN & DASS."

INDIAN CITIZEN.

VOTE FOR

Cock and Horse

Khalsa Press, Nairobi.

Campaign poster supporting Shams-ud-Deen and Isher Dass

to gain support for their campaign against the Kenya (Highlands) Order in Council which was being promulgated to reserve the Highlands for Europeans. Pandya had declared in his presidential address, at the thirteenth session of the EAINC in December 1934, that 'preference was being given not only to the white British subjects of His Majesty the King but also to the white subjects of other countries of the King in the Empire.' It was at this time that the Secretary of State for the Colonies, Ormsby-Gore, stated that he regarded the Indians as 'mere interlopers in a country that belonged only to Africans and Europeans.'[31]

Shams-ud-Deen and Isher Dass had offered to undertake the mission in spite of the fact that elections for the Legco were round the corner and they intended to defend their seats. Makhan Singh helped to campaign on their behalf and used the platform of the Indian Youth League to exhort workers to vote for the two 'who would best take care of their interests.' A leaflet with the slogan 'Deen and Dass – Vote for Cock and Horse' was circulated urging the Indian community to return the two unopposed as their representatives in the Central Electoral Area. Others, including Chunilal Madan and Vasudev Singh, supported Shams-ud-Deen. Both Deen and Dass were re-elected together with N S Mangat, A C L de Souza and J B Pandya.

WORKMEN'S COMPENSATION, 8-HOUR DAY, 45-HOUR WEEK

✳

The LTUEA was now consolidating its gains. Members were enrolled throughout Kenya and Uganda and branches of the union were established in Mombasa and westwards in Magadi, Nakuru, Miwani, Kisumu, Kitale, Kakamega, Tororo, Soroti and Kampala. The two most difficult structural problems was the collection of fees and establishing branches. The 1938 accounts – the only surviving ones – show an income of KShs 545, plus KShs 253 carried from the previous year, giving a total of KShs 798. A part-time clerk was paid KShs 655 so a paltry KShs 143 remained to run the organisation. The Union did not supply strike pay and members had to be supported by communal organisations and their families.[32] Nevertheless, the union's membership went up to 2,500. African workers had begun to form committees at the places of their employment but avoided coming into the open for fear of victimisation and repression.

In May, 1938, the LTUEA held a conference on workmen's compensation in the Desai Memorial Hall, Nairobi. Makhan Singh was determined to have this issue legalised and he had secured a copy of the colonial office's model compensation ordinance, prepared in 1934. In Kenya, there was no law to ensure that compensation would be paid in cases of injuries or death sustained in the course of doing work. As a result, this hardship was reducing many families to destitution.

The EAINC, the Federation of the Indian Chamber of Commerce, the Indian Elected Members Organisation, the LTUEA, the Kenya Uganda Railway Asiatic Union, the Muslim Labour Union of Kenya and Uganda, the Indian Youth League, the Cutchi Gujerati Welfare Association, the Ramgharia Labour Union of EA and the Press Workers' Union participated. No African association was represented although the Kikuyu Central Association (KCA) sent apologies later.[33] The KCA leaders were suspicious of the motives of the Asians who were, comparatively, well-paid, and declined the invitation. A second session of the conference was held in June. The principle of workmen's compensation was approved and the Kenya government was asked to introduce the necessary legislation.[34] Though the International Labour Organisation had stated this requirement in 1922, and the trade union movement in Kenya had been agitating for it since 1936; the bill was not passed until ten years later, in 1946, after World War II was over.

THIRD ANNUAL CONFERENCE
OF
The Labour Trade Union of East Africa
On SUNDAY, 23rd JULY, 1939, at 9 a.m.
in the GROUND behind DESAI MEMORIAL HALL

Reception Committee
MEMBER

No. 121 SHS. 3.

LTUEA Receipt, 1939

On 31st July, the LTUEA held its second annual conference which was attended by most of the Asian organisations and trade unions.

The British Trades Union Congress, the South African Trades and Labour Council and the International Labour Office sent fraternal greetings. Special thanks were expressed to the EAINC for including trade union matters in its agenda. The conference elected a central committee of six Asians, three of whom were Sikhs. Under the chairmanship of Gulam Mohamed Luhar, it demanded the legalisation of a workmen's compensation statute together with the eight-hour day and 45-hour week. A minimum wage bill was passed by the Legco in 1946.

The unity of the African nationalist organisations was being strengthened as the Kikuyu Central Association, the North Kavirondo Central Association, the Taita Hills Association and the Ukamba Members Association began to work together. They sent a joint memorandum regarding the White Highlands issue to the Secretary of State for the Colonies and Isher Dass presented it in the Legco. One outcome was that the leaders of these associations now began cooperating with the LTUEA, and African workers began to join the union in large numbers.[35]

In March, 1938, the government had passed the Native Lands Trust and the Crown Lands Ordinances which confirmed the reservation of the highlands for European settlement only – which is why they were known as the White Highlands. This meant that the Africans who were the original inhabitants (and therefore owners) of these highlands were now excluded from them except as agricultural workers or

squatters. In this year too
the government began to
force the Wakamba to sell
their cattle against their
will, citing 'overstocking'
as the reason. Samuel
Muindi Mbingu led a
protest march in Nairobi
and was assisted by Isher
Dass. Muindu Mbingu
was   arrested   and
deported to Kismayu on
4th October, 1938, but the
protests   continued.   In

Samuel Muindu Mbingu

December the government relented; forced sales were halted
and a great victory was won.[36] But Muindi Mbingu was kept in
restriction for eight years. In 1939, his wives wrote to A B Patel,
requesting his assistance in ascertaining how much longer the
government intended to detain their husband and, if the release
was not to be soon, 'could the Government give us 100/-
allowance for food and clothing?'

The growing participation of African workers in the trade
union movement led to several resignations from the LTUEA
central committee with the members citing 'lack of time' and
'personal disability.' This was clear evidence that some of the
Asian trade unionists were opposed to cooperating with their
African counterparts.

The Asian community had one foot in the slums, the other in
the respectable middle class. Trade unionism appealed to the
skilled and semi-skilled Asian workers, particularly in the
building trades and on the railway. The middle class used the
EAINC and the Indian chambers of commerce to defend their
interests. Clerical staff formed staff associations – this deprived
the artisans of the leadership of the more educated members of
the community but also ensured that when these workers
organised, they were likely to be more militant.

It was utopian to think that Asian workers who were better paid than Africans often solely on racial grounds, would back a truly multi-racial union. From this time on Makhan Singh was a lone general unable to retain the loyalty of more than a section of the Asian working class and held at a certain distance by the African militants in Nairobi who increasingly looked upon trade unionism as part of the African nationalist struggle in which it was difficult for Asians to participate.[37]

At a mass meeting of Nairobi workers organised by the LTUEA, one of the resolutions congratulated three Sikhs for their sacrifice in enduring prison hardships in the cause of promoting the rights of the workers of East Africa and the LTUEA. Three men who had refused to pay the poll tax as a matter of principle – Amar Singh Chima, Kartar Singh Mehdi and Narinjan Singh – were interned in the Nairobi civil prison. Makhan Singh visited the Revenue Office on behalf of the three regarding the payment of their poll taxes and arranged for advocates to represent them. Shapely, Schwartz & Barett took the case and in April, 1939, sent Makhan Singh a bill for fees of KShs 158.

Makhan Singh was a very kind person; he followed the teachings of the Sikh gurus and his own father's conduct. Hence he was often called on for help. One Tarlok Singh from Muhoroni wanted his examination results from London that had been received by the Director of Education. He requested Makhan Singh to forward them to him. Later, he thanked Makhan Singh for making the necessary enquiries and asked for some books and magazines. Waryam Singh Gharjakhia sought help regarding remission of school fees for his son Teja Singh.

Makhan Singh participated in the Social Service Flag Day and the Spanish Children's Relief Fund. In August, he joined classes run by the Red Cross Society on precautions to be taken during an air raid. He, together with eight other Indians and forty Europeans, was awarded a certificate and enrolled on the list of persons available for duty. Later he wrote an article on

'How Indians should prepare themselves to meet an emergency in case of war.' He himself practiced physical fitness; one of the teachings he followed was called 'Scientific Body Massage and Instructions on Physical Culture.'

A telegram from one Hazara Singh, a Ghadrite in Mombasa, addressed to Makhan Singh read, 'Start today's train urgent shop condition bad.' Hazara Singh used to assist fellow revolutionaries with embarkation procedures at the port and in this instance there was a serious hitch. He requested Makhan Singh to travel to Mombasa and help him to sort out the problem. It is recorded that in October, 1937, Hazara Singh facilitated the movement of Harnam Singh Sodhi from Russia to Goa via Mombasa.[38]

All the while Makhan Singh continued to compose poetry, and to present his poems at cultural fora. In April the Shri Sanatana Dharama invited him, as on previous occasions, together with other Hindu, Muslim and Sikh poets to a *Kavi Darbar* (Poetry Gathering). In August he attended a *Kavi Sammalan* (Poetry Session) organised by the Arya Samaj. The invitation stipulated that the poems must be moral and social in character and could be written in Hindi, Urdu or Punjabi. The following year he participated in a *Bazm-I-Adab* (Poetry Session) held at the Railway Indian Institute, in which English, Hindi and Punjabi were added to the traditional Urdu languages of expression.

On 29th October, 1939, Makhan Singh was invited to participate in an Inter-religious Conference held in Nairobi. Its agenda was 'to impart true knowledge to followers of all religions and promote goodwill among various religious communities.'

Though his main attention was focussed on trade unionism and freedom from colonialism, Makhan Singh was well aware that for the anticipated changes to be accomplished, the larger society would need to be progressively reformed and mobilised. He had, since his student days, been an avid reader of historical, political and religious writings and was in the habit of making copious notes for his personal use. He now directed the knowledge he had, and continued to acquire, into educating and inspiring his fellow unionists, community members and colleagues.

He had written at length on the labour movement in Kenya. Although largely for his own perusal, his writings were read by fellow trade unionists and occasionally published by the press. From time to time he prepared handwritten notes that he used for reference in a discussion group called the Monday Club. The group appears to have had a clandestine existence; it is not known who the members were or how often they met. It may well have been the precursor of the Marxist study group he was part of much later, in 1948.

In August, he wrote at length on 'the present international chaos,' which he attributed to 'Britain's post-war foreign policy.' He maintained that the wars in Spain and China were a threat to democracy and that they were strengthening the chains of the colonised peoples. His notes included a 'Commercial and Strategic Map of the British Empire' showing naval stations, fortified points, trade routes and the proposed Cape to Cairo railway and telephone lines.

In November, 1938, the secretary of the Tanganyika League wrote to Makhan Singh enclosing three sets of literature on the organisation and twelve enrolment forms. A Major F W Cavendish-Bentinck had formed the League 'to assist the British citizens of Tanganyika to remain an integral part of the Empire.' It was in response to a German pronouncement that she intended to reclaim her colonies. The matter was hotly debated as there was a fear that, as a gesture of goodwill for Germany's fight against communism, Britain might consider abandoning the mandated territory. The League insisted that the interests of Kenya and Uganda were one with those of Tanganyika. The people of the territory supported this view. The EAINC put out a circular highlighting the issue and supported the stand of the League. The British Conservative Party stated that 'Tanganyika in foreign hands would weaken the strategic unity of the whole British Empire.'

This position was by no means unanimous in the Indian community. The *Kenya Daily Mail* in its 13th November issue asked, 'You say just as we claim equal rights we must give our full co-operation. Quite right. But have you got equal rights?' It went on to urge, 'Bargain now – strike while the iron is hot. We need definite promise of equality in the status of our community in all three territories.' The *Colonial Times* in December asked if the EAINC was 'with the League or under it?' Letters from India, while stating an objection to the transfer of Tanganyika to Germany, insisted that 'no single power should possess any colony,' and bemoaned the total drain of wealth from India by the colonial power.

The *Colonial Times* of 26th November, 1938, carried an article by Makhan Singh in which he decried the poor performance of the Indian representatives in the Legco. He was particularly concerned about the lack consultation and joint decision-making amongst them. This translated into the absence of a united front which was so necessary if the Asian members were to succeed in passing legislation in a settler-dominated Legco. He drew attention to the 'hiatus between our representation and the represented and the somnambulant state of the Indian community' and concluded, 'We pray for the return of leaders like Desai.'

Makhan Singh was a delegate to the fifteenth session of the EAINC held on 31st December, 1938, and 1st January, 1939, in the Desai Memorial Hall. It was the Congress' Silver Jubilee Year and it reiterated its fundamental objective of insisting on Indians getting equality of status with other immigrant races and a common roll with common franchise.

The session debated matters ranging from the clove dispute in Zanzibar, the need for Tanganyika to remain British, the White Highlands and the proposed settlement of Jewish refugees in East Africa to inclusion of Indians in defence schemes, the improvement of educational and health facilities for them and increased Indian representation.

At this meeting, Makhan Singh proposed resolutions concerning the representation of unionists on government bodies in charge of formulating the rules regulating shops in the rural areas, the marketing of native produce, the licensing of transport and the control of the dairy industry. He asked for an improvement in conditions for Indian prisoners and the removal of unfair and unjust restrictions on the trade unions. Citing the rise in the cost of living without any change in the wage structure, he asked the government to enquire into the conditions of workers in all industries and trades. He also wanted the East African governments to introduce an ordinance for workmen's compensation and urged the Kenya Uganda Railways and the Public Works Department to put their Indian artisans back on a permanent basis of employment.

THE MOMBASA GENERAL STRIKE OF 1939

The LTUEA celebrated May Day 1939 by holding a workers' meeting in the Desai Memorial Hall. The handbills publicising the meeting were published in Kiswahili in addition to English, Urdu and Gujerati. For the first time the meeting was attended by large numbers of African workers, with leaders of the Kikuyu Central Association (KCA) such as Jesse Kariuki, Joseph Kangethe and George K. Ndegwa participating. The LTUEA and KCA leaders were now working together in organising the day to day struggles of the workers. Class interests were consolidating, and superseding, racial categories. However, the KCA's support of the Union weakened the enthusiasm of some of the Indian members, many of whom preferred, for understandable reasons, to retain the racial terms of service which gave them better terms than it did the Africans.[39]

Third Annual Conference of the LTUEA in Azad Maidan

On Sunday, 23rd July, 1939, the LTUEA held the open session of its third annual conference on *Azad Maidan* (Freedom Ground) behind Desai Memorial Hall. The chairman was Mota Singh, Kenya's veteran trade union leader, and thousands of African and Asian workers attended. Makhan Singh gave the report on behalf of the central committee. Speakers included Jesse Kariuki and George Ndegwa and Kariuki was elected as one of the two vice-presidents of the union while Makhan Singh was re-elected its general secretary.

The conference established a Tenants Association with Kavi Prem Singh as president, Jesse Kariuki as vice president and Abdul Rauf as secretary, for the purpose of taking steps for a reduction in rents and to deal with matters concerning tenants of all races. A wide range of decisions and resolutions were proposed and accepted, including one on the freedoms of speech, press, meeting, movement and organisation.

Leading members of the LTUEA had earlier managed to get six resolutions pertaining to the demands by workers passed at the annual session of the EAINC. Two members, Makhan Singh and one other, had been elected to the executive committee of

Jesse Kariuki

Joseph Kangethe

George Ndegwa

the EAINC. The All India Congress Committee sent fraternal greetings. The LTUEA held a poetry symposium on the 23rd and eleven invited poets recited in Urdu and Punjabi.

But the highlight of the conference was the joint discussions by Asian and African workers for the first time in East Africa. The demonstration of this unity had an immediate effect on the African workers' struggles.

An on-going strike by African railway apprentices in Mombasa sparked off a series of strikes in Mombasa and by August the entire protest became popularly known as the Mombasa African Workers General Strike of 1939. Thousands of handbills were printed in five languages and distributed in Nairobi, Mombasa and other places. The LTUEA annual conference in July had electrified the strike and the number of strikers grew to 6,000. Baton-wielding police charged in, and picketers and others were arrested. On 5th August, the LTUEA held a mass meeting in Nairobi to express solidarity with the striking workers of Mombasa.

On 8th August, dockworkers in Tanga declared a strike. Membership of the LTUEA now stood at 3,000; trade unionism in Kenya had indisputably forged ahead. The government was alarmed. It set up a Mombasa Labour Inquiry Commission on 19th August. Of the seven members, there was one Indian, one Arab and no African; the rest were all Europeans – and none were workers. The principal labour officer, Percy de Vere Allen, reported that the strike had been organised by Makhan Singh and the KCA but no evidence was ever presented. KCA did not have a branch in

MOMBASA

Watu 6,000 Wana "Strike"

WATU WOTE
WATAKUTANA

Siku ya Jumamosi Tarekhe 5th. August 1939.
Saa kumi na moja na nusu, katika
Desai Memorial Hall.
Habari yote watu watajulishwa. Kutaongewa
Kingereza, na Kiswahili na Kihindi.
Watu wote wafanyao kazi na wale wengine· wote
twaomba wafike.
**MAKHAN SINGH General Secretary,
The Labour Trade Union of E. Africa.**

MOMBASA

Andu 6,000 mena "Strike"

Andu othe makagomana muthenya wa
Jumamosi Mweri 5th. August, 1939 thaa ikumi na
imwe na nuthu, kuria Desai Memorial Hall.

Hindi iyo andu niimakamenyithio uhoro
wothe. Gukario Kingretha, na Githwahiri, na Kihindi.

Andu othe aria marutaga wira, o hamwe na
aria angi othe ni wega magakinya.

**MAKHAN SINGH, General Secretary,
The Labour Trade Union of E. Africa.**

Khalsa Press, Nairobi.

Strike Notice in Kiswahili and Gikuyu

Mombasa and Makhan Singh was in Nairobi at the time. He organised a sympathy meeting and then dashed down to Mombasa to testify before a commission of inquiry headed by H C Willan, the attorney general, and which the government had quickly set up, fearing the outbreak of a similar strike in Nairobi. On 4th October, Makhan Singh, as general secretary of the LTUEA, submitted a memorandum and gave oral evidence for about two hours. The memorandum listed 28 different complaints; later it was translated into Kiswahili and distributed widely.

The workers' grievances were fully ventilated. One of the demands was the introduction of a minimum wage which should be based on the requirements of the family, not the individual. The prevailing wage at the time for African workers ranged from ten to fifteen shillings monthly. Based on the 1939

TANGA

WORKERS' STRIKE.

WORKERS FIRED UPON.
SOLIDARITY
MASS MEETING
on SUNDAY, 13th August, 1939,
at 10 a.m. in Desai Memorial Hall.

Full facts of the strike will be presented. Speeches will
be made in English, Swahili and Hindustani.
All workers and public are requested to attend.

MAKHAN SINGH, General Secretary,
The Labour Trade Union of East Africa.

ટાંગાના કામદારોની હડતાલ

જાહેર સભા

રવીવાર ૧૩-૮-૩૯ ના સવારે ૧૦ વાગે
દેશાઇ મેમોરીયલ હોલમાં ભરાશે.

ટાંગાના હડતાલનું ખરા સમાચારો રજુ કરવામાં આવશે.
સર્વે કામદારો અને જાહેર જનતાને પધારવા વિનંતી છે.

મખન સિંગ, મંત્રી,
લેબર ટ્રેડ યુનીયન ઓફ ઈ. આ.

ਟਾਂਗਾ ਦੇ ਕਿਰਤੀਆਂ ਦੀ ਹੜਤਾਲ

ਹੜਤਾਲੀ ਮਜ਼ਦੂਰਾਂ ਤੇ ਗੋਲੀ ਚਲਾਈ ਗਈ।

ਐਤਵਾਰ, ੧੩-੮-੩੯, ਨੂੰ ਸਵੇਰੇ ੧੦ ਵਜੇ

ਇਸ ਬਾਰੇ ਇਕ ਜ਼ਬਰਦਸਤ ਮੀਟਿੰਗ

ਹੋਵੇਗੀ। ਹੜਤਾਲ ਦੇ ਪੂਰੇ ਹਾਲਾਤ ਪੇਸ਼ ਕੀਤੇ ਜਾਣਗੇ। ਸਾਰੇ ਕਿਰਤੀ ਤੇ
ਪਬਲਿਕ ਜ਼ਰੂਰ ਦਰਸ਼ਨ ਦੇਣ। ਮੱਖਣ ਸਿੰਘ, ਜਨਰਲ ਸਕੱਤਰ,
ਲੇਬਰ ਟਰੇਡ ਯੂਨੀਅਨ ਆਫ ਈਸਟ ਅਫਰੀਕਾ।

Khalsa Press, Nairobi.

A strike poster in English, Gujerati, Gurumukhi and Urdu

cost of living index, the union wanted a minimum monthly wage of fifty shillings. Other demands included regulation of the working hours, improvement of conditions at work, provision of health care, primary education, unemployment insurance, annual leave with pay and old age pensions. Better cooperation with the trade unions and encouragement of the formation of such unions, establishment of rent boards for the control of rents and neat and clean houses at low rents were further demands. The use of unnecessary force against the strikers was condemned.

On the whole, the results of the Mombasa African Workers General Strike were encouraging. Housing or housing allowances began to be provided. The crowded unplanned African locations of Nairobi and Mombasa were singularly depressing places in which to live. Mombasa, in this respect, was among the worst in the colony and slowly between 1939 and 1947 there emerged a class, in addition to the already prevailing race, consciousness among the workers there. The strike seems to have been more of a class than a political protest, some wages were increased, but more importantly it had an electric effect as workers in all trades and industries began to see the need for organisation. The trade union movement in Kenya had received another boost.

The militant Socialist International of London wrote to the LTUEA offering to mail their *Socialist Vanguard*, a monthly journal, on an exchange basis. Makhan Singh replied, 'It is unfortunate our movement is in its initial stages; it publishes no labour or political journals. This is a great drawback in our movement and we are trying to remove it'. He sent information about the LTUEA to the Colonial *Information Bulletin* in London.

On 12th February, he travelled to Mombasa to give a lecture in the Ramgharia Sabha Sikh temple premises. The subject of his talk was 'The conditions of Indian workers in East Africa and the way to redress them.' Later in the year, the LTUEA conducted a trade union course for training its functionaries. The course lectures were based on a book by John A Mahon and one by Creech Jones. Makhan Singh gave 10 lectures in Hindustani to an average attendance of nine. He also conducted a course in English for a Luo member of the union.[40]

On 12th August, he addressed the Literary Meeting of the Indian Youth League in Nairobi and traced for them, the history of the Indian National Congress from its inception in 1885. He noted Gandhi's return to India from South Africa in 1915, the Jallianwala Bagh Massacre in 1919 followed by two years of civil disobedience, the rise of both the labour and youth movements and of terrorism and further radicalisation of the Congress leading to civil disobedience from 1930 to 1932. He emphasised the strengthening of the worker and peasant organisations, which ultimately contributed to the formation of two distinct camps in the Congress, and the parts they played in the freedom struggle.

Soon after the LTUEA conference, the Union wrote to Jomo Kenyatta who was then in England. The World Committee against War and Fascism was holding an international conference on 'Problems of the Defence of Democracy, Peace and Humanity'. It was scheduled for 30th September, and 1st October, in Brussels, Belgium. Makhan Singh informed Kenyatta that the LTUEA could not bear the expenses of the journey from Kenya and requested him to represent it. Kenyatta replied, addressing him as 'Dear Comrade,' thanking him and agreeing to the request. He asked Makhan Singh to send a memorandum and expressed pleasure that Makhan Singh was cooperating with the KCA. The letter was written on a KCA letterhead that stated 'Fort Hall' as its headquarters. But as World War II commenced in the beginning of September, all further correspondence was curtailed and the conference never took place.

THE EFFECTS OF WORLD WAR II

In June, 1939, before the war had been declared, the Indian Manpower Committee, through its Nairobi sub-committee, asked the LTUEA to supply it with the names and addresses of firms employing Indian workers to enable it to enrol them for wartime service. The union wrote back that it was not prepared to comply.[41] The LTUEA had made a clear decision not to support the British war effort.

Interestingly, Isher Dass, the fiery anti-colonialist, accepted the position as director of the Indian Manpower Committee. His job was to control and regulate the supply and cost of Asian artisans to the war effort; and to assist the government in its intention to introduce the kipande, which had hitherto been restricted to Africans, for Asians. Many Indians saw this as a complete betrayal and, at a meeting he called to explain his stand; he was pelted with stones and sticks and had to flee. The explanation for his turnabout possibly lay in Stalin's declaration at the Second Comintern that fascism was a greater enemy than colonialism.[42]

Makhan Singh and his LTUEA colleagues took a neutral stand in the war. Makhan Singh's overriding concern was the oppressed condition of the working class. In his lifelong struggle to mobilise and organise workers, both in Kenya and in India, to liberate themselves; he espoused any ideology, political platform, organisation and leadership which could support him in his cause. Though fully aware of the ideological and political debates, he kept aloof from all that was extraneous to his objective, and studiously avoided becoming embroiled in, to him, irrelevant controversies. He was first and foremost an activist. For him, the need to maintain unity was uppermost in all his work and he would never criticise, or even comment upon, his socialist and anti-colonial associates. Makhan Singh maintained complete independence of thought and his principled commitment was to focus on the rights and responsibilities of the workers. He guarded this independence zealously and this is evident in his refusal to ally the LTUEA to any international trade union or labour movement, east or west.

Throughout his life he neither wrote nor commented on the different sectarian trends in the left movement. For example, he makes no mention anywhere of the Ghadr Movement and yet some of the people he was closest to in Kenya were Gopal Singh, Vasudev Singh and Kavi Prem Singh who were Ghadrite leaders. They were older than Makhan Singh who, initially, was probably too young to be aware of their clandestine activities when he first met them. But given his remarkable intelligence and drive, he could not have remained ignorant for long.

Gopal Singh arrived in Kenya in 1929 and used to accompany Makhan Singh, when he formed the LTU, to all the conferences organised in Nairobi and other towns. In 1932, he returned to India for five years, but then, in 1937, came back to

Kenya. He travelled frequently to India to attend to his family affairs and brought his wife and children to Kenya in 1946. His first job was as a carpenter with the Railways, but in 1939 he settled in Nairobi and started a photographic shop which later became known as Star Studio. Other active Ghadrites were Amar Singh Jalandhari and Hazara Singh, the electrician in Mombasa. Like Hazara Singh and at considerable risk to himself, Gopal Singh used to collect Ghadrites arriving from India at the Mombasa port, take them to his home and arrange for their passage to Moscow. At first, he did not know any English and was known by the pen name, Gopal Singh *Dhukia*, meaning 'wretched or miserable.' In 1947, when India became free, he changed this to Chandan, the name of a well-known bard of Guru Gobind Singh's court[43]. Some of the Ghadr leaders maintained a pro-German/Italian connection and while Makhan Singh would have supported their anti-imperialist ideology, he would have disassociated himself from any partisan preferences. Gopal Singh, Hazara Singh and Ujagar Singh (mentioned earlier) were all members of the LTU.

In India, there were sharp differences between those who supported the British war effort, those who favoured the other side and those who wished to remain neutral. While the Punjab Legislative Assembly, Congress and Gandhi gave their unconditional support to Great Britain, the revolutionary Subhas Chandra Bose trained a small army and joined the Japanese forces.

Even after World War II had started, Makhan Singh and the LTUEA continued to make their demands. They deplored the ineffective protection against the war provided to the civilian population and the Compulsory Service Ordinances passed by the East African governments. In 1940, the LTUEA demanded that workers be compensated for the rise in the cost of living. The *Colonial Times* wrote 'Fresh taxation and the increase in the price of goods have already broken the back of the average citizen'.

Isher Dass continued to present the resolutions of the

LTUEA in the Legco.[44] In September, 1942, he supported a
motion to appoint Africans to the Legco. That was his last
significant contribution as, on 6th November, 1942, he was shot
dead in his office by a Sikh worker. A year earlier, the head of
the (European) Manpower Board in Nairobi, the Earl of Errol,
who was veering away from fascist affiliations, had also been
murdered. Both murders have been officially attributed to
romantic motives, affairs of the heart, but the real reasons may
well lie elsewhere. In the Ghadr Directory of 1934, Isher Dass is
mentioned as a conduit for funds for the Ghadr Kirti Party in
Kenya. Devinder Singh was one of the recipients; money could
have been a possible motive or reason. A fitting epitaph for
Dass is that, whereas to the conservatives he was an extremist,
the people loved him.[45]

FAMILY MATTERS

During all this time, Makhan Singh had had family matters
to attend to. Immediately after his marriage to Satwant Kaur in
1934, he had left her in India and returned to Kenya. She was
feeling the pangs of separation and as we have seen Makhan
Singh sent her a poem to allay her distress. But it was not just
the one poem, he wrote several, using the pseudonym 'Bhan'
which means 'brightness'.

Why this separation should cause
So much pain to the heart
When the very passion
Is teaching us how to fight injustice
And love gives us strength to continue.
This separation of love
Can be the water that nourishes
The plant of sacrifice

Satwant and Bhan have got together
To wipe out the filth of lies and deceit
From our hearts.

He continued to write encouraging words to his wife as can
be seen in this poem.

After the autumn comes the spring
After the thorns come the flowers
After suffering comes happiness
After struggle fulfilment
What kind of humans are we
If we lose hope before achievement
These pangs of separation
Will eventually raise our hearts.

Sohan Singh, Makhan Singh's friend in Gujranwalla,
informed him that his wife would be returning to Lahore on 15th
October. He mentioned being surprised that Satwant Kaur
wept when he instructed her to cover her face when outside the
house as that was the accepted custom. Needless to say,
Makhan Singh must have had different ideas and Satwant Kaur
felt confused. Sohan Singh's father lived in Nairobi in very
poor circumstances and so, in addition, Sohan Singh requested
Makhan Singh to assist him, especially in finding employment.

Meanwhile in June, 1935, Sudh Singh, Makhan Singh's
father, travelled to India via Sri Lanka and Calcutta. Makhan
Singh ran the printing business in his absence and then joined
him in November to attend the wedding of his sister, Kulwant
Kaur to Shivcharan Singh from Peshawar. Makhan Singh
returned to Nairobi in February, 1936, finally bringing his
young wife with him. Sudh Singh travelled with them and his
wife, Isher Kaur, joined him the following August.

Satwant Kaur delivered a baby boy a year later, on 15th
February, 1937 in Nairobi, and they named him Hindpal. The
initial letter 'H' was taken from the Guru Granth Sahib. The

Makhan Singh (second right) as a scout

custom was for a priest in the gurdwara to open the book at random; the first letter on the page would then be the first letter of the child's name. Makhan Singh created the name to encompass his political creed, *pal* meaning 'protector of', *Hind* being India. In August, Satwant Kaur made plans to visit India. Her family seemed anxious to see her, as both her father and her brother wrote several letters enquiring about the date of her departure by ship. She travelled in September, taking little Hindpal with her. In India they first stayed with her brother Harbajan Singh Mahal in New Delhi. Dr Mahal, a chemical analyser in the Bombay Government, seemed to be particularly concerned about his sister's welfare, especially when she was in Kenya. Satwant Kaur kept in touch with Makhan Singh by occasionally adding a few lines in Punjabi to the regular correspondence between her father and her husband in Kenya.

During this period Makhan Singh pursued his interest in the scouting movement. He rose to the position of 'scoutmaster' and participated in training camps held outside Nairobi, and even Kenya.

In May, 1939, Satwant Kaur accompanied Kulwant Kaur and her husband back to Nairobi. The Mahal family was planning the weddings of the two sons, Harbajan Singh and Kartar Singh during the Sikh *Vaisakhi* (New Year) festival which was always held in April, the harvest season. They informed Makhan Singh that he too was expected to attend the wedding. There was a delay in the arrangements as the girl who had been betrothed to Kartar Singh passed away. Then Tara Singh, the groom's father, could not hold the ceremonies during the cotton harvesting season. Moreover, he had been laid up with a bad abscess.

In June, Makhan Singh had requested the LTUEA for leave to visit India for a few months and this was granted in December. He expressly stated that he was taking temporary leave and left Gopal Singh Chandan in charge of the LTUEA.

Gopal Singh Chandan

He left Nairobi by train on 23rd December, and sailed for India from Mombasa on Thursday 28th. His family members embarked on 3rd February, 1940.

CHAPTER FIVE

INDIA
1939-1947

Makhan Singh sailed from Mombasa on Thursday, 28th December, 1939. The steamer stopped at Seychelles and Goa before reaching Bombay on 6th January. Before disembarking he disguised himself as a Muslim. He shaved off his beard and long hair (kesh), put on a Muslim cap and wrapped a *tehmet* (sarong) around his waist.

The LTUEA was not banned but the colonial authorities in Kenya were keeping a close watch on it and knew that it depended for its success, on the initiative of one person; Makhan Singh.[1] Throughout 1935-1939 the trade union movement remained his personal creation, when he left for India, union activity lapsed. And there was no effective political or labour vehicle of protest for the African worker no matter how bad his conditions came to be. The colonists by and large failed to recognise the deteriorating economic and political situation of the African and Asian workers – their attitude can be summed up in the words of one anonymous European, '. . . what we deprecate is the greed, slackness and insolence . . . in households where there is a bwana to kick him in the pants, the native may still be amenable to discipline.'[2]

The government's disapproval of trade unions in general and its hostility to Makhan Singh, the general secretary of the LTUEA, were unmistakable. On 5th January 1940, the acting attorney-general, had, during a debate, informed the Legco that the secretary of the union had left for India. One member, Major Grogan, asked rhetorically if he too could be imprisoned for subversive activities. No reply was given. Makhan Singh's bitter hostility to colonial rule was well known; his ability to organise and mobilise the workers, especially across the racial divide, was a potent threat to the powers-that-were. The leadership role he was purported to have played in the recent Mombasa General Strike and the memorandum he presented to the Inquiry Commission made him a marked man.

He had good reason to be cautious, even in India. Late in 1939, Mota Singh, a former president of the LTUEA and one of the very active communists of his time, had been detained in

India soon after reaching there. Mota Singh had first arrived in Nairobi in 1926 at the age of 22 years. He worked as a stonemason and established a construction company called Dilbagh Singh & Bros. He returned to the Punjab, probably in the early 1930s and in 1934 was framed in a dacoity (banditry) case and jailed. He was released following a visit by Nehru, and then returned to Nairobi. He was arrested again in India in 1939, and was tortured in the infamous Lahore *Shahi Qila* (fort) and remained in prison until 1945.[3]

ARREST AND DETENTION

Makhan Singh was well aware that he too could be arrested. Hence the disguise, but his activist spirit would not allow him to remain idle, even in hiding. In Bombay, he attended the popularly anticipated 'Independence Day' celebrations which used to be held on 26th January. He got in touch with underground comrades and was assigned to work in Ahmedabad, a large industrial city 500 kilometres north of Bombay. He travelled there exactly a month later and began working with a textile union. February, 1940, was taken up organising strike actions with the textile workers demanding, not only better wages and conditions of work, but also *swaraj* or full independence. In the first week of March he addressed a large mass meeting of about 30,000 workers and strikers and later in the month, attended a Ramgharia Session of the Indian National Congress as a fraternal delegate from East Africa. It was in this session that Congress gave full authority to Mahatma Gandhi to launch a *Satyagraha* movement whenever he deemed it necessary.

On 1st May, 1940, Makhan Singh participated in a May Day parade. With the intensification of the freedom struggle and working class movement, political and trade union leaders were being detained without trial. The Defence of India Rules were similar to Kenya's Defence Regulations, promulgated at the beginning of the war. Makhan Singh was arrested in Ahmedabad on 8th May and remained detained and restricted without trial in various parts of India for five years.

In the same month of his arrest in India, 23 prominent leaders of the Kikuyu Central Association, the Ukamba Members Association, the Teita Hills Association and LTUEA were arrested in Kenya and the first three organisations were declared illegal. Those arrested included Jesse Kariuki and George K Ndegwa of the LTUEA. They were sent to a detention camp in Kapenguria and remained there for most of the war. The LTUEA had earlier made representations to the Colonial Office that Kenya's Trade Unions Ordinance of 1937 be amended to allow the unions to function without undue restrictions. The concerted action of Kenya's settlers and reactionary officers in the Colonial Office resulted in the Trade Unions (Amendment) Bill being withdrawn.

In India, Makhan Singh was moved from prison to prison so he got to meet many communist, socialist and revolutionary leaders from all over India. This gave him the opportunity to discuss and debate the politics of the day and the different ideological arguments as well as to inform his fellow prisoners about conditions in Kenya. From 9th May to 2nd June he was detained in the historic jail in Sabarmati. Then he was taken by train to Lahore to start a month's internment in Lahore Fort.

Satwant Kaur and little Hindpal were staying with her father in Lahore so they came to the railway station. Makhan Singh had not seen his wife and son for over two years and on seeing his father behind bars of the railway carriage, four-year old Hindpal began to cry. A policeman standing near to him put his hand on his shoulder and said to him, 'Why are you crying? Your father is such a brave man, you must be brave too.' Makhan Singh's name was obviously already well known in the Punjab. It was especially known in police circles as, on an earlier occasion, Makhan Singh had slapped a policeman, a fellow Sikh who had used abusive language to him. Makhan Singh, who was only 5ft 3ins in height, had climbed on to a chair and chastised him.[4] The only time he is known to have protested physically.

On 6th July, 1940 he was taken by train to Muzaffar jail where he remained until 20th October. From there he was moved to Deoli Detention Camp, where he remained incarcerated for almost fourteen months, his longest prison sojourn. Between October and November he went on a hunger strike with 160 other detainees there. The strike lasted for 16 days and ended successfully with the welfare conditions of the detainees being radically improved. On 19th January, 1942 he was taken by train to Gujrat jail. Six months later, on 25th July, 1942, he was finally released from prison but restricted to his village, Gharjakh, and ordered to report every week to the police station in Gujranwala.

Satwant Kaur and Hindpal joined him in Gharjhak. Hindpal

Detainees released from Gujarat Jail. Comrade Ram Chandra, S Rattan Singh, S Sher Singh, Mubarak Sapar, S Chhaja Singh, Des Raj Chadha, S Makhan Singh. Photographed at Lahore Railway Station. Picture publised in the Tribune, 27th July 1942.

attended school in Gujranwala, Satwant Kaur, although she did not enjoy the village life, kept busy with household chores. Makhan Singh had never owned anything, not even a bicycle. Now he bought himself a cow, but this investment was a failure. The cow consumed more than the value of the milk she produced and one day died. That was his first and last attempt at 'ownership'.[5]

In India, Makhan Singh always wore white kurta pyjamas made of *khadi*, India's homespun cloth, a summer jacket and a white turban. His beard was trimmed. In no time he was gathering the young village children and regaling them with stories about the injustices of British imperialism and India's valiant freedom fighters. The parents, however, were not amused and tried to keep the children away from him. He already carried the label 'communist' – a tag that imperialism had made akin to a red rag to a bull. His comrades often referred to him as their 'Bhagat Singh', in reference to one of India's most famous revolutionaries who was hanged in Lahore, in 1931, by the British at the age of 24. Bhagat Singh's birthplace was not far from Gharjakh.

JOINING THE COMMUNIST PARTY

The label was correct. Makhan Singh had become a member of the Communist Party of India and was contributing to the theoretical and organisational work of the party. He spent his time in prison translating Marx's *Das Kapital* into Punjabi using the Gurumukhi script.[6] In 1942, Jagjit Singh Anand, editor of *Jang-I-Azadi* (Struggle for Freedom), organ of the Communist Party, received a translation into Punjabi by Makhan Singh of Dialectical Materialism, a chapter in *Das Kapital*. Anand, a contemporary of Makhan Singh, recalls his deep impression of

Makhan Singh's grasp of theory as well as his mastery of the Punjabi language. The two men worked on the editorial board of *Jang-I-Azadi* until the time Makhan Singh left India for Kenya in 1947.

In December, 1943, Makhan Singh finalised the constitution on which he had been working, of the Punjab Students Federation. The organisation brought all the students in the Punjab under one umbrella and enabled them to interact with other student bodies in India. The principal objectives were to encourage cultural and intellectual cooperation, to work for a sound educational system, to safeguard the rights of the student community and to prepare students for citizenship by arousing their political, social and economic consciousness.

In February, 1944, he was arrested again on the charge that he had broken a restriction order by publishing an article. He was jailed in Gujranwala until June when he was acquitted, his convincing argument being that he had written an article but it had not been published.

On 11th January, 1945, F C Bourne, Chief Secretary, Government of the Punjab, signed Order No 7414A D. S. B. cancelling the restriction order that had been placed on 30th November, 1943, on Makhan Singh. All restrictions were lifted unconditionally on the 19th and Makhan Singh then moved with his family to his in-laws' house in Model Town, Lahore. A month later, he visited the Lahore hospital to have his spectacles up-dated. He had spent four and a half years in detention in India and the imprisonment had affected his eyesight. Makhan Singh and Satwant Kaur's second child was born on 2nd July, 1945 in Lahore. It was a girl and the Mahals, who held the naming ceremony for her, named her Inderjeet. The selection of the first letter 'I' was done at the Panjsaheb shrine near Islamabad; it was a family joke that had Makhan Singh had his way he would have named his daughter, *Inquilab* or Revolution.[7]

From February, 1945, to July, 1947, Makhan Singh was not only working with Jagjit Singh Anand on *Jangi-I-Azadi* but he was also actively involved in mobilising the peasants through the Communist Party's *Kisan Sabha* (Peasant Movement). In spite of his weakened condition at the time, he remained constantly on the move. He travelled by bus everyday from Model Town to the *Jangi-I-Azadi* offices and press. Hindpal remembers accompanying his father once to the press, where he, a curious youngster of eight, lifted a tray and the type-set letters all fell out. Typical of Makhan Singh, there was no fuss or scolding and the type-setters just settled down to the extra work. The party gave him just enough money for his bus fare and a simple diet, Sudh Singh used to augment this by sending 50-60 rupees every month. Makhan Singh worked heart and soul for the peasants and the Kisan Sabha would not release him in spite of appeals from his Kenyan comrades. Makhan Singh himself was torn between remaining in India and returning to Kenya.

Ambu Patel noted that when Makhan Singh left for India 'EATU[C] was in decline and I lost touch with him; but when I went to India I contacted him again. I knew that he had joined the communist party at Lahore. While he was with the communist party his father sent him a good sum of money which he donated to the party work like other comrades. He was working in the party's press and was getting a living hourly allowance. While working for the party he was briefly arrested. He was offered release and 'something big' on the condition that he give up the party and political work and [join] a government contract. Makhan Singh refused to do so.'[8]

With Makhan Singh involved in party work in India, Sudh Singh had returned to Kenya where he continued to run his Khalsa press and support the family. Initially, his financial position was not so good but this improved during the war years. He planned to stay on in Kenya and, in 1944, sold the old machines of the Khalsa Press to Reliance Press and renamed it the 'Punjab Press'. The following year he moved the press, for a brief period, to Kirinyaga Road and then finally to Duruma Road (Varma Road then) off River Road. The same year, he built himself a residential house in Park Road in the Ngara area and moved out of the house he had been renting. His wife, their daughter and her husband lived with him.

During this period his wife, Isher Kaur, developed a chronic skin disease which afflicted her badly. Years of hardship and child-bearing had taken their toll and she did not have as sturdy a physique as the rest of the family. In 1945, Sudh Singh took her to India for a year for treatment but they did not succeed in finding a cure.[9]

PREPARING TO RETURN TO KENYA

World War II ended in August 1945. Makhan Singh termed it a 'complete victory over fascism, both in Europe and the Far East' and began to make plans for leaving India. On 9th October, 1945, the principal immigration officer in Nairobi wrote to Sudh Singh, Makhan Singh's father, informing him that 'there will be no objection to the re-entry into Kenya Colony of Mr. Makhan Singh from India.' A copy was sent to the immigration office in Mombasa. But a later event rang a warning bell. When, in June 1946, a journalist with the *Colonial Times*, W L Sohan, was released after serving a jail term of four months' hard labour in Kenya for sedition, his re-entry permit, which would have allowed him to travel out of Kenya and return, was cancelled.

Sudh Singh began to send his son press clippings relevant to the political and labour scene in Kenya. Makhan Singh noted some observations on the differences in the situation of the Indian community between 1926 and 1946. In 1926, the Indians had been united, the European settlers were not very strong, the government of India had considerable influence, and there were few vocal Africans.

But now, in 1946, the Indians were divided, with Muslims favouring separate representation. The Europeans were united, vehemently against an open-door immigration policy, and in a strong position. The government of India had lost its influence over the British government and many Africans were making their demands and opinions heard.

On 9th October, 1945, Sudh Singh had applied for and been given a re-entry permit into Kenya for Makhan Singh. The number was CIDIS 49/A/83470/, issued in Nairobi. Some months later he received the news that the permit might have been cancelled. On 22nd February, 1947, Makhan Singh wrote to Kenya's chief secretary enquiring about a possible ban on his entry into Kenya. He sent copies of his letter to Jawaharlal Nehru, Jomo Kenyatta, the EAINC and LTUEA. Two weeks later he received a telegram from Sudh Singh saying: 'Entry permit not cancelled. Come immediately.'

Makhan Singh needed to get a new passport, as the previous one had expired. Inordinate delays on the part of the Punjab government forced him ultimately, in 1947, to appeal to Jawaharlal Nehru, who personally intervened and Passport No 93397 was issued to him on 11th July. (He gave his last permanent address as '18C Model Town, Lahore.') That same month, Sudh Singh sent particulars of Makhan Singh's entry permit to the immigration authorities in Bombay, stating that his son was coming to join him in business and requesting them to allow him to 'embark without any hindrance.' He also remitted rupees 2,000 by air to Makhan Singh for his steamer fare. In July, a police informer in India known as IB made a report that the Kenya police were anxious to ensure that 'Punjab Police Suspect 191 was not allowed to enter British East Africa because of his meddling in anti-British and subversive activities during his stay there.'

In April, S G Amin, president of the EAINC, travelled to India to join James Beauttah at the Asia Conference being held in Delhi. Makhan Singh met with them there for three days and had useful discussions. Beauttah, writing about the talks later,

said that he had urged
Makhan Singh to return to
Kenya to 'help organise
the unions in such a way
that they would help in
the political struggle.' He
was particularly
concerned that the unions
manage themselves, as
opposed to being
government-sponsored
and therefore,
government-controlled.[10]

Writing to his father in
May, Makhan Singh
thanked him for his three

James Beauttah

letters and apologised for the delay in replying. 'The riots have
started,' he said in reference to the Indo-Pakistan conflict on the
eve of independence. 'It takes time to decide one's direction in
life. Though I have decided now, the conditions are very
difficult. We are still safe from the riots, only sporadic ones in
Lahore, but the curfews are on. I am going to a peasants'
conference in Uttar Pradesh. I have received the monies you
sent me.' He also informed his father that Hindpal had passed
his school examinations.

It was a time of great upheaval on the Indian subcontinent
and especially in the Punjab as large populations of Hindus,
Muslims and Sikhs relocated themselves. The creation of
Pakistan while giving a new home to many also evicted others
and the region became engulfed in one of the most brutal
conflicts the sub-continent had ever witnessed. Gharjhak,
Gujranwala and Lahore were all ceded to Pakistan. Makhan
Singh's own family and his wife's family both moved to India,
leaving behind their ancestral homes. Four truckloads of the
Mahal possessions were looted in Lahore and they arrived in
their new home with virtually only the clothes they were

James Beauttah with Pandit Jawaharlal Nehru at Asia Conference

wearing.

Makhan Singh arrived in Bombay on 30th July, his wife and the two children two days later. He sent a telegram to Nehru informing him that he was going back to East Africa after eight years' of participation in the freedom struggle in India. 'Remained detenue five years,' he stated and went on to suggest that Nehru 'wire an independence message for East Africa's two lakh Indians.' He signed himself as 'Ex-member Executive Committee, East Africa Indian National Congress.'

Leaving his wife and children in Bombay with her brother Harbajan Singh Mahal, he sailed on 6th August, on the SS Shirala, travelling third class, and arrived on the 20th in Mombasa. On 15th August, crew and passengers celebrated India's Independence Day on board. In his own words, 'One aim of my life, the freedom of India, has been achieved.' A day prior to disembarking his passport was, through an oversight, stamped as 'allowed to land'. Unbeknown to him, in May he had been declared a prohibited immigrant in Kenya and his re-

entry permit had in fact been cancelled while he was on the
high seas.

CHAPTER SIX

KENYA
1947-1950

When Makhan Singh disembarked, Sudh Singh telegraphed his friend Gurbukshrai of Mbaraki Workshop in Mombasa to receive his son.

Those who went to meet Makhan Singh must have been aware of the government's intentions, for they took him through a side entrance and managed to secretly whisk him out of the harbour, past the immigration officers. He left the very same evening by train for Nairobi, arriving there on 22nd August.

The *Kenya Daily Mail* of 27th August ran a headline announcing Makhan Singh's arrival. But, on the same day, the government issued a Quit Order. Citing an Immigration Restriction Ordinance, the principal immigration officer declared Makhan Singh an 'undesirable immigrant who had been allowed to land through an oversight.' His status was now that of a 'prohibited immigrant' and he was ordered to leave the colony within 30 days.

The six years of World War II had been tense and difficult. Nevertheless, the struggles and strikes continued unabated. On the trade union front, the LTUEA had appointed Gopal Singh, Makhan Singh's close friend and colleague, to serve as acting general secretary in the latter's absence. Not only did these actions unite the workers but they also helped to strengthen the nationalist struggle for justice and equality. Two important events, the World Trade Union Conference in London in February, 1945 and the Pan-African Congress in Manchester eight months later, greatly encouraged the trade union movement in Kenya.[1]

The major consequence of proscribing African political organisations and the only labour organisation, the LTUEA, was that a dangerous political vacuum was created. During this period, there was no political or trade union organisation which could speak for the African masses, many of whom were being asked to make great sacrifices in order to support an imperialist war. On the other hand, it was during this time that the white settlers in Kenya attempted through various pressure groups, political and economic, to wring maximum privileges and benefits from the colonial government.[2]

THE MOMBASA GENERAL STRIKE OF 1947

On 13th January, 1947, 15,000 African workers of Mombasa started another general strike, which lasted until 25th January. The overall result was that, in addition to winning an increase in wages for nearly all workers of Kenya, the strike created a tremendous awakening for the rights of workers and a national consciousness. The African Workers Union, led by the 28-year old Chege Kibachia, was renamed the African Workers' Federation to avoid confusion with the Kenya African Union (KAU) which had been formed in 1944. Kibachia was well read, including in the works of Karl Marx, but did not have any theoretical or practical experience of trade union organising. This resulted in short term success but the agitation could not be sustained. The strike did paralyse Mombasa for almost two weeks but efforts to spread the African Workers' Federation nationally and to merge it with KAU were not successful, despite the fact that James Beauttah had formed a branch of KAU in Mombasa.

Judge Ransley Thacker, who three years later was to send Makhan Singh into detention, chaired the tribunal to look into the strike. In his submission, Kibachia gave the motives behind the strike as the refusal of employers to pay Africans on the

Chege Kibachia

same scale as workers of other races who were doing the same jobs and the disrespect shown to the African worker wherever he was employed.

The strike had involved 15,000 men and the government became seriously alarmed. The *Mombasa Times* was convinced that the strike was part of a large-scale conspiracy. However, only one serious charge was brought, that was against Haroon Ahmed, editor of the *Daily Chronicle*. Handsome and good-natured but serious, he was imprisoned for six months for making a false statement likely to cause fear and alarm. The publisher was fined KPounds 200. The article claimed that the police had instructions to fire on the strikers but had been delayed by bad weather at Nairobi airport. It was based on information given to Haroon Ahmed by Gurwand Sheth, a civil servant, but, in court, Haroon Ahmed refused to divulge his source. On 22nd August, the same day that Makhan Singh disembarked in Mombasa, Kibachia, together with eighteen other leaders of the African Workers' Federation, was arrested. Three advocates, O'Brien, D N Nene and C A Patel, defended him, but in September he was found guilty, detained and restricted to Kabarnet in Baringo District for ten years.[3]

The strike spirit spread countrywide and the Federation headquarters were moved from Mombasa to Nairobi. But with the arrest of its leaders, the organisation was collapsing. Makhan Singh took it over and, in a show of bravado, appointed Chege Kibachia, in detention, as president. The government reacted sharply by arresting more trade unionists in Mombasa, but Makhan Singh remained undaunted. However, the Federation was largely a paper organisation.

Rather than organise, Makhan Singh preferred to use the name of Kibachia as a stick with which to beat the administration. Later, in March, 1950, Makhan Singh called a meeting at Kaloleni Hall in Nairobi to start a massive campaign for freeing Kibachia but, as a result, more union officials were arrested. Nevertheless, the events of 1947 had shocked the colony and forced the government to consider seriously the causes of labour unrest and created a labour legend which later labour leaders could invoke.

Makhan Singh's return to Kenya aroused the gravest apprehensions among the colonial authorities as they were well aware of his record as a very effective trade union leader prior to World War II. A lengthy biographical note in an intelligence report sent to the under-secretary of state in London from Kenya in November, 1949, tersely summed up his activities in 1936 as 'Worked to affect Moscow control over Nairobi Trade Unions'. As stated earlier, according to the Kenya historian Bethwell A Ogot, 'trade unionism in Kenya from 1935 to 1950 owes its success to the vision, dedication and selflessness of one person: Makhan Singh.'[4] It was not surprising that the government had become so wary of him.

THE QUIT ORDER

Shorn of technical detail, the Quit Order issued on 27th August, 1947, by the principal immigration officer read:

'Whereas you Makhan Singh . . . were deemed on the 13th May, 1947, by the Principal Immigration Officer to be an Undesirable Immigrant under Sec.5(f) of the Immigration Restriction Ordinance and whereas such decision was confirmed by the Governor in Council on the 23rd May, 1947, and whereas you . . . did enter . . . Kenya on or about the 21st August, 1947, having been allowed to land through an oversight . . . Now therefore, in exercise of the powers conferred upon me by Sec.8, I hereby order you . . ., a prohibited immigrant, within the meaning of Sub-section (f) of Sec.5, to leave the Colony within 30 days from the date of service of this Order.

Failure to comply with this Order is an offence under Section 8 and any person so convicted may, in addition to liability to removal or otherwise, be imprisoned with or without hard labour for any term not exceeding six months, provided such imprisonment shall cease if and when arrangements are made for the deportation of any offender from the Colony.'5

The *Daily Chronicle* and the *Kenya Daily Mail* newspapers gave full publicity to the Quit Order. They published photographs of Makhan Singh, who demanded to know why he was not informed by the authorities when his re-entry was cancelled. Nor, he added, had the newspapers, which consistently kept their readers informed of every development, reported the matter. Makhan Singh wrote to the EAINC, to the Hon. A B Patel, to Prime Minister Nehru and to the India League in London. The EAINC in turn wrote to the government of India.

The press also highlighted the Immigration Bill that had been introduced by the government, the main purpose of which was to control and limit the entry of Indians into the colony. Chanan Singh (once a clerk for the Kenya Railway who had, by self-education, qualified as a lawyer, edited a newspaper called *Forward* and later rose to become chief justice) wrote a booklet entitled *The Indian Case against the Immigration Bill*. He stated that, owing to the food and housing shortages, more Indians were leaving rather than entering the colony. The recent arrivals were those brought in by the manpower committees. He argued that statistics showed that the Indian population was increasing no faster than the European one. The per capita income of the Indian was a quarter that of the European. He justified the immigration of

Indians on the basis that Indians employed large numbers of Africans, and there was no question of competition as the wages earned by the Indian were 200% higher than those paid to the African.

However, Hon. Eluid Mathu, the African who had been appointed as a member of the Legco in 1944 at the constant insistence of Isher Dass and other Indian MPs, supported the Bill 'because Africans ought to be protected from unfair competition.'

Chanan Singh held brief for Makhan Singh. Much later, in 1976, he wrote 'I had been practising for two years when a young Indian, Makhan Singh, approached me for assistance in a legal battle which he thought he should have to fight against the government. This, if I agreed, should give me an opportunity to test some of my ideas about the constitutional rights of subjects. I was pleased that I had been approached and I unhesitatingly agreed to act for him. I did not know then that I would have to fight for him in several courts for several years.'[6]

Chanan Singh then petitioned H E the Governor-in-Council on Makhan Singh's behalf and wrote to the Acting Member for Law and Order requesting an interview. He asked that the case be reviewed on the ground that Makhan Singh was an ordinary resident of Kenya, not an immigrant, and that the object of the law in question could not possibly be the expulsion of Kenyans: it was the keeping out of non-Kenyans. The petition, however, did not succeed and the government confirmed that the Quit Order could not be rescinded, or even extended, and that Makhan Singh had to leave on or before 26th September or by the earliest boat. The governor had himself considered the petition but was not prepared to intervene in the matter. In fact the petition was never placed before the Legco, in spite of A B Patel's repeated efforts.

CIVIL CASE NO 371
OF 1947

Chanan Singh

On 24th September, two days before Makhan Singh was expected to leave, Chanan Singh wrote to the principal immigration officer informing him that 'my client has decided to test the validity of the Order in a court of law.' Civil Case No 371 of 1947, Makhan Singh versus Principal Immigration Officer was registered. The application was filed in His Majesty's Supreme Court for an *Order Nisi* (interim order) by way of *Certiorari* (to quash an illegal decision), asking the principal immigration officer to show cause why his order should not be quashed. Makhan Singh signed an affidavit stating, amongst other facts, that he had been a member of the Communist Party of India and sub-editor of *Jang-I-Azadi*, the official organ of the Party's Punjab Committee, from February, 1943, to July, 1947. The Commissioner of Oaths this time was Saligram Kapila, (father of Achhroo Kapila, a young patriotic lawyer who defended many of the victims of colonialism); the affidavit was witnessed by Chunilal Madan (later chief justice).

Chanan Singh has explained that 'there were obvious difficulties in Makhan Singh's way. The remedies available to a subject to challenge the actions of government are of a limited scope and are circumscribed by technical rules. They were more so then because Kenya had no Bill of Rights. The Immigration Restriction Ordinance, although enacted as early as 1906, had been little used and had not received judicial interpretation. We were conscious of these difficulties but decided to seek the Court's intervention. The result was to produce in my mind a firm conviction that if a subject has to fight the Government and has the choice of Court he should fight it in a criminal rather than civil court. In a criminal prosecution, the burden of proving the guilt of the accused is on the prosecution. It is true that once a prima facie case is made out, the accused is put on his defence, but the scope of the defence in a criminal case is very wide and the accused is free to call into question actions of the Government which in a civil case it may not be easy or even possible to question.

'We decided to apply for the ancient writ of certiorari which enables the superior courts to examine the acts of persons or bodies of inferior jurisdiction. The acts in question must be of a judicial or a semi-judicial character. My argument was that the Principal Immigration Officer could not act arbitrarily, but had to act on 'information' which naturally meant he had to weigh pros and cons. His act was, therefore, a quasi-judicial act which the court was free to examine.

'In a short Order, Mr. Justice M C Nageon (later Sir Clement) de Lestang, one of the ablest judges who have adorned the Kenya bench, dismissed the application because the granting of certiorari would, in effect, amount to an interference by the Court with an executive act of the Governor-in-Council which the Court cannot properly do by way of certiorari.'[7]

The application was dismissed on 2nd October, 1947, on the ground that the Order of the Principal Immigration Officer was an administrative act and the 'Writ of Certiorari did not lie.'

On 9th October Justice Lestang granted leave to appeal the ruling given in Civil Case No 371 of 1947. The next sessions of the Court of Appeal were due to sit on 21st October, in Dar-es-

Salaam; the case was registered as Civil Appeal No 24 of 1947. An adjournment was granted and the date set for 14th November. The *East African Standard* charged that the 'defence are using delaying tactics.' Meanwhile a letter in the *Daily Chronicle* accused the EAINC of 'just fiddling' in the case of Makhan Singh. 'The least it could do,' the writer stated, 'was to publish a record of its activities in connection with the case. This was important both in the interests of its own prestige and for public information.' On 1st October, *Radio Posta*, published in Kisumu by W W W Awori, announced *Sasa ni Safari Mzungu Kumshtaki Muhindi* (Now starts the process for a European to prosecute an Indian).

The India League in London voiced its support for Makhan Singh but the Indian National Congress sent a telegram informing him that the governor and supreme court of Kenya had declined to intervene in the matter and suggesting it be taken to the UK government. The EAINC then requested the government of India to ask Krishna Menon, it's High Commissioner in the UK, to make representations to the Secretary of State for the Colonies. Makhan Singh also wrote to the Indian Overseas Central Association, New Delhi, the Imperial Indian Citizenship Association, Bombay and the Indian Overseas Department of the All-India Congress Committee, Allahabad. 'This case concerns the whole of the Indian community in East Africa because it is an attack upon the Indian political workers and upon such residents who are domiciled in Kenya,' he stated.

The Africa and Overseas Merchants Chamber in Bombay wrote a letter of support. 'It is because of your patriotism that the timid government of Kenya chooses to harass you,' it claimed. It wrote to the Ministry of Foreign and Commonwealth Relations in New Delhi, enclosed Makhan Singh's letter and asked for proper publicity and all necessary steps. 'Are the Kenyan authorities at all right in serving a notice on him? He is an adopted son of the soil. The Immigration Officer seems to have acted on out of date police information from India,' it contended. C P Joshi, leader of the Communist Party of India, sent a message to East African Indians urging them to 'Unify against Imperialist White Supremacy' and praising them for forming an 'Indo-African joint front.'

Two advocates processed the appeal; Chanan Singh who was then secretary of the Nairobi Indian Association and S G Amin, president of the EAINC. They offered their services free of charge as a patriotic duty. Air reservations were made on 16th October, through Thomas Cook & Son Ltd, re-entry permits and certificates of smallpox and yellow fever were required. Two seats were reserved on the coast route, departing on 10th November, and returning five days later.

The *Daily Chronicle* of 22nd October published a letter headed 'Prohibited Immigrant Clause is a Highly Dangerous Weapon in the Government's Armoury.' It quoted J M Nazareth, honorary secretary of the EAINC, who affirmed that 'Prohibiting bona fide residents of Kenya on the plea that in consequence of information received, they are deemed by the Principal Immigration Officer to be undesirable immigrants was . . . a very dangerous power in the hands of the Government.'

The *East African Standard* reported that W Gallacher, a British MP representing the Communist Party had, at question time on 1st November, raised a query in the House of Commons regarding Makhan Singh, wanting to know why he had been refused entry into Kenya. The MP concerned, Hon. Mr Rees-Williams, replied to say that he had been excluded under Section 5(f) of the Immigration Ordinance 'by reason of his activities when he was resident there and refused to interfere with the discretion of the Governor-in-Council. The National Union of Civil Liberties, however, took up cudgels on behalf of Makhan Singh. And on 2nd November, Jomo Kenyatta, speaking at a meeting of the KAU in Kaloleni passed a resolution 'deploring the Deportation Ordinance and requested the Government to revoke it forthwith.'

Both Jomo Kenyatta and Makhan Singh had returned to

Kenya in 1947. Makhan Singh first met Kenyatta in September, 1947, when the latter was the principal of a teacher training college in Githunguri. Jesse Kariuki, a well-known nationalist and trade unionist, had accompanied Makhan Singh who then invited Kenyatta and Kariuki to lunch at his house in Park Road. They met for about an hour and a half. Makhan Singh noted that, 'Kenyatta talked less and listened more. He would reply wisely after weighing every word,' and said he felt honoured by the respect Kenyatta gave him.

CIVIL APPEAL NO 24 OF 1947

Makhan Singh flew to Dar-es-Salaam with Chanan Singh and another advocate, D N Khanna. *The Tanganyika Herald* announced details of the 'Immigration Control Appeal Case.' Civil Appeal No 24 of 1947 in Makhan Singh v Principal Immigration Officer was heard on 14th November, by Judges G Graham Paul (chief justice, Tanganyika), Will Stuart (Tanganyika High Court) and J H B Nihill (chief justice, Kenya).

According to Chanan Singh: 'Mr. D. N. Khanna, an advocate of considerable experience (whose help and encouragement in the early days of my practice had placed me under a great debt of gratitude) was engaged as senior counsel . . . For obvious reasons, neither the Supreme Court nor the Court of Appeal went into the merits of the case. They merely decided that the old remedy by way of certiorari was not available to the applicant because the act of the Government which he was trying to challenge was an administrative, as distinct from a judicial or a quasi-judicial, act.

'The absurdity of the whole position was obvious. One of the judges of the Court of Appeal (Mr. Justice Will Stuart) made a pertinent remark in the course of a witty one-page judgement.

He wrote:

"It is suggested, and apparently admitted by Counsel for the Crown, that the Kenya Immigration law is so drawn that a person domiciled by birth or choice in Kenya who makes the error of leaving Kenya, without losing his domicile can be stopped at the port of entry if his way of life is disagreeable to the authorities. Then he would seem to become a stateless person, as it were a bird without a perch: only on the twig of domicile could he settle as of right and that right could be denied him."

'The rule of international law against taking an action which would make a person stateless was not then so established as it is now. But it should be observed that argument had really turned on domicile. It was not contended that the Government was depriving Makhan Singh of nationality. The right of a British subject to enter British territory was to be argued – without success – in a future case.

'So far as the remedy of certiorari was concerned, a dead-end had been reached with the Judgement of the Court of Appeal. The question of whether the immigration authorities could expel a person domiciled in Kenya remained unanswered. If Makhan Singh's right to remain in Kenya was to be established – his father and he were most anxious that it should be – then some other way would have to be found.

'Mr. D. N. Khanna, Mr. Makhan Singh and I returned from Dar es Salaam in the same aeroplane. When we reached Nairobi Airport, the immigration authorities tried to make Makhan Singh sign a document to the effect that he was entering Kenya for a short period. He, of course, refused to sign. We had foreseen these tactics and I had asked the Principal Immigration Officer for written confirmation that there would be "no objection to his travelling to and from Dar es Salaam by air via Mombasa." A reply had in fact been received before we left Nairobi. This stated that there would be no objection to Makhan Singh's "travelling to Dar es Salaam by air via Mombasa for the purpose of appearing in the Court of

E. A. Appeal at Dar es Salaam and of returning to Kenya via Mombasa for the purpose of appearing in the Court of Resident Magistrate, Nairobi, in C. C. No.4047/47."

'This criminal case had been filed against Makhan Singh while we were fighting for the remedy of certiorari. It charged him with the offence of failing to comply with an Order to leave Kenya within the stipulated 30 days. I had, then, taken this as an unequivocal answer to my question. I now see that it did allow scope for the Immigration Department's argument: the permission to return had been given specifically "for the purpose of appearing" in a criminal case. Nevertheless, all that happened was some delay in getting home; the officer did not persist in his demand.'[8]

The appeal was dismissed with costs on 22nd November, 1947. The judgement, inter alia, stated that 'the appellant cannot be deported from the Colony unless a competent court decides that it is lawful that he should be deported.' It also ruled that there was no need for the appellant to seek the aid of a Writ of Certiorari. Section 5(F) of the Immigration Restriction Ordinance clearly stipulated that 'Nationals of Kenya could not be rendered stateless and homeless.' The Court could not interfere with the decision of the Governor-in-Council. Only a lower court could decide if the appellant, a domicile, had defied a government order. Makhan Singh immediately telegraphed his father, 'Appeal dismissed today. Matter left open for argument in criminal case.' The *Colonial Times* of the same month wrote that, 'the trials showed that no quarter and no co-operation [from the government] could be expected.'

On 17th November, Makhan Singh wrote to the secretary of the Colonial Advisory Committee of the Trade Union Congress (TUC) in London. He expressed surprise that the TUC could not take any action to protest his deportation order. 'We consider this to be the biggest attack on the trade union movement, not only in Kenya but in the whole of East Africa. Is it not the duty of the British TUC to save the colonial trade union from such attacks?' he asked and added, 'The matter deserves full publicity in the British Labour press.'

On the same date he wrote to Gallacher thanking him for a copy of the British *Hansard* and explaining the Appeal court judgement. 'The struggle here is mainly not based on a legal fight, but we have seen that such a fight in a colonial country does help the main agitation . . . the Indian and African communities have already seen the far reaching importance of this case not only for the labour and progressive movements here but also for the domicile rights of all the communities. The judgment of the court has made it still more clear.'

With the appeal dismissed, the case reverted to a lower court in Nairobi. Makhan Singh wrote to the Ministry of Foreign Affairs and Commonwealth Relations in India asking 'what has the Government of India done in this matter . . . no reply has been received . . . ' A B Patel appealed for better relations saying 'Stop treating Africans as a commodity and Indians as a problem.'

Radio Posta reported the dismissal of Makhan Singh's appeal and quoted a judge who warned that the Deportation Ordinance 'could cause even greater hardship to Kenya Africans.' The *East African Standard* interpreted it as 'Appeal Court Judge says Indian Must Leave' and 'Indian On Charge of Disobeying Order To Go.' The *Goan Voice* and the *Colonial Times* published the Appeal Court judgment in full.

In early December, the *Daily Chronicle* reported 'Indian Government Pleads for Makhan Singh Representations to the Kenya Government.' The *East African Standard* noted that an essential ingredient of the prosecution's case was whether Makhan Singh was an immigrant or not. The *Forum* headline read 'British-dominated Kenya deports a Respectable Indian Citizen.'

The initial court case declaring Makhan Singh a prohibited immigrant, now resumed. Chanan Singh wrote in his summary, 'The Resident Magistrate's criminal case to which reference was made in the written reply of the Immigration Department had been filed against Makhan Singh for failing to leave Kenya in compliance with the Principal Immigration Officer's Order. It had been adjourned to enable the appeal to the Court of Appeal to be determined.

'The criminal trial started on 26th November, before Mr. R. A. Campbell, Resident Magistrate, Nairobi (later the Chief Justice of Aden). Mr. S. G. Amin, Mr. D. N. Khanna and I appeared for the defence. Mr. Khanna, who led the defence team, took care to stress the merits of the case while neglecting no technical point, however important it might seem. The point that ultimately proved fruitful was a technical one. It concerned the proof of a document.

'It was necessary for the prosecution to prove that the decision of the Principal Immigration Officer ("deeming" Makhan Singh an Undesirable Immigrant) had been confirmed by the Governor-in-Council that is the Executive Council of the colony. This, in effect, required proof of the relevant minute of the Council. The minutes are confidential. At first, the prosecution called an officer of the Secretariat who was in charge of the Immigration Section there and he produced a copy of the minute marked "certified true copy". It was obviously a copy of a copy received by the Immigration Section and was inadmissible in evidence.

'The following day, the prosecution called the Clerk of the Executi[on] Council. He produced another copy certified by himself. This proved inadmissible, in the end, because the Indian law of evidence which applied to the colony required such documents to be certified by the head of the department concerned. The head was, admittedly, the Governor, not the Clerk of the Council.

'At the conclusion of the prosecution case, the defence submitted that there was no case for the accused to answer, the confirmation by the Governor-in Council of the decision of the Principal Immigration Officer not having been proved by admissible evidence. The learned Magistrate accepted this submission and acquitted Makhan Singh on 22nd December.

'Thus concluded the second phase of this protracted

litigation. Makhan Singh was to remain a free man for another nine months.'[9]

The *Daily Chronicle, Colonial Times* and *Radio Posta* all announced the acquittal. On 21st December, Makhan Singh thanked the Indian government for its 'strong representation to the Kenya government,' but added 'I am not out of the woods yet.' Makhan Singh was acquitted on the basis that the copy of the minutes of the Governor's Executive Council was not valid because they were not certified by the Governor himself.

The African and Overseas Merchants Chamber of Bombay congratulated Makhan Singh on his victory but added, 'May I drop a friendly hint that, you being a labour leader, you should beware of communistic tendencies in Kenya. I believe labour should go socialist but socialism is a middle course between communism and fascism. Both are to be eschewed. Socialism is the only choice as it points to 'One World' by evolution as opposed to revolution.'

On his return from India in 1947 Makhan Singh at first involved himself in political activities. He worked with the EAINC in the election of 1948, but he was never trusted or accepted by the hierarchy of the Congress which was powerful enough to keep him on the fringes of the movement. Nor does he seem to have associated too closely with the young and radical Asian intellectuals and journalists who were much involved in the *Daily Chronicle*. Insetad he revived the LTU in 1948, and devoted his time fully to it.

It would seem that he tried to make the LTU once again an all-embracing general organisation for the workers of Nairobi. For some time he was a one-man secretariat. He made press statements concerning government's legislation . . . he was reported extensively in the *Daily Chronicle* and fairly frequently, though with disapproval, in the *East African Standard*.[10]

EAST AFRICAN STUDENTS
FEDERATION AND
KENYA YOUTH CONFERENCE

The East Africa Students Federation, also for the Asian youth, was formulated with conservative aims such as body building, general education and the like. Earlier, in April 1947, the Federation had held a conference and revised its constitution, making the organisation open to all students of both sexes between the ages of 13 and 25 years. The following year Makhan Singh did attend some of the Federation's meetings.

While Makhan Singh had been sailing westwards, a young Kenyan named Eric arap Seroney set off on 12th August, 1947, on the MV Sangola to journey in the opposite direction. He was one of the first five lucky Africans selected to go to India for higher education under the Government of India's scholarships for Africans scheme. But his own people had let him down and he had had no money to travel to Allahabad. The *Colonial Times*, the Arya Samaj, students and individual Indians had contributed at short notice to 'get him out of an awkward situation and make it possible for him to avail of the scholarship.' 'For me this was a practical demonstration of the goodwill of the Indians towards the Africans,' wrote Seroney.

The Kenya Youth Conference had been founded in early December 1947. It was an initiative of the Indian Youth League which had been in existence for ten years and had a history of erratic activism. The president was Haroon Ahmed, the secretary, Achhroo Kapila and the treasurer, Shanti Pandit. Makhan

Eric arap Seroney

Singh, as a member of the League, was the vice-president of the Conference together with R P Joshi and O P Sachdeva. The following year, when Haroon Ahmed had to travel to India, Makhan Singh took his place as president.

On 25th and 26th December, 1947, the first session of the Kenya Youth Conference was held in the Desai Memorial Hall. It represented all the Asian youths of Kenya. Over 200 delegates attended drawn from Eldoret, Kericho, Kisumu, Mombasa, Nairobi, Nakuru and Thika, and were comprised of adult as well as student leaders.

Makhan Singh especially urged Muslim and Goan youths to attend. The Muslim community, feeling it was losing ground both economically and politically in the EAINC, had begun to organise separately. A Central Muslim Association and a Muslim Chamber of Commerce had been formed in 1945 and 1946, respectively. However, no Muslims, except for a few Ahmadiyyas, attended the Conference, and only two Goans, J M Nazareth and M Roderigues, were present. In total, 190 delegates and African and Arab

J M Nazareth

Haroon Ahmed

Shanti Pandit

observers, attended. Haroon Ahmed presided,

Achhroo Kapila was the secretary and Councillor Shanti Pandit was chairman of the Reception Committee.

Messages of goodwill were received from overseas from the Students Labour Federation of Democratic Youth, the Young Communist League of London and the Natal Indian Congress. The Communist Party of India message read, 'Hope Asian youths in Kenya will forge bonds of solidarity and comradeship with African youth to fight for independence and democracy.' Other messages came in from the EAINC, the Indian Merchants Chamber, the Siri Guru Singh Sabha, the Social Service League, the Bhagini Samaj, the Kisumu Youth League and the Kisumu Ladies. From Elburgon, the iconoclastic radical Goan, Eddie H Pereira, telegraphed, 'The king of youth, Jay Prakash Narain, has his hands on your youthful pulse so on with socialism in all your resolutions. British colony my foot! Youth have a right to shape their destiny on socialist lines.'

In his presidential address, Haroon Ahmed dwelt on the social, political and economic discriminations faced by Asians and Africans in the colony. The main thrust of the Conference was on the need for unity, a spirit of service and for closer Indo-African cooperation. The fact that it was recognised and recorded that 'the privileged classes will resist' gave the Conference a decidedly left orientation. His closing remarks were to urge the youth to pass responsible resolutions 'with a determination of action behind them.'

Makhan Singh's personal notes emphasised 'Kenya is our home. . .cast away communalism . . . unite learn serve . . . unity is strength . . . future is yours . . . Asian and African youths unite and eradicate illiteracy.'

He was elected as one of its three vice-presidents and appointed convenor of the constitution drafting committee together with Haroon Ahmed and R C Gautama. In January, 1948, he was the convenor of the literacy subcommittee with Haroon Ahmed and J M Nazareth and served on a subcommittee on 'Minimum Wages.' As one of its first activities, the Conference decided to start a literacy campaign, first among the Indians, and later on among the Africans. It was decided to conduct the literacy camps in Gujerati, Gurumukhi, Hindustani and English and have a class in Kiswahili for prospective teachers.

The executive committee of the Kenya Youth Conference held its fifth meeting in July, 1948. Present were Haroon Ahmed (presiding), Makhan Singh, B M Kapila, G S Gahir, S T Thakore and V P Mandal. On minimum wages, Makhan Singh reported that nothing had been done to date. On hostel accommodation, he presented a rough memorandum, on Asian representation in the Legco, he was the only member opposed to sending the conference resolution to the Legco's Indian Representation Committee. Concerning the proposed literacy camp he presented a short report. The chairman asked him to 'take some pains' and prepare the reports before the next central council.

Clearly, Makhan Singh was overburdened with the work

Makhan Singh Park Road residence, as at 2005

Makhan Singh's office, door on the right, as at 2005

Sudh Singh behind the counter of his printing press

that was being allocated to him by different organisations. Meticulous and fastidious as he was, he must have felt extremely pressured, especially as his main interest was the affairs of the labour movement. In addition he read widely, as evidenced by the detailed summaries he wrote. He never failed to keep abreast of international news. For example, in spite of his heavy schedule, he sent, in July, forty shillings to Bombay as a renewal of his subscription to *People's Age*.

Makhan Singh's family now lived in a house which Sudh Singh had acquired on Park Road, in the Ngara area. The house had many rooms, some of which they rented out.

Makhan Singh worked from a small

office on Ndumberi Road near the junction of Duruma Road (previously Varma Road) and River Road, just across from the Casino Cinema. At the junction was Hayat Building which housed the offices of the LTUEA. Down Varma Road, next to the Surat Building, was Sudh Singh's Punjab Press.

Makhan Singh's office was rather dark and dingy with very little space,' remembers Nanalal Sheth, president of the East African Students Federation from 1946 to 1951.

We used to meet there in the evenings, my brother Pranlal, Haroon, Rawal and others and discuss mainly trade union matters. Makhan Singh did his own typing. He had an old Remington typewriter and could never get the letters aligned quite right. He was a very intense person, fiery and dedicated.[11]

THE ASIAN-OWNED PRESS

The Asian-owned newspapers of this period took a firmly anti-imperialist and anti-colonialist line. The main ones were the *Kenya Daily Mail*, the *Colonial Times* and the *Daily Chronicle*. The Pandya family in Mombasa published the *Kenya Daily Mail* (1927-1964), G L Vidyarthi of Nairobi started the *Colonial Times* in 1933, as a slim bi-lingual weekly bound in yellow covers. In 1943, he recruited a team of gifted young journalists and up-graded it, with D K Sharda responsible for the English section, Haroon Ahmed for the Gujerati, and Pranlal Sheth one of its outstanding journalists and main reporter. The paper became a great success due to the lively style of writing and incisive reporting and its coverage of the local struggle of Asians and Africans for equal rights, but more especially because of its coverage of the independence movement in India. In 1945,

Vidyarthi was charged with sedition and jailed for four months with hard labour.

Soon after the entire editorial team resigned en masse and in 1947, they founded the *Daily Chronicle* which ran till 1962. India (and Pakistan) was soon to become independent and the focus of attention shifted to the growing clamour of the nationalists and trade unionists in Kenya. Ideologically, the paper moved to the left as the team of journalists had a socialist orientation; this was further accentuated after Makhan Singh returned to Kenya in 1947 and became a frequent visitor to the press. Kenyan and East African issues were moved to the forefront, putting the paper on a collision course both with the colonialists and some of the local Indian leaders. Jaramogi Odinga has stated that 'it was the first and only English language paper in Kenya to advocate a militant nationalist policy.'[12]

'Association with Makhan Singh made us much more conscious of the class dimension of the East African situation,' says Piyo Rattansi.

Makhan Singh began to call at the *Chronicle* offices, and took an increasingly active role at public meetings of the Congress and the Indian Association . . . we were perhaps more prepared to respond to his brand of left-wing socialism because of growing disillusionment with the policies of the Labour Government then in power in Britain . . . . We used to be ardent followers of the Fabian Society, the Labour Party's think-tank, and read the writings of Margery Perham and Arthur Creech-Jones who commented on the injustices of the colonial system and what Labour policy should be.

When Creech-Jones was appointed colonial secretary, he wrote Sessional Paper 191 which all of us, including Makhan Singh, supported as he advocated equal rights for all. The Kenya settlers were enraged. But Creech-Jones then produced a second paper in which he did a surprising *volte-face* and sided with the settlers in their plan to take over control in Kenya on the Southern Rhodesian model.[13]

Between 1947 and 1950, the team at the *Daily Chronicle* was a closely-knit group of mostly young, gifted left-wing intellectuals determined to expose and oppose colonial injustices in Kenya. Inspired by Gandhi's independence struggle in India and the ideals of the Russian Revolution, these nationalists worked hard and passionately and kept in touch with the African masses largely through Makhan Singh. Many years later the Corfield Report singled out the *Chronicle* as having contributed to the origin and growth of the Mau Mau through its 'blatant bias against both against Government and the European, never missing an opportunity of supporting African claims, however fantastic or subversive.'

Piyo Rattansi, who had joined the *Chronicle* team as a teenage reporter in the interim period between high school and university, remembers Makhan Singh as 'always cheerful and positive'. In retrospect he realised that Makhan Singh never spoke about his family and Piyo never met any of them. He hardly ever even spoke about himself and it was only many years later that Piyo learnt about Makhan Singh's role in the trade union movement prior to 1947. Piyo did, however, know that he had been detained in India and Piyo once asked him, 'What did you do during all those years in detention?' 'I translated *Das Kapital* into Punjabi,' replied Makhan Singh matter-of-factly. On hearing this D K Sharda, the editor who was a great bilingual punster, joked '*Mein to Das Kapital ka Das hoon*'. (Das in Hindustani is Master, so 'I am the master of *Das Kapital*'). Makhan Singh began to visit the *Chronicle* offices regularly and a bond grew between him and the journalists. They would attend EAINC meetings and participate in them actively. It was a true camaraderie.[14]

Some of the Chronicle team and others, including Makhan Singh, even started a communal chicken and fruit farm on a plot in Ruaraka, some 15 kilometres north of Nairobi. Hassan Rattansi, Piyo's older brother, remembered the lawyer Achhroo

Fred Kubai

Pranlal Sheth

Kapila going there on his bicycle. Pranlal Sheth, Fred Kubai, D K Sharda, A S Rao and Dave were some of the others in the group which was akin to a cell. The project was abandoned when the chickens all died.[15]

Many were the conversations in which bitterness about the colour bar, racism and exploitation would be expressed and lamented about but the invariable conclusion would be a hopeless 'yes, but what can we do?' 'We can do something. I know what we can do,' Makhan Singh would assert and captivate the others.

'In discussions,' Piyo reminisced,

Makhan Singh would constantly remind his comrades to analyse the contradictions. "Class struggle hey bhai (brother)" he would say. He had an extraordinary way of thinking. If you took a query to him he would sit you down and say "tell me." Then he would think in front of you there and then. Often he would take off his pagri (turban) as if his head had become too warm. After a couple of minutes, he would offer an analysis.

Although at first cautious because of his self-professed communist allegiance, which in the cold war atmosphere of the time turned him into a 'tool of Moscow', the *Chronicle* team became increasingly impressed by his total sincerity and commitment to the cause of all Kenyans, his sympathy for the oppressed and disadvantaged, his organisational and constructive abilities and skills, and his use of peaceful mass agitation to mobilise the power of workers to improve their conditions and obtain justice from employers. Pranlal Sheth joined him in unionising the workers and held the post of president of the LTUEA when Fred Kubai became more involved in the Transport & Allied Workers Union.

MARXIST STUDY GROUP

Makhan Singh used to hold classes on Marxism for the *Daily Chronicle* team. Together with Govind Rawal, Pranlal Sheth, D K Sharda, Piyo Rattansi and T P O'Brien[16], he also formed a small study group. Haroon Ahmed distanced himself from the group as he disagreed with their increasingly left-wing ideology. On one occasion the United States Embassy sent the *Chronicle* a selection of articles by Marx and Lenin. The intention was to educate its staff on the 'fallacy and pitfalls of communist ideology.' They were exactly what the study group needed and Piyo was persuaded to visit the embassy and ask for more.

Y Dadoo and G M Naicker of the South African Communist Party would stop over in Kenya and meet with the group. Their visits were always shrouded in secrecy and on one occasion when Piyo, Rawal, Sharda, Sheth and Indu Desai met Dadoo, Piyo remembers Makhan Singh asking Dadoo a lot of detailed questions and following up on news of several individuals. The group wrestled with divided loyalties as it became increasingly radicalised. 'We'll have to watch China to see how she behaves with her neighbours,' said one in reference to the Indo-China territorial dispute. 'Why, is there a problem?' asked Makhan

Singh. For him there was no doubt which side he would support.[17]

GOVERNMENT'S ELECTORAL ROLL ON RELIGIOUS LINES

On 30th December, 1947, Makhan Singh attended an Executive Committee meeting of the EAINC held in Desai Memorial Hall. In the minutes of the meeting, Minute 18/E/7/10/K referred to the proposed issuance of a statement by the EAINC protesting against Makhan Singh's deportation order. Dr Adalja, the acting secretary, was not in favour of issuing it as 'it might lead to legal complications.' The statement was, ultimately, published after modification. Makhan Singh's main concern was the government's introduction of separate electorates on religious lines – Hindu and Muslim – for the Indians. He termed it 'a deadly evil which elsewhere has done so much nefarious work.'

SATURDAY, 3rd JANUARY 1948

"A Free Press Is The Sentinel of Peoples' Rights."

Shall We Be Divided ?

'Colonial Times' editorial

The editorial in the *Colonial Times* of 3ʳᵈ January, 1948, was headed 'Shall We Be Divided?' A certain section of the Indian Muslims had asked the government to introduce separate electoral rolls for them and the government had promised to consider this demand. The *Colonial Times* saw this as 'the age-old imperialistic game of divide and rule', and compared it to the Simla Conference which had formalised the division of India and Pakistan. It called for a boycott of elections based on religious franchise.

Towards the end of the month, the Governor, Sir Philip Mitchell, called a conference to discuss the issue of separate electorates. The conference failed to reach any agreement and the EAINC stated that the proposals were unacceptable. The EAINC resolved that as a protest against the division on the basis of religion of the Indian seats on the Kenya Legco, Indian members elected on a Congress ticket should boycott the Legco sittings until the offending amendment was repealed.

The Legco, established in 1907, allowed the white settlers to participate in direct rule. One Indian, A M Jeevanjee, had been nominated in 1908. In 1923, the Devonshire Paper had introduced elections for Indians, but on a communal, and later religious, electoral roll. The portfolio for African interests was initially allocated to an European member but after the Second World War, Africans were nominated to the Legco. However, election of African members did not take place until 1957.

The EAINC resolved to contest the forthcoming Legco elections itself and appointed a board consisting of S G Amin, J D Byramji, T J Inamdar, S D Karve and J M Nazareth to select its candidates. Each would have to pay a fee of KShs 1,000, which would be refundable for non-selection. It reached a stalemate on a proposed boycott of the elections. The Congress secretariat remained reticent but rumours revealed a difficult and confusing situation. Several candidates were preparing to stand independently and the Sikh community threatened to walk out of the EAINC if one of them was not selected as a candidate. Makhan Singh condemned this 'deplorable attitude.' The EAINC never really managed to pull the Indian communities together as each remained trapped within its communal and religious confines.

It was agreed finally, by a very narrow majority, that the successful candidates should not participate in the Legco proceedings. Makhan Singh offered himself as a candidate for the Nairobi Central Area and sent in the required cheque, signed by his father, together with an assurance that he would not contest the elections if not selected by the EAINC. Initially, he refused to appear before the selection board but later he agreed. At another time, during the annual elections for the EAINC office bearers in Nairobi, Makhan Singh and two others were elected but then he stepped down in favour of someone else. 'This instance showed that he had no desire for fame,' wrote Ambu Patel.[18]

The other applications were from Bhagat Singh Biant, A R Cockar, Bachulal Gathani, Chunilal Madan, Pritam Singh Lal, D Puri, A B Patel and Chanan Singh. The *Kenya Daily Mail* appeared to support Barrister C Madan whom it described as 'a young but intelligent politician and diplomat who is very popular among the younger generation of the capital and the candidate most likely to promote and preserve the solidarity of the Indian community.' Patel (Eastern), Lal (Western) and Madan (Central) were nominated. Cockar was selected to contest the Muslim seat but he withdrew in favour of Ibrahim Nathoo. Biant decided to stand independently. The African nominees were J Jeremiah, Kipsugut, E Mathu and B A Ohanga.

In April, one G S Gahir wrote to the *East African Standard* and the *Daily Chronicle* asking the EAINC to publicly state its policy towards the Indian communists. He also related the 'betrayal' and 'treachery' by India's Communist Party when it sided with the imperialists during World War II and its resultant defeat in the 1945 general elections. He claimed the party dominated the All-India Trades Union Congress and exploited the workers.

In the same month, the Nairobi Indian Association elected

Makhan Singh to serve on its executive committee and to convene a sub-committee on Asian housing. In August, 1948, he was re-elected to the executive and standing committees of the EAINC. Apart from his trade union activities, he regularly attended meetings of the EAINC, the Kenya Youth Conference and the East African Students Federation. He proposed that the Indian Association should hold a public meeting on 18ᵗʰ April, to discuss the Trades Union Amendment Bill, the new Valuation Roll and the government Indian schools in Nairobi. This would be the day G L Vidhyarthi was to be released from prison and he would be asked to address the gathering. He was asked to draft a memorandum on the Valuation Roll.

On 31ˢᵗ January, 1948, Mahatma Gandhi was assassinated. Makhan Singh was one of the speakers at the condolence meeting, it was one of the rare occasions when he appeared in public wearing the traditional *kurta*/pyjama outfit with a short sleeveless waistcoat.

The Central Muslim Association put out a notice stating that 'owing to the tragic death of Mahatma Gandhi, all Muslim shopkeepers and businessmen are requested to keep their shops closed.' The Kenya Youth Conference paid tribute, sent condolences to Nehru and requested the EAINC to consider erecting a monument to Gandhi.

Despite the tragic events in India, Makhan Singh at this time appeared to be in a very up-beat mood, which is captured in his poem entitled 'A New Age Has Dawned'.

The whole world has changed
A new dawn has arisen
He rejoices at the defeat of fascism and anticipates a rule of
Workers and peasants
Artisans and weavers
Blacksmiths and intellectuals . . .
The India of the Englishman
Has come to an end . . .
There is turmoil in Africa

Addressing the crowd in Nairobi, following the assassination of Mahatma Gandhi in 1948

But Africa is also changing . . .
The hatred of colour is still remaining
The practice of slavery is still going on.
Don't ignore the warnings
It is time to act . . .
We have to bring change into Kenya
As the new age has dawned.

In May the *Daily Chronicle* published a particularly important letter by Makhan Singh. 'The next week is going to be the most decisive in the history of Indian national movement in this country. In this week the election in the Central Area will decide whether the forces of nationalism and progress as represented by the Indian National Congress will advance forward in the struggle for equal rights in East Africa, or the forces of disruption and reaction, as represented by Mr. Bhagat Singh Biant will hinder our democratic progress in this country.

'The Kenya British settlers like Sir Alfred Vincent are planning the union of British territories in Africa, which would be nothing else than an open rule of generals like Smuts and suppression of all the progressive and labour movements. The fate of South Africa's Indians and Africans would also become the fate of Indians and Africans in this part of the world. In East Africa, the Indian National Congress is the main organisation among Indians, which, with the help of the East African labour movement and other progressive forces can or can be made to check this nefarious move of the imperialists. The role of Mr. Biant in defying the Congress and fanning the forces of disruption and reaction only plays into the hands of our common opponents. It has nothing to do with the interests of labour, of the Indian workers and artisans.

'The duty of Indian workers and artisans is quite clear. They can only support the forces of nationalism and progress, which in this case are the forces of Congress. The support for reactionary and disruptive forces would mean the disruption of the labour movement in East Africa, and the weakening of the workers' struggle for better conditions.

'The contest in this case is not between a labour leader and a capitalist candidate. Individually both the candidates are of capitalist ideology. Neither Mr. Madan nor Mr. Biant has any record of service for the Labour movement. But as one represents the forces of nationalism and progress and the other represents the forces of nationalism and reaction, the choice of the Indian workers and artisans can only lie with the Congress candidate.'

Another letter to the *Daily Chronicle*, signed 'A Worker', was in Makhan Singh's handwriting. It referred to Bhagat Singh Biant's decision to offer himself for election and so defy the Indian National Congress. 'He proclaims himself a labour leader; he is not known in the LTUEA and acts as a communal leader – will this communalism not work against the interests of the Indian artisans and workers?' the letter asked. By 'communalism' Makhan Singh meant religious and sectarian categories such as Sikh, Hindu, Muslim and Goan, Gujerati and Punjabi. Unlike African ethnic categorisation which is based on tribal identity, Asian communities are based on religious affiliation. Makhan Singh constantly encouraged workers to regard themselves in economic or class terms, rather than according to their communal, religious or tribal affiliations.

A T E N - D A Y F A S T

On 8th June, the *Daily Chronicle* published a startling letter by Makhan Singh. 'From 7 a.m. today I have commenced a ten-day fast. I am risking my health, and it may be my life, in a supreme effort to raise the honest consciousness of the Indian people, and that of the leaders of the East African Indian National Congress and other organisations. At this critical juncture when all our efforts should have been concentrated for a real unity of the Indian people, our energies are being frittered away in useless controversies and mutual bitterness.

'The communal passions aroused on account of the compromising and no-boycott policies of a section of the Congress leadership, and by the hate propaganda of a few disruptive elements in the Indian community are the biggest danger facing us at the present moment. They imperil not only the present, but also our entire future, our national struggle, and the entire working class movement in this part of the world.

'Who will fight for our democratic rights and for the economic demands of the working class, if our common and joint organisations are disrupted and weakened? Who will defend us from the onslaughts of the anti-Indian and racial policies of the white settlers, if we ourselves are not in a position to unitedly face them? Unity and solidarity of the Indian community should be the main aim of every Indian national, and their promotion is the sole object of my fast. My humble desire is that during and after my fast every Indian citizen and every worker and artisan should do his utmost for the sacred cause of unity. Let there be no communal bitterness in his feelings. Let there be sober thinking over all the issues facing us. Let every Congress leader be approached to change the weak-kneed policies pursued by a section of the leadership. Let the leaders of the Congress and other organisations take immediate and prompt steps for the unity and solidarity of the Indian community.

'My fast will last for ten days. It would be a complete fast. I would take nothing except water. It could be stopped even before the completion of the period, if I see that real efforts are being made for achieving the solidarity of the Indian community. To avoid any misunderstanding I may add that I do not intend to stand as a candidate in any forthcoming election to the Legislative Council. I hope that with the help of you all, the purpose of my fast will be achieved.'

The executive committee of the Nairobi Indian Association

met on the same evening. Chanan Singh was in the chair, other members were H Ahmed, B Gathani, R Gautama, P C Handa, J Kapila, T Nath, D Patel, D Puri, H Patel, Dr Patwardhan and K P Shah. They discussed Makhan Singh's fast and passed three resolutions. One appealed to the Indian community to give serious consideration to the issues he had raised and the second expressed appreciation of the action taken by him and assured him that the Association would take all possible steps to achieve the objectives he espoused. The third urged the EAINC to take steps to achieve complete unity of Indians residing in Kenya and to see if the decisions taken regarding the elections could be reviewed.

The *East African Standard* wrote 'Indian Fasts to Rouse the Community.' However four days into the fast, the *Daily Chronicle* wrote 'Community's Leaders Ignore A Fasting Man'. The high sounding resolutions of the Association did not translate into any action, the EAINC was too busy criticising the *Chronicle* and trying to get an extra seat in the Legco. It stated that 'the factors which prevent the achievement of unity are not entirely within the control of the Indian community of Kenya. Many of our troubles are an overflow of the situation in India.'

Makhan Singh ended his ten-day 'unity fast' on the seventh day. On the previous evening a deputation of representatives of the Congress, Indian elected members and representatives of various organisations visited him and informed him of the efforts they were making to respond to the concerns he had raised. Makhan Singh was convinced of their sincerity but said that, for obvious reasons, he could not reveal the nature of the efforts and solutions.

The *Daily Chronicle* editorial of 23rd June, was not in agreement. 'Makhan Singh claims to have fasted for communal unity, not to patch up any personal antagonisms with some of the 'leaders' . . . communal unity is a public matter. How can any group of people dispose of it secretly and among themselves? The people have a right to know those vital developments . . .'

On 7th July, a letter by Makhan Singh himself clarified the matter. 'After the publication today of the official communiqué about appointment of a special Legislative Council Committee to consider and make recommendations as to the form and strength of Indian representation in the Legislative Council, I am now in a position to state that it was the information that the leaders of the community were making serious efforts to have the whole question reconsidered in some such way, that led me to ending my fast on the seventh day.

'As I said in my previous statement of the 16th June, "whether the proposed solutions (recommendations of the Committee if

Daily Chronicle's view of the present leadership

appointed) would ultimately succeed or not, it is for the community to see." But with the appointment of the Committee the whole question of Asian representation has been reopened, and all the honest and healthy elements among the community have got the opportunity to unitedly work for a real solution, which, in my opinion, should not be based on religion, but which should ultimately lead us to our cherished goal of a common roll in this country.'

Makhan Singh's commitment to the greater good, his spirit of self-sacrifice and his unbending sense of responsibility and discipline are much in evidence here. The committee met on 17th July with the government expressing much reservation on the wisdom of the decision to reopen the difficult question of Asian representation.

On 26th August the LTUEA submitted a comprehensive memorandum to the Committee. A union delegation consisting of Taj Din, Jesse Kariuki, Gopal Singh, Prabubhai, M J Deman and Makhan Singh gave oral evidence. The memorandum first explained the composition and character of the LTUEA. 'The Union is not a political organisation but one of its aims is to safeguard the general interests of the workers and toiling people in Kenya.' It rejected all three alternatives for Asian representation in the Legco as they were based on racial lines, religious affiliation or attachment to India or Pakistan. It stated that 'labour was not represented in the Legco . . . therefore legislation in the Colony was biased in favour of the employers.'

M J Deman

It proposed the following solution. 'Adult franchise should be granted to all. Elections should take place for all seats on the basis of common roll. Voting should not be for individual candidates as at present but for registered organisations, parties and trade unions. Each of them should be allotted number of seats in proportion to votes received by them.' It further stated that there should be no ex-officio or nominated members in the Council.[19] The government did not accept these recommendations. Instead it passed legislation based on a religious division of the voters' roll, with a certain number of seats reserved separately for Hindus (including Sikhs) and Muslims.

In mid-June, Mombasa Muslims had decided to boycott the EAINC, quoting 'growing discontent or disaffection between the major sections of the Indian community.' The signatories were A H Kaderbhoy, K R Paroo, Dr Najmudean (the author's father), A H Nurmohamed and Y E Jivanjee. As soon as two of the five Indian seats were reserved for Muslims, some prominent Muslim members of the EAINC resigned. The Sikhs had revived their demand for one of the remaining three seats to be reserved for them. Fragmentation of the Indian community was becoming a political reality.

Makhan Singh was very involved in the election process. He advocated the boycott, canvassed widely for the Congress candidates and spoke to Sikh organisations at the Coast, in Kitale and elsewhere. In August, in a delegation with A B Patel, R C Gautama, Chanan Singh and S G Amin, he addressed the Indian Association in Kisumu. He spelt out the problems facing the Indian community and emphasised the importance of unity to safeguard its interests. He decried the lack of good leadership and the policy of compromise without a well thought out strategy. Boycott by itself was not adequate and there was need to take into account the effect on Africans. He recognised the complaints of the Muslims and the Sikhs and the domination of the Hindus in the EAINC; nevertheless he was convinced that secession from the Congress and separate representation were counterproductive. The EAINC had achieved a great deal especially in the areas of immigration, representation in the councils, opposing 'Closer Union' and combating racism. 'Build the organisation,' was his advice, 'educate the masses.' He never failed to remind his listeners of the problems created by the partition of the Indian subcontinent.

Most Indian associations supported the EAINC although Kisumu was taking a contrary line. Five Sikh organisations in Nairobi declared their full support and loyalty to the EAINC and as a gesture of goodwill withdrew their support to any Sikh candidate not duly nominated by the Congress. They did however demand the support of the boycott call as evidence of the EAINC's genuine opposition to separate representation on a religious basis. The resolution was drawn up by Makhan Singh and according to British intelligence reports 'the campaign between Mr. Bhagat Singh Biant and Mr. Madan was conducted with considerable bitterness and Congress through Makhan Singh and his colleagues indulged in some questionable tactics.' It envisaged that, as a result, Makhan Singh would encounter difficulties in recruiting members for the LTUEA which he was trying to revive[20]. Some Sikhs from Eldoret did in fact dispatch a terse telegram to Makhan Singh saying 'Waiting for news of your death. Coffin follows.' Such hostility was, however, felt by a minority although the British intelligence reports portrayed him as being unpopular and also the Congress as an organisation of 'strict regimentation and the enforcement of blind obedience from its followers.'[21]

Piyo Rattansi of the *Daily Chronicle* recalls Makhan Singh walking into the press and showing them the telegram. In his usual serious and analytical method he tried to ascertain if any adverse report had been made about him, especially by the authorities or the special branch. His inquiries did not emanate from any fears but rather from a determination to keep himself as fully informed as possible of the context in which he operated.[22] A letter from Dr A U Sheth to the *Colonial Times* referred to the suicidal policies of the EAINC. 'It ceased to be an East African institution eighteen years ago and became a Kenya body. In the last twenty months it has lost support of the Muslim community. It has isolated the Hindu community from all important elements in the country.' He termed taking responsibility for nominating candidates a foolish decision and the policy reckless.

The boycott question raised a storm of emotions. At one point, the standing committee of the EAINC actually boycotted the boycott! The *Daily Chronicle* on the other hand insisted that

'Boycott Was The Only Way.' 'Three empty seats will be a constant reminder to the government that to all progressive Indians in the Colony, political division on a religious basis is unthinkable, unacceptable and abhorrent.'

ONE BOYCOTT
TO ANOTHER

One outcome of the boycott issue was a war of words between the *Daily Chronicle* and the EAINC. The reporter, Piyo Rattansi, had observed the Hon. A. B. Patel sneak out of the spectators' gallery at tea time, where the boycotting MPs sat, and dash to his official seat to collect the day's business papers. To Patel's chagrin, his failure to adhere to the boycott pledge fully became a news item. Piyo titled his press report: 'The Man Who Could Not Resist.' Piyo's father and other Congress members prevailed upon him to retract his story but he stood by what he had written. This led to the Congress boycotting the newspaper on 9th June[23]. In addition, his father, Rattansi, who was a close associate of A B Patel, withdrew his allowance with the result that Piyo went around in worn-out clothes for some time.

Makhan Singh sought to solve this impasse. On 14th July, he wrote in a letter to the *Daily Chronicle*, 'The present controversy between the *Daily Chronicle* and a section of the Congress leadership headed by Hon. A B Patel is not a personal controversy, as some people seem to think. It is, in my opinion, a controversy between two policies – a policy of active struggle against the racial and reactionary measures of the Government and white settlers; and a policy of compromise and surrender.

'The leaders who dared not boycott the Legislative Council to fight the communal divisions, have today indirectly initiated a move to boycott the *Chronicle*, the only Indian daily in the capital, which has been championing the real cause and declared policies of the Congress for the last so many months. Had it been a reactionary paper supporting the anti-Indian measures and policies of the Government, as was sometimes the case in India, the move for a boycott of the paper would have been understandable. But here the case is quite different.

'The views expressed by the *Chronicle* are in spirit the same as are expressed by the pro-boycott section of the Congress. Does Hon. A. B. Patel desire to suppress the views of the opposition? Will he not be strengthening the hands of the Government to suppress, one by one, the progressive sections of the Indian community? Will such a policy not weaken the organisation of the Congress itself?

'It is high time that responsible leaders of the Congress should awaken to the danger that awaits both the Congress and our daily in the capital. They should immediately call a meeting of the Standing Committee, invite the editors of the *Chronicle* to the same, find out a way, in which the decisions of the Congress secretariat and executive committee could be revised, and freedom of the press to express progressive, critical and constructive views assured.'

Notwithstanding Makhan Singh's intervention, the quarrel was carried a stage further with the EAINC instructing the *Daily Chronicle* to discontinue sending any further copies and asking that its year's subscription be amended to expire as of the previous 30th June.[24]

THE GANDHI MEMORIAL ACADEMY

Though not a member, Makhan Singh was often invited to attend the EAINC standing committee meetings as an observer. He was invited to attend a public meeting on 19th June, postponed to 30th June, the agenda being planning a memorial to Gandhi. The initial intention was to involve the three East African territories but with poor response from Uganda and Tanzania, the Kenyans decided to go it alone. A Gandhi Memorial Committee was later formed in Uganda and linked up with its Kenyan counterpart. At a meeting on 30th October, Makhan Singh proposed that the twelve member Kenyan committee be put under the jurisdiction of the Congress. This was opposed overwhelmingly on the basis that 'other territorial organisations would demand the same right.'

Two schools of thought emerged: one put forward by Haroon Ahmed favoured local memorials at important places in East Africa, the other preferred a central one for the whole region. Makhan Singh and Gopal Singh were appointed to the eleven-member inter-territorial memorial committee. Later, ostensibly to 'strengthen' it, a majority of professionals were added. Makhan Singh objected to this but was over ruled. Ultimately the proposal for a central memorial prevailed and preparations were made to establish a Gandhi Memorial Academy in the University of Nairobi. A portion of Gandhi's ashes were received in Nairobi and after paying homage, the urn was taken to Kampala via several of Kenya's towns. On 14th August, it was immersed in the River Nile at its source in Jinja.

In June, Makhan Singh travelled to Kakamega to investigate the beatings meted out to two Indian employees of the Rosterman Gold Mines. While there, he formed a Labour Union for the Indian workers in the mine.

In July, he reported on various sub-committees. On the valuation roll, the problem was that properties belonging to Asians were valued at a considerably higher price that the properties of the Europeans. The housing sub-committee had asked the municipal engineer to find a suitable site for construction of more housing for Asians. Architects were to be approached to prepare designs and estimates for two, three and four room flats.

Meanwhile, the EAINC passed a resolution suggesting that the division of the electoral roll for Indians could be done on

EAINC group at Nakuru. DD Puri, president with B R Kapila, Shanti Pandit, Makhan Singh, J M Nazareth and G L Vidyarthi

the basis of the candidate's 'attachment to India or Pakistan.' At a meeting of the executive committee meeting of the Indian Association, Makhan Singh proposed that this would not be in the interest of unity and solidarity of the Indian community because to accept the principle of national division would lead to exactly the same results as feared from division along religious lines. It was resolved to request Congress to reject this suggestion.

In the August meeting of the Indian Association, Makhan Singh proposed that a letter be written to the reception committee of the next session of the EAINC to be held in Mombasa, asking it to admit a reporter from the *Daily Chronicle* to the session. The proposal was voted down. At the 19th session of the EAINC held on 20th, 21st and 22nd August, 1948, at the Patel Samaj in Mombasa, Makhan Singh was elected once again to the executive and standing committees, while D D Puri was elected president. Bhagat Singh Biant and his nominees were denied admittance and, in retaliation, they paraded outside and greeted arriving delegates with black flags.[25]

Makhan Singh proposed the following resolution.

'In the opinion of this Congress it should be the privileged and sacred duty of the immigrant communities to assist the Africans in their rapid development economic, social and political so that they may take their rightful place in the country at an early date and become the dominant factor in the government of this country which their number justifies and with this aim in view would instruct all Indians to be helpful to Africans in all their legitimate aspirations and in particular work for the Africans obtaining more land for their use, ameliorating their working conditions and achieving increased representation on the Legislative and Municipal bodies with elective principles.'[26]

Makhan Singh was chosen as one of the group given the task of revising the EAINC's constitution[27]. This was necessary to bring the document in line with the changes on the Indian sub-continent following the achievement of independence in 1947 and the creation of Pakistan.

With J M Nazareth, he prepared a private bill aimed at prohibiting any racial discrimination, either in law, rules or practice. He wrote out a long and detailed list of all discriminatory legislation and regulations, including the exact dates when they were passed. He drafted a memorandum on the subject of Indian Representation for submission to the Legco Inquiry Committee. It read 'the draft, in the main, is consistent with the resolution of the Congress, though not with my personal views which I expressed in Mombasa and still hold . . . . A British commission condemns any sort of electoral division and this makes the stand of the Congress quite ridiculous when it itself demands division of the roll on a Dominion, that is political, basis.'[28] Makhan Singh supported the decision of the EAINC to consult the government of India on the matter. The executive council of the Kenya Youth Conference also sent a letter of protest on the EAINC's proposal concerning the 'division of seats on a Dominion basis.' He reported that the Nairobi Indian Association, owing to internal differences, had not been able to appoint delegates to the forthcoming Congress session.

SATWANT KAUR COMPLAINS

On 13th December, 1947, Makhan Singh's wife, Satwant Kaur, writing from Bombay, and addressing her husband as *sathiji* (comrade), told him she was in the eighth month of her pregnancy and quite ill and had been ordered complete bed rest. Their little daughter, Inderjeet, had been admitted into Standard 3 in Santa Cruz School and was then able to read and write a little Hindi but had to take extra tuition at 25 rupees a month. She thanked her husband for the 200 rupees he had sent, but requested regular monthly payments. 'I only have few clothes. If you cannot bring 4 sarees, bring the material,' she urged. The third child, a boy, was born on 18th January, 1948. Though the usual custom was to select a name from the scriptures, Makhan Singh created a name for him, as he had done for his first son. He chose 'Swarajpal' meaning 'protector of independence.' Hindpal, now ten years old, was able to write to his father in Urdu. He requested for more money for his studies and thanked him on receipt of it. The schools in Bombay,

At a picnic in 1947

he explained, taught in Marathi, so he was looking for a Hindi-medium school.

Satwant Kaur wrote several more letters to Makhan Singh. She clearly had assumed that her husband had returned to Kenya in August, 1947, for a brief visit and would soon be returning to settle in India. She thanked him for another 100 rupees he had sent and gave details of how she had spent the money. She advised him to be careful about expenditure and on his return to India, requested him not to 'go here and there . . . from Gharjakh come to Lahore, then we can go to Delhi,' she wrote. She also sent him some additional letters, one that he was to read and destroy and others that he was to deliver.

By early 1948, she began to sense that Makhan Singh actually intended to remain in Kenya. That she was not too pleased by this change of plans is evidenced by her statement 'if you had intended staying there, you should have taken me.'

Three lengthy letters, written first on 13ᵗʰ February, and then at weekly intervals, portray an anxious period in her life. Her major concern was her father's illness. In spite of consulting the best doctors in Bombay and Delhi, and being given the most expensive medicines, he was not responding to treatment.

She found it distressing to have to ask for help. 'It is different if you are alone but with children . . . you know how it is in Model Town . . . . It is better I just stay with father . . . . Winter is coming and we have no mattress or quilt, so bring yours when you come . . . . How long do you intend staying there?' Then later, 'the children have no winter clothes . . . we have not yet named the baby.' She complained about the baby requiring constant attention and the naughtiness of his sister, Inderjeet.

She appeared reluctant to travel to Kenya and wrote, 'If I am to be treated as before, let me know now. I do not have the strength to suffer again in a strange land . . . . I will miss my father, I can stay on here.' Makhan Singh must have tried to reassure her but she remained unconvinced. 'You have said you will maintain a better relationship but old habits do not change . . . One has to go where Fate takes one.' Her fears were justifiable, as Makhan Singh had once declared to his family, 'I am not made for you. You can die of hunger but I will continue to do what I am doing. That is how I am.' Resignedly, she set about applying for a passport and booking passages on a ship.

The passport was not a problem and tickets were available in all three passenger classes on the ship. Clearly Makhan Singh expected them to travel third class. Satwant was wary. 'I don't know how I shall travel, with no companions and two of the children are young,' but on a more positive note she added, 'It would be good if you could keep a cow for the baby.' Hindpal wrote to his grandfather in Hindi requesting him to send the money for third class tickets, as they intended to sail any time after 15ᵗʰ August, when his exams would be over. He assured his father that he was studying hard for his exams. They ultimately sailed to Kenya in April, 1948.

It was the custom then in Nairobi to hold tea parties to

honour leaders and occasions. The Blue Room in Hardinge
Street (now Kimathi Street) was a popular spot for these get-
togethers. In September, the KAU invited Makhan Singh to a
farewell party for Hon. Eluid Mathu who was leaving for
England.

On 3rd October, 1948, the Cutch Madhapor Patel Guati
Mandal, an Asian communal, working class, organisation
entertained Shrimant Appa Saheb B Pant, who had arrived as
India's first High Commissioner to Kenya. Makhan Singh was
the spokesperson for the Mandal and took the opportunity to
state that the Cutchi community were the labourer and mason
class, who, in order to raise their standard of living, should
demand more wages.

The EAINC also invited him to welcome Shrimant Appa
Saheb Pant. The British government did not view the activities
of the Indian High Commissioner favourably. The *Kenya
Intelligence Review* noted that 'not only is he going beyond the
terms of his appointment but he is also endeavouring to create
a solid bloc of the coloured races in the Colony.' The colonial
government on several occasions requested Nehru to recall him
and in May, 1953, declared him *persona non grata*. He finally left
Kenya in 1954.

In the same meeting Makhan Singh bid the formal farewell
to Hon. A B Patel who was going to London to attend the
African Colonial Conference. Makhan Singh was not too
enthused by the Conference. At an EAINC Executive
Committee meeting held on 27th November, he noted that its
real purpose was to 'prepare a ground for African union and to
plan exploitation of colonial resources for a Third World War.'
He urged the Congress to work towards building a common
front of non-Europeans in Kenya and submitted a proposal for
the KAU and EAINC to form a common front.

Makhan Singh's notes also included denunciations of the
British government for refusing to submit reports to the UNO
on political development in the colonies and recommended
that 'the administration of these colonies be put under UNO

Trust Care for not more than 10 years and that their people be prepared for self-government at the end of that period.' He was keenly aware of the need to attack imperialism at the global level. He denounced the ban imposed on the *Blitz* and *People's Age*, India's left-wing newspapers, and criticised a Mr Adams for saying that colonial people are quite satisfied with British rule. He protested against the racist utterances of Dr Malan in South Africa against Africans and Asians and congratulated the Indian community there for its heroic struggle.

The Nairobi Indian Association held a conference on education. Makhan Singh was selected as convenor, the appointment letter stating, 'Knowing your interest in the younger generation, your sincerity, earnestness and your past services in the interests of the Indian community, the Association has selected you . . . . ' His report to the conference enumerated the number of Indian school children, teachers, school buildings, funds and included a breakdown of the income and expenditure details. He insisted that the question of doubling the fees should only be considered when the allocation for education was made irrespective of race or community. The conference urged the government to establish a technical institute and to enlarge Makerere College in Uganda to enable it to admit Indian students for higher education.

Meanwhile the matter of Makhan Singh's threatened deportation still hung in the air. The EAINC executive committee, at its meeting on 8th October, discussed the unresolved issue of the deportation of Makhan Singh. Minute 2 read 'Political implication of a possible deportation of Makhan Singh, one of our members.' The committee decided to send a deputation to the acting member of Law and Order to get assurance from the government that there would not be undue hurry in this, and future cases. 'The person to be deported must be allowed to fully utilise all legal assistance.' On 12th October, it was reported that the necessary assurance was obtained.

Makhan Singh wrote to the *East African Standard*, the *Colonial Times* and the *Kenya Daily Mail* and to the elected members' organisation and the High Commissioner for India informing them of the government's attempt to deport him. He urged Hon. Madan and Hon. Pritam to raise a question in the Legco and Hon. Gallacher to ask the same in the House of Commons. He also informed the *Daily Worker*, the *Guardian*, the *People's Age*, the *Blitz*, the *Tribune*, the *Hindustan Times* and the *Chronicle*. Clearly the bird was still without a perch!

CHAPTER SEVEN

GOVERNMENT ATTEMPTS DEPORTATION, AGAIN

On 4th October, 1948, J Basil Hobson, acting member for Law and Order under Section 9 of the Immigration (Control) Ordinance 1948, ordered the deportation of Makhan Singh from the colony of Kenya to India. Hobson further ordered that whilst awaiting deportation, as well as being conveyed to the place of his departure, Makhan Singh should be held in prison custody. On 5th October, 1948, Makhan Singh was arrested and jailed.

Gopal Singh Chandan, in his memoirs writes that he remembers receiving a phone call from Makhan Singh asking him to go to the Khalsa Press, as a man from the Criminal Investigation Department had come to arrest him, and his father was not present. At the press, Makhan Singh gave him some of his important papers and informed him that the warrant for his arrest stated that he was to be taken by the 17.30 train to Mombasa and deported to India two days later . . . he asked him to inform Chanan Singh.

On the 8th Chanan Singh and Handa Advocates applied for a hearing of *habeas corpus*. Makhan Singh's affidavit this time was witnessed by M K Bhandari. Gopal Singh Chandan describes the situation:

'We were all frantic. We hastily drove to the prison. Makhan Singh signed the appeal against his deportation orders and it was filed before a special judge. He was brought to court the following morning, his bail application having been rejected on public security grounds . . . the police were well prepared this time, they had obtained information from the Criminal Investigation Department in India.'[1]

Chanan Singh conducted the defence. 'From the beginning of August, 1948, the old Immigration Restriction Ordinance was replaced by a new law, called the Immigration (Control) Ordinance. This authorised the Governor to deport persons whose presence in the colony was unlawful under the repeated Ordinance, and, pending deportation, to keep such persons in prison. The Government now proceeded to exercise its newly-acquired power. The following, fresh Order was addressed, therefore, to Makhan Singh, made by the Acting Member for Law and Order on October 4th, 1948:

"Whereas you . . . entered . . . Kenya from India on or about the 21st day of August, 1947:

"And whereas you . . . were deemed on the 13th day of May, 1947 by the Principal Immigration Officer to be an Undesirable Immigrant under para (f) of section 5 of the Immigration Restriction Ordinance . . .

"And whereas such decision was confirmed by the Acting Governor-in-Council by the 23rd day of May, 1947,

"And whereas in accordance with the provision of section 16 of the Immigration (Control) Ordinance, 1948, your presence in the Colony is unlawful:

"And whereas . . . The Governor in exercise of the powers conferred upon him . . . was pleased to depute the Member for Law and Order . . . to exercise such powers as are conferred upon the Governor by sections 9 and 10 of the Immigration (control) Ordinance, 1948:

"Now, therefore, in exercise of the powers conferred upon the Governor by section 9 . . . I . . . do hereby order the deportation from the Colony to India of you, Makhan Singh . . . whilst awaiting such deportation be detained in prison custody . . ."

APPLICATION FOR 'HABEAS CORPUS'

❋

'This Order was to start the third phase of litigation. It was served on Makhan Singh on October 5th, 1948, and he was taken into custody immediately. His father told me this during the day and asked me to take steps to prevent Makhan Singh's being sent away by that evening's train, with a view to being deported to India. I put in hand the drafting of an application for habeas corpus. Makhan Singh who was held in the Nairobi prison had to be interviewed twice, first to obtain facts and then to get his affidavit approved and sworn. While this was done, I requested the Registrar of the High Court to request one of the Judges to be available in Chambers to hear an urgent habeas corpus application, if necessary after court hours.

'We regarded this development as important, because this would enable us to obtain a decision on the general question of whether a permanent 'resident' could be declared a prohibited immigrant.

'I filed the application in the afternoon, praying that the Superintendent of Prisons, Nairobi, be directed to produce Makhan Singh in Court and show cause why he should not be released from custody.

'Mr. Justice de Lestang was waiting in his Chambers. He made the Order nisi without delay, and we served it on the Superintendent of Prison, thus preventing the removal of Makhan Singh to Mombasa. The hearing was fixed for October 8th, but was later adjourned to October 12th. This postponement enabled me to file an additional affidavit enclosing a copy of the proceedings and judgement in the criminal case.

'The Attorney-General filed an answer and we made a reply. I tried, in the interval to get Makhan Singh released on bail, but the application was refused.

'At the hearing, the Acting Solicitor-General (Mr. A. G. Lowe, a New Zealander and an extremely good-natured man who returned to his country on completion of his tour of service) represented the Crown. My arguments were two. First, Makhan Singh was not an "immigrant" (that is, a person coming into a country for settlement). He had arrived in the colony when only a minor to join his parents who had made their home here. He had completed his education in Nairobi had joined his father in business. He had acquired and had exercised his franchise. He was the only son of his parents, and, therefore, the sole heir under Hindu Law. He had acquired Kenya domicile before he went to India in 1939. On return from that country, therefore, he could not be declared a prohibited "immigrant". Such declaration was illegal and of no effect. The object of the Immigration Restriction Ordinance of 1906 was clear beyond doubt. It concerned "immigration", not mere entry, into the colony. Section 5(f) under which the Principal Immigration Officer had purported to act prohibited the "immigration" of certain classes of persons. Even if Makhan Singh belonged to one of those classes, he was not in 1947 "immigrating" into the colony but only returning home after a temporary visit to India.

'In any case, I argued, - this was my second point – that the Law had given power to the Principal Immigration Officer to "deem" persons undesirable immigrants. The letter addressed by the Immigration Department to the Government asking for the confirmation of the Governor-in-Council had been signed by another officer and stated "hereby deem Makhan Singh . . . to be an Undesirable Immigrant." This was *ultra vires*.

'The judge had listened patiently to the earlier part of my argument but was now showing signs of weariness. Apparently, he had come to a tentative conclusion in his own mind. But experienced Judges tend to conceal their feelings from counsel and there is at that stage no means of knowing these feelings. It is not easy for counsel to give up arguments which may in a certain eventuality be helpful to the client. I was now putting forward my minor arguments and the learned Judge remarked a little impatiently: "Mr. Chanan Singh, you have put forward some very good arguments but now you have resorted to quibbles." I took the hint and curtailed my arguments.

'Mr. Lowe had a difficult task. He performed it as well as any counsel could. He left no doubt in anybody's mind that his clients would not like the decision to go against him. He was speaking with such earnestness and conviction.

'The learned Judge wrote a long judgement in which he examined the whole basis of the 1906 Immigration Law. He came to the conclusion that it did not apply to permanent residents (that is persons domiciled in Kenya). He held that Makhan Singh was such a resident and, therefore, not subject to that Law. He also accepted my second argument and ordered the applicant to be released from custody.

'Thus, the third phase of litigation ended in favour of Makhan Singh, who was again a free man – on October 18th, 1948.'[2]

According to the *Intelligence Review* 'Makhan Singh's arrest caused no repercussions and surprisingly the 'Daily Chronicle' has refrained from comment. The majority feeling, and especially among the Ramgharia Sikhs, is that Makhan Singh has himself to blame for the position he is now in and that he should have kept in the background after his acquittal in the Courts last year. Top ranking Congress leaders discussed his case and the best legal brains were called in for advice, otherwise only the President of the Cutch Madhopor Guati Mandal, which numbers among its members many of the illiterate mason class and the Managing Committees of the Siri [G]uru Singh Sabha and the Gurdwara Bazaar Temples have taken his part.'

The writers of the *Review* appeared to be convinced that Makhan Singh was actively working with communist organisations, and was propagating the ideology among Indians and Africans in Kenya.

The *Review* gives Makhan Singh's names as alias Mohan Singh, alias Balwant Singh, alias Bhugangi and states that 'he joined the Nairobi Kirti (Kisan) Party. In 1934 he raised subscriptions for the 'Kirti' and corresponded with its editor and with Teja Singh alias Lal Sin[g]h of Sansarpur on the subject of communist organisation among Indians and Africans of Kenya. Also asked Lal Singh (above) for rules of the Punjab Kirti Kisan Party and Communist literature. In 1935, with Mota Singh and Vasudev Singh organised the East African Labour Trade Union. In 1936, he visited India and worked for Ghadr and Communist causes and attended conferences and associated with revolutionaries; requested dispatch to Moscow.

On return to Kenya, in 1936, worked to effect Moscow control over Nairobi Trade Unions and corresponded with extremists in India and sent copies of the Gurumuki 'Kenya Worker' to Indian newspapers. In 1938, he contributed to the Kirti Lehar of Meerut and asked the A.I.T.U.C. to ventilate grievances of East African workers. Invited by the 'Friends of Africa' organisation to go to London to study industrial organisation etc. He was friendly with Jessie Kariuki, a former vice-president of the now illegal Kikuyu Central Association and in 1939 with Woresho Mengo, Secretary of the Teita Hills Association, now illegal[3].' In para 282, the Review noted that Makhan Singh regularly received The *Communist* and the *People's Age*, both organs of the Communist Party of India.

On 1st December, 1948, Mr Skinnard, Labour MP for Harrow East, in a parliamentary debate in the House of Commons, asked the secretary of state for the colonies for what reason Makhan Singh had been deported from Kenya to India, if this had any connection with his trade union activities. Arthur Creech Jones replied curtly that Makhan Singh had not been deported. On 17th December, Makhan Singh wrote to the *Guardian* in Cape Town enclosing a copy of the judgement on his deportation case and seven shillings and fifty cents as an annual subscription. He sent a postal order of thirteen shillings for renewal of his subscription to the *Labour Monthly*, which expired that month.

On 30th December, the Communist Party of Britain wrote to congratulate him. 'It is a great tribute to the value of your work in organising Africans and Indians to fight for better conditions and for some democratic rights that the government of Kenya takes so much trouble to try and get rid of you! . . . . it is a most hopeful sign that you have begun to succeed in establishing organisational unity of African and Indian workers, and we hope that the trade union movement in Kenya will go from strength to strength on this basis. . . . There is much greater interest in African affairs now in Britain than there has been for a very long time.' It attributed this to 'the place the African continent now occupies as the last great focal point of imperialist oppression.'

In his letters, Makhan Singh elucidated that he had won the case with the help of the Indian community and the trade union movement. He ascribed the main reason for the second deportation order to the formation of a common front of Indian and African workers. He had revived the activities of the LTUEA which was now a 3,000-strong general labour union with different sections for different industries and trades.

Earlier in July, 1948, he had assisted the Indian artisans employed by the railway to organise for a review of their salaries. His main contact with the railway artisans was Ujagar Singh, a Ghadarite employed on the permanent staff. On 28th July, Makhan Singh wrote an article in the *Daily Chronicle* headed 'Workers demonstrate before Railway Chief.'

A CONFERENCE ON THE COST OF LIVING

❋

In early September, representatives from sixteen unions and staff associations participated in a conference on the cost of living and the wage structure. Its main significance was that Indian and African trade unionists met together, independently of the Labour Department, and jointly discussed the problems facing the workers and had decided to work together in the future. Long hours of work, insufficient pay and inequality of remuneration were the main complaints. A committee was set up to coordinate the activities of the various registered trade unions and help in their functioning and to give every possible aid for the formation and registration of new trade unions.

This committee sent a circular to all unions and associations of workers on 26th September, summarising the resolutions passed at the Conference and asking for their cooperation. The circular went on to say that the committee was preparing a comprehensive memorandum for submission to the select committee on the cost of living and in order to facilitate the work of the committee, a copy of the constitution, number of members, facts and figures about the cost of living of members were asked for.[4] The British government's assessment of the whole purpose of the conference was 'to get non-government employees to unite together and to induce them to nominate Makhan Singh, as secretary of the E. A. Labour Trade Union, as their negotiator and spokesman.'[5]

Earlier in the year, the colonial government had become seriously concerned about the increased trade union activity. African workers were now well organised in the E A Painters Union, the Kenya Government Office Workers Union, the Stone and Masons Quarry Workers Union, the Shopworkers Union and others. With the acquittal of Makhan Singh on 22nd November, 1947, and the failure to deport him; the banning of Chege Kibachia would no longer serve the government's purpose of weakening the African Workers' Federation, because its activities would now be coordinated by the LTUEA.

To deal with the new situation, on 9th March, the government introduced a bill in the Legco to amend the Trade Unions and Trade Disputes Ordinance of 1943. The aim of the amendment was to prevent the registration of general workers' unions and any central organisation of trade unions, and confer more powers of control on the registrar of trade unions. The proposed Ordinance would place many obstacles in the way of the workers' movement including the recognition of unions by the employers and the victimisation of workers by them for their union activities. The *Daily Chronicle* published a report on the bill the following day and Makhan Singh issued a lengthy press statement. 'The Government is . . . resorting to an undemocratic method by not giving time for discussion.' The LTUEA campaigned against the proposal, lobbied the Legco members and other organisations and sent memoranda to the government and trade unions abroad.

E W Mathu, A B Patel and A R Cockar criticised the bill, C K Archer, a prominent European leader, wrote in favour of it. In the *East African Standard* of 23rd March, he said, 'Nothing in these days needs more careful watching than the trend and development of trade unionism in infant communities.' He referred to the recent policy of Atlee, the British prime minister, of promising 'the removal of communists from positions where they are likely to exercise pernicious influence on persons with whom they come into contact' and suggested that 'there might with advantage be a close scrutiny of the past history of some of the self-styled leaders of trade union movements with a view to their elimination.'

What the settlers and some other employers were really afraid of was the part the trade unions had already played and were now playing in intensifying not only the trade union struggles but also the nationalist movement. That had happened in Kenya and was happening in other parts of the colonial empire.[6] Their fears were well grounded. Makhan Singh kept closely in touch with African groups organising themselves politically. His files contained a letter published by *Coro wa Murang'a* (Voice of Murang'a), a Kikuyu newspaper, addressed to 'Sons of Gikuyu and Mumbi, Muranga' by one H W Gathithi. It urged the people of Murang'a to organise themselves and support their leaders and also dealt with issues of education and welfare.

British government intelligence reports on Makhan Singh noted that 'His associates, of a like way of political thought, are already in control of two Sikh temples, and thus are in a position to secure the support of the Indian labourers attending them. Makhan Singh's main theme is equal pay for equal work, irrespective of caste or creed, and he is a factor that will have to be reckoned with in Indian labour politics in the future'.[7]

In spite of the hostility against the trade union movement, the LTUEA held courses in English and Kiswahili on 'What is a Trade Union, its organisation and rules?' Young Bethwell A Ogot gained the highest number of marks and was awarded the first prize. Other students were John Mungai, Fred Kubai and Meschak Okello. The last, who was general secretary of the Transport and Allied Workers Union, was selected by James Patrick, a Scottish trade unionist who had been appointed the Trade Union Labour Officer in Kenya by the Labour government in Britain, for a scholarship to Ruskin College, Oxford. This enabled the much more radical Fred Kubai to take over the leadership of the union. Ogot went on to become a well-known university don who, twenty-five years later, edited Makhan Singh's second book on the history of Kenya's trade union movement.

Repression of what the government viewed as possible hot beds of anti-colonial fervour, and union activity in particular, was widespread. Associations and religious societies were banned, offices searched, leaders were arrested and deported, journalists jailed. Against this background, new trade unions continued to be formed and strikes successfully organised. A noteworthy development was the large enrolment of members in the Transport and Allied Workers Union under the leadership of its new organising secretary, Fred Kubai.

Born in 1917, of a Kikuyu father and a Giriama mother, Kubai was a fiery young man, determined and resolute. He had no formal education but nevertheless was employed by the E A Posts and Telegraphs from 1934 to 1946. He was an organiser in the African Workers Federation in 1946 and general secretary of the Transport and Allied Workers Union between 1947 and 1948. James Patrick described the union as 'one of the most progressive' unions in Kenya.

On 15th July, Asian civil servants met to consider the report of the Civil Servants Salaries Commission. A section of the report stated that, 'the economic law of inducement and other considerations necessitate differential rates of salary for Europeans, Asians and Africans, respectively.' They strongly objected, amongst other issues, to the rejection of the principle of equal pay for equal work. Makhan Singh, in an interview with the *Daily Chronicle* and speaking as the secretary for the

LTUEA, insisted that 'all services maintained on a racial basis should be abolished and that services should be based on the principle of 'equal pay for equal work.' He considered that the salaries proposed for Asians were insufficient and should be increased, commensurate with the rise in the cost of living.

He appealed to Asian and African civil servants to form a united front against what he called the

> grave insult of racial discrimination perpetuated by the Commission. The whole major policy underlying the Report is to perpetuate the two separate sets of conditions; one for the ruler, the Europeans; another for the ruled, the Asians and Africans and to keep racial divisions in the Civil Service. It seems the purpose is to keep the Civil Servants in a weak and crippled position and in a state of constant racial antagonism, so that Civil Servants may never be in a position to struggle unitedly for the amelioration of their conditions and of resisting the onslaughts of their employers.

The *Kenya Intelligence Review* noted that Makhan Singh was in correspondence with the Civil Service Clerical Association in London and had received a copy of the Association's Rules and Constitution. 'This may provide a clue as to his future intentions in this colony,' it concluded. It also mentioned an F M Ruhinda who was helping to activate civil liberties associations in Nairobi and described him as an African who 'harbours anti-British sentiments, is strongly anti-colour bar, and for some time past has been frequenting the offices of the Indian "Daily Chronicle"'[8]. Ambu Patel commented in his notes that on many occasions Makhan Singh had to go to the heads of departments to put workers' grievances before them and he always spoke courageously and no one could move him from his point.

AN APPEAL FOR A UNITED NON-EUROPEAN FRONT

The *Daily Chronicle* of 30th October, 1948, carried a letter headed 'Appeal for a United non-European Front.' It was signed by Benjamin Manguru, Executive Officer of the KAU. On 4th July that year, the KAU had held its fourth annual conference under the chairmanship of Jomo Kenyatta.[9] The letter stated that 'A joint committee of non-Europeans should be formed by representatives of the East African Indian National Congress and the KAU. This joint Committee, if formed, should realise the urgent need of cooperation between the non-European peoples and other democratic forces for the attainment of basic human rights and full citizenship for all sections of the East African people . . . this joint Committee should pledge itself to the task of the fullest cooperation between the African and Indian peoples and appeal to all democratic and freedom loving citizens of East Africa, to support fully and cooperate in this struggle for full franchise and equal economic and industrial rights and opportunities and trading facilities, especially on the African side.' The *Kenya Intelligence Review* was certain that the letter had in fact been drafted by Makhan Singh.[10]

In November, Makhan Singh, together with others, became life members of the Nairobi Indian Association. The Association had been founded by Allidina Visram in 1901; the membership fee now was KShs 100. On 14th November, he attended a dinner at the Sikh Union to celebrate the birthday of Pandit Jawaharlal Nehru. The menu, with descriptions using names of landmarks in Nehru's life, made interesting reading: *Harrow* Chops and *Cambridge* Salad (educational institutions), *Lucknow Jail* Bhajia with *Nabha* Chips (prisons), *Nainital* Poori with *Alipore* Kareila, *Ahmadnagar* Rice with *Cawnpore* Curry and *Palam* Pappar (centres of political activity), *INA* (Indian National Army) Rasgoola with *Lal-Kila* Jalebi (Red Fort in

Delhi), UNO Fruit Sundae and Prime Minister Paan (after-dinner delicacy).

During this period, the LTUEA shifted its offices to Hayat Building at the corner of Canal Road (later Varma Road, then Duruma Road) and River Road. Other unions and workers' associations later joined them in having their headquarters there.

On 10th January, 1949, over a hundred Europeans attended a public meeting at the Thika Club. The majority of participants were settlers, while the government was represented by members of the Legco and officials from the Labour Department, including James Patrick. The rallying theme was opposition to 'Furtherance of Trade Unionism' and support for the establishment of Whitley Councils (industrial, works and staff councils), which would be appointed by the Labour Department and operate under the control of government for the regulation of remuneration and general conditions of employment.

Patrick invited representatives of the LTUEA, the Transport and Allied Workers Union, the Tailors and Garment Workers Union, the Railway Asian Union, the Kenya Asian Civil Service Association and the E A Standard Asian Staff Union, to a conference on 28th January. The conference unanimously decided that representatives of employees on the councils should be appointed by trade unions; that sections in the proposed bill which avoided, bypassed or weakened trade unions should be deleted; and that provisions of the Bill should apply to all workers, including agricultural workers.

At the end of the conference, Fred Kubai, the acting general secretary of the Transport and Allied Workers Union, proposed the formation of a permanent central organisation of trade unions to deal with problems common to all registered unions. The proposal was welcomed by all and Makhan Singh was appointed convenor. An important stage had been reached in the development of trade unionism in Kenya.

PUBLICATIONS AND ORGANISATIONS BANNED

The government reacted by banning, through official gazette notice 202, dated 8th March, 1949, a number of periodicals from abroad. This was done under Section 53 of the Penal Code by His Excellency the Governor in Council. The banned publications included the *Labour Monthly* of London, *New Africa* of New York, *Guardian* of Cape Town and *People's Age* and *Blitz* of Bombay[11]. *Blitz* was reported as having 'communist leanings . . . [which] hurls streams of scurrilous abuse impartially at the British, South African and Indian Governments . . . The *Daily Chronicle* in its issue of 14th October, 1948, had eulogised *Blitz* as the world famous *Socialist weekly* and as a fearless champion of oppressed and exploited peoples everywhere. It exposed imperialist designs in Africa and elsewhere and had a wide circulation in the Colony.'[12]

Makhan Singh responded to the news of the ban immediately; it gave him an opportunity to disseminate the struggle for emancipation. In a letter to the *Daily Chronicle* published on 12th March he wrote: 'So, in the name of preventing the spread of Communism in Africa the drive against the workers and peasants movement goes on in Kenya. This week the announcement of bans on the entry into the colony of three more journals, the 'Labour Monthly' of London, 'New Africa' of New York and 'Guardian' of Cape Town, is the latest development in the drive.

'In the post-war period the drive began at the time of Mombasa African workers strike in 1947. In addition to imprisonment of many strike leaders on various counts, the chief leader of Mombasa Workers, Chege Kibachia, was deported. In the strike was seen a tremendous upsurge among the African working class. But the upsurge among the African peasants and agricultural workers was even greater. Arising from the need of satisfying the African hunger for land, a number of religious sects sprang up in the African reserves. Though their form was religious, the content was the urge for more land and improvement of working conditions of agricultural workers and squatters. Three of these sects were banned in 1948 for "their existence was contrary to public interest". They were as follows:

'Dini ya Misambwa. Meaning "Religion of the Original People." Led by Elijah Masinde, the sect had three main slogans: 'Don't want foreign religion, Land should belong to the original people' and 'No unoriginal man should stay here.'

'Dini ya Jesu Kristo. Led by Reuben Kihiko, who was later on sentenced to death on a charge of murder of a police officer, the sect had these slogans beside others: 'Land should belong to the people' and 'Give us land for building our own churches and schools.'

'Nandi Kipsigis Union. Led by a man who had received his education at Kenya Teacher Training College, the union concentrated its activities in the Kericho area famous for tea plantations employing about 25000 tea labourers.

'In addition to these three, Somali Youth League, which demanded a United Somaliland and which was active in the frontier districts of Kenya, was also banned last year. The Kikuyu Central Association, which was banned during the war, still remained under a ban. Mr. George K N'degwa was sentenced to one year's imprisonment for acting as a secretary of this banned association. The bans on all these organisations were followed by bans on the journals, whose only 'crime' is that they wholeheartedly support the cause and defend the true interests of the colonised people, and work for their emancipation and democratic rights.

'Wherein lies the significance of all these bans and the drive against the workers and peasants movement? The significance lies in the fact that Africa is the only continent in the world, upon which the British and American ruling classes have to depend for cheap raw materials, intensive exploitation of land and mineral resources, and development of a vast base of their plans of not only keeping the African people under subjugation but also reconquering the people of the rest of the world, who are either free since long or have recently won a partial freedom, such as the people of India and Burma. The significance of the bans further lies in the belief of the imperialists that a genuine movement of workers and peasants would upset their plans and that the movement might be checked with the bans. It also lies in the fact that the peoples' movement has become stronger to organise in the ways or read those publications, which are in the best interests of the people of the Colony, and which the people consider as such.

'The question is being asked where will this drive and bans ultimately end. Certainly the experience of other colonial countries shows that they cannot and would not succeed in their purpose. The voice of the United Nations and of the people everywhere would be too strong.'

In a letter dated 18th January, R Palme Dutt, editor of the *Labour Monthly*, wrote to Makhan Singh 'My stay in Kashmir with you has always remained with me as a very vivid memory in which I deeply appreciated your companionship and comradeship. Since then we have been following with the greatest interest the news that has reached us of the splendid work that you have been doing in Kenya.'

In early March, the editor of *People's Age* informed Makhan Singh that the Congress Ministry of Bombay had prohibited the New Age Printing Press from publishing for a month. 'This attack of the bourgeois government on *People's Age* and communist and other papers of the Communist Party is part of the offensive to suppress the voice of the toiling people, to destroy freedom of the press and to establish a complete fascist regime. You must raise your powerful voice of protest to fight back this onslaught.'

Govan Mbeki and Yusuf Daddoo of the *Guardian* wrote 'It is deplorable that you should be prevented from reading what matter you wish to . . . we have lodged protests with the government, the colonial secretary and the prime minister and have asked certain members of Parliament in Britain to raise our case in the House.' For a communist, Makhan Singh was always eclectic in his sources of information.

APPLICATION FOR A CERTIFICATE OF PERMANENT RESIDENCE

Chanan Singh wrote: 'Having won a major victory in court in October, 1948, Makhan Singh became more ambitious and now sought a certificate of Permanent Residence. This started the fourth phase of litigation. The new law, introduced in 1948, provided for a new class of resident called a "Permanent Resident" defined as "a person born in the colony" or "a person who permanently resides in the colony" or "a person who is in possession of a valid certificate or is entitled to be issued with a certificate of permanent residence." The Principal Immigration Officer was given the power to endorse a certificate of Permanent Residence on the passport of a person who satisfied him that, "he was permanently and lawfully resident in the Colony."

'The Supreme Court having already held that Makhan Singh was not an 'immigrant' but a permanent resident, it seemed a certificate of permanent residence could not be refused. An application for such a certificate was made on 20th November, 1948.

'This application was not dealt with by the authorities until the law was changed. The changed law gave the Governor-in-Council power to exclude from the definition of a "Permanent Resident" a person who was not born in the Colony, if the Governor-in-Council considered such exclusion in the interests of the Colony. Then, on January 14th, 1949 the Principal Immigration Officer informed Makhan Singh that His Excellency had excluded him from the definition of a

Permanent Resident and that, therefore, the certificate asked for could not be issued to him.

'The application was heard by Mr. Justice Thacker. The Attorney-General Sir Kenneth O'Connor, assisted by Mr. A. G. Somerhough, appeared for the Principal Immigration Officer. He immediately applied for leave to cross-examine Makhan Singh on his affidavit which had been filed in support of the application. Makhan Singh was present in the court and leave was readily granted. In reply to the Attorney-General's questions, he made statements to the following effect:

'He remembered *habeas corpus* proceedings in which his object was to show that he was a permanent resident of Kenya.

'The Judgement of Mr. Justice de Lestang in those proceedings was based on the facts stated in his affidavit. One sentence in that Judgement read: "The applicant lived in Kenya for 13 years without break." This was apparently based on Makhan Singh's statement in his affidavit that he had arrived in Kenya in May, 1927, and had left for India on a temporary visit in December, 1939.

'He agreed that, in fact, he had made two visits to India between 1927 and 1939, so that his stay was not unbroken. He had gone there on the first occasion for his own marriage and on the second occasion to attend his sister's marriage.

'He needed a passport when in India from 1939 to 1947 and on the application form had given his "domicile or ordinary place of residence" as "18.C Model Town, Lahore (Punjab)."

'When returning to Kenya after his first visit he had stated on the Immigration form his probable duration of stay in Kenya in the words "I can't say" and after the second visit as five years."

'The purpose of the Attorney-General's questions was to show, first, that Makhan Singh regarded India as his home, not Kenya, and, secondly, that, in his affidavit sworn in the *habeas corpus* proceedings, he had not disclosed his two visits to India between 1927 and 1939 and had misled the Judge into believing that his stay in Kenya between these years was unbroken. The suggestion was that the finding that Mr. Justice de Lestang made (namely, that Makhan Singh was a permanent resident of Kenya) might not have been made if the two visits had been disclosed.

'Makhan Singh stated in reply to other questions that during his visits to India he had engaged in political activities in association with the Communist Party of India as well as with the Indian National Congress. But he denied the suggestion that he worked for India's freedom because India was his "home" or "homeland." He explained: "My principle is freedom for all countries." The first two visits were of a short duration, but his third visit was prolonged by circumstances beyond his control. For part of the time he was detained without trial and, later, he was restricted to his village for some time.

'He gave his Lahore address in his application for a passport because that was where he was staying: he did not know the meaning of the word "domicile". His ancestral home in India was not in Lahore, but in Gharjakh in Gujranwala district in the Punjab. He had not disclosed his first two visits to India in the habeas corpus proceedings because he did not think they were relevant. They were so short and each was for an obviously temporary purpose - his own marriage and the marriage of his sister.

'For us, this questioning had come unexpectedly, but, as a layman, Makhan Singh did not do badly. It can hardly be said that he fell into any trap, although some of the answers were used against him later. The points that I emphasised in court were these:

'On the date when Makhan Singh applied for a certificate of Permanent Residence – that is, on November 20th, 1948 the relevant Regulation read as follows:-

'3(1) – Each of the following persons shall be entitled on application to the Principal Immigration Officer, to have endorsed on his passport by the Principal Immigration Officer, a certificate of permanent residence, namely:-

'A person who satisfies the Principal Immigration Officer that he was permanently and lawfully resident in the Colony at the date of the coming into operation of the Ordinance and is permanently and lawfully resident in the Colony at the time he makes his application for the endorsement.

'There were certain exceptions which did not apply to Makhan Singh's case. Clauses (a) and (c) also did not apply.

'The new law enabling the Governor-in-Council to exclude a person from the definition of a "permanent resident" came into operation on December 24th, 1948 and was not retroactive. It could not be applied to Makhan Singh who was already a "permanent resident" which term was defined in law to mean:-

a person born in the Colony;

a person who permanently resided in the Colony;

a person who was in possession of a certificate of permanent residence or who was entitled to be issued with one.

'Makhan Singh belonged to two of these categories at the date that the new law came into force.

'His application had been turned down because the Governor-in-Council had excluded him from the definition, not because he was not a permanent resident.

'The Principal Immigration Officer had, in refusing Makhan Singh's application for a certificate of permanent residence, replied solely on the decision of the Governor-in-Council under the new law to exclude Makhan Singh from the definition – see his letter No.R.1131/PIO/23 of January 14th, 1949. He was now putting forward an additional ground for refusal, namely that he was not satisfied that the applicant was in fact a permanent resident. I argued that he should not be allowed to change his stand at that stage.

'In the alternative, I argued that my client had complied with that condition also. He had to show that he was a permanent resident on August 1st, 1948 (the date on which the Ordinance came into force) and on November 20th, 1948 (the date of his application). The High Court having already held (in the *habeas corpus* proceedings) that Makhan Singh was a permanent resident, the Principal Immigration Officer could not reasonably say that he was not; his "satisfaction" or non-satisfaction had to be founded on reasonable grounds.

'The non-disclosure by Makhan Singh of two visits to India could not be said to affect the result of the habeas corpus application. If the learned Judge could regard a visit of eight years' duration (1939-1947) as temporary, although Makhan Singh had during it taken part in the political movement in India, then it was hardly likely that two obviously temporary visits, each of a few months' duration would be held to break a person's permanent residence.

'The Attorney-General pressed several points in his argument. The Principal Immigration Officer had a discretion in this matter and he had exercised it against Makhan Singh. He had obtained from India a photostat copy of the application form which Makhan Singh had completed to obtain a new passport. This had shown his domicile as India. If Makhan Singh had a Kenya domicile, then he had changed it. The Judgement of Mr. Justice de Lestang in the *habeas corpus* proceedings was not conclusive on the issue of permanent residence because it was given:-

under an Ordinance which had since been repealed.

on an application for habeas corpus from which there was no appeal.

in the absence of certain facts which the applicant had not disclosed (two visits to India and declaration of "18.C Model Town, Lahore, Punjab" as domicile).

'The hearing lasted two days. The judgement delivered about a week later dismissed the application for *Mandamus*. (A writ issued by courts of superior jurisdiction and directed to subordinate courts commanding them to do something therin specified.) Makhan Singh could do nothing further. An appeal was filed against the refusal of Mr. Justice Ransley Thacker to grant a writ of Mandamus. It was dismissed.'

Makhan Singh's affidavit was a frank and comprehensive statement of his arrival in Kenya and his work, travels and activities since then. It included his period of imprisonment and detention in India and his work with the Communist Party there. He made no attempt to omit or gloss over any information that might have damaged his case.

Nevertheless, the affidavit of the principal immigration officer, John Anthony Palfreman, claimed that Makhan Singh had misled the court. 'His passport application shows the domicile of the plaintiff as "British India, District Lahore," therefore he is not domiciled and permanently resident in Kenya.'

Justice Thacker delivered his judgement on 7th October. 'The grant of a writ of Mandamus is, as a general rule, discretionary in the court. It is not a writ of right and it is not issued as a matter of course. It will lie to require public officials to carry out their duties but it will not be granted in order to require a public official to exercise his discretion, where he has a discretion, in a particular way, and where it has not been shown that his discretion has been improperly exercised. Upon the facts and the law as I understand them I refuse to make the rule absolute and in the result the Rule Nisi is discharged.' Makhan Singh's case against the principal immigration officer was thus dismissed.

Ransley Samuel Thacker, Q C, was a retired Kenya High Court judge who had served since 1938, and opted to spend his retirement in Nairobi. He had then been re-appointed as a First Class magistrate. Being a man of renowned conservative persuasions, his appointment had been met with warm approval by Kenya's white settlers[14]

On 14th January, the principal immigration officer wrote to Makhan Singh that his application dated 20th November, 1948, for a certificate of permanent residence had been rejected as 'he was a person not born in this colony'. His passport (No 93397) and the ten shillings fee were returned to him.

Makhan Singh had applied under Immigration (Control) Regulations of 1948. The government introduced an amendment to the bill in the Legco adding the proviso 'if it is in the interests of the colony.' All three readings were gone through the same night of 21ˢᵗ December, 1948, even before the bill was gazetted, and it was published on 4ᵗʰ January, 1949.

Makhan Singh wrote a private and confidential letter dated 29ᵗʰ April, 1949, to the Indian High Commission for East Africa in Nairobi.

He stated that the government's refusal to grant him status of permanent residence was of 'fundamental importance not only to me, but also to all the residents, who, though not born in the Colony, have acquired the status of permanent residence through their long stay[s] in the Colony and on account of various other reasons.' He pointed out that the refusal negated the ruling in his legal case of 1949, that stipulated that no permanent resident would be declared a prohibited immigrant, which meant that the governor would have the power to oust the Indian community from the colony and to use it against persons whose views were not palatable to the government, to deny the right of domicile and the fundamental human right to freedom of movement and residence. He requested the Commission to make representations to the government of India, the British government through the Indian High Commission in London and bring the matter to the United Nations and any other inter-dominion conference. The Asian newspapers foresaw the residence clause as a weapon the government intended to use against Makhan Singh, and strongly attacked it.

THE BOYCOTT
OF INDIAN SHOPS
✳

While Makhan Singh was battling for his certificate of permanent residence, he had many other concerns. In November, 1948, he had noted the boycott of Indian shops organised by Africans in Elburgon, Molo and Mau Summit. The move had been initiated in Limuru. In Nakuru, Indian-owned clothing shops in the market were closed down. The DC there was encouraging Africans to open their own shops and get their supplies from the Kenya Farmers' Association.

The EAINC became very concerned about these developments and assigned Chunilal Madan the task of visiting Limuru, Fort Hall and Nyeri and neighbouring areas to ascertain the actual situation. Madan made an extensive tour and met with the traders themselves. Here, threats of boycott had been made but no action taken. This was unlike the situation on the Nairobi-Nakuru route where the Kikuyus were keeping away from Indian shops. In Naivasha there was practically no trade. At a meeting organised by Hon. Pritam Singh Lal in Molo, the Africans even refused to discuss the matter. Hon. Mathu, a Kikuyu MLC who had been requested to attend by his fellow legislator, failed to turn up.

Madan reported, 'One is struck by the growth of the African and his obvious entry into the arena of commerce, agriculture and social spheres.' He viewed the large number of new, well-built and well-equipped buildings of stone as a 'concerted effort to set-up competitive stores and trading places which would ultimately oust the Indian trader from these areas.'

'The Indian trader living in . . . old fashioned miserable looking buildings, temporary in nature, undignified in appearance, and unstable in structure, has in my opinion failed to ingratiate himself into the heart of the African to consolidate the position of Indian settlement. The Indian trader must make progress in his ideas, to be able to march with the rapidly changing conditions . . . it is but natural that the ordinary African, while indulging in ordinary trading, should prefer to deal with his own countrymen . . . gradually also, therefore, the Indian trader will be ousted from these areas as he has very little else to hold him there . . . . The Indian is not in contact with the African as much as the European . . . the Indian trader is not trusted by the African. He has lost his reputation. Most of this could be due to subversive propaganda against the Indian community, some of it is due to our shortcomings, and the rest to direct attacks.'

Madan advised the Indian traders to create a better relationship with the Africans and to switch from retailing to production, to manufacturing. He recognised that to do this the Indian needed 'guidance and education.' While talking, the Indian traders also brought up the issue of the lack of schools for their children.

Makhan Singh's response to the problem can be ascertained from an article of his published by the *Daily Chronicle* on 12th February, 1949. In clear and uncertain terms he wrote: 'The Political Morass In Kenya . . . And The Way Out. What is to be done? This is the common question, which is being more and more asked by the Indian political workers, as they see the Indian community in Kenya going down deeper and deeper in a serious political crisis of an enormous magnitude.

'What they see is a depressing picture. The old prestige and influence of the political organisations like the E. A. Indian National Congress is not the same; it has dwindled. The old workers and leaders are retiring from the political field. The youth leagues, trade unions and the chambers of commerce are not active. Disruption is rampant. The enemies of the community are active in every field.

'Is there any way out of this situation? Yes, there is. In the following lines I briefly give my views. I hope others will follow suit, and contribute to evolve a practical solution.

'The main task before us is to forge a strong unity among ourselves and with the Africans for the common cause of democratic public advance in the country. To fulfil this task this is what should be done: We should concretely define our aim. Till now our aim according to the constitution of the Congress has been "to achieve full and equal rights of citizenship for all races in East Africa." This is quite vague. In the present-day world, when most of the colonial people including India, have achieved political freedom, "equal right of citizenship" does not inspire enough enthusiasm. In my opinion our aim should be: "To strive for the establishment of a democratic Government in Kenya, with equal franchise, adult suffrage and common roll for all on the representation in the legislature according to votes received by each party or institution." This reorientation of our aim would inspire all the honest and sincere people among all races, and would help in forging the common front.

'But reorientation of our aim is not alone enough. Unless unity is there, no achievement of aims is possible. For this we would have to convince our people by their own experience that unity is possible. Nowadays most of our public workers and common people think that no unity is possible either among us or with the Africans. It is our duty to struggle against this defeatist mentality. How?

'We should not emphasise our differences. Our emphasis should be on common interests and common problems. Even if we are in a position to go one step further unitedly let us do that. The achievements of one thing, how small it may be, with unity, would convince our people that unity is possible, and efforts for unity on other things should be continued. The united effort for raising funds for South African Indians and the Cost of Living and Wages conference, attended by Indian and African participants was a great achievement. The resolution of big differences would certainly take time. Let us begin with small things, on which unity is possible, and which can be achieved with some united effort.

'But we should never refuse to do a thing even when complete unity is not possible, or somebody refuses to join in. Let every effort be made to bring in others, but if some of them refuse, we should begin with maximum unity achievable at a given time. In due course others would be persuaded to join in.

'The problems of education, intolerable immigration restrictions and struggle against rising cost of living are some of the questions on which relative unity can be built, and a start can be made. In due course higher issues can be taken up.

'The duty for building up this unity primarily lies upon the public workers. They should set up a personal example first. *They should shake off their old prejudices.* They should be prepared to cooperate with anybody for a common aim, though they can have differences with him on any other issue. Service should be their aim. They should have the capacity to face criticism and admit mistakes or reply in a democratic constructive manner. This would bring out our public workers from the depths of defeatism and demoralisation.

'There is plenty to do for all. Organise joint fronts of Indian Association, African unions, Pakistani organisations, trade unions, chambers of commerce, youth leagues and other influential organisations for common problems. Form joint clubs, consisting of peoples from all races. Form trade unions consisting of all workers, united chambers of commerce of both Indian and African trades and united youth leagues. Establish common high schools where possible. Support every just struggle of the people. Support the struggle for civil liberties, whether in the towns or in the reserves. But never break struggles for just demands, such as strikes, etc. Fight every reactionary move from whatever quarter in the language of the people, Swahili. Teach the best of your culture; learn the best of African culture.

'All this should be done, as far as possible, keeping our political aim in view, and in the best Indian traditions. Kenya is our home, and we have to make it a free liv[e]able home. Let our public workers and common people do their best for our united efforts. This would enthuse both the leaders and the people, and inspire confidence in each other.

'So let the common people in whatever organisation or association you are working at present, start moving it towards a common effort and common front. Make a united start from small issues, on which unity is possible, and go forward to bigger ones.

'This way lies our salvation, and this is the way out.'

THE SETTLERS' SCHEME
FOR A UNITED FRONT

The following week, on 19ᵗʰ February, Makhan Singh explained at length, in an article headed 'Capricorn Conference Is A Conspiracy Against Democracy,' the significance of the Capricorn Conference being held then in Southern Rhodesia. The Capricorn Society had been established in Tanzania in 1947 by wealthy Europeans and Asians who were opposed to the demand for independence.

As always, Makhan Singh was most concerned about the action that could, and should, be taken. He wrote, 'This week a very important Conference of white rulers of Central Africa, with a white observer from Kenya, has been held at Victoria Falls in Southern Rhodesia, and a decision for federating the Rhodesias and Nyasaland has been taken. The decision is such that it would have far reaching effects, and if its materialisation is not checked in time, it would lead to permanent imperialist subjugation of the African people and to ousting of Indian population from all the African territories.

'The plan behind this move for a Central African Union is this: First form this Union, then prepare the way for Union of East Africa, and then amalgamate these two Unions with the Union of South Africa. This amalgamation of Unions from Uganda to Cape Town would be a basis for the formation of United States of Africa, comprising all the British and non-British Dominions and colonies in Africa. This is the plan that is being envisaged by white leaders like Sir Alfred Vincent and white rulers like Malan and Smuts.

'One can say; what is the harm if all African territories are united into a single African Union? If you consider from the viewpoint of imperialist rulers, then there is no harm. But if you consider the matter from the interests of the African and Indian people, then you would see harm and nothing but harm. How? This Union of Africa would not be a Union of free democratic people working in the interests of the overwhelming majority.

'It would be a Union of imperialists; under whom the African and Indian people would keep on groaning under same conditions as at present. The South African pattern of Fascist life would become the general pattern. The imperialist masters would have at their disposal tremendous resources for exploitation and for their preparations of aggressive wars. They would have enormous armies and police forces for suppressing the democratic and freedom movements of the people.

'Thus all these plans for United Front of imperialist masters are a conspiracy against the African and Indian people struggling for freedom and democratic rights. These plans developed in the post-war period, when the imperialists were compelled to renounce some of their imperial interests in India, Pakistan, Burma, Ceylon and Egypt. They further developed in the period when movements of oppressed African and Indian people began to develop in South Africa and all the colonies in the form of Satyagrahas and trade union struggles for better living conditions. In East Africa these plans took the form of paper No. 210. The present East Africa High Commission and Central Assembly is the first step towards the achievement of the plans.

'The African and Indian political organisations in East Africa have not remained silent spectators. They opposed these schemes. But the basic weakness has been this: the closer union, under which the white masters are able to further strengthen their hegemony and supremacy, has been accepted by the Congress and the KAU "under protest."

'There is still time when our premier organisations should revise their policies in the light of the new experiences. They should think what would be the position of African and Indian people, if the white masters are allowed to materialise their plans for the Union of Africa, dominated by South African fascists and American imperialists.

'But only revision of policies is not enough. Our political

organisations should immediately have joint discussions to form a United Front to struggle against the nefarious plans of the imperialists. An Indo-African United Front is the only guarantee that these plans would not succeed. A section of the Indian and African leadership is under the illusion that these plans are only the plans of white rulers and settlers in Africa, and the Labour Government is not supporting them.

'This section is mistaken. We should have no such illusions. The present Labour Government is not so strong that it would be able to stand against the pressure of white settlers here. One should recall how the Paper No. 191, which provided for racial equality, was changed into Paper 210, which assures white supremacy in the Central Assembly. One should also see how the Labour Government, bending before the American imperialists, has played a prominent role in organising the Western Union in Europe. All this has been done in the name of anti-communism. Now similar arguments are being used by the white settlers here. Sir Alfred Vincent says; "The African Union can be the best guarantee against the spread of Communism in Africa." And according to his statement last March "every trade unionist is a potential communist". So the game is quite clear. As communists today are the spearhead of every genuine democratic and trade union movement, they are being characterised as the biggest enemies of imperialist interests, and therefore behind the smoke- screen of anti-communism the Africa Union is being planned to impress the democratic struggles of Africa and Indian people. The danger against which we should guard is that some of our own people might fall into this trap of anti-communism.

'The policy of acceptance under protest should be renounced. The danger involved in the plans should be immediately felt and the people should be warned against it. A strong non-European front is the primary task. Only this way the plans for Union of (imperialist masters of) Africa can be combated, and a democratic advance assured.'

THE EAINC MARGINALISES MAKHAN SINGH

All the while, Makhan Singh was working with the EAINC, attending its executive and standing committee meetings. He suggested the EAINC approach African organisations to build a united non-European front but was overruled. Members felt 'it would be better to bring about better understanding and closer cooperation between African and Indian communities through personal efforts.' A disturbing alliance had begun to gel between the conservative Asian leadership and the colonial government.

Makhan Singh was appointed to a sub-committee to draft resolutions. He drafted one to the UNO demanding that powers administering non-self-governing territories submit regular reports. He conveyed fraternal greetings to the All India Congress and stated that 'we expect greater support from our mother country.' One resolution supported the 'heroic and just demands of the Mombasa Indian students' in protesting against the doubling of school fees and urged the Indian Associations to support them. It further condemned the action of the Indian elected members for not opposing the amendment when the Bill was introduced.

The executive committee of the EAINC meeting on 5th March observed a two minute silence for the late Sarojini Naidu, Nehru's sister who had presided over the EAINC in 1924. Regarding the government's circular prohibiting government servants from participating in politics, A B Patel and Chanan Singh supported it but Makhan Singh was opposed to it. He also raised the issue of the government's withdrawal of the LTUEA's authority to attest passport applications. These items, together with the matter of the refusal to grant him a certificate of permanent residence, were deferred to the standing committee. This committee met on the 18th March when Chanan Singh reported that as the matter of the certificate was likely to go to court, 'no action should be taken by this Congress.'

The March 1949 meeting of the EAINC observed a two-minute silence for the late A R Cockar, member of the Legco and an executive member of the EAINC, then got down to business. The EAINC had already opposed national registration. Now, Makhan Singh proposed that the EAINC should approach the KAU for possible joint action but was unable to get a seconder. He differed with others too on the publication of EAINC minutes in the *Colonial Times*. This had been done without official approval and he felt the issue deserved sterner action.

A special meeting of the EAINC executive committee was called, to discuss the forthcoming municipal elections and the participation of the four members of the Indian Association. It was resolved that the members should reject election on a religious basis and instead demand proportional representation on the basis of a single transferable vote. If the government was unable to implement this immediately, it should at least give an undertaking to introduce this system. To avoid postponement of the election, nomination to the four seats should be accepted. Makhan Singh was totally opposed to the system of nomination, but was overruled by an overwhelming majority.

Three days later, at a meeting of the standing committee, he again proposed the deletion of 'the agreement to nomination by the Government for all seats as a temporary measure'. He was seconded but again defeated overwhelmingly. An earlier minute stated that the government's circular prohibiting government servants form participating in political institutions was supported and carried unanimously. Makhan Singh, being both opposed to the ban and a stickler for accuracy and correctness, raised an objection to the word 'unanimously' as he had not been present - he had joined the committee a few minutes later.

The EAINC published a monthly bulletin issued by the authority of the executive committee, which it distributed to 63

Indian associations all over Kenya. There was however no organised system of membership and subscription. As could be expected, there was criticism of the EAINC in some of the associations. In June, the secretary of the Eldoret Indian Association wrote to Makhan Singh saying that the majority of the Hindus and some of the Sikhs were opposed to the leadership of the EAINC. He, however, recognised that the EAINC was the only organisation that could safeguard their interests and requested Makhan Singh to visit Eldoret. 'The EAINC should travel to all the centres and explain itself,' he insisted.

Makhan Singh replied immediately. 'Sardar Pritam Singh Ji, I do remember meeting you in Eldoret last year . . . I appreciate your sentiments . . . the information given by you in connection with anti-Congress propaganda is incomplete . . . if you could describe in detail the allegations and arguments . . . I shall then write to you in detail. Meanwhile you should officially write to the Congress Secretariat on behalf of the Indian Association. Please do write to me occasionally. Sat Siri Akal. Yours sincerely.'

Pritam Singh Lal wrote saying 'Most of the propaganda is without foundation . . . but it is high time the Congress proves to the public that it is functioning and is not a dead body. Lot of people are against the President, D. D. Puri . . . . Press is the biggest backbone of any institution. The *Daily Chronicle* is against the Congress and it is the most widely read Indian daily. The *Kenya Daily Mail* and the *Colonial Times* are not popular, nor favourites.'

In May, Chanan Singh convened a meeting to 'devise ways and means of combating the bad practice of "black market"'. The meeting was held in the offices of the Indian High Commissioner and consisted of five consumers, five retailers and five representatives of the Nairobi Chamber of Commerce. Makhan Singh was on the committee.

In April, 1949, Makhan Singh was elected one of the three vice-presidents of the Indian Youth League. He was invited to a performance by a team of girls from Baroda, India, staged at the Empire Theatre by the East African Students Federation. Later, in August, the Federation held a conference under the chairmanship of Nanalal Sheth, president of the Nairobi Students Federation. Makhan Singh did not participate. It sought to coordinate the scattered activities and unifying the conflicting attitudes of the various student organisations. Its main objective was to struggle for free and compulsory primary education but had neither any political concerns nor action-based programmes.

Following a conference resolution, the Indian Youth League wrote to the EAINC seeking directions about celebrating India's Independence Day. A copy of the letter was sent to the *Daily Chronicle*; Makhan Singh thought this was in order, but the EAINC objected to such letters being sent to the press. Minute 8 raised the issue of EAINC members of the Legco not attending the opening sessions of the Legco as a symbol of the boycott. (The boycott had been agreed on by the EAINC in January, 1948) At the meeting of 9th August, a discussion was scheduled on the motion on 'steps to be taken to repeal the Immigration (Control) Ordinance of 1948'. Hon. A B Patel was the proposer of the motion and if he did not attend the opening session of the Legco, the motion would be lost. In spite of the fact that this motion had a direct bearing on him, Makhan Singh was the only person in the meeting to oppose the decision to allow its members to attend the opening sessions of the Legco.

Meanwhile, with the rising tide of the national and trade union movements, the European settlers had begun worrying that the British Labour government might give in to some of the African demands. In September, they formed an 'Electors' Union' and published a 'Kenya Plan' with an accompanying brochure entitled *We Are Here To Stay*. Among its objectives was ensuring the increase and permanency of British settlement and the paramountcy of control and leadership in a British East Africa Dominion. It was in fact a blue print for substituting colonial government rule with European settler rule. The aim was to form a federation in East and Central Africa and link it to the south. The South African foreign minister, Eric Louw, made an official visit to Kenya and warned of the 'communist peril.' The colonial office in Britain could not see any economic background to the rising political unrest and militancy, not even after the Mau Mau revolt began. Elspeth Huxley, a settler spokesperson, attributed the unrest to 'social maladjustment which must be dealt with on a psychological plane,' and branded Kenyatta as a 'small-scale African Hitler.' In April, 1949, Michael Blundell spoke in favour of 'proper unions and negotiating machinery' but denounced the EATUC as 'claptrap.' He urged that those who used free speech to promote bitterness and hatred 'must be dealt with and they must be dealt with firmly.'[15]

The KAU reacted strongly against the 'Kenya Plan' and sent Mbiyu Koinange, the veteran nationalist leader, to personally present a petition to the King. The Hon. Mathu, in a statement to the *East African Standard* of 6th October, called the plan 'tantamount to a declaration of war.'[16] The EAINC, on the other hand, in its usual cautious and equivocal manner, appointed Makhan Singh, Chanan Singh, J M Nazareth and D D Puri to a committee to study the plan and submit a report.

ACCUSATIONS OF COMMUNIST SUPPORT

※

At the same meeting in September, Makhan Singh raised a point as to whether the Hon. A B Patel was in order when he indulged in anti-communist remarks against the trade union movement in Kenya, in the course of a Legco debate. While opposing, with Mathu and Madan, the Trade Union Re-registration Bill, Patel had stated that 'he held no brief for agitators and was not against the exercise of proper supervision of trade unions'.

He accused the LTUEA of receiving covert funds from the World Federation of Trade Unions (WFTU) . . . alleging that it had fallen under undue communist influence. He also alleged that the *Daily Chronicle* was receiving a financial subsidy from the Soviet weekly, *Isvestia*, an allegation he could only have made after reading an intelligence report. But he gave not one iota of proof for either accusation. The denunciation marked the high point of a concerted attack by the colonial government and the conservative Asian leadership on the trade unions and the *Daily Chronicle*. Ultimately, it led to the dispersion of the *Chronicle* team of journalists who had, for seven years, fearlessly used the pen to spearhead the anti-colonial struggle.

The president of the EAINC ruled that Makhan Singh should submit a memorandum to be put before the next executive meeting. The latter said he would reconsider the matter. In the *Daily Chronicle* offices the matter raised some humorous comments. 'I wish we were getting some money,' said Haroon Ahmed, one of the editors. People would ask Piyo Rattansi: 'Is it true?' and when he adamantly denied it, they would question, 'but how do you know, you are only a reporter?' Sharda laughingly suggested to Makhan Singh that he should file a civil suit complaining that 'my colleagues are not giving me my share of the Moscow gold' and he should appoint A B Patel as his lawyer![17]

The *Daily Chronicle* published an article under the heading 'Drastic Education Tax in the Offing' and condemned the betrayal of the Asian community by the Hon. A B Patel and Hon. I E Nathoo. It termed the Hartwell Committee Report on Indian education a 'Foul Plot to Hoodwink The People.' In brief, the Report argued that if the Indians wanted full schooling facilities for their children, they must raise money from their own sources, or else be content with things as they are. Hon. A B Patel had supported it as a short-term measure and on condition that the Indian community would not be permitted to split the education system into communal sections.

The EAINC's November meeting opened with a condolence message for the family of the Hon. General Secretary, Romesh Chandra Gautama, who had died at the age of 32. It went on to deal with the nationality question. Once again, as on the boycott issue, Makhan Singh was the only member opposed to Indian residents in Kenya possessing dual citizenship that is Indian and British. He was overruled when he demanded that the committee appointed to look into the matter 'disclose the line it was going to take.' The matter was discussed at length later in December, when it was unanimously resolved to inform all Indian associations to advise their members not to take any hurried steps which might 'prejudice the acquisition or retention by Indians residents here of local citizenship or citizenship rights.'

A letter from the KAU enclosing copies of the resolutions passed at its annual conference was read and merely noted and the secretary directed to 'send a suitable reply.' No discussion followed, as surely Makhan Singh would have expected.

The select committee report on Indian education prepared by a sub-committee comprised of Chanan Singh, Makhan Singh and Dr K V Adalja was presented. It rejected the existing situation of racial taxation and stated that all social services should be paid for out of general revenue. Terming the Hartwell Report 'a deliberate and premeditated economic assault on the poor', it demanded more Indian civil servants in the education service, proper terms of service for teachers, bursaries for needy students and asserted that education was a basic right.

The 19th Session of the EAINC held in August, 1948, had appointed a committee to draft a new constitution and a new name. The members were, Haroon Ahmed, Bachulal Gathani, Joshi, A R Kapila, J M Nazareth, S Pandit, J B Pandya, Makhan Singh and Hon. Patel and Hon. Madan. A draft was prepared by Nazareth for adoption. Makhan Singh's notes indicate his queries and alternative suggestions were not incorporated. Instead of the new name 'Kenya Indian Congress'; he would have preferred 'The Kenya Congress' or 'East African National Congress', thus opening the organisation to all races. He wanted the aim of the organisation to be not just 'to achieve full and equal rights of citizenship for all races in East Africa' but 'the complete independence and freedom of East Africa'. His interest in specific rights was evident in the aim 'to strive for establishment of a free democratic government in Kenya with equal franchise, adult suffrage and common roll for all races.' He objected to the clause 'the decision of the president on any question of interpretation of the constitution shall be final' and opted for replacing 'president' with 'executive'. Clearly, the problem of concentrating power in one individual is not a recent phenomenon in Kenya. He also pushed for a democratic and countrywide structure rather than the centralised organisation of the EAINC as it was.

LAUNCHING THE EAST AFRICAN TRADE UNION CONGRESS

'Sunday, the 1ˢᵗ May, 1949 was a historic day in the history of Kenya's trade union movement,' because on that day a central organisation of trade unions was officially launched, the East African Trade Union Congress. The decision to form the EATUC was taken at a meeting held in Hayat Building under the chairmanship of Fred Kubai.

Five registered trade unions attended: the LTUEA, the Transport and Allied Workers Union, the Tailors and Garment Workers Union, the Typographical Union of Kenya and the Shoemaker Workmen's Union. Twenty-five representatives, five from each union, participated in the meeting. Three unions, the Kenya Asian Civil Service Association, the Railway Asian Union and the E A Ramgharia Artisan Union, did not respond to the letter inviting them to the meeting, the Railway African Staff Union and African Civil Servants Association too did not attend.

Agitation and dissatisfaction were prevalent among the workers and some of them were already on strike. Just before the EATUC was officially born, the Indian Shoemakers Association had struck and stayed out for a month. As a result, their working hours were reduced from 63 to 49. As all shoemaking businesses were owned by Asians, this is an interesting indication of the degree of exploitation prevalent among Asian employers.[18]

The basic objective was the 'amelioration of the economic, social, cultural and other conditions of the East African working class and co-ordination of the aims and activities of all organised workers in East Africa'. A central council of 25 members was appointed with the following officials: Fred Kubai (president), Nelson Kagao and B J Bharucha (vice presidents), Makhan Singh (general secretary), H M Stanley

---

EAST AFRICAN TRADE UNIONS CONGRESS

HAYAT BUILDING - CANAL RD.

AIR MAIL REGISTERED.   P. O. BOX 1207

NAIROBI

KENYA COLONY - B. E. AFRICA

4th April, 1950.

D. N. Pritt, Esq.,
K. C.,
4. Essex Court,
Temple, E. C. 4.

Dear Sir,

Yesterday we sent you under a separate registered cover the whole record of Mr. Makan Singh's Case, which we hope you would receive along with this letter.

The East African Trade Unions Congress letterhead

and Pranlal Sheth (assistant secretaries), Chhaganlal (treasurer) and Richard K. Munyatta (assistant treasurer).

The formation of the EATUC was announced at a huge May Day meeting held that afternoon in the Desai Memorial Hall. The government had turned down a request for a May Day parade but allowed the meeting. The pledge for independence was reiterated here and it was also announced that attempts would be made to organise the railway and agricultural workers. Jomo Kenyatta, the president of the KAU, made a rousing speech emphasising the need for unity and sacrifice. Other African leaders present were Eluid Mathu, Mbiyu Koinange and Jesse Kariuki. The British Trade Union Congress and the World Federation of Trade Unions sent messages of support.[19]

The government's attitude was dependent on the 'conduct it [the EATUC] shows . . . if it proves to be an attempt by communist elements to obtain control of organised labour for subversive objects, government will be strongly opposed to it.' James Patrick, the government's trade union officer, viewed the functions of a union to be purely industrial and eschewing all political interest.

The *East African Standard* of 17th August disparagingly wrote that 'the new EATUC is apparently trying to run with the hare and hunt with the hounds . . . . Communism is not a criminal offence, particularly in a democratic country where there is still great liberty of thought, but those who profess the creed will be aware that it is not nowadays above suspicion, or welcomed, in British Colonies.'

Baraza headed its article 'Linked with the Communists' and published the same in Kiswahili. 'It [the EATUC] was formed by a small group headed by an Indian who is known to be, if not an actual communist, at least a man who is extremely sympathetic to the doctrines of Russia . . . the World Federation of Trade Unions is a communist-dominated body, the free democracies headed by Great Britain and America very properly decided to withdraw from it . . . the EATUC is headed by a committee consisting in the main of Indians and Kikuyus and . . . has aligned itself with the communists.' It went on to urge trade union members in East Africa to disassociate themselves from the EATUC and added, 'the LTUEA called Chege Kibachia "the beloved leader of the Kenyan working class." *Baraza* considers him 'a scoundrel who terrorised the workers of Mombasa and headed the dreaded *Afisi ya Maskini*.' (The 'Office of the Poor', so named by Makhan Singh, was a branch of the LTUEA situated in Shauri Moyo, a working class district of Nairobi).

In theory, the EATUC got its money from dues, twenty-five shillings from each union and 10 cents per member, of which there were initially over 500. But neither the Congress nor its affiliates was ever able to organise a satisfactory system for collecting subscriptions. Paid collectors were used but money stuck to their hands. Police and employers were hostile while workers were too poor and, when immediate results were not obtained, too fickle. Most of the money came from collections at public rallies. Contrary to what some people assumed, no financial aid was received from the British Trade Union Congress or the WFTU.

100 African and Asian waiters in Indian sweetmeat shops went on strike and won a wage increase. The *East African*

The famous tree on the right bank of the Nairobi River where Afisi Ya Maskini was established in 1947

Standard of 30th September, 1949, reported a dispute between the LTU and United Motor Works regarding the dismissal of six employees. The hand of Makhan Singh could be seen in both these disputes for they primarily concerned Asians.[21]

In this atmosphere of united workers' and nationalist struggles on the one side and adamant opposition from the

employers and European
settlers on the other, the
Transport and Allied
Workers Union declared a
strike on 4th October. The
union had sought redress
from the Nairobi
municipality's new taxi-
cab by-laws for three
years with no success. The
by-laws were designed to
raise driving standards
and to fight crime, but the
union felt they were
unduly restrictive, unfair
to those who already had
licences and would impose unreasonable financial demands on
the poorer taxi drivers.

M A O Ndisi

Two thousand workers were involved, led by their
secretary, Fred Kubai, who had temporarily taken over from
Meshak Ndisi[22].

Makhan Singh, as general secretary of the EATUC, assured
them that the strike was a lawful one. The Association of
Chambers of Commerce and Industry of Eastern Africa
supported the strike that threatened to become a general strike.
The EATUC met with the various relevant authorities, as a
result of which high government officials assured the strike
committee of a 'sympathetic hearing by the municipal council.'
The strike by all taxi drivers in Nairobi was supported by a
sympathy strike at the Kenya Bus Company and lasted sixteen
days, after which time it was called off. Efforts to spread the
strike failed and the city council upheld the by-laws but
allowed a right of appeal to the attorney general – a concession
of little interest to the union. It was a great demonstration of
unity, solidarity and discipline of the workers. In November,
the union prepared a memorandum tabling its demands and

distributed it widely. In mid-December, the municipal council responded. The union was not satisfied and the struggle continued.

Jomo Kenyatta on the other hand expressed disapproval. At a meeting in Kaloleni Hall in September, 1947, he and W W W Awori urged a

> moderate and business-like approach. Write your demands on paper, give them to your employers, give them notice of intention to strike and then strike if need be – that is the proper way. But lightening, illegal strikes, without notice and without the people really knowing what they are about or what they want, are useless,

Kenyatta advised[23]. The following year in June, Mbotela denounced EATUC at a KAU meeting in Nakuru. 'Africans ought to learn to strike in a civilised manner,' he harangued and strongly criticised those who had played a leading part in the disturbance, and had followed a Sikh who had claimed to know everything.[24]

Kenyatta seemed to have been willing to associate with Makhan Singh, Kubai or Kibachia as long as their organisations were subordinate to the KAU. It is clear from Bildad Kaggia's autobiography, *Roots of Freedom*, that the radical unionists in KAU, especially Fred Kubai and Bildad Kaggia, regarded the LTUEA as a ginger group within KAU[25]. Having become disillusioned by the KAU leadership, Kaggia turned to the trade union movement for support for a more militant political struggle. After hearing Makhan Singh speak at the EATUC meeting, he decided to join the Congress. 'He had the fire I admired and was a real revolutionary,' he wrote. However, he could only join the EATUC if he belonged to a union and there was no clerks' union at the time. So he formed the Clerks and Commercial Workers Union. 'In those days there were few trade unions and educated people were not interested in them,' he lamented. Later when the EATUC was banned, his union joined the LTU of which he then became president.[26]

Between May Day, 1949 and mid-May, 1950, the EATUC mounted a vigorous campaign, with more and more publicity, and attacked white oligarchy in a practical way. Between January and April, 1950, the KAU issued a stream of press releases and sponsored 25 to 30 meetings, the tenor becoming more and more radical.

Meanwhile, the International Confederation of Free Trade Unions (ICFTU) based in the USA, had come into existence. The EATUC had declined to be affiliated to either the ICFTU or the WFTU. The African Workers Federation changed its name to East African Workers Federation, appointed Chege Kibachia as its president, even though he was under restriction, and applied for registration.[27]

Notwithstanding a slander campaign by the conservatives, the workers continued to build and strengthen their organisations. Makhan Singh drafted the necessary documents, including a constitution for the Municipal African Tenants' Association of Nairobi and a memorandum on labour problems in East Africa that he and Kubai presented, through the assistant labour advisor, in November to the British secretary of state when he visited Kenya.

In April, the management committee of Waithaka Secondary School invited Makhan Singh to a tea party to honour Mbiyu Koinange for the good services he had rendered to the people of East Africa. In the same month, the Hon. Mathu voiced his opposition to the practice of finger printing for registration purposes; the issue became known as the 'Kipande Controversy'. (A system of identification by registration was instituted and the *kipande*, or document, had to be carried at all times in a metal locket to be worn around the neck).

On 2nd October, the Indian Youth League of Nairobi celebrated Gandhi Jayanti, the 81st anniversary of Mahatma Gandhi's birth. They arranged an exhibition, which was visited by thousands of Asians, Africans and Europeans. Spinning of cotton yarn as Gandhi used to do, artefacts from his ashram and texts in Gandhi's own hand-writing formed the main attractions of the exhibition, which also included portraits, oil paintings and a selection of various other subjects connected with Gandhi. On the first day of the three day event, a young Indian girl spun continuously for almost twelve hours. The flag-day, the prayer meeting and the fireworks display were well attended. (There were, however, a few Asians who were critical of Gandhi; in August, Makhan Singh had received an abusive letter from an anonymous writer berating him for paying tribute to Gandhi.)

In early May, the KAU presented a memorandum to Britain's secretary of state during his visit to Nairobi. The issues raised were African taxation, unsatisfactory representation in the Legco and the Executive Council, land shortage and the racial aspect of voter registration.

In December, 1949, Tom Mbotela, vice president of the KAU, issued a pamphlet entitled 'Implementation of the Universal Declaration of Human Rights'. He placed the onus of the implementation on the United Nations Organisation. While agreeing with the demand that 'the African community should be recognised and treated on the same level as other races', Makhan Singh queried the concluding paragraph which read, 'It would not be out of place to place on record the fact that the British people have a good policy of colonial administration but they only fail in the equal treatment of "black" and "white". (This does not, of course, apply to the British people and to the British Government of Great Britain, but to the British people in the colonies.) On the whole, no one can deny their ability, level-mindedness and sense of justice. There are no doubt weaknesses in their policy but such difficulties could be overcome by cooperation. No nation in the world can be perfect. It is hoped that the British people will offer all possible help to the United Nations Organisation to achieve implementation of human rights.' As far as Makhan Singh was concerned, Mbotela's understanding of imperialism and colonialism left much to be desired.

A mass meeting of Nairobi workers was held on Saturday 14th January, 1950, under the auspices of the EATUC in the Desai Memorial Hall. Fred Kubai, Makhan Singh, John Mungai, L K Kigume, Moses, Ujagar Singh, Tom Mbotela and James Beauttah all made speeches. They fully supported the demands of the unions for an increase in wages, an 8-hour day and 45-hour week, 14 days local leave with pay, paid gazetted holidays, equal pay for equal work, one month's notice for termination of services for all categories of workers, sick leave with pay and schemes for provident fund or pensions. A campaign was launched and more than 5,000 signatures collected for the release of Chege Kibachia. Resolutions were adopted concerning, among other things, full recognition and representation of the EATUC, registration of trade unions and withdrawal of the forced labour legislation.

The following day, an even bigger meeting was held in the Kaloleni Social Hall under the chairmanship of Dishon Kahiato, a veteran trade union leader. On that day, the forced labour legislation was coming into force in the form of an ordinance to 'make provision for the employment of certain Voluntarily Unemployed Persons' and was to be applied as a first step to Nairobi and its adjoining areas. A large number of workers attended the meeting, money was collected and the EATUC sent cables to the United Nations and the Secretary of State for the Colonies.

On 26th January, the governor, Sir Philip Mitchell, in a lengthy speech at the Rotary Club of Nairobi, spoke of the

Dishon Kahiato

'The New Tyranny,' in reference to the menace of communism. Makhan Singh underlined certain passages in the written version, notably, 'There are a few people here, who are known to be Communists, that is to say, in fact, revolutionaries . . . . There is no openly organised revolutionary party in Kenya, and there is no organised propagation of party ideology.'

Mitchell described various ploys to 'manufacture grievances, real or imaginary,' and the promotion of discontent and unrest. Ascribing all ills to 'imperialism', 'capitalism' and so on, infiltration of labour and trade union organisations, promotion of strikes and disturbances, propaganda in schools and terrorist acts were the major methods he highlighted.

He described the idealised form of Marxist theory attractive to intellectuals, especially adolescent intellectuals, as 'emotional Socialism'. He averred that the vast majority of 'educated' Africans 'are people with the sort of education that our children have by the time they are 12 years of age.' The solution he proposed was, interestingly, quite progressive.

What we have got to concentrate on, and to take active measures about, is not so much either the teachings of political theory or the manifestations of subversive revolutionary forces, but the political, economic and social conditions which exist in fact in Kenya, and the extent to which they are in themselves either causes of, or at least inducements to such discontents as may give opportunities for disruptive and revolutionary activities.

The settlers' paper, the *Kenya Weekly News*, supported Mitchell and called for laws which would enable 'restraint and sanctions to be imposed upon those who seek to use it for subversive agitation and for designs destructive of the true wealth of East Africa.'[28]

BOYCOTT OF CITY CHARTER CELEBRATIONS

Meanwhile, it had been announced that Nairobi was to be raised to the status of 'city' on 30th March, 1950. Celebrations for the occasion had been planned on a big scale but there was a mounting resistance and resentment amongst the workers and others against the policies of the British and Kenya governments and the Nairobi municipal council. On 19th February, the E A Painters and Decorators Union passed a resolution asking the EATUC to organise a boycott of the celebrations.

On 4th March, the EATUC called a mass meeting of workers which was held in Nairobi's Kaloleni Hall and it was decided to boycott the forthcoming celebrations. This was reiterated the next day at a meeting of the Domestic and Hotel Workers Union. The *Daily Chronicle* reported that 'A total boycott of all Civic Week celebrations in Nairobi was unanimously decided upon by over a thousand Africans who met in the Pumwani Memorial Hall . . . a vigorous speech by Mr. Fred Kubai described the celebrations as "a mere propaganda trick" designed to make it appear to the outside world that democracy was on the march in this country. "We see no change in our status", declared Mr. Kubai, adding that housing for the worker was still expensive, wages were low and even so basic a need as water was not available to him in adequate quantity. How could the workers under such conditions, honestly join in the celebrations?'

'The celebrations,' demanded Mr. Kubai, 'should be boycotted and no worker should accept any sweets, meat or posho distributed by the Municipal Council . . . nor should he participate in any dances organised . . . in this connection.' Mr Makhan Singh declared that, 'there were two Nairobis – that of the rich and that of the poor. The status of the latter Nairobi had not changed and there is nothing for us to celebrate.

Celebrations will be justified on the day when this country's Government becomes truly democratic, with the workers fully sharing in the tasks of Government.

'How can the workers be pleased when out of 28 Municipal Councillors, 17 are Europeans, dominating the entire show, despite the fact that they represent only an insignificant minority in Nairobi? As against this, only two Africans were nominated to represent more than a hundred thousand Africans, mainly workers. How can we be pleased with fireworks when the fire of hunger gnaws in our stomachs? The workers will have plenty of fire-works when they became free from the rule of the rich.'

A statement issued by the EATUC on 20th March claimed that the boycott was of the utmost importance and that it had arisen from the indignation of the workers and the trade union movement against the anti-working class, anti-trade union, anti-democratic and racial policies and practices of the Nairobi Municipal Council and the Kenya Government.

'How can the workers take part in the 'celebrations' and share the 'pleasure',' it asked, 'When the municipal council is dominated by a white majority supported by other vested interests and nominated members; When an overwhelming majority of workers in Nairobi have no right to elect the Councillors; When thousands of workers have to live in the dirty and unhealthy slums of Pumwani, Shauri Moyo, Marurani and River Road areas and when the roads in these areas are of the worst type in Nairobi; When the workers already burdened by a high cost of living are further burdened by the Municipal Council with high rents, with meagre water and latrine facilities; When the workers' children are not getting sufficient education and hospital facilities and when there is no future social security for workers; When the capitalist-dominated municipal council ignores the representations made by the Transport and Allied Workers Union to repeal the repressive taxi-cab by-laws, against which the heroic transport workers had to declare a big strike in

October last year. When plans are being secretly hatched to add to Nairobi more land of Africans.

'. . . By their boycott they [the workers] wish to demonstrate that the so-called 'progress' is not the progress of the millions of toiling people but a handful of capitalists. By their boycott, the workers will be protesting against the anti-trade union policies of the Kenya government and the British government; their refusal to recognise the East African Trade Unions Congress; their silence over the question of registration of some of the unions, their refusal to release Chege Kibachia, their refusal to repeal the forced labour legislation and anti-strike laws, their refusal to remove the *kipande* system and finally their refusal to democratise the government in which the workers could have their own share.'

Fred Kubai and Makhan Singh, as president and general secretary of the EATUC, signed the statement. On 23rd March, at a joint meeting of all the executive committees of its member unions, the EATUC decided on a complete boycott of the city celebrations and resolved to apply for permission for a

Kiburi House

procession of workers on 'Charter Day'. It would start and end at Kiburi House (the home of the trade unions and KAU situated in Grogan Road),

Passing through the African localities and avoiding the areas where the celebrations would be held. Twelve different slogans were chosen for the banners.

The police refused to give the permission for the march. The *Daily Chronicle* team suggested setting fire to the main VIP stage but Makhan Singh would not hear of it. He had a strong Gandhian streak in him and in addition to his preference for non-violent methods and mass movements; he was a stickler for legality and honesty. 'We communists don't believe in individual terrorism,' he stated. Sharda, in his usual jovial and impish manner, teasingly rejoined, 'You believe in collective terrorism!'

On 30ᵗʰ March, when the Duke of Gloucester presented the City Charter to the mayor, the overwhelming majority of workers of Nairobi and the adjoining areas remained at home. Most of the national leaders, headed by Jomo Kenyatta and ex-senior chief Koinange, who had been officially invited to take part in the celebrations, did not attend. The organisers brought in people from far-off *shambas* to line the routes but even amongst them there was 'a lack of enthusiasm'.

Eluid Mathu, Tom Mbotela (vice-president of the KAU) and Joseph Katithi repudiated the EATUC boycott. In an interview with the DC, Jomo Kenyatta criticised the three and supported Makhan Singh but in order to heal the rift in the KAU, he told a mass meeting held on 15ᵗʰ March, that Makhan Singh and Fred Kubai were harming African unity. The trade union movement was itself affected as Meshack Ndisi, who had returned three months earlier, resigned from the Transport and Allied Workers Union saying, 'the policy of the union is influenced by persons outside it, who are supporters of the communist-dominated WFTU.'[29]

The degree to which the campaign and the boycott upset the settlers and their leaders can be gauged by the settler newspaper's reaction. The *Kenya Weekly News*, under the headline 'Wicked Mischief' published the full text of the EATUC statement. The editor wrote of the 'evil in their midst' and went on to vilify Makhan Singh as 'an avowed communist.' 'He has sought to affiliate the trade union movement in Kenya with the World Federation of Trade Unions, a communist controlled organisation. During the war and since the war Makhan Singh has shown himself to be antagonistic to Great Britain and to the Commonwealth. Personal gain has no place in his mind but he is a fanatic revolutionary who would probably seek to overthrow the social order of Utopia. He uses the common technique of which His Excellency the governor spoke in a recent speech – exploitation of grievances, poverty and discontent, racialism and nationalism; magnification of anything that can do harm to the repute of government; ascription of all ills to imperialism, capitalism and so on; and the distortion of the trade union movement away from its proper purpose, and the creation of 'phoney' unions. The simple fact is that there is no room for a Labour Department and for Makhan Singh in Kenya . . . . In my view the continued tolerance of Makhan Singh's activities is a gross betrayal of the true interests of the Africans whom he seeks to deceive and to lead astray. It is high time that Kenya [were] rid of him and of others like him.'

A few days later, Sir (then Mr) Michael Blundell, a leading member of the Legco, referred to the EATUC statement as 'most utter claptrap,' and went on to declare 'these men must be dealt with and they must be dealt with firmly.' The boycott enraged the ultra-conservative and passionately monarchical settlers and their reactions were reported by the *Daily Chronicle* on 7th, 21st and 25th March.

A DEMAND FOR COMPLETE INDEPENDENCE

While the struggles of the trade unions and the EATUC were continuing and intensifying, a major event took place on Kenya's national scene on Sunday 23rd April, 1950. The KAU and the EAINC jointly held a huge meeting of about 20,000 people in Kaloleni Social Hall under the chairmanship of Hon. Eluid Mathu with fellow legislators I E Nathoo, Mbiyu Koinange and Chanan Singh also present. A B Patel, supported by Tom Mbotela, moved a motion strongly condemning the aggressive and racist agitation by the European settlers against the proposal to grant equal unofficial representation to Africans and non-Africans in Tanganyika's Legislative Council, with provision for the election of members on a common roll. They appealed to national and international bodies to 'save [the Territory] from the designs of the domination by the Europeans of East and Central Africa.'

Makhan Singh, seconded by Fred Kubai, then moved an addendum to the resolution. It declared that

the real solution of the problem is not this or that small reform, but the complete independence and sovereignty of the East African territories and establishment in all these territories of democratic government elected by the people and responsible to the people of these territories only, and that the solution should be implemented at an early date.

After a long debate the whole resolution, including the addendum, was passed unanimously. Jomo Kenyatta, the president of the KAU, in his speech said,

I always like cooperation, but I do not want the cooperation of the cat and mouse. We must support our

Kaloleni Hall

friends in Tanganyika, and unitedly continue our struggle for independence.

Piyo Rattansi attended the Kaloleni meeting and saw Makhan Singh address the predominantly African crowd and was amazed at the transformation in the man. 'He climbed up to the podium his pockets bulging with fountain pens and addressed the crowd in a shrill tone, almost screaming.' A reporter from the BBC's *Listener* described him as 'burnt out with anger.' The audience was rapt and attentive and seemed to sway to the tirade against British colonialism.

When asked, Makhan Singh had publicly stated, 'Yes I am a communist. I am fighting for the freedom of all countries in the world.[30] When Makhan Singh declared himself a communist, he probably meant that he was a generally Russian-oriented Marxist; not a disciplined member of a communist structure since there did not appear to have been any formal communist organisation in Kenya at that time. Nor does the EATUC seem to have received any practical support from the WFTU or from other communist bodies. He had the worst of both worlds. He alienated many Asians and Africans by his declaration and gave the Europeans an effective handle with which to beat the labour movement without securing any practical advantage for himself or the EATUC.[31] The treasurer of KAU, Ambrose Ofafa, joined with Asian leaders in attacking Makhan Singh.

The government refused the EATUC permission to hold a May Day procession and rally stating that it had done so because the organisation was not registered. In his May Day article Makhan Singh wrote: 'May 1st – the International Workers' Day is being celebrated throughout the world . . . In East Africa we are celebrating it as "FREEDOM DAY" . . . The EATUC is celebrating the Day also as its first birthday. It was on 1st May, 1949, when it was formed by five registered trade unions whose number has now risen to nine and membership from about 5,000 to about 12,000.' He highlighted the increasing Indo-African unity and claimed that it had begun to influence the politics of the country. He referred to the Kaloleni meeting as a 'peoples' front and pledged that the EATUC and all its members would strive to make themselves efficient and capable to be able to effect the resolutions which were passed at the meeting.

In its 3rd May issue, the *Daily Chronicle* ran a headline 'Mombasa Whites Jittery Over Kaloleni Resolution.' It quoted a Mr Robinson as declaring that 'it is time to take the matter seriously. We cannot allow this thing to develop while Government apparently takes the attitude that pretending it [communism] does not exist [in Kenya] will give us peace in their time.' In response to it, the *Daily Chronicle* wrote 'who but a genius like you could have conceived the remarkable idea that the people who talk of freedom should be deprived of it? Purely in a spirit of cooperation you should agitate with all the saw-dust in your brain to try and have the definition of "sedition" altered in the Penal Code. Define sedition as the unforgivable sin of demanding freedom for anyone the colour of whose skin is not colourless. THEN you can put the handcuffs on the chaps who seek to dislodge you from your cosy positions of exploitation.'

As was to be expected the government introduced bills in the Legco for the restriction of meetings and organisations and tightened and extended the sedition laws. On 9th May, the Government of Uganda banned the importation of the *Daily Chronicle* from Nairobi. (By then the editors were D K Sharda for the English section and Indu Desai for the Gujerati section.) The EATUC denounced the ban as 'victimisation of the paper for its support of working class and trade union movement[s] and its solidarity with the demand for freedom and democratic liberties.' It also termed it 'a serious attack upon the freedom of the press.'[32]

In addition to his trade union activities and attending to the government's court cases against him, Makhan Singh was occupied with drafting a constitution and a report on the Kenya Plan for the EAINC Meanwhile in March, the EAINC executive committee had resolved to resume sending communiqués to the *Daily Chronicle* as 'Congress activities were not getting sufficient publicity.' On the constitution, he laid emphasis on including the word 'national' in the name of the organisation and wanted its main objective to be 'to achieve the complete independence and sovereignty of the people of East Africa. In addition 'it should endeavour to form joint fronts with other organisations on matters of common interest . . . . A member could be suspended for participating in any communal political body or any organisation which engages in racial political activity . . . . Executive members must be recruited nationally and not only from Nairobi . . . . Voting and decision-making must be democratic.'

Regarding the Kenya Plan he made extensive notes on the problems facing Kenya. He placed them in three categories: political, economic and social. Under political he listed the constitution, franchise, representation, law and justice and the question of closer union with other East African territories and with the Central African territories. Economic issues concerned land, immigration and settlement, government finances, labour and trade union matters, civil and railway service terms, trade and commerce and social services. In the social sphere, his concerns were the colour bar and segregation in residential areas.

Earlier, in January, the executive committee of the EAINC held a special meeting to discuss the forthcoming Indian Republic Day on the 26th of the month. Members decided to celebrate it by organising a dinner at a charge of fifty shillings per couple, subsidised by a donation of KShs 1,000 from the president. Makhan Singh, though in favour of holding a function, preferred a 'garden party or a peoples' dinner' where the expenses would be reasonable and affordable. Chanan Singh supported him but they were both overruled. As it so happened, at a subsequent meeting the president, who had not been present at the earlier meeting, declined to offer the required donation. It was then decided to mark the occasion with a 'peoples' dinner which large numbers of less wealthy members could attend.

Ambu Patel remembers that 'once Makhan Singh and a team of five or six active members went to protest at the Parklands Club to prevent the replacement of old workers. Makhan Singh, with all of us there, was arrested and fined by the court. He said he would not pay the fine so we all said the same. I don't remember how we were released but I am sure that none of us paid the fine. Makhan Singh remained firm and did not hesitate to go to jail for the cause he believed in.'[33]

Makhan Singh had a phenomenal capacity for work. His singleness of purpose and his selfless dedication and commitment seemed to provide him with boundless energy and fervour. He seemed deceptively young, at least ten years less than his actual age. At the *Daily Chronicle* press, they worked from nine in the morning to nine at night. The team would then meet with Makhan Singh and others for a chit-chat. Makhan Singh often brought his writings to the press with a request to have them 'polished up.' Piyo Rattansi narrates how just as they were closing down for the night, Makhan Singh would come in with a request for an article to be reviewed. 'But Makhan Singh,' Piyo would remonstrate, 'it is late and we are closing.' Makhan Singh would look taken aback, amazed at Piyo's attitude. *'Magar raat apni hein,'* (But the night is ours), he would contend[34]. However, clearly there were times when he could not cope with the workload. In April, the secretary of the Indian Youth League had to request him to attend the meetings after he had failed to be present two consecutive times.

Makhan Singh had an exceptionally high degree of self-discipline and focus of purpose. He always knew what he was doing and why; he was resolute, ever hopeful and convinced of the rightness of his cause. Friendly and approachable, he was never moody. He structured his entire life-style and thinking to minimise dependency on material needs and personal considerations.

'Up to the time of his detention I never once saw in him any sign of fear or anxiety for his own personal safety,' Piyo attests.

> While appreciating the companionship and support of his comrades, he was always careful not to incriminate them in any way. He was very conscious about security and taught me never to speak sensitive matters on the phone, to use false names and say only what was necessary and only to those whom it concerned.

Makhan Singh's discretion was such that despite being in regular contact with Makhan Singh from 1947 to 1950, Piyo himself remained unaware of his friend's life and activities prior to that time.[35]

AN APPEAL TO
THE PRIVY COUNCIL

A matter which continued to be of grave concern to Makhan Singh was the dismissal of his case by the Court of Appeal for Eastern Africa and hence the Kenya government's refusal to grant him a certificate of permanent residence. Following the rejection, in November, 1948, of Makhan Singh's application for a certificate for permanent residence, the EAINC sent a telegram to His Majesty requesting him to 'exercise his power of disallowance in respect of Immigration (Control) Amendment Ordinance 1948.' Makhan Singh also wrote a letter dated 28th May, 1949, to William Gallacher, MP, House of Commons, London, requesting, on behalf of Chanan Singh, the advice of D N Pritt, K C regarding his case which is 'a fight against the reactionary clauses of the Kenya government's Immigration Laws and against the efforts of the government to impose restrictions upon the trade union workers and progressive elements . . . I was the first victim of the new ordinance whereby the Governor-in-Council can refuse to grant me a certificate of permanent residence . . . Please do spare your valuable time for this struggle, as you have been doing in the past. Yours fraternally . . . '

In February, 1950, he asked the EAINC committee if it would consider forwarding his case to the Privy Council in Britain(and, of course, bear the expenses). However, the majority of members felt that litigation was not the proper approach to fight for political rights of this nature.

In March, he wrote to the attorney general in reference to Civil Case No 329 of 1949 and Civil Appeal No 1 of 1950, Makhan Singh versus Principal Immigration Officer. 'I propose to appeal to the Privy Council against the Judgement of the Supreme Court of Kenya. The papers are being prepared and in the course of the next few days would be sent to my solicitors in London,' he informed him.

The attorney general wrote back, 'I shall be glad to be informed under what provision of law it is suggested that an appeal lies to the Privy Council . . . it would appear that the object is merely delay.' Makhan Singh replied that the appeal was being filed in accordance with the laws of the colony and Great Britain. 'I must point out,' he added, 'that there is no delay on my part. In fact, the delay is on the part of the Kenya Government which is delaying the endorsement of a certificate of permanent residence on my passport.'

On 4th April, Fred Kubai and Makhan Singh wrote to the advocate D N Pritt in London enclosing the whole record of the case. 'The Government of Kenya has been making consistent endeavours to deport Mr. Makhan Singh since August 1947,' the letter stated. 'Makhan Singh filed an application in the Supreme Court of Kenya praying for an order by way of Mandamus calling upon the Principal Immigration Officer to endorse on his passport a Certificate of Permanent Residence. Judgement was given against him. Then he appealed to the Court of Appeal for Eastern Africa; but the latter Court decided that it had no jurisdiction to hear appeals from refusal of prerogative writs.

'. . . because Makhan Singh is the General Secretary of the E. A. Trade Unions Congress, and has been consistent fighter for the working class since 1935, for more than 15 years, and has suffered imprisonment for the cause while in India . . . the Congress is determined to resist all attacks on its functionaries . . . . It, therefore, requests you to help the East African trade union movement by championing Mr. Makhan Singh's appeal in the Privy Council in the manner the local patriotic advocates have been doing here, that is without fees. The movement here is trying to raise some funds for bearing the other costs of the appeal.'

Two weeks later the firm of Privy Council Appeal Agents and Solicitors wrote to Chanan Singh & Handa, Advocates stating that they were sympathetic to 'the political views which your client seems to hold,' and that a petition could properly be presented to the Privy Council as it concerned the civil rights of a British subject. The firm estimated the total cost would be 500 pounds sterling.

On 5th May, Makhan Singh wrote to Pritt and H S L Pollak requesting them to act patriotically. 'It would be a great contribution on your part towards the defence of trade unionism and human rights in the colonies.' Pritt replied that he was willing to act without fees in the appeal to the Privy Council and Makhan Singh applied to have his case lodged as a 'pauper', as especially most of the trade union leaders were in prison and, therefore, unable to help. To Pollak he wrote, 'Your devotion to the cause of the colonial people is well known.' He sent a copy to 'Comrade Dutt.' Palme Dutt of the British Communist Party replied assuring him that 'all friends here are very much concerned over the position and that we are taking all possible steps.' Dutt's encouraging letter was received by Sudh Singh as it arrived after Makhan Singh had been arrested.

CHAPTER EIGHT

ARREST AND
DETENTION CASE 1950

Monday, 15ᵗʰ May, 1950, dawned dramatically. At 6.30 a. m. Fred Kubai and Makhan Singh were arrested at their respective homes in Pumwani and on Park Road. Police officials searched their houses, the office of the EATUC in Hayat Building, and the Punjab Printing Press, where Makhan Singh worked. They seized files, documents, books and photographs, and sealed them in 9 bags (one from Fred Kubai's house, two from Makhan Singh's house, four from the EATUC office and two from the press). The court ordered, in spite of their objection, that all the bags be handed over to the C I D for documentation, although the magistrate agreed that such documentation be done in their presence. The offices of the EATUC and several unions were closed and sealed by the C I D.

FRED KUBAI AND MAKHAN SINGH ARRESTED

News of the arrests spread like wildfire. The workers were outraged. Members of EATUC's central council met at Kiburi House and decided to declare a general strike in Nairobi and other parts of Kenya. Their demands were:
- The release of Makhan Singh, Fred Kubai and Chege Kibachia.
- A minimum wage of KShs 100.
- The abolition of the municipal by-laws regarding taxi drivers.
- An end to workers being arrested at night in their houses.
- Freedom for all workers and freedom of East African territories.

The strike notice was signed by Chege Kiburu as president and Mwangi Macharia as general secretary, and a strike committee was formed under the chairmanship of John Mungai.

The general strike began in the afternoon on Tuesday 16th May. The government immediately extended the list of 'essential services' in which it was illegal to hold a strike. By Wednesday morning, the strike was in full force. The Public Works Department and the city administration were the most affected, employees of central government and the railway were involved to a lesser extent.

The same day a bonfire was lit on the left bank of the Nairobi River in the valley of Pumwani and Shauri Moyo and was kept perpetually burning with trunks and branches of trees from the nearby areas. The fire became a symbol of the fighting spirit of the strikers as well as of the people of Kenya for freedom and independence. 'MOTO! MOTO!' (Fire! Fire!) was the slogan everywhere. As Bethwell Ogot was to write many years later, 'When we use it we should remember the brave Kenyan workers who in 1950 organised, without their leaders, the first successful countrywide strike in defiance of colonial authorities and white settlerism.' Over one hundred workers were arrested and imprisoned including Chege Kibiru who was sentenced to eleven months.[1] Food was donated by the workers for the

The historic place in Shauri Moyo

strikers and their families on a large scale.

Though the *East African Standard* insistently reported it as a 'Nairobi strike', all the major towns — Mombasa, Nakuru, Kisumu – as well as others such as Thika, Nyeri, Nanyuki, Kakamega and Kisii were affected, with hundreds of employees going on strike. Workers from the Railways, the Public Works Department, and the Power and Lighting Company were initially slower to respond than those from the smaller firms. On Friday, a 20-year-old youth, Jarnail Singh Liddar, who had resigned his job in the Nairobi post office a day or two earlier, went to the railway central workshops and called upon railway workers to join the strike. In Shauri Moyo, he addressed the strikers and urged them to maintain their solidarity and unity. He was arrested and sentenced to six months' hard labour.[2]

When Mathu and Jeremiah, both members of the Legco, tried to inform the strikers that the strike was illegal and suggested setting up a committee to look into their grievances, they met with a hostile reaction. The police attacked the strikers with baton charges and broke up their meetings. The police enrolled Luos as special constables since they were frequently the victims of the strikers and were 'itching to get even with their Kikuyu assailants.'[3]

By Tuesday the 23rd, 345 arrests had been made, but the strike continued unabated. Repression was not succeeding. More than a hundred thousand people throughout Kenya participated in the general strike which lasted 10 days, showing unprecedented courage, heroism and discipline in defying the colonial authorities and employers. Women played a significant role especially in the Limuru area.[4] The government declared an increase of six shillings to the minimum wage. The strike committee decided to call it off on Thursday, 25th May, acknowledging that a great anti-imperialist demonstration had taken place.

The charge against Makhan Singh and Fred Kubai was that of being officials of an 'unregistered trade union', the East

African Trade Unions Congress, and of having not dissolved the Congress within three months after the Trade Unions and Trade Disputes Ordinance turned down its application for registration. Against Makhan Singh there was a second warrant, which was under the Deportation (Immigrant British Subjects) Ordinance, 1949. This case was to commence proceedings before a judge of the Supreme Court and if found guilty, a restriction order could be issued against him. Bail was refused and they were incarcerated in Nairobi prison as remand prisoners.[5] A radically new situation arose for Makhan Singh and the trade union movement in Kenya.

Makhan Singh and Fred Kubai had been arrested and placed in remand in Nairobi Prison on Monday, 15th May, 1950. The member for law and order had justified the arrest of Makhan Singh by stating that, 'in this country today certain not too well educated persons, mainly Africans, are being seduced from their own way of life by an Asian brand of Communism. They remind me of animals confronted by a snake –

Mwangi Macharia

Chege Kiburu

John Mungai

mesmerised, bemused and swaying to the rhythm.'[6]

They were taken to court the same day to appear before the Nairobi Resident Magistrate, F Miller and charged with failure to dissolve the EATUC. Both of them denied the charge, the trial took place on 6th and 7th July, 1950. Fred Kubai argued that the EATUC was an association of trade unions and therefore, as in other countries, did not require to be registered, as the adviser to the Secretary of State for the Colonies and Labour Affairs had already affirmed.[7]

Makhan Singh instructed his father to prepare an affidavit. Sudh Singh and an advocate by the name of Bhandari brought it to the prison at 3.40 p. m. and after a quick glance at it, Makhan Singh signed it.

The authorities charged Fred Kubai with the attempted murder of Councillor Muchohi Gikonyo and with an attempt to buy a pistol without a permit. They brought one more case –a perjury case – against Makhan Singh. The perjury case was listed as Criminal Case No 861 of 1950 and was heard in the Resident Magistrate's Court in Nairobi. It was adjourned repeatedly and was finally heard on the 27th, starting from 8.30 a.m. It continued the whole day and the same on the 29th and the morning of the 30th. The Magistrate ruled that there was a case to answer. Makhan Singh spoke briefly, spelling out his rights. No witnesses were called.

The frequent change of times of the court hearings is evidence of the government's nervousness in its prosecution of Makhan Singh. Thousands of Africans were attending the court hearings and the government had to circumvent the massive public support and concern for the accused as well as ensure the accused had minimum time and facilities to prepare his legal arguments. Judgement on this case was delivered on 2nd June, 1950, when Makhan Singh was already in detention in Lokitaung. He was ordered a prison term of three months on the first count and acquitted on the second one.

CRIMINAL CASE NO. 5
OF 1950

Meanwhile, the general strike was becoming increasingly difficult for the government to control. It then decided to relocate Makhan Singh, whom it considered as the focal point of the strike. In the early hours of Sunday morning on 21st May, Makhan Singh was removed to Nyeri prison, 158 kilometres from Nairobi. In Nyeri, he was informed that the restriction proceedings against him under the Deportation Ordinance would he heard there instead of in Nairobi and would start the next day. The case brought against him was based mainly on his trade union activities as general secretary of the EATUC and was conducted in the Supreme Court of Kenya under Justice Ransley Samuel Thacker, Q C.[9]

D N Khanna Advocates were unable to appear for the defence at such short notice and telegraphed Sudh Singh in Nyeri offering to refund the fees paid. On the 22nd, the first day of the hearing, Justice Thacker adjourned the case in order to secure a lawyer to defend Makhan Singh. The latter had informed him that he had been unable to obtain the services of a good advocate, as none he had approached would appear on his behalf. Chanan Singh was persuaded by Justice Thacker to undertake the defendant's defence and the court then sat from 23rd to 27th May, including on the 24th, a public holiday to observe Empire Day.

The charge sheet read: 'In the Supreme Court of Kenya at Nyeri, Miscellaneous Criminal Application No: 5 of 1950. In the matter of the deportation (Immigrant British subjects) Ordinance, 1949 AND In the matter of Makhan Singh s/o Sudh Singh.' The judge was Justice Ransley Thacker. The Crown case was presented by the Attorney General, Mr K K O'Connor, assisted by the Crown Counsel, Mr A G C Somerhough. Mr Chanan Singh appeared for the defendant.

The opening address was made by the Attorney General.

Other witnesses for the prosecution who were examined and cross-examined were:

+ James Roland Ross – Registrar.
+ Elizabeth May Green – Assistant inspector of police, women, and confidential secretary to the assistant superintendent of police, Nairobi Division.
+ Norman Francis Harris – Deputy mayor of Nairobi.
+ Cecil Penfold - Director of Intelligence and Security for the Kenya Colony.
+ Ernest Lloyd Parkar - Assistant Superintendent of Police.
+ Constable Nzioka – No 250, Constable Mwangi Musau – No 402 Constable Kiplangat – No 287. Constables Nzioka and Mwangi had been detailed to attend all political meetings with special instructions to cover Makhan Singh for the past year. Both were illiterate, so they reported from memory.
+ Kenneth Meadows and John Riseborough, the town clerk, were additional witnesses.

The defendant called no witnesses other than himself.

The attorney general served the following notice on the defendant in accordance with Section 7, Sub-section 3 of the Ordinance within 24 hours of his being apprehended:

"TAKE NOTICE that the Supreme Court will be moved on the 22nd day of May, 1950 at 10 o'clock in the forenoon, or as soon as thereafter as Counsel can be heard, by the Attorney General that a report to the Governor under subsection (2) of Section 8 of the above Ordinance be made together with recommendation that a Restriction Order with or without a Security Order should be made against you pursuant to the said Ordinance on the grounds that you are an undesirable person within the meaning of the said Ordinance. Particulars as to the nature of the facts alleged against you are contained in the affidavit of Cecil Penfold, sworn and filed herein on the thirteenth day of May, 1950."

The attorney general further clarified that 'Restriction Order' meant an order prohibiting the person in respect of whom it was made from entering or leaving an area within Kenya without the consent of the officer specified in the order. 'Undesirable Person' meant a person who was or had been conducting himself so as to be dangerous to peace, good order, good government, or public morals, or was or had been attending or conducting himself in a manner calculated, to raise discontent or disaffection amongst His Majesty's subjects or inhabitants of the colony, or to promote feelings of ill-will and hostility between different classes of the population of the colony.

The attorney general then read from the affidavit presented by Cecil Penfold, director of intelligence and security for the colony, Kenya. Some of the main points were that:

1. According to secret information derived from the then government of India, Makhan Singh, while in India in 1935 worked for communist causes and requested to be sent to Moscow.[10]

2. While in India he was detained under the Defence of India rules from the 8th of May, 1940, to 22nd July, 1942, and he was interned in his village in the Punjab from the latter date till the 18th of January, 1945. He was prosecuted under the Defence of India Rules in 1944 for violating one of the conditions of his restriction order.

3. He had stated in his affidavit that, while in India, he took party in the activities of the Communist Party of India, being sub-editor of the official organ of the Punjab Committee, from February, 1945, to July, 1947, and that he returned to Kenya in August, 1947. Quoting from the affidavit the attorney general read: "While in India I took part in the activities of The Indian National Congress, the Mill Kamdar Union, Ahmedabad, and the Communist Party of India." He went on to add that since his return from India he had taken a leading part in various strikes.

4. In 1948, he was receiving Communist publications, one

being The *Communist*, the monthly organ of the Communist Party of India, and the other being the *People's Age*, the official organ of the same Party. In 1949, he was receiving copies of the *Labour Monthly* which is the official organ of the Communist Party of Great Britain and *Africa Newsletter* which is produced by the African Committee of the Communist Party, 16 King St, London. One copy included a reference to the EATUC – sub-headed 'Growing Strength of East Africa TUC'. The importation of both these publications was now banned in Kenya.

5. On 12th March, 1949, he wrote in the *Daily Chronicle*, Nairobi that 'Repression in Kenya is Mounting.' On 15th January, 1950, he addressed a meeting of the shop workers Section of the EATUC. He referred to the Voluntary Unemployed Persons Ordinance, which had been passed some months before as the 'Spiv' Bill. He said it was a slave law.

6. Makhan Singh endeavoured to organise a boycott of the civic celebrations held on the occasion of the conferment by His Majesty the King of a Charter raising Nairobi to City Status. At a joint meeting of the executive committees of LTUEA, Transport and Allied Workers Union including Railway workers, Typographical Union of Kenya, Tailors and Garments Workers, Shoemaker Workmen's Union, Domestic and Hotel Workers Union and E A Painters and Decorators Union, he encouraged the workers to wear black mourning armbands. The attorney general then produced copies of a leaflet which was distributed on 29th March, 1950, urging all workers from 30th March, 1950, to wear black arm bands on the left arm near the elbow or to wear black badges which would be distributed by the EATUC. (Penfield had translated the Swahili word susia to mean 'prevent' the celebrations. Chanan Singh clarified that it meant 'boycott' the celebrations). Constable Mwangi Musau had testified that Makhan Singh said, ' . . . that if people will not attend, the King's son will observe that Africans are not happy and he will also observe that there is slavery and that there are slaves.'

7. On 19th February, 1950, he addressed some 150 workers on the city status issue and encouraged them to strike, on 15th April, 1950, he addressed 500 workers in support of Transport and Allied Workers Union which had been on strike.

8. On 25th March, 1950, he applied to the superintendent of police, Nairobi for permission to hold a workers' procession on Charter Day from 9.00 a.m. to 12.00 noon on 30th March, 1950, which was a public holiday. The route was from Kiburi House along Race Course Road, Kariokor, Pumwani, Shauri Moyo, Kaloleni, Landies Road, Duke Street, Government Road, River Road, Race Course Road, Kiburi House. Slogans were to be: 'Long Live the Workers Unity, Recognise the EATUC, Release our Leader – Chege Kibachia, Higher Wages and Better Housing, Repeal Forced Labour Laws, Repeal Anti-strike Laws, We don't want Kipande and Pass Laws, Workers Representation on Municipal and Legislative Councils, Education for Workers Children, Medical Facilities for Workers, Boycott Civic Celebrations, No more African Land for Nairobi.'[11]

9. Makhan Singh had been in correspondence with the World Federation of Trade Unions which is a communist dominated body, pro-Slav and anti-British in outlook.

10. A manifesto detailing workers rights, conditions, etc. in Swahili was produced for May Day with translations. On 23rd April, 1950, at a joint meeting of EATUC and the KAU, Makhan Singh declared that 'the only solution was complete independence and sovereignty of the East African territories.' On 1st May, 1950, the *Daily Chronicle* printed an article entitled 'May Day – The Freedom of East Africa Day' by Makhan Singh.

MAKHAN SINGH'S DEFENCE

The attorney general then closed the case and the judge asked Makhan Singh to make his defence. He was given three options: He could give evidence on oath from the witness box which meant that he could be cross examined; he could make an unsworn statement from where he then stood; or he could remain silent. Justice Thacker cautioned Makhan Singh that with either of the first two options he could not be cross examined but that he, Justice Thacker, attached more weight to sworn evidence. Makhan Singh then declared that he would give evidence upon oath.

His evidence was lengthy and detailed and consisted of precise responses to each accusation made against him. Some of the points he objected to were regarding:

Accusation 2. The 1944 prosecution case in India. One of the restrictions had been that he could not publish a book while under internment. He had in fact written a manuscript but this had not been published, therefore he had been acquitted. Penfield had failed to mention this.

Accusation 5. In the speech made by him on 14 January, in Desai Memorial Hall, he had said that there were no capitalists in the Soviet Union, there was no racialism and no exploitation of man by man. He had not said slavery existed in Kenya.

Accusation 3. Strikes. Yes, he did take a leading part in all the strikes organised by the unions affiliated to the EATUC. None of these strikes had been declared illegal.

Accusation 5. The article 'Repression is Mounting in Kenya' in the March 1949 *Daily Chronicle*. The factors which prompted him to write this article were mainly the policy of the Kenya Government to ban the entry into the colony of all such publications which supported the cause of the working classes and which opposed the capitalist system.

Accusation 6. The boycott of the city civic celebrations. Yes, he had taken a very prominent part in it.

Justice Thacker intervened to ask, 'What word did you use for worker in Swahili?'

Makhan Singh: 'Wafanyakazi'

Justice Thacker: 'You do not consider that I work?'

Makhan Singh: 'Yes, as an employee of the Government.'

Justice Thacker: 'Is it not dangerous to address a meeting of Africans and call them workers. Is not the inference that employers are not workers?'

Makhan Singh: 'They are not, Sir. The main source of their livelihood is not their work as individuals; it is the profits earned from the labour of others.'

Chanan Singh then cross-examined Makhan Singh asking, 'Did you tell the meeting that if the celebrations continued without the African, then an all out strike would stop the celebrations?'

Makhan Singh: 'Never Sir, not in any meeting. Whenever I spoke in any meeting I spoke as a responsible official of the Trade Unions Congress and I always knew the meaning of what I uttered and why I uttered it. In my affidavit I stated that I had instructed that no man was allowed to fight or throw stones at anybody. My exact words were, 'Peace is required and if it is possible let everybody stay in his house if he is not at work. No-one is allowed to eat meat or to drink *pombe* or to take any sweet things which will be given out for those who delight in the city.' I would like to further add that I do consider strikes are a very dangerous weapon both for the workers as well as for the employers. The policy of the trade unions and the EATUC was to use the strike weapon only as a last resort and only when all other attempts had failed.'

Attorney General: 'Were you active in supporting the strike of the Transport and Allied Workers Union that took place in October, 1949?'

Makhan Singh: 'Yes, I was very active. The Union had been making representations to the Municipal Council since 1946 but they had not been able to get justice . . . they wanted certain by-laws removed. For example, such as the introduction of special new licences which put the taxi drivers at the mercy of the town clerk and the superintendent of police.'

Attorney General: 'And your position on the civic celebrations?'

Makhan Singh: 'I spoke of *matajiri* and *wafanyakazi*. I never used the term 'Africans'. I said workers should not rejoice in the celebrations. I never referred to anybody as Chege Kibachia the second – it was impossible to say like that. I never asked the workers 'What would you do if I am arrested' nor did I encourage them to strike. The boycott was the unanimous decision of all the executive committees of the affiliated unions of the EATUC. We did not take out the procession after the police refused us permission. In the route we had planned we had avoided Delamere Avenue, Sadler Street and Gulzar Street so that the processions should not touch each other.'

Attorney General: 'What was the policy line of the EATUC?'

Makhan Singh: 'To help the workers in different trades to join the unions in existence and to affiliate those unions to the EATUC, and to help the formation of new unions in new trades. To endeavour to explore every channel before calling a strike to get the grievances of the workers redressed. The EATUC itself had no right to declare a strike. The decision to go on strike is taken by the executive committees of the different unions. There was no question of promoting discontent between the working classes and the employers as this was already a reality, the question was how to remove this discontent. The EATUC uses all constitutional methods and never terrorist tactics – my habit is what I say I do. What I don't believe, I never put into practice.'

Makhan Singh: 'Regarding the World Federation of Trade Unions, the EATUC is not affiliated to it – it only maintains fraternal relations with it as it does with the British Trade Unions Congress. The World Federation of Trade Unions is a democratic body of trade unions to which any trade unions' congress or any trade union organisation can affiliate irrespective of their political opinion or policies. This can be seen in the correspondence which was taken from the EATUC office – three large files.'

Attorney General: 'Tell us about the meeting of 23rd April, 1950, at Kaloleni Hall. A resolution was first proposed and then you proposed an amendment.'

Makhan Singh: 'The amendment I proposed was in the form of an addendum at the end of the resolution that complete independence and sovereignty of the East African territories should be implemented at an early date . . . . And that no foreign power had the right to rule over us.'

Attorney General: 'Do you include His Majesty in that phrase?'

Makhan Singh: 'Yes, His Majesty's Government has no right to rule over this country. Also I said "I am a communist" because, at the meeting, Mr Nene had made a speech opposing my amendment and alleging that I was a communist and it was my duty to play a destructive role. This is not correct. My role is to construct a new society in which the people are free and where they have got equal opportunities.'

Chanan Singh (in his cross examination of police superintendent Penfold): 'What is the significance of that small sentence "I am a communist"? He does not become an outlaw by saying this, does he?'

Justice Thacker: 'I would like to ask the witness what he means by 'complete independence and sovereignty? I am wondering where you would get your judges for instance? As far as I know there is not a single qualified African in law.'

Makhan Singh: 'Before the advent of the British, the Africans were able to judge their own matters and they can do so even now. I am not in favour of making illiterate people judges, but workers educated in the new law as decided by the new parliament can perform these duties.'

Justice Thacker: 'I wish you would refrain from using the word 'worker' – it sounds like propaganda. I consider myself as much a worker as you consider yourself. I rather resent the arrogation to yourself and the people whom you pretend to serve as 'workers'. You would impress me more if you would drop that propaganda and call them employees. I do not like the use of the word 'workers'. I do not think that the people you refer to are the only workers. I think all of us are working very hard in this court. Thousands of people who are employers work, don't they?'

Makhan Singh: 'Your Lordship I do not consider employers as workers, I am stating facts and nothing but facts. My definition is: the worker is employed to work for the employer whose main source of livelihood is from work done for the employer.'

Chanan Singh: 'You were telling us about the EATUC.'

Makhan Singh: 'Since the formation of the trade unions and the unity in the EATUC, racial divisions amongst the workers have decreased to a very great extent.'

Attorney General: 'And the International Confederation of Free Trade Unions?'

Makhan Singh: The International Confederation of Free Trade Unions is a scab international of strike breakers. It is a special organisation in the imperialist struggle against the World Federation of Trade Unions and bears the stamp of the betrayal of the interests of the working class.'

Attorney General: 'Were you and Mr. Kubai the moving spirits in the strike by the Transport and Allied Workers last year?'

Makhan Singh: 'The leaders of the Transport and Allied Workers, along with the officials of the EATUC, were the moving spirits in the strike.'

Attorney General: 'Who is the dominant spirit in the EATUC, is it not you?'

Makhan Singh: 'Policy is not made by only one person, the EATUC Central Committee takes the decision as a whole and those decisions are binding upon me and upon Mr. Fred Kubai as president.'

Attorney General: 'Mr. Kubai is your political pupil?'

Makhan Singh: 'I do not consider him as such.'

Attorney General: 'You are a communist – I put it to you that the main aim of the communist parties all over the world is to get control of organised labour.'

Makhan Singh: 'No Sir.'

Attorney General: 'You swear that?'

Makhan Singh: 'Yes, I am on oath. My Lord in England there are trade unions and there are communist officials also, but the government never victimises any union because its official is a communist, and that is why I still say that I am a communist, let the government try me for being a communist if it is illegal. But how can the government try to discourage trade unions because one of the officials is a communist?'

Attorney General (reading from *African Newsletter*): "Determined to maintain her hold, Britain is undertaking so-called development schemes and using her old tactics of combating fake 'concessions' with increased oppression of the popular movements." Do you agree with this, he asked?'

Makhan Singh: 'I do. As far as Anglo-American imperialism is concerned their plan is directed against the Soviet Union and other free countries of the world, and if the Soviet Union is conquered, and if other free countries are conquered, which in my opinion could never be conquered, there is no guarantee that the British and American imperialists will not try to re-conquer India also . . . the base at Mackinnon Road along with other bases of the American and British ruling classes are to be used against the free people of the world.'

Makhan Singh objected to the bans on *Dini ya Msamwa* and *Dini ya Jesu Kristo* (two indigenous Christian sects). The attorney general insisted they were responsible for arson and murder.

Makhan Singh: 'The government has not submitted any facts. If anybody makes a breach of the law, he can be prosecuted, but the whole organisation should not be banned.'

Attorney General: 'Are you aware that police officers were killed by members of these sects?'

Makhan Singh: 'I have read certain allegations in the press.'

Attorney General: 'Would you take it from me that it is so?'

Makhan Singh: 'I am not prepared to accept your opinion.'

Attorney General: 'Do you accept the statement that you read in the press?'

Makhan Singh: 'I am not prepared to believe that statement . . . unless the facts are before me, and unless the facts are expressed by an unofficial tribunal, I cannot express any opinion.'

Chanan Singh: 'Now the murder and arson by certain members of a certain religious sect, do you approve of these methods?'

Makhan Singh: 'I do not approve of the methods of murder and arson.'

Attorney general: 'And the report of the workers' meeting by the police officers? Are you saying these police officers have gone into the witness box and perjured themselves?'

Makhan Singh: 'Yes, of course.'

Justice Thacker: 'Why do you say 'of course'?'

Makhan Singh: 'I am sorry I used the words 'of course'. That was incorrect.'

The attorney general then named officials of the EATUC. Kubai - president (Secretary of Transport and Allied Workers union), B J Bharucha - vice president, Makhan Singh - general secretary and assistant treasurer, Pranlal Seth - assistant secretary, Nelson Kagau, Gichuri Galeni, Githoro Kamau, R D Patel, Manchila and John Mungai.

Makhan Singh refused to confirm or reveal the names the EATUC officials or their positions and insisted that they are all 'inactive'. 'I consider that this matter does not concern the case,' he added. On the issue of 'Secret plans to add to Nairobi more of African-owned land', Makhan Singh claimed there was some sort of haggling going on formally or informally. Chief Koinange had raised the matter in connection with the extent of the City Charter and the boundaries it had drawn. The deputy mayor, Norman Harris, had asserted that the Council had no secret plans to take over African land in Nairobi and then under cross examination by Chanan Singh added 'except for health reasons'.

Regarding the Kenya Government's stand vis-a-vis the trade unions, Makhan Singh said, 'In words they say everything, but in practice the Government is against the Trade Union Movement in Kenya. These remarks are based on my own experience and my own dealings as General Secretary of the Trade Unions Congress with the Labour Department as well as the Kenya Government.'

Responding to Makhan Singh's description of 'the Voluntary Unemployed Persons Ordinance' as 'forced labour laws of the colony amounting to slavery', the attorney general gave a legal definition of slavery.

Makhan Singh: 'That was slavery of olden times and this is slavery of new times. It is a great hardship because a man will not freely accept wages that are very low. The committee implementing the Ordinance are from the community of unemployed persons but these are yes-men of the Government.'

Attorney General: 'What about the persons who are genuinely not seeking work and who have no means of livelihood?'

Makhan Singh: 'Government should not have the power to repatriate anyone out of their town or country. I do not accept the principle of repatriation.'

The Attorney General challenged Makhan Singh to name any who had been thus repatriated. Makhan Singh refused to do so and was accused of concealing information.

Attorney General: 'There is no comparison whatever between this Ordinance and slavery?'

Attorney General: 'There is, Sir. The form has changed but the content of the whole thing is the same.'

Attorney General: 'Who are "the imperialists who desire to enslave the world?"

Makhan Singh: 'They are Great Britain, America and some other countries. Not India . . . opposition to imperialists in a country does not mean opposition to that particular country.'

Attorney General: 'You say "peace-loving peoples are realising that the Marshall Plan, the Atlantic pact, the attempts to organise a Pacific Pact, as well as point 4 of the Truman programme, are all part of the policy of the American imperialists' mad drive to dominate the world." Do you include His Majesty's Government in the description of imperialists who are making a mad drive to dominate the world?'

Makhan Singh: 'Yes. I do.'

Attorney General: 'The Scab International – we know it is the International Confederation of Free Trade Unions of which the principal constituent is the British Trade Unions Congress. Are you aware that the British Trade Unions Congress broke away from the World Federation of Trade Unions because of its communist policy?'

Makhan Singh: 'That is not the real reason. The World Federation of Trade Unions is not anti-British, nor is it communist.'

Attorney General: 'Are you aware that those fighting in Malaya are not the people of that country but Chinese communists?'

Makhan Singh: 'They are the inhabitants and they have every right to fight for freedom of their country.'

The Attorney General then suggested that the membership of the various trade unions as stated by Makhan Singh was grossly overestimated and that those members merely filled out forms but did not actually subscribe any dues.

Makhan Singh: 'All those members have filled in forms, and we consider them as paying members and they actually pay dues.' He did, however, admit that there were only fifty-five shillings in the Transport and Allied Workers Union account and forty-eight shillings in that of the Garment Workers Union.

Attorney General: 'It is part of your policy to stir up disaffection, ill will, and hostility . . . . You hoped to get yourself in a position where, if the law moved against you and arrested you, that would immediately be followed by a general strike.'

Makhan Singh: 'A strike did take place, but we neither prepared for it, nor gave instructions for it, nor create an atmosphere for it.'

Letters to Makhan Singh from S Rostovsky and Louis Saillant of the WFTU were produced at the trial, the first asking for ' . . . any information you may possess on the trade union organisation activity and the economic and social situation of the countries bordering on Kenya, particularly Tanganyika. We ourselves have only vague information, for example about the Dar-es-salaam dockers' strike which seems to us of considerable importance.' The second merely sent a May Day manifes to and urged publicity. Makhan Singh also sent three letters to the WFTU, one listing the unions affiliated to the EATUC, and two containing protests about labour legislation and the internment of Chege Kibachia.[12]

Chanan Singh, after refuting the various charges, submitted that the defendant could not be regarded as an undesirable person. The attorney general, in his summing up, stated that it was not necessary to show that the defendant had broken some law. He was undesirable because he was responsible for a long campaign of producing ill will and disaffection, produced by deliberate misrepresentation. He cited the following examples:

1. Calling the Voluntary Unemployed Persons Ordinance a 'Spiv bill or slave law'.

2. Claiming that secret plans were being hatched to take land from native land units in Nairobi.

3. Writing an article entitled 'Repression is Mounting in Kenya – an Attack on Imperialism'.

4. Protesting against the banning of Dini ya Msamwa and Dini ya Jesu Kristo.

5. Characterising His Majesty's government as a foreign power and asserting that it has no right to rule in Kenya.

6. Boycotting the civic celebrations and stating that it was 'a tale of two cities'.

7. Alleging that the Labour department was trying to keep the trade union movement weak.

The attorney general in his closing argument asserted, in summary, that 'agitators of the type of the defendant care nothing for the rights of the workers; their object is to make trouble . . . . All he stands for are malignant influences and he most emphatically comes within the definition of an undesirable person in this Ordinance.' He asked the court to grant powers to restrict the defendant's activities before it was too late and in so doing to assert, once more, the principle that no one, however an inflated position he may think he has secured, could put himself above the law and substitute mob law and hooliganism for the processes of law.

At 1.00 p.m. on 27th May, 1950, Justice Thacker announced that, based on all the affidavit and oral evidence, he would make his report to the Governor-in-Council. He did so the same day. His main finding was that Makhan Singh had deliberately caused hostility and inflamed the feelings of Africans against the Kenya Government, the Municipal Council and His Majesty's Government and between Europeans on the one hand and Africans and Asians on the other. As evidence, he cited Makhan Singh's statements concerning the 'slave law', plans to take away Native land in Nairobi, the British Government being a 'foreign power' and its imperialist intentions together with that of the USA Government, the Kenya Government paying lip service to the trade union movement, the Tanganyika Government's repression of the dockworkers, the boycott of the civil celebrations in Nairobi and his call for the release of Chege Kibachia.

Though Justice Thacker had no evidence to support his finding, and Makhan Singh denied it too, he remained convinced that the defendant had both fomented the strike of the African taxi drivers as well as planned and organised the general strike beforehand to protest his arrest.

His conclusion was: 'In general, and from the evidence before me, I consider that the defendant is a malignant influence and that he is and will be dangerous to peace, good order and good government, so long as he is free to go about, to speak at public meetings and to write and air his views in press.

'The defendant is not, I am satisfied, content to pursue constitutional methods in order to bring about what he desires. He will continue, I am convinced, unless restricted, to use or threaten to use the strike weapon on the slightest provocation and even upon no provocation at all. He glorifies the strike weapon and is a protagonist of class hatred. He is very anti-British.

'It is a moot question whether he is a Communist, who really sincerely believes in the ideologies of that creed. [Earlier he had stated that 'This, however, appears to be no offence according to Kenya law'.] It is, whatever may be the correct answer to the question, certain that he is an unscrupulous and clever self-seeker who undoubtedly has obtained an increasing influence over many ignorant and easily persuaded Africans. He uses his talents in the fomenting of disaffection and ill will amongst Africans particularly against Great Britain, the Kenya Government and Europeans. Nor am I satisfied that he is entirely unsympathetic with acts of violence committed directly or indirectly on behalf of the cause which he represents.' It is interesting to note that the same judge, R S Thacker, was to preside in 1953 at the trial of Jomo Kenyatta and the Kapenguria Six and have them detained in the same detention centres to which Makhan Singh was sent. Kenyatta in his final submission in court had declared, 'We are not guilty and we do not accept your findings'.

JUSTICE THACKER RULES FOR RESTRICTION ORDER

＊

Justice Thacker therefore recommended that the defendant be declared an undesirable person within the meaning of Section 2 of the Ordinance and that a Restriction Order, as defined in the same Section, is made concerning him. He further ordered that the defendant be detained in the civil prison at Nyeri or Nairobi, whichever was convenient, until the expiration of 28 days after his said recommendation or until the Governor-in-Council decided to make or not to make a Restriction Order or Security Order or both, whichever of the said dates should be earlier.

The restriction order was issued on 5th June, 1950, and signed by John Dalzell Rankine, the acting governor, after consultation with the executive council. Makhan Singh was restricted to the township of Lokitaung in the Northern Frontier District, twenty kilometres south of the Sudanese border, and a few kilometres from the north western shore of Lake Turkana, (then called Lake Rudolph). It was 965 kilometres from Nairobi. It was so remote that the colonial government found it a useful place to house prisoners and political detainees. There was little chance of escape, no crowds to create a disturbance; no great need even to provide a secure prison, for few escapees could survive in that desert.[13]

In Lokitaung, he was banned from visiting the Kenya police and tribal police lines, the school, all labour lines, all shops other than any shop or shops to which access might be permitted by writing under the hand of the DC, and any telegraph office or station.

The *East African Standard* reported the proceedings on a daily basis with such sensational headlines as 'Sheer Nonsense, says the Judge' and 'Am I a Worker? asked Judge of Union Leader'.

The gross miscarriage of justice is demonstrated by the

speed and stealth with which the hearings were held, the total disregard for justifiable evidence and the failure to show that the defendant had contravened any law. Chanan Singh in his closing remarks had submitted that 'to prove a person dangerous to peace, good order and good government, it was necessary to show he had broken some law and that unless the evidence which had been produced was sufficient to convict the defendant of the crime of sedition he could not be regarded as an undesirable person.'

CHANAN SINGH'S SUMMARY

Chanan Singh had not been able to get a transcript of the case when he wrote the following summary, 'Makhan Singh did not give the Government an excuse to forget him. He continued with the type of activity that had annoyed the Government in the past. It seemed the immediate need and the desire of the Government was to immobilise him. The attempts to deport him had failed. In any case, the deportation of nationals was not in accord with current thinking. I had myself argued in the Mandamus proceedings that the effect of refusing to Makhan Singh a certificate of permanent residence was to deprive him of the right to return to Kenya if he happened to go out. I had quoted the Universal Declaration of Human Rights and the Magna Carta. The learned Judge had dismissed – as he could properly do – the Universal Declaration as mere "resolutions of the United Nations." So far as the Magna Carta was concerned, one should have thought it deserved more serious consideration, but all that happened was that the learned Judge expressed a desire to see the document because he had heard of it but had never seen it. I handed him a copy, he looked at it and returned it to me saying, "Thank you". The Attorney-General's comment was that Makhan Singh was free to go out and that the question of his return to Kenya did not arise at that stage. It should be pointed out that the present Constitution of Kenya guarantees freedom of movement to citizens so that they are free to go out and to come back at will. In colonial days, the Magna Carta and the rules of International Law and Declarations should have achieved the same purpose but they were not enforced in colonies.

'The Government had apparently been thinking about the fundamental issues raised by Makhan Singh's cases. It had tried to deport him but had not succeeded because he was a British subject domiciled in Kenya. It was now intent on restricting Makhan Singh's activities which it regarded as harmful. This time, it made use of another law.

'An Ordinance called the Deportation of Offenders and Dangerous Persons' Ordinance had been on the statute book since 1923 but it was not in consonance with current constitutional thinking because it made no distinction between nationals and aliens. Therefore, it was repealed and two new Ordinances were passed in its place. One (No. 36 of 1949) with the Deportation of Aliens and the other (No. 37 of 1949) with the Deportation of Undesirable British Subjects. Both came into force on September 8th, 1949.

'The latter authorised the making of "deportation orders" as well as "restriction orders." If an immigrant British subject did "not belong to Kenya" he could be deported, but if he belonged to Kenya he could be either restricted to a specified part of the country of deported out of the country. But no order of any type could be made in respect of an "immigrant British Subject" except on the recommendation of a court. An Alien could be deported (under Ordinance No. 36) without any court formalities.

'The Government now thought of using against Makhan Singh the provisions of the new Ordinance dealing with Immigrant British Subjects. Accordingly, a Notice of Motion was taken out by the Attorney-General on May 18th, 1950, and served on Makhan Singh requiring him to appear before a Judge of the Supreme Court at 10 a.m. on May 22nd, 1950, when the Attorney-General was to apply for the making of a Restriction Order against him.

'The hearing was fixed before Mr. Justice Thacker who was at that time sitting at Nyeri, a small town situated 90 miles to the north of Nairobi. I told Makhan Singh that he should now employ another advocate who would be able to bring a fresh mind to bear on his problems. What had kept me attached to this litigation was the nature of issues involved. There was no question of earning fees. I had regarded this litigation as part of my public work but now thought I had done my share and it was about time somebody else came in. Makhan Singh agreed and told me he would try to find another advocate.

'When the hearing started at Nyeri, Makhan Singh got up and asked for an adjournment to enable him to engage an advocate from outside Kenya. From the notes he gave me later, I see that he informed the Judge that his father had approached seven Nairobi advocates all of whom had refused to act for him. He mentioned the names of the advocates concerned and also the reason which each had given. One had said that he could not take the case because his wife was ill. Another had said:

"Not feeling to take case" (meaning, perhaps, "I don't like such cases").

A third had said that he was "going to India'. The remaining four had given a "flat refusal". The points that Makhan Singh made are summarised in his notes as follows":-

"Not prepared to appear. Government created such atmosphere that none of them is forthcoming. They seem to be terrified. Traditions of legal professions are to defend persons of any political opinion. It seems these traditions are breaking down in Kenya."

'It was agreed that the hearing be adjourned and that the Attorney-General should contact me by telephone to see if I was willing to act. The Attorney-General telephoned me and asked me "as the head of the Kenya Bar" to come to the assistance of Makhan Singh if he was prepared to pay me a reasonable fee. He added that, if I agreed, the Government would place an aeroplane at my disposal and that I could travel to Nyeri immediately. Without talking to Makhan Singh or to his father I told the Attorney-General that I would come. I left Nairobi immediately and arrived at Nyeri at noon. The question of a fee was never discussed, but on my return from Nyeri at the end of the cases Makhan Singh's father paid me a sum of five hundred shillings.

'On arrival at the Law Courts at Nyeri I found a large crowd of people waiting outside. Among them was the old Senior Chief Koinange. He told me that he thought the Government was accusing Makhan Singh of making public statements to the effect that the City Council of Nairobi was contemplating taking once African land just outside the boundaries of the city. If so, he was prepared to give evidence in support of Makhan Singh. We thanked the old Chief for taking the trouble to travel so far but told him that his assistance would not be needed because the issue before the Court was not whether the City Council had in the past taken over African land – an issue on which he could speak from personal knowledge – but whether the Council intended to take more land now.

'In front of the Court, I found a European police officer who greeted me but immediately added: "But I can tell you one thing; this is not doing you any good." I realised that the remark was probably well-founded and, certainly, well-meant, but I was already convinced that some risk was always involved in defending rebels against an established order. I was an advocate helping an accused person to defend himself according to law and according to the rules of the profession.

'Hearing commenced on May 23rd, 1950, and lasted until May 27th, 1950. The Crown was represented by Mr. (later Sir) Kenneth O'Connor assisted by Mr. A. G. Somerhough. Makhan Singh realised from the beginning that he would not leave the Court a free man this time. He was in no mood to compromise his principles. He wanted to re-iterate them emphatically in open court and requested me to frame my questions in such a way as to give him an opportunity to state his views at some length. We were helped in this by the Government's own case which was that Makhan Singh held views and followed policies which made him an undesirable person in the context of Kenya. Throughout the five days of hearing, nobody really lost his temper. I had never seen Mr. Justice Thacker in such an amiable mood. He lost his temper once or twice but on the whole he showed commendable patience, so that Makhan Singh was able to make short speeches in answer to many of the questions.

'The Government case was contained mainly in the affidavit of Mr. Cecil Penfold, Kenya's Director of Intelligence and Security. It emphasised what it regarded as Makhan Singh's communist links. He was accused of receiving periodicals with communist leanings actually published by Communist Parties. The strong language used by him in describing the disabilities of workers and peasants was quoted. He had called the so-called Spiv Bill "a slave law". He had advocated the boycott of the celebrations to be held on the occasion of raising Nairobi to "City" status and called for an all-out strike. It was alleged that Makhan Singh had been active in support of the strike called by the Transport and Allied Workers' Union in support of taxi drivers. He had applied for permission to hold a workers' procession on the day that Nairobi was to be made a "City".

'Makhan Singh had been instrumental in forming the East African Trade Union Congress which, according to the affidavit, had been "active in promoting discontent between the working classes and employers since its formation." To the affidavit were attached several extracts from the Daily Chronicle which was stated to be giving "wide publicity and support to Makhan Singh and the East African Trade Union Congress."

'It was alleged that on April 23rd, 1950, at a public meeting called jointly by the KAU and the East African Indian National

Congress, Makhan Singh had "moved an addendum to the resolution before the meeting declaring that complete independence and sovereignty of the East African Territories was the only solution." He had told the meeting that the time had come for the people to say that the country was theirs and that no foreign power had the right to rule it.

'Makhan Singh was also alleged to have written an article headed "May Day; the Freedom for East Africa Day" and also to have been in correspondence with the World Federation of Trade Unions which was stated to be a "Communist-dominated body, pro-slave and anti-British in outlook."

'The affidavit even stated that an African Municipal Councillor who was co-operating in the "City" celebrations "was attacked" by somebody and that another African who was a co-author of the Communiqué issued by the KAU dissociating that body from the boycott move was "threatened with a fire-arm by an African who escaped," and it was suggested that this violence was used by the minority "disappointed at their lack of success with the boycott." It was stated that this was "a result of the efforts of Makhan Singh and the Trades Union Congress and the publicity given to their attempted boycott" which had created "ill-feeling" among "a certain proportion of the African population of Nairobi; though the majority remained loyal."

'The Government also filed supporting affidavits sworn by Councillor Muchohi Gikonyo and Tom Mbotela, Vice-President of the KAU.

'The first witness to give evidence for the Government was Mr. N. F. Harris, the Deputy Mayor of Nairobi, who stated that there was no proposal to increase the area of the Nairobi City, and that, therefore, there was no foundation for the statement that the Government intended to take over African land to extend the boundaries of Nairobi. He was supported later by Mr. John R[e]seborough, the Town Clerk of Nairobi, who also spoke about the grievances of the drivers. Superintendent Penfold, then, confirmed what he had stated in his affidavit. At one stage, when I was questioning the Superintendent on the accuracy of translation of certain documents on which the Government relied, the Judge got a little upset and suggested we should get down to facts such as the expression that

"The Kenya Government does not like workers' Unions". He added: "In my knowledge that is not a true statement; the Government encouraged them and showed how trade unions should be run, I will require justification of that statement when and if Mr. Makhan Singh comes into the witness box."

'In describing these particular proceedings I shall be relying on the reports in the East African Standard. There was nobody to take notes when I was cross-examining Makhan Singh in chief. Looking through the reports that appeared in that newspaper twenty six years ago I am impressed by them. They are a reliable record of what happened during the trial. I think Makhan Singh or his father obtained a copy of the Judges' notes but I have not seen them.

'This remark made by the trial judge at an early state of the proceedings, coming as it did after a strong opening speech by the Attorney-General indicated to us what we were up against.

'An African Constable attached to the Special Branch told the Court that he was present at two meetings addressed by Makhan Singh. The parts of Makhan Singh's speeches which he quoted to the Court were as follows:-

1. If Chege Kibachia (a trade union leader then in detention) is not released, Makhan Singh said, "We the Russians, Japanese and Germans were not their enemies."

2. Makhan Singh asked the audience what they would do if he was arrested; the reply was, "Strike".

3. The "Spiv" Bill must be opposed as it was slave law.

4. If Nairobi was to be a city, Africans should have the same type of houses as Europeans and Asians.

5. Europeans and Indians would never employ domestic servants in their own countries. In Kenya, they employ a large staff of African servants.

6. The Government was at fault for not teaching Africans

trade.

'Another African Constable gave evidence about what happened at Mr. Tom Mbotela's house when an African tried to shoot him. The last witness for the Crown was Assistant Superintendent Lloyd Parker who spoke about the strike of the Transport and Allied Workers' Union. He told the Court that during the previous five months, the Police had covered 25 to 30 meetings, suggesting in effect that the unions had been active.

'Now, Makhan Singh entered the witness box. He did not mince his words – he did not intend to – in examination in chief. During cross-examination, he was even more candid. He never hesitated to admit facts which he knew to be true. The Attorney-General had no difficulty in this account. Makhan Singh did not attempt to prevarication or argument. He made denials here and there if what he was asked to affirm was not true. On the whole, there was little dispute on facts: the dispute was what these facts meant. The Attorney-General thought they showed that Makhan Singh was an "undesirable person" whose activities ought to be restricted. On the other hand, Makhan Singh thought they showed that he had been saying or doing no more than what a public man and trade unionist was entitled to say and do. Makhan Singh seemed to think he had a mission which he was trying to fulfil. He said more than once that he was a Communist in his political views and that he had worked for the Communist Party during his short stay in India. He considered it his duty to work for the liberation of subject countries. In Kenya, his main interest and field of work was trade unionism. As Secretary of the E. A. Trade Union Congress, he had been involved in workers' strikes. He did not believe in strikes for their own sake: a strike was a serious matter and should not be resorted to except in the last resort. He was an opponent of Imperialism and even believed that if the opportunity arose, British Imperialism would set up in this part of the world a base from which to launch an attack on India. It was all right calling Nairobi a "City" but there were in fact two cities, one for the poor people and other for the rich.

'The Attorney-General was a skilful advocate and used statements like these to good purpose.

'At the end of the trial and addresses by me and the Attorney-General, the Judge adjourned the Court for a short while and then announced his decision which was that he was recommending to the Governor that a Restriction Order be made against Makhan Singh. He had not accepted my argument that the definition of an "Undesirable person" in the Ordinance (namely a person who is "dangerous to peace, good order, good government, or public morals, or is or has been attempting, or conducting himself in a manner calculated to raise discontent or disaffection amongst His Majesty's subjects or inhabitants of the Colony, or to promote feelings of ill-will and hostility between different classes of the population of the Colony) required a more strict proof – at least, as strict as in a charge of sedition – than the Crown had offered. As a trade unionist, he had to safeguard the interests of workers and might have to criticise employers, but that otherwise, my client had tried to bring the workers together on a common platform.'

To accuse Makhan Singh of using unconstitutional methods, to insist that he preferred strike action to negotiation and to describe him as 'unscrupulous' and a 'self-seeker' was a most blatant misrepresentation.

It is worthy of note that though Makhan Singh could have called any number of witnesses, he declined to do so. He believed in fighting his own battles with legal help and without incriminating others. He also knew only too well that the Government had passed judgement on him even before the case commenced and there was no point in prolonging the process. His decision to give evidence on oath was based on his determination to establish the truth. His compelling gaze, forthright manner and steadfast adherence to principles left no doubt about his honesty and his commitment.

BIAS IN THE
LEGISLATIVE COUNCIL
*

Not only was the court biased, there could be no expectation of a fair hearing in the Legco. Makhan Singh was exiled out of Nairobi into a remote part of Kenya by the colonial government. The non-European elected members of the Legco kept up the pressure on the government for his release. The following is an example of the debate, which used to take place (Hansard 1st May to 9th July, 1957, Vol.LXX11, Part 11, 166):

'Tom Mboya, then African elected member for Nairobi area, asked the Minister for Internal Security and Defence (Mr Cusack) to state the number of persons detained under detention orders issued under Emergency Regulation No 2. Mr Cusack replied that the number of persons detained under orders issued under Emergency Regulations Number 2 was 26181 on 30th April, 1957.

Mr Mboya: Will the Minister state the racial breakdown of detainees?

Mr Cusack: There is one Asian, all the rest are Africans.

Mr Madan: Mr Speaker, Sir, arising out of that reply...

The Speaker: (Sir Ferdinand Cavendish-Bentinck): You cannot ask supplementary questions on replies to supplementary questions, you can only ask supplementaries on the original reply.

Mr Madan: Arising out of all the replies, Sir, would the Hon. Minister consider release of the Asian as the odd man out.

Mr Cusack: No

Mr Harris: The odd man in.

Mr Mboya: Arising out of the reply, Sir, would the Minister tell us, in the case of the Asian detainee, whether it is true that when his father was seriously sick, he or his family asked that he should be allowed to visit his father who was apparently a civil servant in this Government for over 20 years, and that permission was refused.

The Speaker: I cannot allow that, it is going too much into detail. If you wish a reply to that last question, I am sure the Minister will give you a reply in writing.

Sir Charles Markham: Hear, hear Mr. Speaker, arising out of the original reply is it not true that the one Asian detained was also a trade union leader?

Mr Cusack: No, Sir.

The Speaker: We will pass on to the next order.'

'The Indian elected members and the African elected members had the force of inalienable rights and undeniable facts on their side but we were too few to topple the government benches which were packed with civil servants and nominated members whose survival as members of Legislative Council depended upon voting for the Government without thinking. On such subjects the European elected members also voted government.'

The Restriction Order was not the end of the Government's crusade against Makhan Singh. Having succeeded in confining him under its control and jurisdiction, it further sought to discredit him and to disable and dismantle the organisation he had built over the years. With this in view, two more prosecutions were filed against him. In one case, he was charged with having committed perjury. In the second case, Fred Kubai and himself were charged as officials of the EATUC for operating an unregistered trade union.

TRIAL FOR PERJURY

Chanan Singh's written summary states that, 'The proceedings before Judge Thacker which resulted in Makhan Singh's being detained in a remote corner of Kenya did no more than put him out of the way. The Government was – it now appears – on the lookout for some evidence which would do more. The purpose of cross-examining Makhan Singh on the subject of his visits to India in the previous proceedings was, it now appears, to get an admission that he had told a lie in court proceedings. He stated in the affidavit filed in support of his application for habeas corpus that he had arrived in Kenya for the first time in 1927 and that he left for India in 1939 on a temporary visit. From this, Mr. Justice de Lestang had concluded:

"The applicant lived in Kenya for 13 years without break . . ." (Miscellaneous Cv. Application 16/1948)

'Makhan Singh had admitted in cross-examination in a later case that the learned Judge's finding was made on the basis of his own affidavit.

'The Attorney-General's Department apparently thought Makhan Singh had perjured himself by not disclosing his two visits to India between 1927 and 1939. These visits Makhan Singh had always unhesitatingly admitted but had maintained that they could not interrupt his domicile.

'The Prosecution evidence during the trial for perjury was largely concerned with proving:

That Makhan Singh had sworn an affidavit in habeas corpus proceedings saying that he had arrived from India in 1927 and that he had gone to India on a temporary visit in 1939.

That Mr. Justice de Lestang had stated in his Judgement in those proceedings that Makhan Singh had been in Kenya for 13 years without a break.

That Makhan Singh had admitted in other proceedings that between 1927 and 1939 he had made two visits to India.

That the Immigration Department's file had forms filled in by Makhan Singh on the occasion of those two visits.

'Makhan Singh had never denied these facts. The only question was whether Makhan Singh could still truthfully say that he had been in Kenya from 1927 to 1939 without qualifying that statement by mentioning his two short visits. There could hardly be doubt about the temporary nature of these two visits: he had gone to get married on one occasion and to attend the marriage of his sister on the other. The Prosecution's contention was that the two visits were material facts in both habeas corpus and Mandamus proceedings and that Mr. Justice de Lestang (who held that Makhan Singh was a "permanent resident", not an "immigrant") might have come to a different conclusion if the two visits to India had been disclosed.

'One rather interesting incident in the trial might be mentioned. One of the witnesses for the Prosecution was Mr. A. G. Somerhough (a Crown Counsel, later a Judge in the Rhodesias). Mr. D. N. Khanna who appeared for Makhan Singh – I assisted him – asked Mr. Somerhough, in cross-examination, for details of his legal experience. The list of the posts he had held since his call to the Bar in 1936 was impressive. His last assignment had been connected with the War Criminal' Trials in Germany. Thereafter he had come to Kenya. Then, Mr. Khanna asked him: "How long have you been in Kenya?" The answer was prompt: "Ever since February 14, 1949."

'Mr. Khanna asked him if he had not been to Uganda in the interval. Mr. Somerhough now gave a smile of embarrassment and said that he had been to Uganda for three days: "You have trapped me, Mr. Khanna."

'Mr. Khanna's purpose was to show that temporary visits easily slipped from memory. If a trained and experienced lawyer could omit to mention his temporary absence from the country when stating his period of stay, then it was not surprising that a layman like Makhan Singh had stated that he was in Kenya from 1927 to 1939 when actually he had been to India for two short periods in the interval.

'But Mr. Somerhough was now on his guard. He argued that the idea of residence "without a break" first appeared in the judgement of Mr. Justice de Lestang. Makhan Singh had not used the words "without a break" in his affidavits. He also stated that in ordinary conversation he would say that he had worked in the Attorney-General's Chambers from 1949 to 1952, but that in drafting an affidavit he could be accurate and would mention 6 days' leave.

'The learned Resident Magistrate, Nyeri, convicted Makhan Singh of perjury as charged and sentenced him to imprisonment for three months. An appeal to the Supreme Court followed. Makhan Singh's Cases were now exciting international interest. The following paragraph in the London Times of 28th July, 1950, conveyed the result of the appeal to the world community:

"Nairobi, July 27th

"Makhan Singh, an Indian Communist and formerly General Secretary of the East African Trade Union Congress, today won his appeal in the Kenya Supreme Court against a magistrate's conviction and sentence of three months' imprisonment on a charge of perjury. The Court held that the magistrate had put an unreasonable interpretation on an immigration declaration made by the appellant in which he said he had resided in Kenya for some years, whereas during that time he had spent two periods in India. It was held that such visits did not legally interrupt his residence in Kenya."

'The case against Fred Kubai and Makhan Singh, on the charge of operating an unregistered trade union, was heard on July 6th and 7th, 1950. Advocate A R Kapila appeared for both defendants, the proceedings have been narrated by Chanan Singh thus: 'Makhan Singh's desire to strengthen trade unionism led him to the formation of a central body which would control and co-ordinate the activities of trade unions. His friends and co-workers in the field agreed with him and they formed the East African Trade Union Congress on Sunday, the 1st May, 1949.

'On June 17th, 1949, an application was made to the Registrar of Trade Unions for the registration of the Congress. The application was turned down on September 6th, 1949, because the Registrar did not think the Congress was a trade union (i.e. a body concerned with the regulation of relations between the employees and their employer) within the meaning of the definition of the term in the Trade Unions and Trade Disputes Ordinance. He said that he was refusing registration under subsections (d) and (f) of section (10) (1). Makhan Singh thought the reply was "purposely vague". If the Congress was not a trade union – Makhan Singh accepted this position – the question of refusing registration under the law referred to would not seem to arise. Clause (d) empowered the Registrar to refuse registration if an already registered trade union was "sufficiently representative of the whole or of a substantial proportion of the interests in respect of which the applicants seek registration." This did not seem relevant. Clause (f) would apply if the combination seeking registration was "an organisation consisting of persons engaged in . . . more than one trade or calling, and . . . its constitution" did "not contain suitable provision for the protection . . . of their respective sectional industrial interests."

'The Congress was intended to be a central body of registered trade unions (i.e. a body concerned with the regulation of relations among trade unions, not between the employees and their employer). The constituent unions already had in their respective constitutions sufficient provision for the protection of the interests of members.

'Convinced that the Government did not think the Congress needed registration, Makhan Singh and fellow workers continued to run the organisation. On May 15th, 1950, however, both Makhan Singh and Fred Kubai were [ousted] on a charge of being officials of an unregistered trade union. Fred Kubai made the following statement on arrest:-

"I have heard about this, but regarding being President of the East African Trade Union Congress I have something to say. The Congress is not, as in other countries, registered; it is an association of registered trade unions. We had a long talk with Mr. Perry, adviser to the Secretary of State for the Colonies and Labour Affairs on October 20th, 1949, who told us it was not necessary to register. That was after receiving the letter from the Registrar of Trade Unions."

'Both accused were produced the same morning before Mr. F. Miller, a Resident Magistrate in Nairobi. Both pleaded 'not guilty'. The trial took place on July 6th and 7th, 1950. Mr. A. G. Somerhough, Crown Counsel, was the prosecutor. Mr. A. R. Kapila appeared for both accused. Judgement was given on July 21st, 1950. Both accused were found guilty and convicted and fined a sum of Shs. 110/- each. An appeal against the judgement was filed on behalf of Makhan Singh and was heard by Sir Barclay Nihill, C. J., and Modera J., on October 18th, 1950. The following are extracts from the judgement:

" . . . the learned Magistrate . . . was satisfied that the provisions of the constitution (of the Congress) by themselves sufficiently disclosed that the Congress was combination whose principal purposes were the regulation of the relations between workmen and master and therefore fall between the four corners of the definition (of a trade union). We go further and say that even if it could be argued that the learned Magistrate might have come to some other finding had he not also addressed his mind to conduct we should not ourselves have been able to support any other conclusion.

"Mr. Kapila had argued that the principal purpose of the Trade Union Congress . . . . were the affiliation of registered trade unions and the co-ordination of their activities. This undoubtedly was one of the purposes of the organisation, but it is equally clear, taking rules 2 and 3 of the Constitution as a whole, that the purpose of the co-ordinating activity was to achieve the amelioration of the economic, social and political conditions of the working classes . . . and that . . . the organisation proposed to take upon itself the duty of 'watching, promoting, safeguarding and furthering the interests, rights and privileges of the workers in all matters relating to their employment.' . . . In one view, therefore, the Appellant had been properly convicted . . . . . and his appeal must be dismissed."

'Mr. Somerhough asked that the sentence imposed on the Appellant be enhanced. This the Supreme Court refused to do for two reasons:-

1. "Mr. Somerhough has conceded that a Trade Union

Congress might not require registration under the Ordinance as a trade union if its constitution was drawn in such a way so as to preclude the direct regulation of relations between workmen and master."

2. "The Appellant had acted in good faith."

'The judgement on Makhan Singh's appeal case was delivered on 27th July, 1950. Mr. Justice Modera and the Acting Chief Justice, Mr. Connel, allowed the appeal. The conviction was quashed and the sentence of 3 months' simple imprisonment imposed on him by the Nyeri Resident Magistrate, some 8 weeks previously, was set aside. The appellant was discharged. Makhan Singh was a free man for two minutes, for immediately on coming out of the court, he was served with the Restriction Order.'

Makhan Singh was moved to Nairobi prison. He was taken out at 5.00 a. m. on Tuesday, 1st August, 1950, and transferred to Kitale prison where he remained until the 5th when he was removed to Lokitaung via Lodwar, arriving there on the 6th, a distance of 483 kilometres from Kitale.

Meanwhile, Chege Kiburu, the acting president of the EATUC had been sentenced to 12 months' imprisonment and was removed to Wajir Prison to serve his sentence. The acting general secretary, Mwangi Macharia, was sentenced to 10 months and 27 days hard labour. In his statement to the court he had said: 'I am going to do more than I have done.' At the end of his sentence he was restricted to Marsabit in the Northern Frontier District and remained there until 1960. He was then transferred to his home district and released a year later. Fred Kubai remained in Nairobi prison until the middle of February, 1951 when he was released.

On leaving Kitale, Makhan Singh was given rations sufficient for eight days. On arrival in Lokitaung he requested toilet articles, medical attention, and minor repairs to his quarters, newspapers and a copy of the official gazette. He informed the DO that he could not agree to have the cost to be deducted from his account. 'These are requirements, not luxuries . . . in case any other course is not possible for you, I am prepared to return all those articles.'

CHARGE OF FAILURE TO DISSOLVE THE EATUC

*

On 6th and 7th July the hearing of the case against Makhan Singh and Fred Kubai on a charge of failure to dissolve the EATUC took place before F Miller, the Resident Magistrate. A G Somerhough, the Crown Counsel, appeared for the prosecution and A R Kapila represented both the defendants. The latter had asked for the Labour adviser to the colonial secretary to appear as a defence witness, but were told that the government was not prepared to pay for his passage.

Judgement was passed on 21st July. The magistrate in his ruling, which took 40 minutes to read, ruled that the EATUC was a trade union and that both its officials were guilty of the offence mentioned in the charge sheet. He fined each of them KShs. 110. The significance for the government was that the illegality of the EATUC had been established. Later, from Lokitaung, Makhan Singh asked Kapila to appeal to the Supreme Court against the judgement. The appeal was heard on 18th October by chief justice Sir Barclay Nihill and Justice Modera. They declined to quash the conviction and the fine imposed by the magistrate.

The principal point for consideration was whether or not the EATUC was in fact a trade union and, therefore, required to be registered. Kapila argued that it was actually a coordinating body but the judges ruled that it was a trade union because 'the purpose of the coordinating activity was to achieve the amelioration of the economic, social and political conditions of the working classes in East Africa.' They, however, allowed the nominal fine of KShs. 110 to stand as 'there had been something in the nature of condonation by certain departments of Government,' and hence the appellant had 'acted in good faith.'

The judgement meant the final proscription of the EATUC. After this, it was decided not to appeal further, but to form another central organisation of trade unions in due course. Meanwhile, the workers continued to organise for securing their rights. The Typographical Union had a successful outcome of their strike when most of their demands were met. Their chief leaders were B J Bharucha (president), C V Patel (secretary), J W Okakah (asst secretary) and Gerald Olola. The Tailors and Garment Workers Union signed an agreement with the Master Tailors Association and from 1 August, the minimum wages in all the main towns of Kenya were increased.

J W Okakah

Gerald Olola

These successes reflected the increasing awakening, mobilisation and unity of workers and other peoples of Kenya generated by the EATUC and by the general strike. They greatly advanced the struggle for freedom in Kenya and the other East African territories.

Makhan Singh's daughter, Inderjeet Gill, writing from Birmingham, UK in 2004 expressed her feelings about her father's arrest thus: 'My papaji (father) was the most dear person for me and I loved him greatly. I only have his loving memories and don't remember him ever scolding me. Before his arrest I remember how in the morning he used to pick me and my younger brother Sawrajpal up to say bye bye before leaving home for his day's jobs. On Sundays sometimes he used to take us all to the movies – this of course did not last very long! The most hurtful feelings I still have and when I remember them they form a very dark / thick cloud over me. May be by putting them down on paper they will vanish from my psyche – that is the morning when he was arrested – I can still see him being taken away by two white policemen flanked on either side, in a black car which was parked on the foot path along Park Road, Ngara, Nairobi across from our house, while I was clinging to my biji's (mum's) leg. Being a child I could not understand what was going on, that my papaji was being taken away from me – was a very traumatic episode. I do not remember anything else afterwards other than what my biji told me that for quite sometime I became very quiet, withdrawn and sickly looking.'

CHAPTER NINE

DETENTION
1950 -1961

On Sunday, 6th August, 1950, Makhan Singh was taken to Lokitaung. The road leaving Nairobi entered the Rift Valley Province and passed through Naivasha, Gilgil, Nakuru and Eldoret up to Kitale and Kapenguria. The area was commonly known as the 'White Highlands' as it had been carved into large, lush green farmlands owned by European settlers. Beyond Kapenguria the landscape changed to arid and semi-desert vistas. The road became increasingly rough and bumpy with very sparse human habitation and miles and miles of nothingness. A road sign, conspicuously displayed, warned 'Private burial ground for reckless drivers.'

The Northern Frontier Province, popularly and notoriously known as the NFD (Northern Frontier District), was a restricted area. Forming nearly half the land area of Kenya, it was very parched with a small population of pastoral people, largely Turkana and Somali. This harsh terrain held no attractions for British settlement and in order to avoid any exploitation of the pastoralists, the British had cut off the area by a security curtain. Hence, there was very little traffic and visitors to the

Kaka's Truck

area needed a permit to enter and were subjected to police and border checks.[1]

Between Kitale and Lokitaung a weekly 'bus service' was provided by Kaka's Transport; leaving Kitale on Thursday and returning the next day. Kaka was a Muslim Punjabi, a Pathan, who was based in Kitale. He had a 3-ton army type truck and had been the government contractor for the Turkana District for many years. He carried out his transport business under very adverse conditions and at considerable personal risk providing transport, rations, foodstuffs, building materials and other essentials to the government officials, police and locals in the region.[2] There were no tarmac roads in this part of the Northern Frontier District, just rough dirt roads and these were criss-crossed by many streams. During the rains a flash flood could cause a delay of many hours to a motor vehicle.[3]

The very next day Makhan Singh wrote to his wife, Satwant Kaur, and his father, Sudh Singh, in Punjabi, telling them about his journey from Nairobi prison and describing Lokitaung as 'desolate, hilly and volcanic with lava deposits.' Situated in Turkana District, it was a sub-station; Lodwar was the administrative headquarters. Kenyatta was briefly detained at Lodwar and desribed it as 'hell on earth, where you sweat from morning to evening – if you are not sweating, you are covered in dust!' Lokitaung was not only very remote but it too was hot and dry with inhospitable, semi-desert conditions. It was a place of sandstorms and hellish heat. However, as it lay in a range of hills, its climate was somewhat cooler than that in Lodwar. Also, though surrounded by sand and lava, it did have a spring of water oozing out of a rock at the head of a dried-up river bed.[4] So though the average rainfall was less than one inch per annum; the local DO had a swimming pool full of clean water! And yet, the Kapenguria Six, who were later detained there, complained of a chronic water shortage making bathing or washing clothes an occasional luxury.[5]

Lokitaung was a tiny police and administrative post, with a few small shops. There was no electricity or piped water, (an

Turkana woman

Indian neighbour who worked for the government had a kerosene fridge). Mail delivery was once a week and was brought by Kaka's Transport, together with whatever rations and other items ordered the week before. The local population consisted of the pastoral Turkana who herded their livestock and lived in extremely harsh and primitive conditions. They were constantly on the move, were scantily clad, and led a simple and fuss-free life-style. They were a law-abiding people who had minimal contact with the rest of Kenya.

The house allocated to Makhan Singh in Lokitaung was a colonial structure built of stone and consisted of two large rooms, a kitchen and a veranda. He was restricted to movement within a two-mile radius, banned from visiting certain shops and offices and not allowed to work. Police officers checked in on him twice a day. He was not allowed visitors except by special permission. Local residents who wanted to visit him had to be vetted by the DO and those from outside Lokitaung had to get permission from the commissioner of police in Nairobi or the DC for Turkana, Leslie E Whitehouse, a middle-aged Englishman based at Lodwar. He was a hard taskmaster with a fiery temper who never seemed to want to move out of the district! All Makhan Singh's out-going and incoming letters and packages were censored. Letters written in English were censored by the DC but those written in Punjabi had to be sent to the attorney general. Communication, owing to the censorship requirements, was generally delayed by several months.

From 1950-51, Lokitaung had two DOs, Patrick Crichton and Brian Keith, Oliver Knowles took the position in 1951-52. A civil servant, a Goan by the name of Mervyn Maciel, was there in the early fifties and remembers the swimming pool well. He was the district clerk cum cashier. 'Because of the racial status quo at the time, we were kept as mere "karanis" even though we often did the work which normally a DO would do,' Mervyn wrote, many years later, in his book, *Bwana Karani*. He added, 'We the Goan staff (Administration and Police) used to go for long walks and also meet at the swimming pool. This is where we would meet Makhan Singh. I cannot remember us mixing freely with him since we were civil servants. I remember him as a quiet individual. Conscious of the fact that we were government employees, we never talked "politics". I can't remember inviting him to our house and doubt we would have been allowed to. He always went under a police escort (things might have changed later).'[6]

Immediately on his arrival, Makhan Singh asked the DC to allow his wife and children to visit him and reminded him that the government was obliged to provide them with transport. (Women, as a rule, were not allowed into the Turkana District – the only exception being wives of officials in Lokitaung). Two days later he was told that this would be possible if they were willing to accept the same restrictions. Makhan Singh wrote to his wife in Punjabi, 'Here I am in a jail and kept under strict surveillance, it will be the same for you. You will eat the same food. Discuss this matter with father and others and then decide.' He then hastened to reassure her: 'Please do not despair, these difficulties will pass. Because of the strict censorship I am unable to write much.' Signed, 'Your beloved Makhan Singh.' He asked his father to remind his advocate, Achhroo Kapila, to file an appeal of his detention case and requested him to send him books in English and Kiswahili.

On the 17th, Makhan Singh wrote to his father requesting him to send him books, newspapers and magazines from his own library as well as from the Desai Memorial Library, the Patwa News Agency and the Jai Hind Bookshop. He asked for books on Kenya, East Africa, Africa and Nehru. He also asked that all issues of the *East African Standard, Daily Chronicle, Baraza* and *Kenya Weekly News* be sent to him. The government however refused to allow him to receive the *Daily Chronicle.* Copies of the *Colonial Times* and *East African Standard* of 20th and 21st February, 1951, in which trade union matters were discussed, were also retained by the censor. The *Daily Chronicle* issues were returned to Sudh Singh and Makhan Singh asked his father to retain the papers for his future use.

By the 18th Makhan Singh was feeling unwell. He wrote to the governor requesting a transfer on the grounds that the climate and water were unsuitable. He also asked for a monthly allowance of 50 pounds as he had a wife and children to support and, again, permission for them to stay with him. On the legal front, he decided to concentrate on getting the restriction order revoked and asked Chanan Singh to look into all possible legal actions.

Makhan Singh wrote to Kapila to appeal to the Supreme Court concerning the judgement against the EATUC. The appeal was scheduled for hearing on 18th October. Sudh Singh telegraphed Makhan Singh that the government was prepared to allow him to be present at the hearing, provided he paid his own expenses. 'Should we adjourn the appeal to the next session?' he asked and went on to warn that Justice Thacker might replace Judge Nihill then. Important as it was for Makhan Singh to avail himself of this opportunity, he insisted that the government had to fulfil its obligations and pay his expenses. He asked them to proceed with the appeal case without delay. The appeal was heard on 18th October and took up the whole day. It was dismissed for the same reasons as stated by the previous magistrate. Kapila advised against appealing further to an East African Court of Appeal, as it would be futile. Regarding the appeal to the Privy Council, Sudh Singh said that, even if the legal representation were free, he could not afford the fee of KShs 15 to 20,000.

On 26ᵗʰ October, Makhan Singh wrote to tell his father that the government had given permission for Satwant Kaur to visit him but refused the same for any other family member. It had also refused to pay their transport expenses, (KShs 700 from Kitale to Lokitaung), and the maintenance allowance he had requested, nor any education allowance for Hindpal, who was now fourteen and entering secondary school.

The restriction order had stated that Makhan Singh was to be given seven shillings daily, as subsistence allowance. Yet on 26ᵗʰ September when he asked for ten shillings from his account, the Lokitaung assistant superintendent of police, C Finnegan, declined saying, 'There being no apparent reason why you should require any ready use for money, I have to refuse your request.' In an exchange of notes Makhan Singh remonstrated, 'This is my personal account and I am fully entitled to withdraw as much as I like.' Finnegan later relented and forwarded the ten shillings and he also allowed him to borrow copies of the *East African Standard* papers received by the police.

Makhan Singh requested his lawyers to demand that either he be transferred to Nairobi where he could find employment or the government should provide an allowance for his family. The refusal by the government, he said, was an indication that it was treating him differently from all other detainees whose families had been allowed to join them at government expense and were being maintained by the government. On 26ᵗʰ November, he was informed that the government was not prepared to allow his family to join him, not even his wife now, and had turned down his petition for having the restriction order revoked. In addition, his family was instructed to desist from sending him issues of the *Daily Chronicle*. Makhan Singh wrote to the governor, Sir Philip Mitchell saying, 'the decision to disallow me the *Daily Chronicle* is totally incorrect. It is a legal publication.'

In December, he was told that his family would be able to

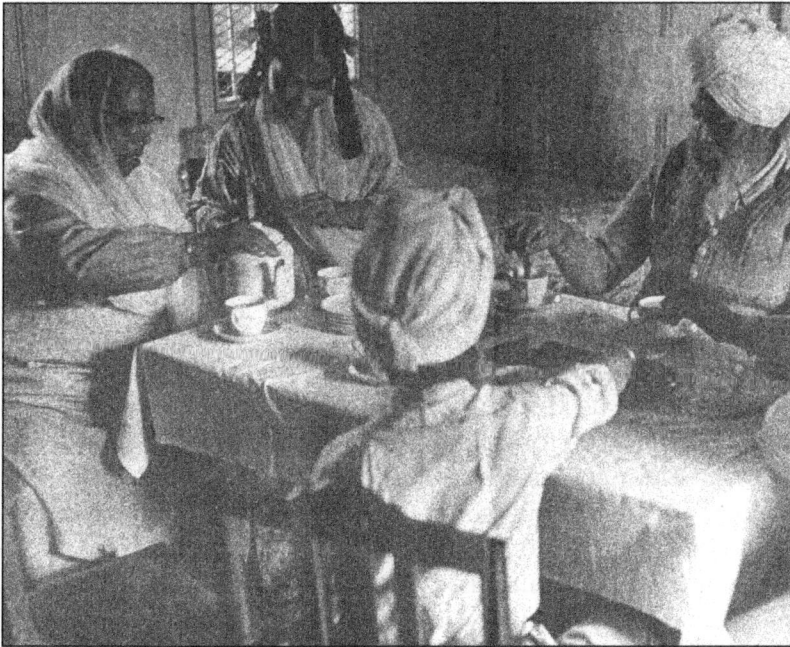

Makhan Singh's family at the dinner table

visit him if he could deposit KShs 2,820. 'The government has detained me from any means of livelihood to support my family, and it is reasonable that my family should be allowed to stay with me and their expenses should be borne by the government. The families of all other deportees are being maintained by the government and they have been allowed to join them,' Makhan Singh protested.

Family problems were a cause for worry. Satwant Kaur had suffered a miscarriage in September and Hindpal complained about the constant quarrelling between bibiji, his mother, and bebeji, his grandmother. Friction between mothers-in-law and daughters-in-law can be acute in Indian households; in Makhan Singh's family it was exacerbated by constant financial worries and his being in detention and therefore unable to mediate. At one point, Satwant Kaur, normally meek, spoke out bluntly: 'I even cannot bear [this] for another day. Why is the Government refusing to give us a house allowance?' Makhan Singh offered to send some of his allowance but his mother declined the offer saying, 'God will help you and you will be successful and meet us joyfully at home.' Whenever there was tension and conflict in Makhan Singh's family, his mother invariably rose to his defence. Satwant Kaur expressed a readiness to join her husband until August 1951 and then return for three months to supervise Hindpal's school examination preparations, if the necessary arrangements could be made. Once again, Makhan Singh requested the government to provide the necessary transport.

He told his son to write to him at least weekly, especially as Satwant Kaur could only write in Punjabi and the censorship rules made this cumbersome. He told his wife not to worry as 'circumstances are bound to change – you might join me here or I join you in Nairobi.' On a more positive note he was pleased with Hindpal's good exam results and sent him a book of general knowledge and one on English grammar as a prize.

In November, Achhroo Kapila married Kumari Krishna Assanand and sent Makhan Singh an invitation. Makhan Singh, needless to say, could not accept and telegraphed, 'Kapilaji, Regrets and sincere congratulations, insignificant present of twenty-one shillings for Achhroo and bride.'

In the same month, A S Rao, a trade unionist, informed him that the LTUEA had received a notice of dissolution effective from 8th December, 1950. Sudh Singh informed his son that in India, the deputy prime minister, Sardar Vallabhai Patel, had passed away and suggested that Makhan Singh should send a telegram to Nehru and Appa Saheb Pant. This Makhan Singh did.

On 27th December he received a telegram from his father wishing him 'birthday greetings from all friends and family and long and patriotic life.' Makhan Singh was 38 years old. 'I celebrated in my own simple way,' he wrote in his thank-you note. 'The only company I had was my assistant Bwana Mrefu.

Don't misunderstand him from his name. He is of small size like myself.' (Remember, Makhan Singh was just 5ft 3ins.) The family sent him a parcel of clothes and some dry fruit.

Makhan Singh asked for more books and correspondence regarding his legal affairs. He kept a record of all the written material that had not been delivered to him and complained of the constant delays by the censor in releasing his correspondence with his lawyers in Kenya and the UK as well as his legal documents. At the suggestion of his lawyers, he wrote a petition dated 23rd December, 1950, to the governor requesting him to lift the restriction order.

' L E A V E ,   A N D   D O   N O T   R E T U R N '

The governor rejected his petition. His letter dated 1st February, 1951, reached Makhan Singh a week later. The governor, it stated, felt it was 'amply proved' that he (Makhan Singh) was an 'undesirable person' and agreed with the restriction order. However, it added, 'if you wish to leave the Colony for a destination other than an East African territory, H E the Governor will consider permitting you to do so, on condition that you do not return.' The offer was repeated at a later date, and at that time included arrangements for his wife and children to accompany him abroad. The government was clearly extremely anxious to get Makhan Singh out of Kenya permanently.

In the same letter, the government wrote that Makhan Singh's wife and two younger children were permitted to join him in Lokitaung, if Makhan Singh so wished, and the government would pay for their transport. However, he turned down Makhan Singh's request for support 'in the absence of any proof of destitution.' Makhan Singh had stated that the government had debarred him from any means of livelihood.

'On the contrary,' the government wrote, 'you have yourself chosen a course of conduct which has resulted in your being so debarred. Government is supporting you, though under the Ordinance your property could be sold to defray the cost of your maintenance.'

Makhan Singh's reply, sent on the 8th was brief and adamant. 'Immediately I wish to make it absolutely clear that I have not even slight intention of leaving Kenya, my home, on condition of not returning.' Later in October, Dr Mahal offered him a vacant house that he had in Bombay 'if he had any idea of settling there.' Makhan Singh's response was 'We are already permanently settled in this country, we have no idea of settling anywhere.'

He then told his father that he would like his lawyers Chanan Singh and Achhroo Kapila to meet him in Kitale to discuss his petition to the secretary of state for the colonies.

On 26th February, 1951, Hindpal informed his father that lawyers Chanan Singh and Achhroo Kapila were filing the appeal to the Privy Council in London and needed the restriction proceedings. Regarding the transport arrangements for the family, the government was not responding to their requests. He then passed on a message from his mother, 'If my health does not remain good here what is the use of us living here? Send us to India.'

On 8th March Makhan Singh wrote to his wife explaining that 'due to censorship difficulties, I could not write to you regularly. I hope you will excuse me.' He then told her that there was no question of her going to India until Hindpal completed his studies in Kenya and passed his London Matriculation exams. 'I know you are suffering great hardships for my sake. I can never forget your sacrifices for me. Even your living here with me in a sort of jail would be a great sacrifice. I do appreciate all this.'

Satwant Kaur's father, Tara Singh Mahal, on the other hand was encouraging her to return to India. Hindpal wrote that 'Mother says you should not stop us from going to India because you don't know what happens here. She knows that perfectly well and therefore you should allow us to leave.' Makhan Singh appealed to her to be more patient. 'I hope you would gladly bear the hardship. The days are not going to remain as they are, they are bound to change. Be cheerful. Be brave. With hearty love ...' He requested his parents to speak with Satwant Kaur and reassure her but this was of no avail. The relationship between Satwant Kaur and her in-laws was tense and in April she told Makhan Singh that if he did not allow her and the children to go to India then he should get them to Lokitaung because 'we cannot live here,' she insisted. Satwant Kaur wrote to the government herself asking for a maintenance allowance, for education expenses for Hindpal and to be allowed to stay in Lokitaung.

Makhan Singh had made friends with some Asians – a medical officer i/c, Dr R D Singh, a Dr Bowry and an Asian mechanic, as well as a few Africans. In March, the DC of Lokitaung placed further restrictions on Makhan Singh's movements by insisting that all visits, except those to one shop, to the doctor, the mechanic and the tennis court in the police compound, required formal invitations that had to be vetted. And the visits were not to exceed more than half an hour. Makhan Singh could walk around freely but was not allowed to visit any home or receive visitors.

In mid March, he received the minutes of a meeting of the central committee of the LTUEA that had been held on 20th November of the previous year. Owing to the absence of the president, the vice president, the general secretary and their assistants, Mushegi Karanja was elected acting president and A S Rao, acting general secretary. Rao wrote to Makhan Singh on 15th February 1951 informing him that Fred Kubai had been released, the murder charge against him being unproven; that Pranlal Sheth was visiting India and that the LTUEA was awaiting registration. He also sent him some magazines from the International Labour Organisation, which Makhan Singh received exactly a month later.

In April, Sudh Singh telegraphed Makhan Singh that the turban-tying ceremony was being arranged for his younger son, Swarajpal, and his nephew, Tarlochan. (The ceremony, called *Dastaar Bandhan*, was performed in a gurdwara when a boy first ties a turban.) Later Sudh Singh sent his son a box of sweetmeats and a photograph of the event. Makhan Singh wrote, 'Swarajpal, my young philosopher, is very thoughtful under the pressure of the heavy turban . . . I greatly appreciate what you are doing in the matter of the Appeal to the Privy Council . . . I have placed too much burden upon you.'

Makhan Singh was now concerned about the travel arrangements for his family, his appeal to the Privy Council and the absence of letters and newspapers. His lawyers were advising against filing the case with the Privy Council. The secretary of state for the colonies, James Griffiths, was due to arrive in Kisumu on 17th May; Makhan Singh wrote to the chief secretary in Nairobi requesting a meeting with Griffiths to study the situation of the trade union movement and to review the dissolution, deportation and restriction orders. 'Your forthcoming visit can be in real interests of people if you try see other side also,' his telegram read. 'Employers and their organisations have full freedom. Trade union movement and its functionaries should have the same.' A copy of the telegram was allowed to reach his father and was published in the *Daily Chronicle*.

In May, Fred Kubai sent him a telegram saying 'Our thoughts are with you this May Day.' On 10th June, 1951, Kubai was elected chairman of the Nairobi branch of KAU with John Mungai as vice-chairman, Bildad Kaggia as secretary and Paul Ngei as assistant secretary. All of them were active trade unionists. Fred Kubai expressed the prevailing mood when he declared 'self-government for Africans within three years and achievement of human rights were the policies which would be implemented,' in an editorial in *Sauti ya Mwafrika*, the newspaper he edited.

In the same month, Hindpal wrote that the government had

Hon. A B Patel

agreed for Satwant Kaur to visit him but 'grandfather can only escort her, not visit you.' Later, the DC allowed Sudh Singh to stay for a week. Then the government demanded a bond of KShs 2,000 each from Satwant Kaur and Sudh Singh and two sureties of KShs 1,000 each. On the other hand, Makhan Singh was now allowed visits from Asian staff of the government in Lokitaung, to carry a panga and long stick for self-defence and to employ a 'boy', a worker whom he called his office messenger. The government now allocated a daily allowance of seven shillings for Satwant Kaur, but regarding Hindpal's school fees, he was advised to seek remission from the Government Indian School.

Addressing his father as 'My dear friend,' 14-year old Hindpal informed him that Hon. A B Patel had taken over the *Daily Chronicle* and that the journalists D K Sharda and Haroon Ahmed had resigned.[8] Hindpal asked for KShs 500 for purchasing items for the visit. (Makhan Singh had told them to bring extra beds, mosquito nets, chairs, mats, curtains, foodstuffs, utensils, crockery and linen as he had not been supplied with any of these.) The list included books in English which were lying at home or in the press.[9] 'Some English schoolbooks for Satwant Kaur,' probably meant that he intended teaching his wife English. Hindpal requested his father to 'write your letters in a neat handwriting as we cannot read them.' Makhan Singh then started writing in block letters which Sudh Singh was able to decipher. He also wrote to his brothers-in-law in India to write in English, 'regularly but briefly'.

FINANCIAL CONSTRAINTS

Sudh Singh, Satwant Kaur, Inderjeet and Swarajpal left Nairobi on 15th July, for Lokitaung. Sudh Singh returned on the 31st, having spent three days on the journey each way. The health of Sudh Singh's wife, Isher Kaur, was poor and financial constraints seemed to be a major concern. In August, Hindpal wrote, 'Nowadays there is no job in our press . . . grandfather says 'I cannot give you expenses of studying and living, you should pay the money yourself.' Hindpal asked Makhan Singh to write to the government to help while Satwant Kaur's father sent some money from India.

On 27th August, Madan Shah Advocates wrote to the member for law and order in the secretariat regarding provision for an allowance for Hindpal and forwarded copies of their letter to Makhan Singh, Sudh Singh and Chanan Singh. On receipt, Makhan Singh immediately sent the secretariat a telegram. 'While fully agreeing and endorsing the request made therein, I strongly disagree with their remarks in same letter about my being misguided man. They had no right or authority to write in such totally wrong tone.' The letter had been drafted by Fitz de Souza at Madan's request; clearly the lawyers thought that such a statement would serve to appease the government. Madan writing about it later explained: 'Makhan Singh's father believed I could perform a miracle and obtain his son's release from detention. How to achieve this end? I decided to adopt an artifice to cajole the Chief Secretary of the day for the release of Makhan Singh. I wrote to him saying among many other things that I believed Makhan Singh was probably misguided. I sent a copy of my supplication on his behalf to Makhan Singh. He promptly wrote back to the chief secretary that I was entirely wrong. He was polite enough not to say that I was the one who was misguided.'[10]

Makhan Singh, though very concerned about his son's education, would not agree to compromise his principles by 'begging' for financial help. He was not pleased about the boy's examination results and wrote to his father. 'Hindpal must increase his general knowledge. He must read regularly daily and weekly newspapers and books of general interest in addition to his schoolbooks. He should improve his spelling. I hope nowadays he wakes up early in the morning for his studies,' he urged. 'The English language as expressed in his letters is generally incorrect. He must improve it.'

On 16th August, he sent a telegram to Griffiths, Secretary of State for the Colonies, through the chief secretary in Nairobi. 'Sent three telegrams for you through Kenya Secretariat on 4th and 12th, May, and 16th June, but no reply. Such attitude extremely deplorable. I reiterate that situation in Kenya demands immediate revocation of restriction order against me and Chege Kibachia and also revocation of dissolution in the interests of trade union movement. Your intervention necessary for the revocation. If you cannot, please let me know reasons for not doing so.' The telegram was replied to on 12th October by the member for law and order: 'In view of the fact that these restriction orders are subject to review from time to time, he [Secretary of State for the Colonies] is not prepared to intervene.' Makhan Singh nevertheless continued to petition for intervention.

In September, he informed advocates Chanan Singh & Handa that he had given the DO in Lokitaung his completed affidavit and notice of intention to appeal against the court proceedings and the restriction order. The lawyers then forwarded the affidavit to London. Pollak, Pritt's fellow advocate, advised delaying the application till after the British elections and then identifying a member of parliament who could 'ventilate' the matter.

Subsequent to receipt of the letter from the member for law and order, Makhan Singh sent a telegram to the governor of Kenya on 26th October. 'These orders and their indefinite continuation and dissolution of former East African Trade Unions Congress etc are against solemn declaration of British Government and seriously infringe conventions of International Labour Organisation ratified by UK government and declarations and charters of UNO and UNESCO approved by British government regarding freedom of association of trade unions and protection of rights to organise them. These conventions apply to non-metropolitan territories including Kenya. These orders cannot be justified before the people, before above organisations and before history.'

The following month, he instructed his father to apply for a permit and transport for Hindpal, as the government had given permission for the boy to visit Lokitaung during the school's Christmas holidays. Meanwhile, he applied for a permit for his mother, Isher Kaur, to visit him. On the 28th the government granted permits to both Hindpal and Isher Kaur and said two seats were available on a government mail lorry, for a fee. Makhan Singh immediately wrote back, 'Charges not acceptable. Cancel all travel plans.' He advised his son to use the vacation to improve in his studies, if he wished to pass the Form Five exams. 'Your detailed result is totally unsatisfactory,' he admonished. He then applied for an extension to Satwant Kaur's permit to stay with him in Lokitaung as it was due to expire on 31st December. His birthday fell on 27th December, and Sudh Singh sent him a telegram of good wishes.

From 14th to 26th January, 1951, Makhan Singh went on a ten-day hunger strike. It was in protest at the introduction of a franchise based on separate communal rolls delineated along religious lines, the continued dissolution of the EATUC, the continued restriction of Chege Kibachia and himself and the refusal of the secretary of state for the colonies to intervene in these matters. The hunger strike went largely unnoticed as his telegram to the press was not forwarded. He asked that his daily allowance of seven shillings not be paid to him as long as he was on strike.

Even in the March school holidays Hindpal did not visit his father, as the government had refused him free transport. Makhan Singh then requested that he, together with his wife and two children be allowed to spend a month in Nairobi because the adverse climate was affecting their health. A permit was required for him or any of his family to visit the local hospital and Makhan Singh protested against this. In the course of the discussion, the DO said, 'If we cannot prosecute, we can at least persecute you.' He was, however, given a radio for his use.

In May 1952, the member for law and order gave permission for his mother, Isher Kaur, and Hindpal to travel free on government transport between Kitale and Lokitaung. Makhan Singh requested an increase of not less than 50% in his subsistence allowance and that the subsistence allowance for his wife be continued when she was in Nairobi. Both requests were denied and he was informed that there would be no change in the censorship rules and no Marxist literature, including the *Tribune* newspaper, would be allowed to reach him.

The special leave to appeal against the finding of Justice Thacker in the Supreme Court of Kenya, in May 1950, that he was an 'undesirable person' and that he had conducted himself in a manner calculated to raise discontent and disaffection among the inhabitants of Kenya, was heard by the Judicial Committee of the Privy Council on 20th November, 1952. The board consisted of Lord Oaksey, Lord Reid, Lord Asquith and Sir Lionel Leach. D N Pritt, QC and Ralph Milner appeared for the petitioner. Makhan Singh's appeal was dismissed. 'Petition by Communist Dismissed' was the headline in the *East African Standard* of 29th November.

In December 1952, D N Pritt came back to Kenya at the invitation of the KAU to defend Jomo Kenyatta and five of his political associates. The charges were of managing a proscribed organisation and the trial was held from November 1952 to March 1953 in an air-less school house in Kapenguria, a small administrative centre on the slopes of the Cherangany Hills, suitably isolated in the Northern Frontier Province, 450 kilometres north-west of Nairobi. Justice Thacker presided over the case and was later handsomely paid 'for his troubles'.[11] The conviction and detention of the Kapenguria Six was based principally on the evidence of one witness, Rawson Macharia, who in 1958 withdrew his evidence by affidavit alleging 'government bribery'.[12]

Pritt was a London barrister and a member of the Communist Party of Britain and had been elected to Parliament. In Kenya, his movements were constantly monitored and restricted and the government had to provide him with an armed guard to protect him from the settlers who wanted to shoot him on sight. Because of the apartheid-style social system, he could only consult with his fellow lawyers like Kapila and Chaman Lal who were non-white when sitting out in the open air, amongst a crowd of curious and admiring Africans.[13] In Kitale, the only decent hotel operated a colour bar and the Defence Counsel had to meet in a dump called the 'North End Arms'.[14]

Makhan Singh wrote to Pritt requesting a meeting with him in Kapenguria to seek further legal advice. The meeting in Kapenguria was not sanctioned and Pritt and his co-counsel in the trial applied to visit Makhan Singh in Lokitaung. In January 1953, the DC, L E Whitehouse, informed Makhan Singh that Sudh Singh had been refused permission to be accompanied by the lawyers. Makhan Singh protested and Pritt left for the UK.

TRANSFER TO MARALAL

✳

The Kapenguria Six (see Chapter 10) had been convicted in Kapenguria and detained in Lokitaung where they were kept under heavy guard both before and after their trial. Kenyatta's camp was surrounded by barbed wire and stood about a hundred metres from Makhan Singh's house.

Achieng Oneko was one of the Kapenguria Six and has recounted their 'meeting' with Makhan Singh thus:

Two or three days after our arrival in Lokitaung we saw an Asian standing on the hillside, a gulley divided us. We were surprised as we knew that the Turkanas and only a few Europeans lived here. The Asian had a beard and he raised both his arms with clenched fists, seemingly in a gesture of solidarity. It was either Kenyatta or Kubai who recognised Makhan Singh – we had not heard of him for three or four years and had

The detention tin rondavals at Maralal

assumed that he had been sent back to India.

Though we were not allowed to meet, or even talk to him, we were soon sending messages to each other. Once he warned us, "Do not eat that goat meat, it is not fit even for the dogs." We were not allowed newspapers, so he sent us his and scribbled messages in them. Unfortunately the authorities found out and after a few weeks, transferred him to Maralal.

Though Oneko had heard of the trade union leader he had met him only once in Nairobi in 1950 in the company of G L Vidyarthi. Oneko was trying to publish his Ramogi paper and was not too interested in trade unionism.

> Trade unionism was a very new idea; many workers thought it was some form of business but Makhan Singh took the trouble to explain and to organise. Fred Kubai learnt a lot from Makhan Singh and the two were close friends. He probably was the only one close to Makhan Singh – Singh was a solo man. He did not go to the people to entice them to shout slogans . . . he was solid, he taught the workers to know their rights. Many of us got a lot of help at the Desai Memorial Hall and I might have met him there.

To avoid any further contact or communication between the Kapenguria Six and Makhan Singh, the latter was relocated. On 26th June, 1953, he was transferred to Maralal, approximately 400 kilometres to the south of Lokitaung. His family then left for Nairobi.

Maralal, though also very isolated, was a much more congenial location than Lokitaung. Situated at an altitude of 2,500 metres above sea level in a hilly area, it was a clean little township with a pleasant climate and a clear view of snow-capped Mount Kenya. A Greek proprietor owned the main shop in this one-street town and supplied all the provisions,

Jomo Kenyatta at Maralal

similar to Kaka's store in Kitale. Makhan Singh was housed in three tin rondavals located a kilometre uphill from the town. He used two as bedrooms and one as a living room. In Maralal too there was no electricity or piped water.

On his return in June, Pritt applied for permission to meet Makhan Singh and was flatly refused. The reason given was that the visitor's pass issued by the Kenya Immigration Department was restricted to the purpose of allowing Pritt to appear for the appellants in the Kapenguria trial. Makhan Singh then applied for an extension to the pass but to no avail. On 1ˢᵗ September he wrote to Pritt stating that 'the fundamental right of a restrictee to consult his counsel and for the counsel to advise his client is at stake.' Pritt agreed and planned to take up the matter on his next visit to Kenya. Meanwhile, Pritt was having his own legal battles. The *Daily Telegraph* of London had published a letter in which it was implied that Pritt was an apologist for Mau Mau. On 9th September it published an apology to Pritt and agreed to pay his costs.

In Maralal, the deliberate harassment of Makhan Singh continued. He had to repeatedly ask for water as the water drums in his rondaval were leaking. Satwant Kaur in Nairobi had developed heart trouble and rheumatism. Makhan Singh's sister, Kulwant Kaur, and her son Gurdev, were refused permission to visit him. Makhan Singh himself had problems with his eyesight and dentures. New conditions were imposed for his wife and children to visit him and when he protested about the restrictions, the DC bluntly retorted 'We know you don't like them.'

Delivery of correspondence and telegrams was increasingly delayed; the excuse given by the authorities was that the censor had been away. This was particularly aggravating for Makhan Singh as Pritt's London office even in his absence, was very prompt and regular in responding to him. An appeal to the Privy Council was being processed for the Kapenguria case and Pritt visited Kenya in December.

He came to Kitale but was refused permission to meet with Makhan Singh. 'He can meet any local

"Sorry Mr. Pritt", Daily Telegraph Apologises

LONDON:— The London daily The Daily Telegraph has apoligised and agreed to pay Mr. Pritt's costs after an out-of-court settlement was reached in the Vacation Court here.

Mr. Pritt had sued the paper for an alleged libel. The paper had published a letter in which it was implied that Mr. Pritt was an apologist for Mau Mau.

Mr. Pritt had made a statutory declaration saying: "I share with all right-thinking people an abhorrence for the crimes of violence which have taken place in Kenya, and would do everything in my power to discourage such crimes and to punish their perpetrators."

The Daily Telegraph has published an apology.

'Daily Telegraph' apology to Mr. Pritt

Pritt Refused Permission To Visit Makhan Singh

Nairobi—It is reliably understood that Mr. D. N. Pritt, Q.C., senior counsel in the defence of Jomo Kenyatta and 5 others, has been once again refused permission to visit Mr. Makhan Singh, veteran trade union leader, now in detention at Maralal, an outpost some 75 miles from Rumuruti.

Earlier, Mr. Makhan Singh had sent a telegram to Mr. D. N. Pritt at Kitale in which he stated that he had wired to the Chief Secretary to release him from the restriction order which had been served on him, or, in the alternative, to allow Mr. Pritt and a local lawyer of his choice to visit him at Maralal.

Mr. Pritt, who had, while in England, communicated with the Secretary of State for the Colonies, sent a long cable to the Chief Secretary on the subject. After an absence of a few days, the Chief Secretary has informed Mr. D. N. Pritt that he cannot allow him to visit Mr. Makhan Singh. It was Mr. Pritt who had appealed to the Privy Council on behalf of Mr. Makhan Singh.

Dennis Pritt denied access to visit Makhan Singh.

counsel,' was the rejoinder. In January 1954, Pritt protested directly and strongly to the secretary of state for the colonies about the delays in correspondence and the refusals to permit a meeting.

In February, the government sanctioned Hirabhai Patel, a partner of Fitz de Souza, to meet Makhan Singh in Maralal. Sudh Singh wished to accompany Patel but was initially refused permission on the grounds that he had recently visited his son. Then a new requirement was imposed, stating that the family would be responsible for meeting their own costs. Makhan Singh expressed his strong resentment to the DC of Maralal and informed his wife not to accept the new conditions and instead apply for their deletion. Finally, the government relented and Patel, Satwant Kaur and Sudh Singh visited Makhan Singh on 18th and 19th April, travelling by air from Nairobi to Kitale and back and by road between Kitale and Maralal.

In March, Makhan Singh sent the secretary of state for the colonies a telegram through the Kenya secretariat requesting 'immediate release through prompt impartial review in interests of strong trade union movement which is important part of solution of Kenya's problems as also recognised by parliamentary delegation.' There was no response and so in September Makhan Singh complained to Pritt of the deplorable behaviour of the secretary of state for the colonies. He received an undated reply from the secretary of state for the colonies, stating that he was not prepared to question the exercise of the Kenya government's discretion in this case. In August, Pritt's secretary wrote 'You must feel very despondent over these appalling delays and over every failure to deal with your communications . . . be sure that in any matter with which Mr. Pritt is concerned he does expedite it to the best of his ability.'

A THREAT TO THE HIGHEST LAW IN THE UK

Nine months later, according to the postmark on the envelope, an undated reply was received. Pritt was extremely dissatisfied and wrote a vigorous protest declaring that Makhan Singh was 'clearly a threat to the highest law in the U.K.' The matter was raised in the House of Commons on 15th December. The colonial secretary, Lennox Boyd, told Geoffrey Bing (Labour) that 'there were no special restrictions placed by the Government of Kenya on British barristers and solicitors desiring to see their clients in Kenya . . . in Kenya, as in all colonial territories, they were subject to immigration controls for intending visitors.' Later, the British government in an unsigned letter to Pritt informed him that he had no right to practise in colonial territories. These were threats they could not enforce.

Pritt, in March, won a case in which a left wing leader of a party in British Guyana was charged with sedition. In August, he was busy defending university students in Singapore. Makhan Singh was a threat to the capitalist interests of the British ruling establishment, which consequently engaged in duplicity and hypocrisy to ensure that he was silenced. Understandably, the British (and Kenyan) governments were adamant about not allowing Pritt to even meet Makhan Singh, let alone take up his case.

Makhan Singh was very particular about remembering the birthdays of family members, and now that he was in detention, he would send them greetings by telegram. That year Hindpal was most upset. 'I have not yet been married, nor do I intend getting married soon,' he protested. 'This telegram has nothing to do with my birthday which is tomorrow.' Apparently the wrong message had been delivered as the telegram read 'Heaven's choicest blessing be showered on you both.' Sudh Singh regularly sent his son parcels of dry fruit, sweetmeats and books. Makhan Singh now requested copies of the weekly *Africa Samachaar*, published by his friend Haroon Ahmed of the *Daily Chronicle* team, and sent his subscription to the Desai Memorial Library. He also asked for a wooden roller for making chapattis as his old one had broken.

Hindpal, now seventeen, was nearing completion of his secondary school studies and was looking into various possibilities for further education. He had chosen teaching as a career but his father discouraged him saying that he should never work for the government. His mother was keen to visit her family in India and wrote to her brothers that she was suffering from heart trouble and rheumatism. Her father, Tara Singh Mahal, requested Makhan Singh to send the family to India by mid-August and Makhan Singh agreed. Tara Singh was also of the opinion that Hindpal should try to get into a university in England rather than in India. Hindpal had, however, learnt that the Indian high commission offered scholarships to colonial students for higher education in India and put in an application in October 1954, to study engineering. As an engineer he could, if he chose to, work for the East African Power & Lighting Company which was run by private shareholders; it was not until 1965 that the government took a majority shareholding in it.

Prior to this, he and his mother had applied for registration as British citizens in order to get new passports. Makhan Singh's passport was held by the Supreme Court of Kenya but he was registered as a citizen of the United Kingdom and Colonies on 6th May, 1954. Satwant Kaur had been registered earlier on 29th January, but was refused a certificate of permanent residence in Kenya on the grounds that she was not born in the colony. According to Makhan Singh, this was 'totally wrong, as she had been a resident for more than eight years.' Inderjeet and Swarajpal were registered as British citizens on 14th May, 1954.

Satwant Kaur had to delay her trip to India as her mother-in-law, Isher Kaur with whom she lived in Nairobi, was in very poor health. But she did manage to go to Maralal in July. The DC, C G Hill, had confirmed in writing that she could continue to get her subsistence allowance as well as medical and transport expenses while in Maralal. But once again, Hindpal was refused transport expenses to visit his father.

Early in 1955 Makhan Singh received confirmation that his son's application for a scholarship had been successful. He had been offered a fellowship to study electrical engineering in the University of Roorkie, one of the best in India. The Indian high commission had, no doubt, given tacit but practical recognition to Makhan Singh's valiant struggle.

Hindpal planned to leave for India in April or May and sent the application forms for a passport to his father to sign. Makhan Singh now agreed for his wife and the two younger children to accompany Hindpal to India and sent Sudh Singh a cheque for KShs 612 to purchase two steamer fares. The cost of deck class with meals was KShs 306 per person; Swarajpal, just seven years old, would travel free, Hindpal's fare was included in the scholarship. Makhan Singh informed his father-in-law of their plans and asked him to send body measurements of his children, presumably so that Satwant Kaur could prepare some gifts of clothing for them.

PAYMENTS TO DETAINEES

At some point the payments to the detainees were increased, secretly, without being gazetted. In 1953, Jomo Kenyatta was receiving KShs 400 per month. By 1961, he, Makhan Singh and Bildad Kaggia, were receiving KShs 600 per month regularly. Seventeen detainees who were classified as being of 'superior status' were paid KShs 180 and a total of 91 detainees were paid monthly stipends ranging from KShs 120 to 600.[15] According to Makhan Singh's notes, in 1956 he was paid a subsistence allowance of ten shillings per day and his wife received a similar amount, adding up to KShs 600 per month.

Satwant Kaur's father was, of course, very pleased that his daughter would be visiting India. In a letter to Makhan Singh he described it as 'a fresh lease of life for Vir Kaur [the name he used for her]. . . . There are temperamental outlooks in one's life,' he added, 'just as you could do what you liked and I have the least doubt that you are quite happy about all that you are undergoing in this world. Similarly Vir Kaur's outlook on life had been quite different and so far she never for a moment realised her wish. There is going to be an end of it and it was quite right that she also would soon realise her wishes.'

Makhan Singh did not agree. 'I don't find myself in a position to comment upon some of your remarks in your letter,' he wrote on 3rd March, 1955. 'In this world one cannot get everything of one's own liking and one has to make the best of a given situation.' He enclosed a money order of KShs 152 for Satwant Kaur's use. The government still refused to pay travel costs for Hindpal to visit him in Maralal saying these were only provided for his wife and the younger children. Sudh Singh was allowed to escort them but refused to go to Maralal, without Hindpal. Makhan Singh's lawyer Chanan Singh requested the government to permit Hindpal to visit his father as he was leaving for further studies. Because of the government's deliberate harassment, Hindpal delayed his journey to India and Satwant Kaur sailed with just the two younger children.

In November 1954, Makhan Singh had requested the new DC of Maralal, Terence Gavaghan, to move him and the family into a house nearer to the town. Gavaghan had been a DO in charge of 'rehabilitating' Mau Mau prisoners in the camps at Mwea and had been the mastermind behind the infamous 'dilution technique' which became the model for the Hola massacre.[16] Makhan Singh's tin rondavals were situated on the edge of a forest and elephants had torn down the barbed wire fence leaving them totally exposed to attacks by wild animals. Makhan Singh used to walk to town at least twice daily and had been confronted by elephants and buffaloes on more than one occasion. He requested permission to carry the traditional Sikh dagger, not for religious reasons but for self defence, and complained of loneliness.

Gavaghan refers to Makhan Singh in his book *Of Lions and Dung Beetles*. 'A unique and involuntary guest at Maralal was Makhan Singh, General Secretary of the East African Trade Union Congress, who had close links with the Kenya trade union and Mau Mau leader, Fred Kubai. He was legally restricted to Maralal where we were required to provide secure family accommodation for him and a precise circuit of movement to my office, to the rear of John Cardovillis' shop and back during daylight. His mail was to be censored by me. He was a short, prickly Sikh positively bouncing on his self-importance and his rights, which he would tick off on a meticulous list as often as he could get at me.

'Item: 'Your office boy says you are not in his pocket!' Item: 'Why must I go in Mr. John's backside?' Item: 'When I am climbing to my house, I whistle and my wife whistles to save us from buffaloes; nobody comes!' I liked his spirit and fortitude and passed all his letters and annotated books, save only to underline passages which seemed to balance his more extreme views.

'A bizarre encounter took place outside my office, linking Makhan Singh with one of my next visitors. This was Hugh Fraser, Under Secretary for the Colonies, accompanying William Gorrell-Barnes his official counterpart. Somehow Makhan Singh had expected a Labour party House of Commons 'pair' to be with them and, bristling like a terrier at Fraser's ankles, demanded to know "What has happened to Labour MP?" From his lordly height and in full voice Fraser responded with feigned surprise, "Oh, I shot him!" The rest was silence.'[17]

It is highly unlikely that Makhan Singh used the term 'boy' but the passage does give an insight into the prevailing conditions. After repeated reminders, the rondavals were shifted in March 1955. Makhan Singh's parents, both Sudh Singh and Isher Kaur, then visited him from 17th to 24th March. They travelled by government lorry from Thomson's Falls (now Nyahururu) via Rumuruti on the well-maintained murram road. For some unknown reason, the government consistently refused permission for Makhan Singh's sister, Kulwant Kaur, to visit him.

Finally, on 7th March, 1955, the minister for defence granted Hindpal the travel expenses to enable him to visit his father for seven days and there was a flurry of correspondence between father and son. However, almost immediately, the DO of Maralal informed Makhan Singh of the conditions for the visit: Hindpal would not be permitted to reside with his father and a government official had to be present during all conversations between the two of them. Makhan Singh refused vehemently to accept these, or any other, conditions and instructed his son to cancel the visit in protest. 'I am acutely feeling the imposition of the new conditions by the Government. Please convey to Hindpal warmest greetings from a heavy heart of a father,' he wrote to Sudh Singh.

SON MEETS FATHER, AT LAST!

In early May, the government relented; Hindpal was allowed to visit his father without any restrictions.[18] Postponing his departure to India by a month, Hindpal arrived in Maralal on the evening of Friday, 13th May and stayed for three days, leaving on the morning of the 16th. He had not seen or met his father for five years, so father and son had much to talk about. Hindpal's study programme and stay in India were the main concerns. News about family, friends, colleagues and the politics of the day were other matters of interest.

Hindpal left for India on 23rd June, and a few days after having been given a certificate of permanent residentship. Gurdev Singh, the son of Makhan Singh's sister, Kulwant Kaur, now took on Hindpal's duties of corresponding regularly with his uncle and keeping him supplied with books and other reading material. Makhan Singh wistfully inquired of his wife, 'No letter from you?' He did however receive letters written in English by his daughter, Inderjeet, now ten and schooling in India. On the 15th Makhan Singh wrote to Sudh Singh, '[Today] I have completed five years of restriction and entered the sixth year with full confidence and resolution.' He was however saddened by the news of his mother's deteriorating health.

Although restricted to a tin house at the edge of a forest in an isolated mountain range in Kenya, he kept in touch with the world. He was informed of a historic Asian-African Conference and sent a telegram to Prime Minister Nehru through the Indian high commission in Nairobi, wishing him 'success in achieving aims of freedom, peace, equality, civil liberties and trade union rights.'

In July 1955, the Hon. Ibrahim E Nathoo, a member of the Legco, visited Maralal but Makhan Singh was not allowed to meet him. His subsistence allowance was now raised from nine shillings and ten cents to ten shillings but the harassment continued. The DC refused to meet him or reply to his letters and made a habit of not being available for scheduled appointments.

Almost a year later, on 12th June, 1956, the governor wrote to Makhan Singh. 'Your case is being reviewed periodically – it is not possible for your restriction order to be revoked at present. Owing to your present attitude your only prospect of being released from restriction is to leave Kenya forever.' Makhan Singh replied immediately and informed the governor that 'you are trying to achieve the impossible. No trade unionist or political worker worth his salt would ever take the suicidal course of deportation to get his release.' He sent copies of his reply to Pritt but his communication was withheld and returned to him by the Kenya secretariat. He protested to the governor about this 'totally unjust decision of withholding my letter.' Seven months later, P H Jones, the new DC, verbally told him that 'there was no counsel-client relationship between you and Mr. Pritt.' This was stated in spite of the fact that Pritt had signed Makhan Singh's appeal to the Privy Council and was his counsel.

On 19th January, 1957 Mr R Wainright, the PC of Rift Valley Province, visited Makhan Singh without any prior notification or accompanying officer. Makhan Singh later noted the following main points of the talk: 'I began by saying that it was now about seven years when the Restriction Order was made against me. In my opinion the Order was not justified and its continuation would be unjustified and, therefore, it should be revoked. I added that it was made on account of my trade union activities and expression of political views all of which, though viewed with disfavour by the learned Judge and the Government, were nevertheless lawful. I further said that my activities before and after the making of the Order had been peaceful and within legal and constitutional limits.

'He [the PC] agreed that there was no infringement of law and terms of the Restriction Order by me otherwise I would not be in my present condition, meaning that in that case I would have been in prison. Thereafter he suddenly asked me whether I was still a Communist. I replied that what I had to say I had said at the time of my "trial" at Nyeri in 1950, but since then I had not said anything about the matter, and I had no intention of saying about it while the Restriction Order continued against me. I added that even with regard to the developments in Kenya my reply had always been "No comment please" and that this attitude would continue while the Order lasted. I further said that I had been brought here for expressing ideas and, therefore, I didn't think it would be advisable for me to say anything during the continuation of the Order. He remarked that such an attitude on my part didn't make matters easy. He added that there was no chance of my being released so long as this attitude continued on my part. He reiterated that I could leave Kenya if I liked.

'I reminded him of my reply to H. E. the Governor and said that I would never leave Kenya on the condition of not returning as Kenya was my home to the same extent as it was the home of others. I added that I was always optimistic that the Government would have to release me as it had to release others, that the situation was fast changing even in Kenya, and it would further change to an extent that the Government would consider it advisable to revoke my Order. I further added that I would not repent or withdraw anything and that I would not make any promises for the future in order to get my release.

'He enquired: "Then why should you be released?" I said my arguments were these: My attitude before and after the Order has been peaceful and within legal bounds, and it has been an honest and straight forward attitude. I consider the Order unjustified and the Government thinks it justified but it has already punished me for nearly seven years which is not a small period. Any change or no change in my creed or ideas should have nothing to do with my release. The Government had already punished me for what I did, and it should now order my release in good faith.

'The talk lasted for about an hour and a quarter with the subject being repeated in various forms. During the talk the provincial commissioner revealed that Mr Chege Kibachia, who had been deported and restricted on account of his trade union activities in 1947, had recently been released. At the end he said that he was not going to recommend my release for the time being.'

Makhan Singh told him that he had no illusions but that he had made his position absolutely clear. In February, Makhan Singh wrote to the minister for defence in the Kenya secretariat and was told that the 'Government has nothing to add to what has been conveyed to him previously.' Pritt and Sudh Singh tried to meet Makhan Singh to persuade him to accept the government's condition for his release but were not allowed to do so.

CHILDREN'S MEMORIES

Satwant Kaur and the two younger children, Inderjeet and Swarajpal, visited Makhan Singh at Maralal and spent the school holidays there. 'I understand that it was almost a year before we had been allowed to stay with him in Lokitaung,' Inderjeet reminisces. 'As he was a very organised and methodical person he would structure the day for us children so that we wouldn't get bored. The early part of learning was all from him as I did not start school until fifth standard – he was a good and a very patient teacher. Since many toys did not exist in those days papaji used to improvise and make tiny cups, saucers, plates, and many other things from used bottle tops. During our daily evening walk my brother and I used to collect these tops thrown along roadsides. Whenever we became sick he went back and forth to the doctors getting medications, sitting up all night with us - a very caring and a compassionate father.

'Once we started school, we visited him during each school holiday - travelling on trains, lorries, land rovers - the roads were pretty rough and at times when rains were heavy we could not cross the flooded rivers until the waters went down and had to spend the night sitting up in the lorries – bless my mother who went through these rough times with us two young children. On our arrival papaji would have hot water ready and a meal prepared for us, which would make us forget the tortuous and uncomfortable journey. He helped us with our school work and sorted out our academic weaknesses. He used to enjoy reciting Punjabi poetry from a book and I still remember the words of some of them. He was a voracious reader and used to receive selected books from the Nairobi library. I picked up this quality from him – I read what ever comes my way. During his detention we used to get short, brief letters from him as all his mail was censored. We could not write much either other than all is well. He really cherished getting our school reports and felt very proud to see his children doing well despite his absence. I do not know but may be I worked hard to always perform well at school in order to please my father and get his approval.

'When he was detained I was still quite young and do not remember specific things but all I know is that he never flouted rules and regulations laid upon him, was very conscientious, determined, sincere, truthful and a man of principles. He taught us to respect all mankind, race, colour, creed and religion – if as children we ever used any denigrating terminology we were corrected immediately. I used to have mixed feelings when leaving him – happy to get back home to be with friends away from the lonely rural life but very sad to leave papaji behind all by himself – at times he did not talk to anyone for days.'[19]

Swarajpal remembers his father as a good friend. 'I was never afraid of him,' he said.

He did a lot of writing and reading but Sundays he

devoted to us. We would spend part of the day running a 'workshop' to make toys such as small cars and aeroplanes using bottle tops, acacia tree stems and thorns and such like. Mother would do the cooking, washing, cleaning and sewing. He would take long walks regularly, he was very fit. Father was not a diplomat; he would call a spade a spade. Grandfather would tell him that he was wasting his time in detention, that he would not achieve anything and he would reply: "This is my ambition and I will do it whatever may happen."[20]

In 1958, the government increased the area of restriction thus allowing him greater freedom of movement. Makhan Singh, however, insisted that his restriction order should have been revoked entirely.

Then on 11th February, his mother died. She had suffered for many years and been in constant pain. From 1956 to 1957, her husband had again taken her to India for treatment, but no cure was found. During this visit, they travelled to Pakistan to their village, Gharjakh, and met many relatives and friends. On their return to Kenya, a Dr Aslam diagnosed a malfunctioning liver as the cause of her illness. Under his medication she began to improve and was almost cured when, tragically, she passed away.[21]

ATTENDANCE AT MOTHER'S CREMATION REFUSED

Makhan Singh applied for permission to travel to Nairobi by air to attend the cremation and his appeal was supported by two Asian members of the Legco, but the government would not be moved. This sad incident served to demonstrate his popularity among the Kenyan rank and file. A newspaper editorial said: 'He earned what very few people of a non-indigenous race have ever earned and that was the sincere respect and the lasting admiration of the masses of Kenyans. A large crowd of Africans gathered at his house in Park Road in openly expressed grief. Her last wish, that she be allowed to see her beloved son, was refused by the Government even though several leading personalities gave their assurances that no untoward incident would take place if he was permitted to come to Nairobi for a short while for such a purpose. Such was his hold on the African mind that the authorities could not overcome their fear. His mother passed away without seeing him.'[22]

The government's persecution of Makhan Singh continued. His sister, Kulwant Kaur, was now allowed to visit him, but on the other hand, his telegram of greetings to the annual conference of the KFL did not get past the censor. In September, Sudh Singh planned to take S G Amin, president of the EAINC, to Maralal to persuade his son to 'moderate his attitude in regard to his early release.' 'Amin most welcome,' Makhan Singh telegraphed, 'but not to moderate my attitude. My attitude has always been lawful. It is the Government which is refusing permission.'

Hindpal completed his engineering studies in India and returned to Nairobi where he joined the East African Power & Lighting Company. But he needed further practical training and was exploring study courses offered abroad. Makhan Singh, however, felt that it would be a disgrace for Kenya if qualified students had to go to other countries for practical training. 'The East African Power & Lighting Company has a monopoly and must provide training for post-graduate students and others. It is a question of principle,' he said. He advised Hindpal to speak with the members of the Legco, the ministries of education, land and labour and the employment exchange in the labour department.

Meanwhile, changes and projects were being instituted by the government which were indicative of a radical shift in the colonial policy regarding Kenya. Makhan Singh noted the transfer to Cyprus of J V Prendergast, the chief of the Kenya Police Special Branch who had organised the mass surrenders of the Mau Mau in the Aberdare forests, and the retirement of Robin Wainwright, PC of Rift Valley Province and J W Cossack, Minister of Internal Security and Defence. In July 1959, 40 Labour members of parliament in Britain moved a motion condemning the policy of detention and restriction in Kenya, Northern Rhodesia and Nyasaland.

On 28th April, 1959, the restriction order made against Pio Gama Pinto in 1957 was revoked. (He had been detained in 1954 and later restricted to Kabarnet, a small town in the Cherangany Hills in the Rift Valley Province.) Makhan Singh's petition for release was, however, again turned down. Though his wife and two younger children were given permits to stay in Maralal for the whole of 1959, there was no let-up in the government's uncompromising attitude to Makhan Singh himself. Pritt was once again refused permission to meet him, and two months later, Pritt retired. The *Daily Nation* of 26th June reported that, 'He [Dennis Pritt, QC] had been chairman of several communist-fronted organisations and was the key influence among the most radical section of the English Bar specialising in particular in the defence of left-wingers and nationalists.' His defence of Kenyatta had been one of his most famous briefs.

The government meanwhile continued to insist that Makhan Singh could only be released if he agreed to leave the colony while the minister for internal security and defence ordered that 'Makhan Singh shall not associate with any person or persons except with the prior approval of the DC.' On one occasion, he was asked if he was writing a book. He did not reply to the question but stated that he was aware of the incidents of spying by the government and the loss of some of his materials. His telegram of greetings to the All Africa Peoples Conference in Accra did not get past the censor, nor did the one he sent to Oginga Odinga of CEMO (Constituency

Elected Members Organisation) and Michael Blundell of NKG (New Kenya Group)[23]. Even the copies of these telegrams which he sent to his father were not forwarded.

Some of the other messages Makhan Singh sent and which were not forwarded by the censor included a telegram and letter to the annual session of the Trades Union Congress in London on 26th August, 1955 as well as the copy to Tom Mboya; a telegram to Sir Vincent Tewson, general secretary of the British Trades Union Congress on 21st March, 1957, through the KFL as he was visiting Nairobi; a congratulatory telegram to Tom Mboya on 12th March, 1957, and a telegram to the annual conference of the KFL on 9th September, 1958. He appealed to the minister for defence against the censor's decision but the appeal was dismissed. He then wrote to Griffiths saying: 'The decision of the Kenya Government to refuse to pass the greetings cables cannot be justified.' A year later the DC in Maralal told Makhan Singh:

I regret but I cannot pass these communications because they are designed to draw the attention of political persons and bodies to your present status.

Makhan Singh replied that the reason for the refusal was not correct.

All concerned are already well aware of my status – I have no need to remind them.

On 27th September, Makhan Singh informed the government that he would, in protest, be going on a hunger strike, drinking only plain water, for an indefinite period commencing at 8.00 a.m. on Friday, 2nd October, 1959. He ended his hunger strike twelve days later, on the 13th, on learning of the meeting on the 10th between the governor and six members of the Kenya National Party together with S V Cooke, Masinde Muliro, Bernard Mate, Daniel arap Moi, J N Muimi, J M Nazareth and

Ronald Ngala. They had met with the Governor, Evelyn Baring, and demanded an end to the state of emergency and the release of Jomo Kenyatta and his five colleagues as well as other detainees and restrictees. (No special mention was made of Makhan Singh.)

Soon after the meeting, the Conservative Party came to power in Britain and Iain Macleod replaced Lennox Boyd as colonial secretary. Evelyn Baring left Kenya and Patrick Renison was sent to take his place as governor. Prof W J M MacKenzie, a constitutional expert, arrived in Kenya in November to advise on the making of a constitution. He was supposed to consult with all shades of political opinion but was not allowed to meet Jomo Kenyatta, Makhan Singh and other detainees. The government did, however, forward a letter written by Makhan Singh to him. He also sent telegrams to J M Nazareth, K D Travadi, A Jamidar, A J Pandya, S G Hassan and Zafrud-Deen, all members of the Legco, urging them, respectfully, to fully support the constitutional conference being organised for the establishment of democratic self-government in Kenya. He also wrote to the Kenya Broadcasting Corporation requesting them to improve the reception of their Asian national broadcast.

END OF STATE OF EMERGENCY

✳

On 12th January, 1960, Governor Renison declared an end to the State of Emergency. Makhan Singh promptly once again petitioned for his release. The DC suggested that he should forward his petition to the council of state, which considered matters of racial discrimination. 'If you had been an African you would have been released long ago,' he said. Makhan Singh's response was, 'I do not consider this to be a case of racial discrimination.'

On 30ᵗʰ January, Sudh Singh, by radio telephone, requested Tom Mboya, general secretary of the KFL who was then in London, to press for the release of his son. On 4ᵗʰ February, the African elected members attending the Constitutional Conference decided to fight for the release of Makhan Singh and Walter Odede, detained president of KAU. On the 23ʳᵈ, the Asian delegates to the conference met the colonial secretary, Iain Macleod, and presented the Sikh community's demand for the release of Makhan Singh and other detainees.

In the same month the *Colonial Times* ran articles about Makhan Singh in its Gujerati section. In March the Kiswahili journal *Picha* published an article headed *'Hadithi ya Makhan Singh'* (The story of Makhan Singh) with a large family portrait of Makhan Singh with his parents, wife and children.

The opening paragraph read *'Mwanzishi wa Trades Unions bado kifungoni baada ya miaka kumi.'* (The founder of Trade Unionism is still in detention after ten years.) The writer found Makhan Singh's history interesting because it showed a positive image of communism. 'So many communists have noble intentions but change when they come to power,' he wrote, and cited as examples Hungary and Tibet. He pointed out that Makhan Singh defended the right of freedom of speech in a democracy, urging that this should be respected whether in Britain or Kenya. The writer explained that he wrote at length about communism because the readers were aware that though trade unionism had brought many benefits, communism remained a dangerous ideology for Kenya. It was a mistake, he wrote, to deny a person his freedom for so long, especially when the circumstances had changed. He warned against acceptance of such draconian laws because they could be used not just against communists but to detain and imprison other anti-colonial persons.

On 6ᵗʰ April, the Kenya Indian Congress demanded the release of Makhan Singh, Jomo Kenyatta, ex-senior chief Koinange and all other detainees but, on the 21ˢᵗ, the government rejected Makhan Singh's application to be released. On 5th, May in a parliamentary debate, the Hon. K D Travadi brought up the subject of Makhan Singh.

His name appears very little in the press but I should urge on the Minister of Security and Defence to consider sympathetically his case as well. I know he has been professing communistic teaching ideas, but now we are having a Summit Conference. We are shaking hands with Kruschev and Bulgarin and I think it is now fair that this man should be allowed a little time to breathe freely.

13th March, 1960, was the 25th anniversary of Makhan Singh's commencement of official trade union work. On that date, in 1935, he was appointed the honorary secretary of the Labour Trade Union of Kenya, which was deregistered in 1953. In India, the daily *Milap* published in Jalhandar, Delhi and Hyderabad featured a story on Makhan Singh in its issue of 19th April.

In June 1960, the Corfield Report on 'The Origin and Growth of Mau Mau', which had been sponsored by Governor Evelyn Baring in 1957, was released. It contained a chapter on 'External and Internal Influences on Mau Mau' which dealt with what

Daily Milap story

the author called 'the broad outlines of the activities of the Asian politicians against the recent historical background of the grant of independence to the two great countries of India and Pakistan.' The chapter basically played down African-Asian solidarity saying that 'such Afro-Indian unity as existed was exerted mainly for political purposes, each side endeavouring to use the other to its own advantage, while unity in the sense of human relationship did not exist.' It made much of Jomo

Kenyatta being 'basically anti-Asian' and far-sighted Asians 'whose political outlook was not warped by an anti-European prejudice' as being embarrassed by the activities of a 'fringe' of the Asian community that helped in the spread of subversion and Mau Mau. It stated that 'noticeable among this fringe were the editors of some of the less reputable Asian newspapers and the Asian Press owners who published many of the more seditious vernacular papers . . . some of the "more doubtful" Asian lawyers also contributed their quota to unrest and subversion.'

The report reproduced a dispatch sent by the governor to the secretary of state for the colonies in April 1950. This dispatch referred in particular to the Indian trade unionist Makhan Singh and said '. . . up to about 150 years ago agitators

Makhan Singh in Daily Milap

such as Makhan Singh and the editor and writers of the *Daily Chronicle*, and many others, would have found themselves quickly on Tower Hill.'[24] The immediate outcome of this dispatch had been an amendment to the law investing the courts with the power to confiscate, under certain safeguards, printing presses used in a conviction for sedition. The Corfield Report also said of Makhan Singh that he had 'locally indoctrinated' Mau Mau leaders such as Fred Kubai and other trade union leaders. Though Makhan Singh never took the Mau Mau oath, he was closely involved in the movement. Achieng Oneko has stated categorically that 'Makhan Singh was Mau Mau'[25]. Robert Edgerton in *Mau Mau, An African*

Crucible writes that 'Makhan Singh and Pio de Gama Pinto played important roles in launching the movement'[26]. The divisive propaganda of the Corfield Report was to have a significant impact on the policies of post-independent Kenya.

The *National Guardian* of 4th June, 1960, pointed out in its editorial titled 'Asians and African Nationalism' that Asians had started to fight for African advancement many years prior to the independence of India and Pakistan. This newspaper was published by J Roderigues and Inde Desai who had left the *Daily Chronicle* following the change of ownership and policy. The prolonged detention of Makhan Singh epitomised the British government's policy, since the early colonial era in Kenya, of driving a wedge between the Africans and the Asians and of minimising and down-playing the participation of Asians in the struggle for independence.

In October, Satish Chander Gautama, a lawyer and president of the Kenya Indian Congress (previously known as the EAINC), was interviewed by the *Sunday Nation*. 'Independence must be accepted as being inevitable and the sooner it comes the sooner the country can settle down to peaceful progress,' he said. He felt that Indians, while backing African demands for independence, did not have to become involved in the Kenya African National Union (KANU) v Kenya African Democratic Union (KADU) struggle but should continue to demand the release of Jomo Kenyatta and restricted persons, Makhan Singh amongst them. He also foresaw the need for the Kenya Indian Congress to adapt itself, either becoming a non-racial political party or even ceasing to exist. An 'unadulterated common roll' would ensure that people lived as individuals and not as Africans or Indians. He emphasised the vital importance of maintaining the rule of law.

KANU released its manifesto in the second week of November and it soon became apparent that there were differences of opinion between Oginga Odinga and Tom Mboya, especially on the issue of compensation for land to be acquired from the white settlers. Makhan Singh, in the copy he

A family portrait in 1949. Standing Makhan Singh, Sudh Singh and Shivocharan Singh. Sitting Hindpal Singh, Satwant Kaur with Swarajpal, Isher Kaur, Kultwant Kaur with Amrit, Gurdeo. Front Row Inderjeet, Surinder, Tarlochan

Registered Trade Unions (KFRTU) with only five union affiliates in 1951 . . . it believed that the trade union movement has the right to be interested in politics, to pronounce on political matters and to take appropriate action to assist during the struggle for independence. It joined the International Confederation of Free Trade Unions (ICFTU) because it believed in a 'free and independent trade unionism.' It accepted that the ICFTU was not perfect as in it were countries which had been colonial powers but despite its faults and weaknesses, it was convinced that it stood for 'Bread, Peace and Freedom'. It was aware of the prevailing East/West struggle but submitted that 'continued affiliation with the ICFTU does not lead to it being used as a pawn in this power struggle.'

The KFL supported pan-African trade unionism. Locally, its concerns were the stabilization of labour, sensible wage policies, old age security, housing, industrial relations, civil service and local government policies, and unemployment. Regarding economic development, it termed it a false impression that only immigrant communities were capable of undertaking activities for economic development and that they were indispensable. This inhibited activities that would lead to the creation of capital and the expansion of the local market for home-produced goods. Effective government participation was necessary in addition to whatever private enterprise already existed.

TRANSFER TO DOL DOL

In September 1960, Makhan Singh again complained of the elephants. 'They are many and come near to my house even in the day time,' he protested.

Makhan Singh registered himself as a voter by post and

received his elector's card. But on 11th March, 1961, the DC informed him that he was to be transferred to Dol Dol, about 100 kilometres southeast of Maralal, close to Nanyuki. From Maralal it could only be reached by traversing a long circuitous route on virtually non-existent roads. Smaller than Maralal or even Lokitaung, its climate was similar to that of Maralal. It was an ideal location for detainees and restrictees from the government's point of view as the people in the area had not been involved in the independence struggle or in the Mau Mau. The area was inhabited by the pastoralist Maasai who were more interested in negotiating with the British for the return of the lands they had given up in the 1904 and 1911 treaties.

The relocation was being done in preparation for moving Jomo Kenyatta to Maralal. Kenyatta's fellow detainees, though still restricted, had already been released from detention. Makhan Singh protested strongly against being transferred to Dol Dol and declared to all and sundry that he would be going on a hunger strike for an indefinite period commencing 13th March. To no avail. On the ninth day of his hunger strike he was transferred to Dol Dol, to the house in which Kungu Karumba, one of the Kapenguria Six, had been restricted and who had since been moved to his home in Kiambu. It was an old colonial, two-room outhouse made of wood. Makhan Singh wrote to the International Labour Organisation requesting more documents and informing them of his change of address to Restrictee, c/o DC, PO Box 11, Dol Dol, Nanyuki.

Makhan Singh, as always, remained steadfast in his political principles and his attention to every detail. The Nanyuki Service Store regularly delivered his grocery order, and once he returned an item with the following note: 'I am returning a South African packet of biscuits, please replace with a locally made one.'

Hon. K P Shah, secretary of the KFP, now appealed to the British government to release Kenyatta, Makhan Singh, Jesse Kariuki, James Beauttah, Rev Kigondu, G Ndegwa and all the other detainees. He sought permission to visit Makhan Singh, together with fellow Legco members Fitz de Souza and S K Anjarwalla. In consultation with D Q Erskine (a national member) and Ngala Mwendwa (member from Kitui) they applied to meet the governor. A deputation from the KFL tried to intercede on behalf of Makhan Singh as well. Legco members K P Shah, Mota Singh, A B Jamidar and S S Patel discussed the case with the minister for defence, A C C Swann, who said there was no official objection to his release 'provided he left Kenya or undertook to give up Communism.' Sudh Singh who was then in India, telegraphed Tom Mboya to 'save my son.' Mboya joined with Fitz de Souza and K P Shah in trying to visit Makhan Singh. In Mombasa, the Indian Association appointed its president, (Dr S S Dhillon) and A J Pandya to join with them. The government turned down all the requests. A little later the Kenya Sikh Central Council was granted permission to visit him but Makhan Singh refused to receive their delegation, unless all the others were allowed to visit him too.

The president of the Kenya Indian Congress, S C Gautama, asked the Asian community to observe Sunday, 2nd April, as a day of fast and prayer in sympathy with Makhan Singh.

On 1st April, Gautama wrote to Makhan Singh: 'Your fast for the release of all detainees has stirred the peoples' conscience' but he also implored Makhan Singh to end his fast as there was widespread concern about the danger to his life. The Kenya Central Sikh Council telegraphed Makhan Singh with the same request. Hon. A Jamidar reported that there had been a big response to the fast appeal with about 180,000 people expected to take part. There were some who wanted it to continue for a longer period. And of course there were those within the Asian community who were opposed to both the appeal and to Makhan Singh's ideology.

On 2nd April, KANU's president, James Gichuru, together with Clement Lubembe of the KFL and Tom Mboya returned to Kenya. The *East African Standard* reported that within minutes of leaving the aircraft they were informed of the hunger strike. Mboya was angered by the government's intransigence and

said he would protest to
the governor and planned
to call an emergency
meeting of the KFL to
decide on any further
action. 'Makhan Singh has
my full support,' he
added. 'I am surprised
that the Governor has not
treated it with the urgency
it deserves.' The next day
the secretary of state for
the colonies, Iain
Macleod, touched down
at Eastleigh aerodrome on
his way from Zanzibar to

Clement Lubembe

Aden. He met with delegations from the various Kenyan
political parties. KANU, which had included K P Shah of the
KFP in its delegation, joined the general request for Kenyatta's
release and pleaded for the release of Makhan Singh.

On Monday, 3rd April, following the numerous appeals and
efforts being made for his release, Makhan Singh decided to
end his fast. It had lasted 21 days and the doctor, who had
regularly checked him, now proclaimed his condition to be
'still satisfactory,' although he reportedly had lost eleven
pounds and become very weak and thin. His wife had returned
from India and was with him; his sister, Kulwant Kaur joined
them later. (His family, including his sister at last, had been
given permits to visit him for the entire year.) The *Colonial Times*
of 6th April published articles about him both in English and
Gujerati. The editorial said, 'to keep a man nearly 11 years
under a restriction order in an out-of-the-way place is not only
unreasonable but also callous . . . why is it [the government]
afraid of individuals like Makhan Singh who do their trade
union work in an open manner?' But a letter in the same issue
by Arvind Jamidar, member of the Legco and minister of

Makhan Singh's fast

works, writing in support of another correspondent, declared his own hostility to communists and communism. 'The democratic way of fighting this secular religion is to offer the people a superior faith and ideology with an unmistakable demonstration of its greater effectiveness in the solution of human problems and abatement of human misery,' he argued.

While staying with her husband in Dol Dol, Satwant Kaur fell ill and was operated on in Nanyuki General Hospital. Writing to Makhan Singh in May her father, Tara Singh Mahal, claimed they had no knowledge of Makhan Singh's work and the reasons for his detention. They were only then learning about it on reading articles about him and his hunger strike in the Indian press. He wished him 'best of luck, health and wisdom.' Makhan Singh's extremely private nature, as mentioned earlier by Piyo Rattansi of the *Daily Chronicle*, is again in evidence.

Meanwhile Hindpal, now 24, had become engaged to Joginder, daughter of the Virdi family in Nairobi. Earlier in the year he, together with Sudh Singh, Satwant Kaur, Swarajpal, Inderjeet, his cousin Gurdev and Joginder's brother had travelled in two cars to Maralal to visit his father.[27] Now there being no likelihood of Makhan Singh being released, he drove to Dol Dol with his grandfather, his prospective father and brother-in-law to perform the validation ceremony between the families.

As usual they stopped for refreshments at a furniture shop in Nanyuki. The owner, Mangal Singh, and his wife were close friends of the family and used to host them to and from their visits to see Makhan Singh.

Arthur Ochwada

The Trade Union Congress of Kenya, led by Arthur Ochwada, wrote to Makhan Singh on 12th May. They saluted him and told him 'we have never forgotten your words in 1948 not to divide the workers . . . we have two central organisations as we in the TUC are opposed to . . . the imperialist International Confederation of Free Trade Unions.' They explained that other leaders in the KFL were pro-West, were influenced by the Americans and did not serve the workers. 'We want to be free from any foreign domination, colonial or otherwise,' they asserted. 'We have applied to visit you.' Makhan Singh replied by telegram, 'Thanks letter but regret unable to receive delegation.'

Fred Kubai was released on 27th May. Elijah Masinde, Mbiyu Koinange, Achieng Oneko, Paul Ngei, V. Wokabi and Munyei, though still restricted, were all moved to their home areas.

In mid June, Chanan Singh spoke out in the Legco for the release of Makhan Singh. The Kenya Indian Congress was given permission to visit him, but he refused to receive the delegation. 'I do not desire a situation when one or two delegations are allowed and then others are refused permanently,' contended Makhan Singh wisely and stoically. Five weeks later, the DC informed him that the government had refused to accept his terms regarding the visits.

Makhan Singh received a letter from Tom Mboya written on 8th July. 'Dear Brother Singh, Your father and I meet often and

Tom Mboya's handwritten letter to Makhan Singh

he will confirm to you that I and my colleagues have got you constantly in our minds. Already we have tabled a motion calling for your release which comes up in the Legco next week. On the other hand we are now sure that you shall be free in a few months. You have not suffered for nothing. We are with you till the total liberation of our motherland and the securing of the dignity of labour. Uhuru.'

On 14th August, Jomo Kenyatta was released. Makhan Singh sent him a telegram congratulating him. *Sauti ya Mwafrika* (Voice of the African) of 27th September published a large photograph of Makhan Singh and asked *'Kwa Nini hawajaachilia Makhan Singh – wanafikiri yeye kwa kweli ana nguvu za kutosha kuharibu Kenya nzima siku moja?'* (Why have they not released Makhan Singh yet – do they really think that he has the power to destabilise the whole of Kenya one day?). It termed his continued detention 'oppressive and inhuman'. 'If Makhan Singh were to die in

Sauti ya Mwafrika published a large photograph of Makhan Singh, and termed his continued detention 'oppressive and inhuman'

detention, God would punish all those who had harassed him. The British Government was known for its awareness and wisdom, in this case they should demonstrate this. And if it does so, I assure them that we, together with many other citizens, will march to the Minister of Defence to say "thank you".'

On the same day, *Sauti ya KANU* carried an article headed *'Amepoteza Miaka 12 - ataachiliwa lini?'* (He has lost 12 years – when will he be released?). It drew attention to the pain and suffering this father had undergone and how this had affected his health and eyesight. Could the minister of defence not allow him to spend his remaining years with his son? The article

Makhan Singh at Dol Dol

With wife Satwant Kaur, daughter Inderjeet Kaur and son Swarajpal Singh at DolDol, 1961

pointed out that Makhan Singh's oldest son, Hindpal, was due to get married in December and according to their custom, a father must attend his son's wedding, if he is alive. Makhan Singh, meanwhile wishing to increase his proficiency in the language, had started doing lessons in Kiswahili which appeared regularly in the *Radio Times*.

At the beginning of October seven more restrictees were released: Omolo Agar, Kariuki Chotara, Isaac Gathangu, Mahashon Itote, Babu Kamau, Dedan Mugo and Kamau Wachira. On the 22nd, *Navyug* asked why Makhan Singh was being detained when so many Mau Mau leaders had been freed. 'He has sacrificed everything for Kenya's freedom . . . there is no British justice and African leaders are doing nothing for him except expressing words of sympathy.'

RESTRICTION ORDER REVOKED

And then on 18th October, 1961, without any prior notification, Makhan Singh's restriction order was suddenly revoked.

On the 19th, Arvind Jamidar led a delegation to the chief secretary to plead for his total and unconditional release. Sudh Singh was in the delegation along with S S Patel, Kirpal Singh Sagoo, R B Patel, B S Giani and J S Patel. Jamidar visited Makhan Singh in Dol Dol the next day. 'I have every intention of taking part in the national and trade union movements after my release,' Makhan Singh told him. 'I am still a communist but without being a member of any party.' Jamidar, who had by this time resigned from the Kenya Indian Congress, gave Makhan Singh a detailed account of the factors causing the disagreements between KANU and KADU.

On 22nd October, Makhan Singh left Dol Dol in a government Land-Rover to travel to Nairobi. Hindpal, Swarajpal and

Makhan Singh in Nanyuki with Mr. & Mrs. Mangal Singh and his son, Hindpal

Mohinder Virdi (Joginder's brother) travelled to Dol Dol in their Volkswagen to escort Makhan Singh home. The Volkswagen, however, had to stop for repairs in Nanyuki and hence the sons were not able to witness their father's arrival in Nairobi, after eleven years and two months in detention.[28]

CHAPTER TEN

UHURU AND
BEYOND

During Makhan Singh's long years in detention, remarkable changes had taken place in Kenya. After the banning of the EATUC and the general strike of May 1950, the trade union movement as well as the national movement in Kenya had to work in an atmosphere of intimidation, victimisation and threats of deportation. However, due to the great upsurge generated by the general strike, the movements were able to overcome the difficulties that came in their way.

A major development was the rapid progress of a secret mass organisation, essentially Kikuyu, which had been in existence for some time. The aim of this uhuru-oathing organisation was to unite and mobilise the African people of Kenya in the struggle for independence and began to be popularly known as 'Mau Mau'. Later, when the Mau Mau fighters decided to resort to armed struggle against the colonialists, they called themselves the Kenya Land and Freedom Army. The Kikuyu independent schools were vital centres for mobilisation.[1]

After attacking the unity of Kenya's trade unions by banning their central organisation – the East African Trade Union Congress – the government now aimed to break the workers' unity that was being established in trade unions on a country-wide basis. In July 1950, a bill was introduced in the Legco proposing the formation of wages councils and staff associations but Kenya's trade unions immediately opposed the move. 'Trade unions and nothing but trade unions!' was their slogan.

The government retreated and on 6th October, 1950, F W Carpenter, the acting labour commissioner, stated that the proposed wages councils were not intended to replace the trade unions and then added,

We want our trade unions in Kenya to follow the good example of British trade unions; we absolutely don't desire that they should be led by people like Makhan Singh.

Repression on the one hand and small concessions on the other was an important aspect of colonial policies.

All the trade unions, whose work had been disorganised by the arrests, searches or closing down of their offices, had by this time been able to reorganise themselves. The most affected had been the Labour Trade Union of East Africa and the Transport and Allied Workers Union. Those who helped in the reorganisation included Fred Kubai, Aggrey

J D Kali

Minya, Pio Gama Pinto, A S Rao, Pranlal Sheth, Bildad Kaggia, J J Simon, J D Kali and Kibara Kabutu.[2] Kaggia took over as president, Kubai as vice-president. Kali was the second vice-president and P C Mula became the general secretary.

As soon as the government moved against the EATUC, it collapsed. Why? In their book *Government and Labour in Kenya 1895-1963*, the authors suggest that, 'the Congress was inexperienced and no match for the government . . . . Its most important leader was an Asian [Makhan Singh] who was vulnerable to racial attacks, a fact not overlooked by Mathu, Mbotela and other critics of the Congress. It was not prepared to embark on revolution and it had prepared no plans for going underground. It had developed no bureaucracy – no money, no cells, no cadres or followers, no press or significant overseas support. In the short run it did not matter, but it was no

Aggrey Minya

preparation for a political siege . . . . It was ironical that both KAU and the settlers were suspicious of the EATUC between 1946 and 1952. Other than in the kipande and colour bar issues, Jomo Kenyatta and KAU leaders showed no interest in trade union or labour questions.[3]

The EATUC had collapsed but it had facilitated the rise of these young nationalists and been a training ground for future trade union leaders. Kubai and Kaggia turned more to party politics and incorporated the spirit of the EATUC even though Kenyatta urged Kubai to choose between the trade union and politics. Aggrey Minya, the secretary of the Plantation and Agricultural Workers Union, was more cooperative and two years later became the general secretary of the newly-formed KFRTU.[4]

All the trade unions began intensifying their struggles for increased wages and better conditions of employment. And their officials and members also began taking a more active part in KAU, ostensibly under the leadership of Kenyatta. In 1947 a very militant group headed by very young men emerged. This was called the Forty Group or 'anake a forty'. They were ex-servicemen who had fought either in the Burma forest, India or Madagascar during the Second World War. These men returned home with a lot of experience of the outside world. Soon after their return they found themselves without employment and without land. Yet their European war counterparts had been rewarded for their services with big farms in Kenya as retirement benefits.

In June 1950, Fred Kubai and Bildad Kaggia had taken over the Nairobi branch of KAU as chairman and secretary-general respectively. A Mau Mau Central Committee was formed in Nairobi. This was to co-ordinate Mau Mau activities in the city as well as in the reserves. After the start of the Emergency the Central Committee changed its name to 'War Council'. This became the 'war office' of the whole movement. Contacts were established with Mau Mau fighters in the forests and in the reserves and supplies in the form of guns, clothing, medical supplies and new recruits were passed on to them.[5] The existence and operations of this militant group within KAU were unknown to Kenyatta and the rest of the KAU Committee.

Oginga Odinga describes some of the group's activities: 'Guns were acquired by illegal purchase or stealing; ex-servicemen gave small arms instruction under cover of dynamiting in quarries; the taxi-drivers in Fred Kubai's union were mobilised, black-marketers and prostitutes were enlisted and lines of communication established between the towns and the thick forests of Mount Kenya and the Aberdares where the war between Mau Mau and its opponents was to be fought.'[6]

A meeting of the Domestic and Hotel Workers Union held in Pumwani Memorial Hall on 20th September, 1951, is evidence of the competence and dynamism of the trade union movement at that time. The *East African Standard* reported that 'Five resolutions were passed . . . [the union] claimed over 4,000 members – and they [the resolutions] were to be sent to the Kenya Labour Commissioner' The resolutions criticised the use of the word 'boy' and demanded 'house rent' and 'one month's notice or pay instead of instant dismissal' among others. There were then more than 15,000 members of registered trade unions and 50,000 employees were covered by staff associations.

On 4th November, 1951, KAU held its annual conference in Kaloleni Social Hall. Here its president, Jomo Kenyatta, produced the national flag for Kenya; broad horizontal black, red and green stripes, charged with a shield outlined in yellow, bearing the letters K.A.U. and crossed by a spear and an arrow. He said:

The black represents Africans, the red the blood of

Africans and green the conditions of Africans; land, and the shield, the arrow [and the spear] are weapons to resist our enemies.

The announcement was the sign of the intensification of the national struggle of Kenya's liberation.

During November and December 1951 there were demonstrations in the Fort Hall area by thousands of African women in protest against the compulsory inoculation of cattle against rinderpest. In the same months, hundreds of thousands of signatures were collected on a petition that was presented to the British parliament on the question of Kenya's land. It was backed by tens of thousands signatures in England. The European, Asian and African civil servants expressed their dissatisfaction with the policies of the Kenya government regarding inadequacy of the cost of living allowance and the deteriorating relations between government and civil servants.

On 5th November, a delegation from the ICFTU arrived in the country. The colonial government was keenly watching the attitude of trade unions towards the ICFTU. It had closed all doors for WFTU delegations and banned its publications, but for ICFTU it had opened all doors and was freely allowing all its publications. On 8th January, 1952, the government published a new bill to replace the 1943 Trade Union and Trade Disputes Ordinance. Staff associations, probationary trade unions, literacy in English and cancellation of registration of a trade union were some of the innovations added to the previous bill. It was aimed at killing, or at least weakening, the trade union movement in Kenya.

In January 1952, the demands for the formation of a central organisation of trade unions were stepped up. Makhan Singh, who was under restriction in Lokitaung, had gone on a hunger strike regarding the suppression of the EATUC. The government acquiesced and the KFRTU, made up of seven unions affiliated to the banned EATUC, was established. At a mass meeting in June, the following officials were elected:

Mushegi Karanja (chairman), Aggrey Minya (general secretary) and S Osore (treasurer).

The government was willing to recognise the new workers' body provided that Kubai or Kaggia were not involved in it and provided it had no connection with the Labour Trade Union. Later, after much discussion in Kenya's trade union circles, the KFRTU was affiliated to the

S Osore

ICFTU. Though many trade unionists personally disagreed with the affiliation as it signified a partisan American connection in the cold war, they saw it as an opportunity to secure a better standard of living.

The tempo of the workers' struggles now increased throughout Kenya under the guidance and coordination of the KFRTU and there was an upsurge in the armed struggle being waged by the Mau Mau fighters in the Land and Freedom Army. Several of the trade unionists were also active in the Mau Mau. At 5.00 p. m. on 20th October, 1952, the Governor, Sir Evelyn Baring, signed a proclamation declaring a State of Emergency.[7]

The Emergency was actually planned three or four years earlier to neutralise or liquidate subversive leaders. This was stated in a circular of the Electors' Union dated 7th August, 1952; 183 leaders were arrested and detained.[8] Of these, Jomo Kenyatta, Fred Kubai, Bildad Kaggia, Achieng Oneko, Paul Ngei and Kungu Karumba came to be known as the Kapenguria Six, as they were tried in a school room in the village of Kapenguria, 450 kilometres northwest of Nairobi. They were charged with criminal, rather than political, offences and both the judge and the star witness were heavily compromised. The six were sentenced to seven years rigorous imprisonment, after which they were to be restricted under the deportation ordinance for an indefinite period. Those detained at the commencement of the emergency included many well-known trade union leaders.[9]

Arrests, detentions, relocations, expulsions and victimisations continued throughout the country and were increased further in 1953. But the nationalists remained defiant. On 5th March, the acting president of KAU, F W Odede, installed D N Pritt as an elder (in Desai Memorial Hall) for 'so ably and courageously defending the Kapenguria Six'.[10] KAU was banned on 8th June. In order to strengthen the trade union movement and the national movement as a whole, the KFRTU sought to turn staff associations into trade unions with a view to incorporating them. The Nairobi African Local Government Servants Association took the initiative; Tom Mboya was its secretary.[11]

Tom Mboya was twenty-two years old when the Emergency was declared. He worked in the sanitary department and was an enthusiastic member of the municipal staff association. Outstandingly intelligent, he was a great organiser and could work long hours. He had a fine command of English, spoke several African languages and soon became an orator of repute. KFRTU held its elections on 11th October and Mboya was elected its general secretary. In the same month Field Marshal Dedan Kimathi, on behalf of the Kenya National Defence Council, issued a charter detailing the objectives of the Kenya Land Freedom Army.[12]

Meanwhile, on 24th April, 1954, four days after implementation of the Lyttelton Plan which proposed some constitutional changes, Operation Anvil was launched. This was the biggest sweep of the Emergency when over 35,000 Africans, men and women, were detained. All belonged to the Kikuyu, Embu and Meru tribes, many of them were members of trade unions, and twenty-nine of them were officials of KFRTU.[13] Repressive measures of the colonial regime continued, hundreds of Wakamba railway workers were arrested and on 19th June, Pio Gama Pinto, progressive active leader of the Kenya Indian Congress and editor of the *Daily Chronicle*, was taken into custody and detained.[14] Dread of the implications of African-Asian unity and the notion that Africans were 'ignorant and easily persuaded' were some of the driving forces behind colonial repression in Kenya.

In 1954, the principle of no racial discrimination in the conditions of the civil service was accepted. A Dockworkers union was formed. On 3rd March, 1955, Mombasa dockworkers went on strike and were joined by thousands of other workers. The strike lasted six days and involved 14,400 workers. It was a great victory as the workers had been able to defy the colonial regime and get most of their demands.[15]

In May 1955, the KFRTU changed its name to Kenya Federation of Labour (KFL), the change of name being passed at the annual conference of the KFRTU held on 7th and 8th at Starehe Hall, Nairobi. It was attended by 63 delegates and 10 observers. The eight unions affiliated to the KFRTU were: the Kenya Local Government Workers Union; the E A Federation of Building and Construction Workers Union; the Railway African Union; the Domestic and Hotel Workers Union; the Dock Workers Union; the Tailors, Tent and Sail Makers and Garment Workers Union of Kenya, the Kenya Distributive and Commercial Workers Union and the Typographical Union of Kenya. The Transport and Allied Workers Union, which had not applied for re-affiliation, was allowed to send observers. Officials of the new KFL were president, Hillary Oduol; vice-president, Ben Gituiku; general secretary, Tom Mboya; assistant general secretary, Arthur Ochwada; treasurer, Elijah Odhaimbo David and assistant treasurer, N Marigi. The trustees were S Kweya and D N J Korokoro.[16]

Mboya, as assistant general secretary, called for 'one man one vote guided by the principle of government of the people, by the people and for the people.'[17] The Kenyan government reacted strongly and moved to deregister the KFL. However, as Makhan Singh wrote, 'the unity of Kenya's trade union movement and the solidarity with it from all sections of the international trade union, defeated the attempt by the colonialists to ban the KFL.'[18] In 1956, Mboya met the American Federation of Labour while on a tour of USA and Canada to seek financial help. Whereas before the Emergency union membership stood at 55,000 with adequate funds, the harsh conditions of the last four years had reduced it to 35,000 with irregularly paid dues. In 1953 the KFRTU had five unions affiliated to it, the KFL in 1956 had nine, and the membership was almost totally African.[19] (For a more detailed account read Makhan Singh's paper in Appendix I).

On 21st October, 1956, the Supreme Commander of the Kenya Land Freedom Army, Field Marshal Dedan Kimathi, was captured by the colonial forces. Britain had deployed eleven infantry battalions, 20,000 police and 25,000 Kikuyu loyalists at a cost of 60 million pounds to fight the Mau Mau and their Land Freedom Army. About 700 security forces lost their lives including 63 Europeans and 29 Asians, Mau Mau deaths were estimated to be over 100,000. Fitz de Souza maintains that 2 to 300,000 was a more likely figure.[20] Nearly 80,000 Africans were subjected to 'rehabilitation' while the government made every effort to counter the portrayal of the Land Freedom Army as an organisation for national liberation[21] but it had become patently clear that a political settlement was the only viable solution to the insurgency.

LEAVE IN ORDER TO STAY

The British set out to achieve a peaceful transition to a legally constituted, secure and pro-Western independent Kenya. In the prevailing cold war dimension, the third consideration took on a major significance. A succession of constitutions followed, each of which rapidly proved unworkable. In 1957, the first African MLCs were elected and Oginga Odinga, Tom Mboya and Daniel arap Moi took their seats in the Legco. On 26ᵗʰ June, 1958, Odinga publicly uttered the 'forbidden' name of Jomo Kenyatta and became the torch bearer for Kenyatta's release.

Political parties were formed as fronts for 'multi-racialism'. Europeans and Asians sought a qualitative franchise, the Africans demanded universal suffrage – democratic self-government, one adult one vote and power in the hands of the majority.[22] The KANU was launched on 14ᵗʰ May, 1960, with Jomo Kenyatta (still in detention) as president, James Gichuru as acting president and Oginga Odinga as vice-president. In the following month, the KADU was formed with Ronald Ngala as president, Masinde Muliro as his deputy and Daniel arap Moi as chairman. KADU was an alliance of the small tribes and favoured by the white settlers specifically to counter the Kikuyu-Luo partnership. An election was held in early 1961 when out of the 44 contested seats, KANU won 19 and KADU 11.[23] KANU however refused to form the government until Kenyatta was released so KADU did, with KANU in opposition.

Kenyatta, apart from being central to the problem, now became central to the solution. His continued detention resulted in a decline in investment and a stagnation of the economy. He was released in August 1961 and formally joined KANU in October. The British, who intended to stay on in Kenya, continued their divide and rule tactics. From separating the 'extremists', Kenyatta, Mboya and Odinga, from the 'moderate' Ngala, they moved to splitting the now 'moderate' Mboya from Kenyatta and Odinga and later favoured Kenyatta and Mboya, branding Odinga as the communist.[24]

The neo-colonialists proclaimed that the goals of the independence struggle, namely, Africanization, multi-racialism and nationalism, had been achieved. So why struggle? they argued. The followers of Mau Mau however published their own analysis of historical events, using a working class perspective. Their pamphlet entitled 'The struggle for Kenya's Future' was widely distributed, including at the KANU

Conference held in Nairobi in December, 1961. The context was the two line struggle which was being waged within KANU – for real liberation, land and freedom or for flag independence under neo-colonial control. It's opening statement read: 'The struggle for Kenya's future is being waged today on three distinct though interrelated levels: political, racial and economic. It seems to us that we Africans are being allowed to 'win' in the first two spheres as long as we don't contest the battle being waged on the third, all-important, economic level.'

They outlined the British Master Plan as: 'Carefully relinquish political control to a properly indoctrinated group of the 'right kind' of Africans, i.e. those whose interests are similar to, and comparable with, our own, so that we retain economic control.' In other words: LEAVE IN ORDER TO STAY. The policies of multi-racialism and nationalism were promoted in order to maintain the colonial status quo.[25] Thus already at the eve of Kenya's independence, the struggle between the capitalist-orientated forces and the socialist ideologues had manifested itself.

Early in 1962, a coalition government was formed and this was followed by a second constitutional conference. Odinga was not given a ministerial post and majimbo or federalism was on the agenda. *Majimbo* was the delineation of provinces based on ethnic lines. However, in the elections held in 1963, KANU, after winning a decisive victory, formed the government. Kenyatta became prime minister and appointed, among others, Odinga Minister for Home Affairs and Mboya Minister for Justice and Constitutional Affairs. From his fellow detainees, he made Oneko a minister and Kubai and Kaggia, assistant ministers.

On 12th December, 1963, the flag of Kenya's *uhuru* (freedom) was hoisted. Kenya was now a republic, with Kenyatta as its president. Less than a year later, using a combination of carrots and sticks, Kenyatta got Ngala to dissolve KADU and merge it with KANU, thus ending – for the time being -- the majimbo debate. In January 1964, a mutiny in the army was quickly put down but skirmishes with the Somali secessionists continued for several years. Already the policies of Kenyatta's government, though officially non-aligned, possessed a quite definite tilt towards the west. Nationalist politics matured into ideological politics at independence but this was a brief interlude before the party began to operate on a patron-client basis. It was not long after independence before the internal security apparatus began to be used by the Kenyatta clique against radicals and their 'communist' friends.[26]

The party merger was the turning point in Kenya's political history. The pro-capitalist forces within KADU linked up with their counterparts within KANU and increasingly side-lined those with socialist inclinations. Thus began an ominous saga of intrigue, political patronage and disempowerment of the party with power being centred in the hands of Kenyatta and the civil service. On 24th February, 1965, Pio Gama Pinto, the selfless nationalist and socialist, was gunned down in his driveway in Nairobi. He became independent Kenya's first political martyr. Others followed. On 5th July 1969, Tom Mboya was eliminated and in March 1975, Josiah Mwangi Kariuki was assassinated. Earlier in 1966, Pranlal Sheth, Odinga's close ally, had been deported.

Soon after Pinto's assassination, the left wing lost its parliamentary strength. The Lumumba Institute, an ideological training centre for cadres of local party officials, was closed. People-orientated policy suggestions on land, nationalisation, rewarding of freedom fighters, wealth distribution, international relations and others were frowned upon and a series of organisational and leadership changes in parliament and in the party ensured a bias to the right. A stage-managed party re-organisation conference held in March 1966 left no opportunity for the centre left group to participate in the party hierarchy, and specifically sidelined Odinga.[27]

In April, Odinga, Kenya's stormy petrel, resigned as vice-president. Twenty-eight other parliamentarians, including Kaggia, crossed the floor to sit in opposition. A number of trade union leaders quit KANU in support of Odinga to form the Kenya Peoples Union. In 1969, its leader, Odinga, was detained. The neo-colonial framework was being consolidated and the leading opponents to this grand plan had to be removed. 'While we had the flag and the theoretical power . . . the colonialists and their settler friends still pulled the strings.' This is how Odinga described neo-colonialism.[28]

On the trade union front, in 1962 Mboya was appointed Minister for Labour, his position as general secretary of KFL was taken first by Peter Kibisu and soon after by Clement Lubembe. Dennis Akumu, a militant trade unionist, together with Ochola Mak'Anyengo, Vicky Wachira and others, objecting primarily to KFL's alliance with the ICFTU, formed the Kenya African Workers Congress. Other splinter groups were Kubai's Kenya Trades Union Congress and the Kenya Federation of Progressive Trade Unions.

Between 1964-65, legislation was passed in Parliament effectively making workers' strikes illegal and rendering trade unions ineffective. Kenyatta's hand was now everywhere in the trade union movement, not in order to support the popular workers' demands for better working conditions but so as to promote and protect weak and subservient leadership[29]. In 1965, the government intervened, ostensibly to create an independent umbrella for the trade unions and the Central Organisation for Trade Unions (COTU) was created with Clement Lubembe as its first general secretary, followed by Dennis Akumu in 1969. However, as the President had a direct role in approving the leading officials, COTU actually served to bring the unions under the strict supervision of the Ministry of Labour. The new Kenyan government had opted for curtailment rather than abolition of the trade unions. Its main object was to prevent the unions from becoming a quasi-political party in opposition to the authorities. It restrained the bargaining powers of the individual unions and emphasised their industrial aspects and in government, industrial relations were docketed as 'social services.' Welfare capitalism was preferred to socialism. Kenyatta had never preached revolution in his long political career, having been conservative in both politics as well as in labour.

Left-leaning ideology was articulated in parliament by Odinga and Kaggia and others such as Tom Okelo-Odongo, Z M Anyeini, K N Gichoya and G F Oduya. Increasingly, the government used 'anti-communism' to resist change, the left was out-manoeuvred and ideological issues ceased to be the concern of politics.[30]

It was to this unfolding scenario that Makhan Singh returned on 22nd October, 1961, after spending eleven and a half years in detention. Kenya's Asian community having always stood for a common electoral roll, now faced political irrelevance. The majority of them had no interest in politics and were fearful about the impact of African self-rule on their trading prospects. In their struggle to gain upward mobility, the Africans sought to take over the space occupied by the Asians and racism became a useful tool to exploit. In the years to come, no distinction was made between what the Asians had earned through merit and what they had been given through political patronage. The few who had wholeheartedly supported the African national cause were ideologically to the left or progressive and, like their African comrades, fell out of favour with the Kenyatta regime. Pio Gama Pinto, Fitz de Souza, Haroon Ahmed, Ambu Patel, A R Kapila, Chanan Singh, Pranlal Sheth, J M Desai and Makhan Singh were some of the outstanding nationalists of this minority community who felt the brunt of political disfavour during this first decade of uhuru.

CHAPTER ELEVEN

AFTER RELEASE
1961-1973

Makhan Singh was driven to his home in Park Road, Nairobi, late in the evening of 22nd October, 1961. The family had been informed of his release a week earlier and it had been in all the newspapers. The entire Park Road had been closed to traffic and was packed with a multitude of Sikhs, other Asians and Africans. The crowd was in a joyous mood as they celebrated the return of their hero and a late afternoon shower of rain blessed the occasion. Government ministers and colleagues from the EAINC joined relatives and friends to welcome him back. They garlanded Makhan Singh and carried him shoulder high to his home. Before entering the house he addressed the crowd and answered questions from the journalists. Ambu Patel, diminutive but portly and wearing his usual corduroy jacket, took many photographs that day and later presented an album to the family.

The *East African Standard* headed its report the next day with 'First Duty to Kenya – Makhan Singh' and a photograph of the man garlanded, giving the clenched fist salute and being carried shoulder-high to his home. When asked by a reporter if he was still a communist, Makhan Singh replied

I was a Communist and I am a Communist, but my first duty is to Kenya and East Africa.

Sudh Singh shouted in a vain attempt to try and stop his son from making the statement. When asked if he thought East Africa should join the communist bloc after independence, Makhan Singh replied:

As far as I am concerned neutrality or non-alignment should be the policy of our national movement . . . whether one is a Communist, a non-Communist or an anti-Communist, the first duty is to work for unity in the struggle against imperialism and colonialism.

Makhan Singh had anticipated this question and had

discussed the matter with Hindpal at Maralal. The son had agreed that his father should state his true beliefs. Makhan Singh had then made two requests of Hindpal.

If you cannot support me, please do not oppose me, and when I die, place a red cloth over me.

He clarified that he had never hidden his communist views from the government or the public and denied that he had ever used 'underhand methods' in his political activities. He said he had every intention of continuing his trade union and political activities. 'The slogan for Kenya should be: Unity of all freedom-loving people under the leadership of Jomo Kenyatta,' he declared.

The *Daily Nation* printed the same photograph but its headline was more sensational. 'I Am Still a Red, Declares Makhan Singh.' It highlighted his comments on the differences between KANU and KADU: 'As a result of the collapse of the Maralal spirit new dangers have arisen in Kenya which, if not rectified now, could lead to another Congo. It is the duty of all citizens, regardless of race and party differences, to try and solve the current problems and get Kenya out of the present danger. The deadlock at the Government House constitutional talks came because the two parties had not made adequate preparations . . . . If the talks had been held under the chairmanship of Mr. Kenyatta, or vice president Oginga Odinga, the situation would be much different. Leaders should place the interest of the country first.' Asked whether he would join the Kenya Indian Congress or the Kenya Freedom Party he answered, 'I would like to study the situation first.'

Among the leaders waiting to welcome him home were Ronald Ngala, the Leader of Government Business, Masinde Muliro, the Minister of Commerce, R A Oneko, Fitz de Souza, Chanan Singh, K P Shah, A B Patel, Arvind Jamidar, S G Amin, Haroon Ahmed and K S Sagoo. A few days later Jomo Kenyatta and Oginga Odinga visited him at his home.

Achieng Oneko states that detention did not change Makhan Singh, unlike many of his comrades.

After our release many of us became diplomatic to the extent of lying but Makhan Singh after his release became even harder. We retreated into our own political parties as the special branch was following us and we did not want to go to prison again. We asked for government positions and were given them but Makhan Singh never asked for himself or for the workers. He failed to influence others to follow in his footsteps. "Do not expect me to speak at your rallies," he would say.

So they labeled him a leftist and isolated him, it was easy. The workers began to withdraw from him. Jaramogi and Makhan Singh got on very well as both called a spade a spade.

The Federation of Progressive Trade Unions in Zanzibar congratulated Makhan Singh and sent him copies of its bulletin, *The Worker*. Makhan Singh replied saying, 'My release is a victory for the trade union movement in East Africa.' Later he met with the general secretary of the union.

In addition to the local messages of welcome and congratulations on his release were the greetings and compliments from abroad. The Kisan Sabha (Peasant Party) of Jalhandar said: 'You have spent your lifetime fighting for the working classes, only you could meet the challenges that have faced you . . . freedom for Kenya is important for the people of Asia, Africa and Latin America – we eagerly await the final victory and we will support your struggle. You have undergone many trials and tribulations and now again you have taken up the struggle. This is admirable. We have sent you the January issue of *Kisan Lehr* – a monthly of the Kisan Movement since 1958 – and will send you past issues. Do inform us on how we can support you further.' From Southall in England the *US Kirti* wrote, so did the Communist Party of

Nawan Zamana of Jullunder (India)

India. Replying to Harkishan Surjeet, the general secretary of the Communist Party of India, Makhan Singh said, 'I am happy that the Indian masses are with us. I send my brotherly greetings to all peace-loving and freedom-loving peoples.'

On 26th November, in special Diwali issues, *Nawan Zamana* (a daily paper of the Indian communist party), *Milap* and *Partap* (newspapers in Delhi and Jalhandar), all published photographs of Makhan Singh's triumphant return and his meeting with various leaders including Kenyatta and Odinga, with captions giving a brief history of his detention. Rajwant Singh, a reporter with *Nawan Zamana*, wrote that after his own release from detention in India in 1945, he had rushed to a conference in the Punjab specifically to meet Makhan Singh. 'I wanted to learn how ordinary people in Africa live . . . I found him to be a very simple man, about 30 years of age, in pyjama and *kameez* [long shirt] who greeted us very politely . . . ' To the *Nawan Zamana* Makhan Singh's response was, 'Your unity has brought me back to you.'

Makhan Singh had begun to comment on national issues. *Uhuru wa Mwafrika* (The African Freedom) in its issue of 10th November declared *'Mbeberu Ni Adui Ya Kenyatta'* (the Colonialists are enemies of Kenyatta), and quoted Ngei, Makhan and Kibaki. This was regarding a visit to Britain when League of Empire loyalists had thrown eggs at Kenyatta's car and Kenya's leaders were outraged.

Makhan Singh, accompanied by Hindpal, Ambu Patel and a member of the Koinange family, visited the grave of ex-Senior Chief Koinange in Banana Hill, a suburb of Nairobi. At the time of Makhan Singh's trial in Nyeri in 1950, Chief Koinange had travelled there to give evidence in support of Makhan Singh. The Chief had become a bitter enemy of the colonialists and as a result had been detained, first in Marsabit and then in Kabarnet. He had been released only when he was close to death. Then more than eighty years of age, he died a few weeks after reaching his home in Kiambaa.

JOINS KENYA FREEDOM PARTY

On the 27th, Makhan Singh was part of a Kenya Freedom Party delegation that met with Reginald Maudling, the colonial secretary at Government House, Nairobi. He urged the British government not to delay Kenya's independence as 'a dangerous situation would arise.' He explained,

When I was under restriction I had to depend only on that I read in the newspapers about the outside situation. But since my release I have been able to personally study the situation and the conclusion I have reached is that any delay in our independence can have dire consequences . . . . Our independence can be granted without any interim constitutional measures as the British government did so in the case of British Somaliland when its independence was granted last year within a few weeks without any so-called preparations . . . . The date on which we must have our complete independence is 1st February 1962 – the date jointly decided by KANU and KADU.

He further warned the colonial secretary that the policy of the British and Kenya governments to back KADU and to keep KANU, the majority party, out of power was extremely dangerous and should be renounced. The colonial secretary remarked that KANU itself had declined to enter the government. 'That was on account of Government's refusal to release Jomo Kenyatta,' Makhan Singh retorted.

Early in December Makhan Singh made the following press statement: 'I have today decided to join the Kenya Freedom Party, the Party which is the closest possible alliance with Kenya's premier national organisation – Kenya African National Union – which has already played

Uhuru wa Mwafrika article, 1961

→ FAMILY REUNITED →
Makhan Singh with sister, Kulwant Kaur

✦ HERO OF THE PEOPLE ✦
Welcoming crowd along Park Road

MAKHAN SINGH

RELEASE
FROM
DETENTION

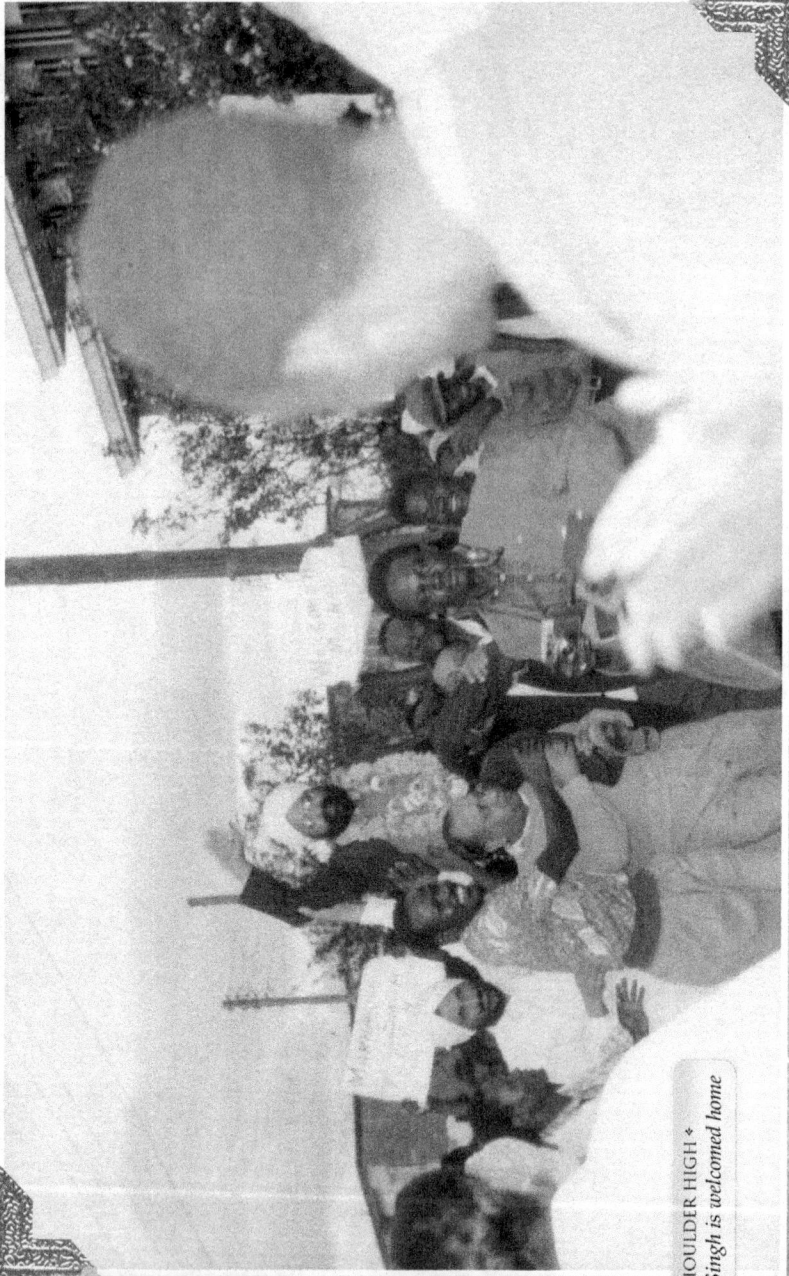

◆ SHOULDER HIGH ◆
Makhan Singh is welcomed home

+ SIGNS OF SUPPORT +
Joyous crowd with placards

✦ TOGETHER AGAIN ✦

Front Row: 1. Sudh Singh 2. Dennis Pritt 4. Makhan Singh 5. Satwant Kaur
Back Row: 1. Inderjeet Kaur 2. Hindpal 3. Joginder Kaur

✦ AT A RALLY AGAIN! ✦
M Chokwe, K P Shah, Gen. Chitia, Makhan Singh at Kaloleni Hall

✦ HOMECOMING ✦
Crowd at Park Road

Makhan Singh and Jaramogi Oginga Odinga

✦ JOYOUS MOMENT ✦
Achieng Oneko, Jomo Kenyatta and Makhan Singh

Kulwant Kaur, Makhan Singh, Satwant Kaur, Achieng Oneko, Jomo Kenyatta, Sudh Singh and Jaramogi Oginga Odinga

Achieng Oneko, Jomo Kenyatta, Makhan Singh and Jaramogi Oginga Odinga

Achhroo Kapila, Makhan Singh, Dennis Pritt and Sudh Singh

✦ HAPPY REUNION ✦

Front Row: 1. Jaramogi Oginga Odinga 2. Chaman Lal 4. Makhan Singh
Back Row: 1. K P Shah 2. Goval Sinoh 4. Chanan Singh 5. Narivan Singh 6. Fitz D'Souza 7. Sudh Singh

At the grave of Chief Koinange

a significant role in the building up of our national unity. With the acceptance of Kanu's leadership and presidentship by the father of the nation, Jomo Kenyatta, it is now the first and foremost duty of all freedom loving people of Kenya – Africans, Asians, Europeans and Arabs and others – to fully support and join Kanu or its closest ally the KFP. Only this way the national unity of all freedom loving people under the leadership of Jomo Kenyatta can be built to achieve our aim of independence now – Uhuru Sasa [Freedom Now].

'I have further decided to resume my active part in Kenya's central trade union organisation – Kenya Federation of Labour. I shall do my best in appealing to all workers and employers – Africans, Asians, Europeans, Arabs and others – to join the unions affiliated to KFL which function in their respective trades, industries or places of employment in order to strengthen the trade union movement and for protection of their interests as workers and employers. A strong national movement and a powerful trade union movement can be the chief mainstay of our society and good human relations for the present and the future.'

Makhan Singh's first choice of a political party was KANU, but it had not opened its doors to non-Africans by then. Welcoming him into the Kenya Freedom Party, the secretary K P Shah said,

We know that as an individual he is a Communist and I am very strongly anti-Communist, but when he has accepted the aims and objects of the Kenya Freedom Party . . . I do not see why we cannot work together for the common cause – independence at the earliest.

On 8th December, Makhan Singh sent a telegram to Mwalimu Julius Nyerere congratulating him on 'attainment of complete independence for Tanzania.' He also visited the British Council to thank the staff for 'continuously sending me books from your library during my restriction.'

He addressed two public functions that month. One was a cocktail party organised by the Kenya Freedom Party to welcome back Appa Saheb Pant, now India's ambassador to Indonesia. In 1954, he had been India's first ambassador to Kenya and had unceremoniously been made to leave the country by the colonial government. Makhan Singh gave the welcoming address and a brief history of Kenya's independence struggle since 1948. He mentioned the hesitation by some Asian leaders to support the movement for independence.

African leadership, and for that matter any leadership, judges by actions and not words. The Kenya Freedom Party had been formed in 1960 to reverse this negative trend among the Asians and it had largely succeeded . . . There is a need to establish unity both at the top and the bottom through KANU, KFP and KFL.

TRANSPORT AND ALLIED WORKERS UNION
MKUTANO! MKUTANO! MKUTANO!

SHABAHA YETU  UMOJA NI NGUV

Majabali hawa watakuwa kwenye mwito wa kwanza wa T.A.W.U. katika SOLIDARITY tarehe 16-12-61 kuanzia saa nane hadi saa 12 kwa minajili ya kumshangilia Bwana Fred Kubai baada ya urudi kwa chama chake.

Pamoja naye kutakuwa na ma'ingwa:—

1. Bw. Makhan Singh aliyekuwa Mwanzilishi wa E.A.T.U.C.
2. Bw. Kaggia mmoja wa viongozi wa vyama vya wafanyIkazi wa zamani.
3. Mhe. Mboya, M.L.C. aliye katibu Mkuu wa K.F.L. pia atahutubia mkutano huu.
4. Bw. Lubembe mwandishi mdogo wa K.F.L.

FRED KUBAI

Mhe. MBOYA

Wasemaji wengine.

1. Francis Muteti Mwenye Rais wa T.A.W.U. Kenya.
2. B. Nyaga   Rais mdogo.
3. Kahuthu Kamau Rais mdogo.
4. Washington Malemo Mwandishi mkuu wa T.A.W.U.
5. Margaret Wanj'ru wa H.Q.
6. Walter Osadho mwenyekiti wa tawi la Nairobi.
7. J. N. Chege Mwandishi wa tawi la Nairobi.
8. Maina Macharia.

Na wengine kwa ruhusa ya mwenye kiti.

B. M. KAGGIA

Kuingia mlangoni kutakua Sh. 1/- tu, kwa kila mtu, kwenye mkutano huu kutauzwa badge za mchango wa kusaidia njaa iliyoletwa na mafuriko ya maji.

MAKHAN SINGH

WASHINTON E. MALEMO,
Mwandishi Mkuu wa T.A.W.U.,
Kenya.

Transport & Allied Workers Union solidarity poster

The other public function was a meeting called by the Transport and Allied Workers Union on 16th December to officially welcome back their secretary general, Fred Kubai, who had finally been released from detention on 27th May of that year, five months before Makhan Singh had been released. Posters announcing the meeting were distributed all over the city and carried photographs of Fred Kubai, Tom Mboya, Bildad Kaggia and Makhan Singh.

Four main speakers addressed the meeting, Makhan Singh, Kaggia, Mboya and Lubembe in that order. The entrance fee was one shilling. Badges were sold in order to raise money to provide food to the people affected by the floods that had inundated vast areas of Kenya that year. On 10th, Makhan Singh had been given a license by the district commissioner to hold a procession from Park Road to the Sikh Ramgharia Hall via Ngara Road, Swamp Road, Government Road, River Road and Race Course Road to express solidarity with the flood victims.

On the same day of the meeting called by the Transport and Allied Workers Union, Makhan Singh's elder son, Hindpal and his nephew, Gurdev Singh, both 24 years old, were married. The brides were Joginder Virdi and Mohinder Sokhi respectively; the double wedding took place in the E A Ramgharia Board gurdwara off Nairobi's Racecourse Road. Harbajan Singh Mahal, Hindpal's maternal uncle, travelled by air from India to attend the wedding and was curious to know from Makhan Singh 'how far you have progressed in rehabilitating yourself in the changed new circumstances.'

On 27th December, Makhan Singh celebrated his 48th birthday. That very day Sudh Singh went away on a brief safari leaving a rather curt note for him. 'I am going and

Sudh Singh's note in Gurumukhi

shall be back on 2nd January. Do not follow me or try to find me.' Clearly there was strife and tension between him and his father, almost certainly due to Makhan Singh's refusal to make any ideological compromises, not even for public consumption. Sudh Singh, who must have hoped for a respite from years of single-handed struggle to keep the family financially afloat, must have been bitterly disappointed by Makhan Singh's apparent lack of concern for family matters. Normally stolid and avuncular, his abrupt departure was not typical, although he had in the past often complained about his 'unworldly' son.[1]

To sum up the old year and celebrate the new, on the 30th Makhan Singh sent a telegram to Harkishan Singh Surjeet, general secretary of the Communist Party of India. It read: 'Fraternal greetings and good wishes to Communists and other freedom loving people, trade unionists and peace fighters in India and all over the world. Today here (in Kenya) all freedom loving people and trade unionists, African, Asians, Europeans and others of all thoughts and creeds are working shoulder to shoulder and are going forward in the struggle.'

He also sent an identical New Year message to the *East African Standard*, the *Daily Nation* and the *Times of India*. 'All the people of Kenya should unite to make this New Year our Uhuru Year, achieving our complete independence in the first half of 1962 and consolidating it in the second half. Imperialists must be faced with a strong united nationalism in the form of a strong united KANU under the leadership of Jomo Kenyatta and supported by all others who have the interest of a genuinely free Kenya at heart.'

A fortnight later the *Times of India* announced the death of Ajoy Ghosh, general secretary of the Communist Party of India, a close compatriot of the revolutionary, Bhagat Singh. Makhan Singh's message to the chairman of the Party in Delhi was: 'His death has caused a great loss not only to the Communist Party of India and the world communist movement but also to the struggle of the colonial people for complete liberation from imperialism, colonialism and neo-colonialism.'

To Sant Inder Singh of Patiala, leader of the Namdari Sikhs, he wrote: 'I remember meeting you and would like to meet with you when I come to India . . . whatever I have contributed to the working class I have been inspired by Sikh history, the Akali movement and national, socialist and communist movements . . . . Although I am not a Namdari, I am inspired by the sacrifices made by them.[2]

CORRESPONDENCE
WITH A COMRADE

Makhan Singh maintained a regular correspondence with his old friend and trade union comrade, Gopal Singh, who had taken charge of the LTUEA when Makhan Singh had been arrested and detained in India. Makhan Singh's letter to Gopal Singh written in January 1962 said, 'I have read both your letters and burnt the first one as per your instructions . . . I cannot fulfil your request as my conscience does not allow it. Please excuse me . . . regarding the question 'do I dye my beard?' ask Swaran who took the photography. But no, it is not my policy to dye my beard.'[3]

The 1962 photographs show Makhan Singh's beard as jet black. Mehraam Yaar, the poet, remembers it as 'completely white' when he met him in 1966.[4] His daughter Inderjeet says her father never dyed his beard. It is possible then that the stress and disappointments of those intervening years had taken their toll. At the end of 1961, Gopal Singh, a Ghadrite himself, had requested Makhan Singh to record the history of the Kenyan Ghadr Party, Makhan Singh wrote back on 31st January 1962, 'I think, the history of the Party should be written after Kenya gains its independence. Let Comrade Sainsra know about it.' (Gurcharan Singh Sainsra was the official historian of the Ghadr Party).

In another letter, Gopal Singh congratulated him on the birth of his grandson – Hindpal's wife had just delivered -- and asked about the political situation and the date of the next elections. 'Britain is delaying the freedom but it will have to give it . . . Teja Singh Swatanter has emerged from the underground . . . In India members of the Communist Party were arrested because of their support to the Movement for the Betterment Levy for the Peasants . . . China has attacked India.' Makhan Singh replied, saying that the political situation was favourable, that elections would be held in May and freedom would be given at the end of the year.

In a letter dated 10th April, 1963, he informed Gopal Singh that he had been given a permanent residency certificate together with a passport as citizen of Kenya. He was overjoyed. 'Now that I have the right to return to Kenya I hope to travel to India and meet old comrades,' he wrote. 'But alas I won't be able to see Arjan Singh Garhgajj, my old colleague in *Jang-e-Azadi*. I feel so sad on his untimely and sudden death. A few days ago I wrote a letter of condolence to Avatar Singh Malhotra, the Punjab Secretary of the Communist Party of India.'

Gopal Singh wrote a full-page article in *Nawa Zamana* of 7th June regarding Kenya's progress to self-government and freedom and the role of Jomo Kenyatta, the Mau Mau and Makhan Singh. A large photograph of Kenyatta, garlanded and cheering, adorned the page. Gopal Singh and Makhan Singh did not meet again after the latter was detained in 1950, as he returned to India in 1957 and died there in 1969.

Tom Mboya and Pamela Odede were married on 20th January, 1962. Makhan Singh and his wife attended the wedding and a week later they attended the 12th anniversary celebration of the Republic Day of India which was graced by H E the Governor and Lady Renison.

Friends had requested Mboya to find Makhan Singh a position in the labour movement, but there were those in the

Invitation to the twelfth anniversary of India's independence, 1962

movement who resisted his participation, as they felt threatened by his superior organisational skills and, given his communist leanings, were wary of upsetting their western donors. He was advised to tone down his socialist fervour and for a few years he did so. He was given a job and an office as director of information in the trade union movement but he soon resigned from it. It was a sinecure with no power and really a ploy to keep him out of the public domain.[5]

Makhan Singh had re-joined the family's Punjab Printing Press, still run by his father, now 70 years old, as an employee. By accepting employment he was able to qualify for membership of the Printing and Kindred Trade Union which was affiliated to the Kenya Federation of Labour. In April of the following year, he was elected as the assistant general secretary of the Typographical Union.

FATE OF
ASIAN CIVIL SERVANTS

❋

Mid-February, 1962, Makhan Singh received a booklet entitled *A Tragedy – A History of the Forgotten Men*, published on behalf of the E A High Commission Asian Staff Association, the E A Railways and Harbours Asian Union (Kenya) and the Asian Postal Union (Kenya). It was a handout designed to give members of the press and public information about the 'sad and disheartening plight' of the Asian civil servants. These civil servants, termed 'non-designated', were recruited locally unlike the European (and a handful of token Asian) 'designated officers' who belonged to His Majesty's Overseas Civil Service. The Asians, however, considered themselves to be non-indigenous and expatriate as they were employed on overseas leave terms and were assured by the British government that 'their interests would not be overlooked.'

Exactly two years earlier, in view of the impending political changes, they, together with their colleagues in Tanganyika and Uganda, had made representations to the colonial secretary for fair and equitable treatment in the matter of compensation for loss of career due to premature retirement, guarantees of their superannuation rights and an option to retire at the time of the change of employer. A cat and mouse game was played with them, until eventually, after much correspondence and many meetings in East Africa and Britain, while getting a pension guarantee, they were denied the right to opt for retirement and all the accompanying benefits. The Asian civil servants termed this 'a niggardly offer' and felt betrayed.

Worse still, they were shocked to learn that the Kenyan government had endeavoured to wreck their efforts to achieve their aims. In the early period of the transition to independence, the government was anxious to retain the services of these civil servants. But in a press handout the Kenyan government issued on 16th January, 1962, it declared its

The 1962 protests by hundreds of 'forgotten men' with their wives and children

intention of rejecting the proposal 'that all non-designated overseas officers should be permitted to opt to retire at the time of independence.' It stated that it 'has not been accepted as it is considered that these officers are local employees of the Government of Kenya and that when Kenya becomes self-governing they will not be subjected to a change of employer as is the case with the designated officers; any fears they may have for the future are not substantially different from those of other persons of all races outside the public service.'

Between 30th April and 2nd February, 1962, hundreds of the 'forgotten men' with their wives and children from all over East Africa staged protest marches and sit-ins in Nairobi.

Makhan Singh appears to have kept his distance from this struggle. On 19th September, when speaking at a Kenya Freedom Party function, he indicated his disapproval of the demand for compensation made by the Asian civil servants. He asked:

What will be the reaction of the African people when they hear that the Asian civil servants are asking for compensation?

Fitz de Souza, then a member of the Legco and deputy speaker, was of the same opinion and, in a meeting with the Kenya Asian civil servants, urged them to demonstrate their loyalty and withdraw their demands. They refused. Soon after, Duncan Ndegwa, secretary to the cabinet and head of the civil service, issued a circular informing all Asian civil servants, citizen and non-citizen, that they were to be dismissed and reemployed on new terms. De Souza and Joseph Murumbi appealed to Kenyatta and the circular was withdrawn but the decision that no non-African would be appointed to the post of permanent secretary remained. In February 1963, Fitz de Souza together with K P Shah, pleaded for abolition of racial discrimination in Kenya's civil service. In hindsight, he is glad that his earlier advice to the Asian civil servants had been rejected by them as by 1964, almost all of the posts held by Asian civil servants were Africanised and they were forced to emigrate. The older ones returned to the Indian sub-continent, the younger ones to the UK and Canada but as their pension funds were transferred to Britain, the emigrants were well financed in their new countries of settlement.[6]

ANTI-ASIAN PARANOIA
※

Anti-Asian sentiments were being manifested in the top echelons of government and Makhan Singh was not the only victim. The *Daily Nation* and *Taifa Leo* of 16th March published a photograph of Ambu Patel, the Nairobi bookbinder and nationalist, garlanding Harry Thuku accompanied by Mrs Thuku.

The accompanying article read: 'Ambulal Patel is a Nairobi bookbinder who for years has demonstrated the most amazing devotion to the person of Jomo Kenyatta, whom he had frequently likened to the great Indian leader, Mahatma Gandhi.

Ambu Patel garlanding Harry Thuku, with Mrs. Thuku looking on

'For years, while Mr. Kenyatta languished in detention and restriction, Mr. Patel devoted himself to the task of getting together a staggeringly complete collection of photographs of his hero, from his earliest

Harry Thuku and Ambu Patel in 1962

years on, to compiling details for a biography, and to organising petitions for his release. Mr. Patel also bec[a]me something of a second father to Mr. Kenyatta's eldest daughter, Margaret, whom he employed in his bookbindery. When Mr. Kenyatta was finally freed last year, Mr. Patel produced a book full of eulogies for his hero, entitled 'Jomo The Great' and attached himself to the Kenyatta entourage as a sort of 'court photographer'.

'But of late, it would seem, relations between master and disciple have cooled off somewhat, And now Mr. Patel has turned his attentions to an even earlier African nationalist leader, Harry Thuku, who was restricted for nine years from 1922 to 1931, and who is now a successful coffee farmer in his native Kiambu District.

'My picture shows Mr. Patel garlanding Mr. Thuku on the occasion of the 40th anniversary of his arrest, the day before yesterday, while Mrs Thuku looks on. Said Mr. Patel later, 'Mr. Kenyatta has rebuked me for paying so much attention to Mr. Thuku, but I told him Mr. Thuku started the struggle for uhuru in 1922 and is therefore a very important man.'

In a letter to the *Daily Nation*, Ambu Patel took strong exception to its description of him as a 'court photographer'. 'I take occasional snaps as a free-lance pictorial news collector in order to satisfy my hobby and have never taken any post as a 'court photographer,' he wrote. 'My relations with Kenyatta are the same today as they have been in the past. Any indication of

---

KENYA FREEDOM PARTY

PUBLIC MEETING

A public meeting will be held at 4.00 p.m. on SATURDAY, 16th June, 1962, in Nairobi South (B) area, opposite the Government Asian Primary School.

Subject:- Present Political Situation.

Speakers:- M/s. Chanan Singh, F. R. S. De Souza, A. Rauf, Makhan Singh and P. G. Pinto.

Noble Stationery Mart, Nairobi.

A public meeting of the Kenya Freedom Party which Makhan Singh attended and addressed

---

cooling off of the relations suggests some discord in our contact which is entirely false and unfounded.'[7]

Makhan Singh did not ever directly refer to any racial discrimination being perpetrated by black Kenyans. At a public meeting held by the Kenya Freedom Party in Nairobi, on 16th June, 1962, he spoke of the London agreement and reminded the audience that while progress had been made, independence had not been achieved. He listed the main tasks ahead as defeating the forces of disruption and disunity, strengthening KANU and joining the trade union movement. Other speakers were Chanan Singh, Bildad Kaggia, Achieng Oneko, Fitz de Souza, I T Inamdar, S K Anjarwalla, Haroon Ahmed, K P Shah, Jaswant Singh and Pio Gama Pinto. In recognition of Makhan Singh's role as an educationist, the Eastleigh Primary School invited him to its annual prize day on 12th April. Hon. Humphrey Slade, MLC, Speaker of the Legco, presided over it.

ODINGA AND MBOYA DIFFER

The differences between Odinga and Mboya, both from the Luo community, were escalating. In May Odinga came under heavy fire from forces within and outside KANU for having allegedly accepted funds from communist sources. Makhan Singh's notes of 1962 addressed this issue. 'Our national movement, and for that matter all other movements in Kenya, should be self-reliant. We should depend on our own resources, based on the patriotism and sacrifices of our people. Any dependence upon foreign money and resources whether Western, Eastern or Neutralist, can only weaken our national and other movements and would make a mockery of their independence of their policy of neutralism. This does not mean that when Kenya becomes free it would refuse brotherly help which is without strings from other countries. Let us not fritter away our energies in making false allegations against each other.'

The *Daily Nation* of 31st May published the following letter by him: 'I should like to say, in my personal capacity, that the public controversy about and between the two prominent nationalist leaders, Tom Mboya and Oginga Odinga, should immediately stop in the interests of Kenya and our national movement. Both Tom Mboya and Oginga Odinga have played an important part in our national struggle. When the colonialists were doing their utmost to prevent the success of our struggle, both of them and millions of others kept the flag of African nationalism flying in Kenya. Not only that. Both of them in their own ways took it abroad. Tom Mboya took the flag to the Western capitalist and other countries and Oginga Odinga took it to the Eastern socialist and other countries. It required great courage to do so. Both of them have used to the best of their capacity the resources of the West and the East for national, educational and trade union development of Kenya.'

However, Makhan Singh's intention of steering a middle course in the widening ideological gap became increasingly untenable. On one occasion, Tom Mboya confronted Makhan Singh and asked him to state whether he was with him or with Odinga. Makhan Singh started by saying, 'That is a difficult question,' whereupon Mboya retorted, 'If it is difficult then you are not with us.'[8] Makhan Singh would, no doubt, have liked to play the role of arbitrator and conciliator but, in the absence of any systematic theoretical debate, the contending viewpoints degenerated into a power struggle. It was a situation which Makhan Singh was neither familiar with, nor in which he would wish to participate. He therefore turned his attention more to the realm of trade unionism; a world he had developed and directed and about which he thought he was more knowledgeable.

P J Muinde was the chairman and Makhan Singh a member of the general council of the KFL. A committee comprised of 'brothers' Makhan Singh (chairman), Ochola Mak'Anyengo, Herman Oduor, Mutuku Ngei, Apolo Owiti, A W Karumba and Juma Boy prepared a memorandum to present to the constitutional conference to be held in February. The memorandum was a progressive and lucid statement detailing workers' needs and rights. The committee also appointed a legislative committee to 'collect, consolidate and produce material that will become actual proposals to amend the [labour] legislation.'

Speaking in Kiswahili at a KFL meeting on 12th May, Makhan Singh said:

We have gathered together to pay tribute to Comrade Tom Mboya for his sterling work. In the 50s the colonialists resorted to a direct attack on the trade union and national movements. Hundreds of leaders of both movements were put behind bars. It was at that time that Tom took over. He and his colleagues, with their hard work, patience and persistence defeated all the efforts of the rulers and employers to weaken our movement. Under their leadership, our movement went forward from strength to strength so much so that at present our movement is one of the strongest in the whole of Africa.

His handwritten draft for the speech was much longer and included a brief history of the trade union movement since the 1920s and linked it to the struggles against the kipande system, forced labour, low wages, landlessness and the colonial system as a whole. It mentioned the participation of 'Africans, Indians and some progressive Europeans' and support from the British Trade Union Congress, the national movement of India and other labour and national movements. Destruction of the colonialists' dream of establishing another South Africa or Southern Rhodesia in Kenya and the deportation of Harry Thuku were also included.

The omission of these topics in the final speech and its brevity suggests some form of censorship, self imposed or otherwise. Had Makhan Singh at the meeting sensed that the post independent trade unionists had not only no interest in the earlier history of labour, but actually wanted to obliterate it? He may even have been advised not to dwell on past history. It is not uncommon in present-day Kenya to read statements which ascribe the birth of trade unionism to the founding of the KFL in 1952.

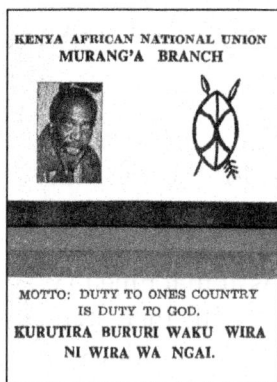

KENYA AFRICAN NATIONAL UNION
MURANG'A BRANCH

MOTTO: DUTY TO ONES COUNTRY
IS DUTY TO GOD.
KURUTIRA BURURI WAKU WIRA
NI WIRA WA NGAI.

KANU Membership Card, 1962

In June 1962, Makhan Singh led negotiations between the KFL and the ministry of Labour. He sent greetings and good wishes to the editor of KFL's *Mfanyi Kazi*, saying it was the workers' own paper and the organ of their united voice. (The weekly newspaper had been established on 30th May, 1962, with West German and US funding but did not do well.)

The Hon. Mbiyu Koinange, on 6th June, presented Makhan Singh with a membership card of the Kenya African

National Union, Muranga Branch, costing one shilling. Interestingly KANU was still officially restricted to Africans only, so had Koinange decided to breach the rules? It was not till 22nd October that year that membership of the party was opened to all citizens of Kenya.

Taifa Leo's issue of 9th July showed a photograph of Makhan Singh in close conversation with a garlanded Waruhiu Itote. Itote, a Mau Mau fighter better known as 'General China', was attending a function in his honour held in Pumwani Hall and organised by the Nyeri Mathera KANU branch. Julius Kiano and Mwai Kibaki attended too, and General China was referred to as 'General wa Uhuru.'

CHAI KWA CHINA

MAMIA ya Waafrika waliohudhuria karamu kuu ambayo ilikuwa imetayarishwa na KANU tawi la Mathera Nyeri, katika Pumwani Hall jana, ya kumkaribisha Bw. Waruhiu Itote, aliyekuwa akijiita "General China," wakati wa hali ya hatari, waliambiwa kwamba "General China" ni "Generali wa Uhuru."
Bw. Joseph Mathenge aliyekuwa Mjumbe wa Nyeri, aliambia umati huo kwamba Wazungu wanaita "General China" kama "General" wa kiliita lakini "sisi tunamjua kama General wa uhuru."
Akiendelea Bw. Mathenge alidai kwamba Kenya itakapopata uhuru General China hatasahauliwa.
Viongozi wengine kama Dr. Kiano na Bw. Mwai Kibaki walihudhuria karamu hiyo.
● Picha ya juu yamwonyesha Bw. W. Itote akiongea na Bw. Makhan Singh.

In close conversation with General China

At a public meeting of the Kenya Freedom Party, Makhan Singh, together with Chanan Singh, Fitz de Souza, A Rauf and Pio Gama Pinto spoke on 'The Present Political Situation in Kenya.' In its memorandum to the government's Economic Commission the Party stated 'there should be no immediate retrenchment in the lower grades of [the civil] service as this, we feel, will aggravate the unemployment situation. Any retrenchment contemplated should be in the higher ranks of the service where replacement of the present incumbents could be effected by recruitment, training and employment of local people.'

Describing Fred Kubai's Sauti ya Mwafrika as 'the voice of our national movement,' he sent them this message: 'Our

Jomo Kenyatta, Ambu Patel and Makhan Singh

national independence would mean prosperity for all and not for the few. It would mean democracy of the people and not of the rich. It would mean working in unity through the national movement (KANU), through the trade union movement (KFL), through the cooperative movement and through other types of peoples' organisations. In short our national independence would mean full development of our land and industry without the exploitation of man by man.'

Ambu Patel sent a circular to Makhan Singh in July informing him of the 'Exhibition of Historical Documents of Kenya' he planned to hold between 20th and 31st October, in the Patel Brotherhood Hall in Duke Street, (Now Ronald Ngala Street). Subjects to be covered included 'Illustrated life story of Freedom fighters for Kenya, Portraits of Personalities, Arts and Crafts of Kenya, Paintings and Bronze statues and important

Press Cuttings and Literature, concerning the History of Kenya Newspapers . . . ' He requested Makhan Singh's assistance in compiling the material, his advice and suggestions as well as his own autobiography. The exhibition opened on schedule and was closed officially by Jomo Kenyatta.

Ambu Patel had spent 15 of his 17 years in Kenya collecting these materials on the political history of Kenya and on Mau Mau and had dedicated himself to the political support of Kenyatta. Shortly thereafter, a group of KANU youth wingers ransacked Ambu Patel's shop, London Book Binders, in Duke Street. Although Patel pleaded with them in Gikuyu, they stole many of his exhibition documents and photographs, in addition to his work equipment. He was 'hurt and disillusioned that the Africans can do this to me when I am always working for them.'

He then told the *Nation* reporter of a series of thefts and indignities starting when he used to mail large food parcels on behalf of the Asian community to Kenyatta at Maralal; three times while doing so, his bicycle, which he had parked outside the post office, was stolen. But most humiliating of all was the laughter with which some KANU leaders greeted his complaints about the theft of his exhibition materials. 'I know how they feel about me now,' he said. 'They are not interested in history, only in themselves.' Not that he got much joy from the Asian community either. Narain Singh Toofan and others vilified him for portraying the Mau Mau movement as 'heroic.' Why did he not show, in his exhibition, the horrendous atrocities perpetrated by their so-called generals, they asked? 'I hang my head in shame at the very thought that an Asian has stooped to glorify Mau Mau,' wrote another. In the early 1950s, Patel had distributed, nationally and internationally, copies of the proceedings of the Kapenguria Trial. He had organised printing facilities opposite Parklands Police Station and at Mathare Valley for Mau Mau publications and was the organising secretary of the 'Release Jomo Kenyatta and Other Detainees' committee.[9] In spite of these criticisms, Ambu Patel soldiered on, saying he had faith in the masses and would work for them.[10]

Makhan Singh did not attend functions organised by the Kenya Indian Congress or community-centred ones of the Sikh Students' Federation or other Sikh associations. This appears to have been deliberate as he did not even respond to the invitations or offer any excuses whereas normally he was extremely prompt and particular about the smallest detail. (For instance, in that same month he wrote to the inspector of police at Dol Dol just to tell him that he had found the books he had earlier reported as missing.) He seems to have been anxious to portray a national, rather than communal or religious, identity.

He did maintain his international contacts. In June, he apologised to the International Labour Organisation in Geneva for the delay in settling his account of fifteen shillings in 1961 when he was in detention. (On 29th September, 1959, when in detention, he had thanked the ILO for 'so long allowing me your publications on credit and for having been very helpful in so many ways'). He further requested a reduction in their subscription prices for the *International Labour Review* and their official bulletin. 'These are beyond my means,' he wrote. He also requested mimeographed documents concerning worker education (India and Singapore), the printing and training centre (Malaya), the draft labour code (Sudan), manpower and labour administration (Libya), the national employment service (Indonesia) and co-operative development (West Indies).

In August, he attended a Kenya Education Fund Fete held in the playground of his old school, the Duke of Gloucester. The *Daily Nation* published a short history of the Duke of Gloucester School, reminding the reader that it had been founded as a railway educational centre in 1906, then became the Government Indian School, and then in 1955, after the presentation of the 'city' charter by the Duke of Gloucester in 1950, took his name. The article listed Sir Eboo Pirbhai, Allah Ditta Qureshi, Mohammed Sadiq, Narain Singh, S K Khanna and K K Sethi who were mentioned as some of the prominent citizens who had studied there. Makhan Singh's name was not included. The Asian community was distancing itself from Makhan Singh in keeping with the government's policy towards him.

In September, while he ignored an invitation from the Kenya Central Sikh Council to a reception for the Indian High Commissioner, he did attend the opening ceremony of the E A Ramgharia Sikh Dispensary, built for all races, in Eastleigh and donated a quilt and utensils to a home for aged Asian destitutes. It was situated in Pangani, Nairobi and Davinder Lamba, its secretary and the present director of the Mazingira Institute, wrote to thank him and invited him to visit the home.

On the night of 8th October, 1962, he was present at the Uganda Peoples' Independence celebrations in Kaloleni Hall on Doonholm Road. On the 20th he received a flyer announcing a Kenyatta Day Rally to 'commemorate the arrest of Jomo Kenyatta ten years earlier.' The flyer was signed by John Keen (KANU National Organising Secretary) and K P Shah (KFP Hon. Secretary).

He went to a party at the Pumwani Memorial Hall to welcome Nahashon Hiuhu, a prime mover of the Independence Schools (conducted in the 1940s to counter the pro-colonial educational institutions), and one at Bahati Community Centre for Ndirangu Kabebe. Both were ex-detainees. He was unable to go to the one held by the Igana Friendly Society as he was tied up in a KFP General Council Meeting and was in Mombasa when the KANU Bahati sub-branch held a tea-party to honour its party leaders. As mentioned earlier, KANU opened its membership to non-Africans on 22nd October, 1962. However it appears that the rank and file considered Makhan Singh to be a member of KANU even prior to that date.

On the 31st, KANU held a public meeting to explain the constitutional developments, registration of voters and the forthcoming general elections. The official speakers were Tom

Mboya, John Keen, K P Shah, Chanan Singh and Zafrud-Deen. Makhan Singh attended and spoke in Kiswahili in support of Kenyatta's conciliatory approach to the Indo-China frontier dispute and the latter's telegrams to Nehru and Chou en Lai.

On the trade union front, in August, officials of more than seven trade unions had issued a press statement attacking a speech made by Mboya, as Minister of Economic Planning, at the City Stadium. They challenged him to come out openly and tell everyone what programme he had to elevate employment and the present economical position of the country. They demanded clarification of the 'imperialists' and 'insects' he had mentioned. Who were they? 'Where does Mr. Kenyatta expect to get the money to develop this country?' they asked. 'We hope not from the East, as he is against imperialist money.'

They accused Mboya of undemocratically calling a meeting without the cooperation of the Nairobi KANU branch and called upon the government ministers, regardless of their party affiliation, to surrender half their salaries to help provide jobs for the unemployed. As a foreboding of present-day concerns, they said, 'We have had enough of the disunity in Kenya politics; we do not want any more of this tribal game.'

Makhan Singh issued a counter press statement stating that 'there is absolutely no necessity or justification for the statement of a few trade unionists issued in their personal and not representative capacity.' He claimed that it was 'undemocratic elements of Kanu's Nairobi branch [who] had tried to prevent him [Kenyatta] from addressing the people of Nairobi.' Kenyatta's condemnation of foreign money did not include the friendly aid of the West and the East which was given without strings attached. 'He was rightly condemning the financing and corrupting of individuals, which is done for perpetuating colonialist and imperialist domination in new forms.' He ended with a call for unity.

The prospect of independence brought forth some of the contradictions that until then had lain dormant in Kenyan society. The *Daily Nation* in its issue on 17th September published an article headlined, 'Line Up Or Get Out' Asians Told'. It was reporting on the statement made by the KANU vice-president, Oginga Odinga, at a meeting of the Kenya Freedom Party in Kisumu which read 'Kenya Asians must line up behind African nationalists otherwise there is no future for them in an independent Kenya'. Odinga accused the Asians of being followers of KADU while pretending to support KANU. He told the meeting that he had been promised support from the Soviet Union but the Western powers were trying to force Kenya not to be friendly with the Eastern bloc 'because they want to keep us here as slaves for years after Kenya's independence.'

In a rejoinder the chairman of the KFP categorically clarified that at no time had Odinga said 'line up or get out,' and termed the *Daily Nation*'s article a 'gross prevarication.' Odinga did express grave concern at the reports of Kisumu Asians' alleged financial assistance to KADU but also asserted that 'Asians were as much a part of this country as the Africans.' He further spoke of the 'lack of adequate manpower resources, the great potential of industrial development in the Nyanza province and his cordial relations with many Asian traders.' He also affirmed he was neither anti-British nor anti-American.

AFRICA FOR AFRICANS

With the prospect of uhuru assured, Kenya's Africans moved to take greater control of their destiny, not just in the political field but, more importantly, in the economic sphere. Having been severely disadvantaged with their lands grabbed and their earning power eroded, they were understandably impatient to redress the imbalances created by the colonialists. The commanding heights of the economy were, and remained, firmly entrenched in the hands of the British Government and its imperialist allies. There was no way the upcoming Africans could dislodge the economic giants; the granting of uhuru was about the transfer of political power, not economic control.

The path of least resistance then was to go for the smaller Asian enterprises and the *dukawalla* became a target of envy and appropriation. The slogan of 'Africa for the Africans' took root and in the years ahead, the wave of anti-Asian hysteria swelled. The age-old colonial policy of 'divide and rule', when the Asians were continuously portrayed as the obstacle to African advance, now took on an added meaning for the African hopefuls. But as so often happens, the basic concerns were soon swamped in a general animosity directed against the entire Asian community. The positive contribution of Asian patriots in the fight for independence was forgotten and the negative aspects of the community were increasingly emphasised. The more responsible and patriotic leaders, Asian and African, struggled to deflect these divisive and sectarian tendencies.

On 19th September, 1962, Makhan Singh addressed a KFP meeting.

Other speakers included Joe Murumbi, Bildad Kaggia, Fitz de Souza, Mwai Kibaki, Chanan Singh, Krishan Gautama and Haroon Ahmed. He said:

In an independent Kenya no past prejudices will be tolerated. We Asians must participate in the process of nation-building, particularly the national movement . . . . In Africa, Africans should be supreme and hence the slogan "Africa for Africans." During the Indian Independence struggle even we shouted "India for Indians, Quit India." . . . Those who have acquired land by exploitation will lose it. Their property will be taken away. Compensation? That will depend on their attitudes. Those who have exploited will be thrown into the sea.

Makhan Singh here was speaking about extremely sensitive and controversial issues. He seemed oblivious of the full import of the ideals he was expressing. The demand for 'Land' had been at the centre of the struggle for independence, with the advent of uhuru, it became a subject of major controversy and corruption, a conflict that remains unresolved even in this year of 2005.

Makhan Singh asked.

To them it only means one thing – that we would like British rule to continue. What will be the reaction of the African people when they hear that the Asian civil servants are asking for compensation?' And that if that is not possible we would not like to serve the African government . . . . KADU is a tribal organisation. The Kenya Freedom Party is a part of KANU.

He then called for KANU to open its doors to other nationals and lambasted the press for not publishing the KFP's statement on the subject of Africanisation and compensation.

With independence on the horizon, a spate of verbal attacks on the Kenyan Asian community was unleashed. KADU made no bones about its dislike for the Asians. On 19th October, 1961, after two Asian members of the Legco had crossed the floor to join KANU, Daniel arap Moi threatened to expel all Asians from East Africa. The Hon. Arvind Jamidar declared that he was willing to continue working with Moi as a colleague but in spite of that, Ronald Ngala, (the KADU chairman), together with Paul Ngei, Liyayi, Wilson Mukuna, Kenneth Matiba and others maintained their anti-Asian rhetoric.

KANU tried to be more diplomatic, but even so, John Keen, its national organising secretary also hurled abuse at the Asians. When some of the Asian parliamentarians voiced a mild protest, he said 'I don't care a damn about these Shahs, Patels and Lals.' (The last was in reference to Diwan Chaman Lal who had been sent by Nehru, prime minister of India, in

Addressing a trade union meeting in 1962

1952 to defend the Kapenguria Six.) He went on to threaten the Asian community throughout East Africa with wholesale ruin if they voted for KADU. In February 1963, Keen proposed a boycott of Asian shops. 'I am starting a new movement,' he announced. *'Sisi kwa sisi* – Africans should buy only from Africans.' In reference to the purchase of 9,000 acres of farmland near Nakuru by a prominent Asian, he said, 'They will buy up the whole of Kenya and there will be no place for Africans.' However the next day Jomo Kenyatta disassociated himself from the statement and Keen hastily claimed that he had been misunderstood.

Tom Mboya, Joseph Murumbi and Mbiyu Koinange publicly deplored their KANU colleague's statements but Mboya played a double game as he then went on to criticise Asians and Europeans for not attending public rallies. In July 1962, he announced that all non-Africans in Kenya had to become citizens or leave. As a guest of honour at the 27th session of the Kenya Indian Congress he stated that 'cocktail' integration was not enough and that integration in independent Kenya had to lead to intermarriage.

MAKHAN SINGH SPEECH COMES UNDER FIRE

N S Toofan (a pen name meaning 'Storm' in Punjabi), a *Daily Nation* correspondent and editor of the *Sunday Post*, wrote a scathing attack on Makhan Singh in the 22nd September issue. 'The most ominous speeches and statements so far made by the most intransigent African leaders cannot collectively prove as injurious to the interests of the local Asian community as the shots fired by the self-professed Communist, Makhan Singh,' he wrote, under the heading 'Makhan Singh's Speech Comes Under Fire.' 'Due to his unique past position as an Asian creator of a largely African mass movement, Makhan Singh still retains an emotional place in the minds of many people,' he admitted, and then went on to state that 'Makhan Singh is instinctively bound to be closer to Oginga Odinga.' He particularly reprimanded him for his support of the Mau Mau 'before a people who are supposed to honour the creed of non-violence'.

'Would Makhan Singh care to explain what he means by the term 'exploitation'?' One of the notorious ways whereby Communists seek to make headway in every country in Africa is by pointing to all European and of course Asian-owned properties as examples of 'exploitation'. They resolutely refuse to see that the very creation of these properties, of a type that never existed previously, is tangible and permanent proof of the development of the country and its people . . . but for the Asians the movement for independence would have taken many more years to find its initiative. By originally inspiring it

Navyug's article on Makhan Singh

in South Africa and then in Kenya, it was the Asians who started the real struggle to liberate the entire continent of Africa.' He counted on the 'Asian political and commercial leaders to denounce Makhan Singh.' But his concluding paragraph contradicted much of his diatribe. 'But perhaps the saddest thing of all about Makhan Singh's speech is not that he said the sort of things we should have expected from him, but that he was loudly and repeatedly applauded by his Asian audience.'

An editorial, in the Gujerati tabloid, *Navyug*, on the other hand, supported some of Makhan Singh's views, though not all. 'We do not agree with his politics but we always fought for his freedom,' it said. 'Makhan Singh says we should fight injustice but who will decide who is unjust . . . he says Africa is for the Africans . . .' The editor concluded that 'such irresponsible and non-cooperative statements do not help anybody.'

Navyug published Makhan Singh's reply on the 29th. He claimed that the report was completely distorted and had missed the main theme of his speech which was the policy of 'Africanisation' and that it should be supported in the interests of national unity. 'I spoke as a citizen and therefore did not at any time use the words "We Asians" or "We Indians", he asserted. 'I clearly stated that African meant one who was resident of and loyal to Africa; and how it was necessary for all of us to actively participate in the national movement and in the process of nation-building . . . . I also mentioned those who had "miles and miles and miles of land," and the mention of "throwing into the sea" in the metaphorical sense was in connection with those who in free Kenya would continue their active opposition to the national movement and national reconstruction . . . . Further I said that people of non-African origin who belonged to and were loyal to Africa and Kenya should consider themselves Africans.'

The editor's note read, 'We are surprised that Mr. Makhan Singh has found out five days after the publication of the story that our reporters (repeat reporters) had distorted the report of his speech. The reporters who covered the meeting have, in fact, been congratulated by the officials of the Kenya Freedom Party for their fair and accurate reporting.'

KANU ADMITS NON-AFRICANS

On 22nd October, 1962, KANU opened its membership to non-Africans and Makhan Singh was the first to join. The Nairobi branch, situated in Nandhra Building on Jeevanjee Street (now Mfangamano Street), gave him a receipt for his membership card no 226.

Douglas Rogers was the second one. Rogers was the editor of *Pan Africa*, a bi-monthly paper which reviewed pan-African affairs and was published in Nairobi. Pio Gama Pinto was the director and secretary of the Pan African press which he had established and which also published *Nyanza Times* in Dholuo and *Sauti ya Mwafrika* in Kiswahili, both weeklies. It is interesting that the first two non-Africans to join KANU subscribed to Marxist ideology.

In December, Makhan Singh wrote to Kenyatta as President of KANU: 'Dear Mzee, I hereby apply for my selection as a

Rogers, Koinange, Kenyatta and Makhan Singh

KANU candidate to contest one of the Nairobi seats for the Lower House in the forthcoming elections.' In the 14th April, 1963, issue of *Taifa Leo* Kenyatta requested Asian and European supporters of KANU to be patient. 'Even if we are unable to nominate you for the Lower House or KANU Branch seats, we will, where possible, appoint you in special posts.' Makhan Singh, who had requested nomination to the Lower House, was not selected.

Following the opening of membership in KANU to non-Africans, the Kenya Freedom Party announced its impending dissolution. The Kenya Indian Congress had already amended its constitution which had as one of its objectives: 'to protect and further the political rights of the Indian community in Kenya.' This was changed to 'further the economic and social rights,' and the issue of 'political rights' was deleted. The decision was announced by the president-elect, S G Amin, at the 27th session of the Congress in July, 1962.

S G Amin

The amendment was arrived at after long, and often heated, debates both in committee and open session. S P Vaid, a Nairobi delegate, termed the change 'premature and dangerous.'

In September 1961, a trade dispute had arisen in the E A Railways & Harbours, when 23 Asian locomotive drivers, clerks and footplate staff had claimed that promotions were being effected on a racial basis. 'Africans and Asians have a higher standard of education and have outclassed their European counterparts,' they had said. 'Further, young Europeans were being recruited as so-called 'experienced expatriates' to supersede them to higher grades.' The Railway Asian Union had appealed to K P Shah of the KFP who in turn wrote to the Ministry of Commerce and Industry and the E A Railways & Harbours.

Makhan Singh met with J S Sagoo, the Railway Asian Union representative, in December 1961 and advised him to

make your position clear about the Railway African Union demands for higher wages and the possibility of strike action.

The Minister for Labour, Mr. Mboya, speaking at the meeting yesterday between the Federation of Kenya Employers' representatives (on the right) and the Kenya Federation of Labour (left) on the subject of an Industrial Relations Charter. On Mr. Mboya's right is the Industrial Relations Officer, Mr. R. A. J. Domerell, and on his left

Industrial Relations Charter meeting

K P Shah had requested Sagoo to negotiate with the KFL and the Railway African Union regarding the procedure for entry into the latter union. Shah advised the Railway Asian Union that

the best and permanent solution will, of course, be to have a non-racial union – there is need for a complete understanding between you and the African Union.

On 9th January, 1962, a Mr Ottenyo of the Railway African Union met with Makhan Singh and informed him that

the Executive Committee has decided to open the doors and the issue of joint representation is on the agenda.

In spite of this, the memorandum of agreement published in July by the Industrial Relations Machinery of the E A Railways

& Harbours retained the individual European, Asian and African unions in the three territories. Meanwhile, the Ministry of Commerce and Industry informed Shah that 'no discrimination is exercised against Asians and Africans in selection, appointment and promotion.'

TRADE UNION MATTERS

Seventy-seven members attended a special general meeting of the KFL held on 29th April, 1962. It was reported that 'Brother Makhan Singh stated that since World War II started, it was in 1937 that the colonial government introduced the trade union law. But now, because we have our own government, we should remove all the colonial rules which are hindering the workers' progress.' Makhan Singh then proposed that a committee should be appointed to go into the existing regulations and recommend those that need to be amended. According to him it would take only a week to go through the law books. Makhan Singh was appointed to chair a committee of six.

The KFL also selected Makhan Singh to chair its legislation committee 'to collect, consolidate and produce material that will become the actual proposals to amend labour legislation.' After amending several drafts and revisions, on 16th May he submitted a typed memorandum to Peter Kibisu, the acting general secretary of the KFL. A trade union leaders' conference was held on 26th May under the auspices of the KFL. Presidents and general secretaries (or, as per Makhan Singh's suggestion, their representatives) of all the organisations affiliated to the KFL attended. Makhan Singh was proposed as chairman but he declined in favour of Peter Kibisu.

Item number two on the agenda read 'Trade Union Legislation – Report of the Legislation Committee, Document

No 1.' There was a lengthy and somewhat heated exchange of views between those who wanted the report discussed and those who refused to deliberate on it until they had studied it. There were calls of 'we must adhere to the agenda' versus 'we cannot discuss anything here unless agreed to in principal.' Ultimately the item was deferred to the next meeting.

AFRICANISATION

Two of the resolutions passed at the conference were: 1) Present ministers in the Coalition Government must be asked to serve their country with a normal salary instead of earning enormous salaries which do not differentiate them from colonial ministers. 2) The present policy of 'Localisation' be changed to one of 'Africanisation'. The term 'Africanisation' had first been introduced by the KADU chairman, Ronald Ngala in 1961 when he was the first African minister for labour. The term itself is ambiguous as the designation 'African' can be used racially or geographically and therefore may or may not include non-black citizens. Ngala clearly was implying preference to black Kenyans.

Regarding the issue of disputes in the unions, Makhan Singh suggested that an advisory committee be formed within KFL to solve the problems. In his address to the conference, the newly appointed chairman, Peter Kibisu cautioned the workers. 'The economic situation is grim, . . . in the past economic activity was dictated from the UK or New Delhi, now we have our own leaders therefore the right to strike must be the result of exhaustion of all available machinery . . . can we hold out on strikes with an economic depression, or with a labour market much in excess of demand?' he asked.

On 4th June, the Plantation Workers' Union invited Makhan Singh to be one of the speakers at a public meeting of all

workers in the tea industry. The meeting was to be held at
Kericho stadium on 8th July. Makhan Singh replied
immediately, saying that he had no objection to accepting.
However, five days later, he wrote again saying that it would be
more appropriate if they sent the invitation through the
organising committee or general secretary of the KFL.

On 6th June, Makhan Singh attended a meeting with Tom
Mboya who was then Minister for Labour. Mboya complained
about the wave of strikes and stressed that the machinery of
negotiation must be fully exhausted. He explained that he had
instituted the right to hire and fire to 'help the unions out of a
dilemma,' and felt a lack of appreciation. He said:

Government is with you but appeals to you to recognise
the national interest . . . the impact of strikes is the worst
possible publicity.

Makhan Singh made rough notes which included the
following comments: 'Present strikes are not political . . . every
one of them has a real grievance at the bottom. Attitude of some
of the employers is provocative . . . . No victimisation of any
one for his trade union activities . . . if the employers don't
change the workers would have to compel them to change . . .
Government is of our own national leaders, they understand
our problems better than anyone else . . . the Labour minister
can work hand in hand and make the employers change their
ways . . . labour are not going to continue with old injustices
indefinitely . . . we are not going to be blackmailed or allow the
Government minister to be blackmailed . . . we wish to fully
share in the fruits of labour.'

Makhan Singh did recognise that there was 'a tremendous
task of economic reconstruction and development ahead,' but
he maintained that the trade union movement was the 'motive
power of the country.' He stated that both the trade unions and
the employers associations had to act responsibly and rejected
the 'big brother type of authoritarianism and a populace cowed

in obedience.'

The following day, Makhan Singh attended a KFL executive committee meeting and was selected to be part of a joint KFL/ Federation of Kenya Employers delegation to meet with the Minister of Labour. The ten KFL members were all union officials; Makhan Singh represented the Printing & Kindred Trades Workers Union (P&KTWU). The points to be raised were: 1) Clarification of Hon. T Mboya's statements which were being misused by the employers. 2) Maintaining good industrial relations. 3) Informing Brother Tom that he was misused by the employers to exploit the workers.

On the 15th he participated in a meeting called by the management board of the Federation of Kenya Employers. Present were Mboya, the Commissioner of Lands, the Industrial Relations Officer, Clement Lumembe, O O Mak'Anyengo, Apolo Owiti and Babu Kamau. Makhan Singh also served on the Joint Disputes Commission of the KFL and Federation of Kenya Employers. Other KFL members on that Commission were Lumembe, Mak'Anyengo, Avulala and Morris Mulema. The terms of reference were to settle outstanding claims consequent on the award of the Arbitration Tribunal. However meetings of the Commission were adjourned several times owing to members of one or the other organisation being absent. Makhan Singh attended consistently. On 28th June it was recorded that the Commission could not continue sitting without an agreement on the terms of reference.

Makhan Singh, however, was able to facilitate the resolution of several disputes. He chaired a meeting between the Domestic and Hotel Workers Union and Z R Block, owner of the Norfolk Hotel, their agreement being signed on 22nd June. The next month Zimmerman Ltd met with the Kenya Shoe and Leatherworkers Union. The follow-up meetings were adjourned several times owing to non-attendance of the commission members but on the 23rd the matter was finalised. In August, he facilitated negotiations between the Kenya

Distributive and Commercial Workers Union and the Education Supply Association Bookshop.

Makhan Singh was more than willing to share his wide-ranging expertise in labour movement matters with the relevant authorities. On one occasion, when the government planned to draft an industrial charter, it included him in its deliberations.

At a tripartite meeting of Government, KFL and the Federation of Kenya Employers held on 3rd and 5th July, the main task was one of drafting an Industrial Relations Charter. Makhan Singh had been appointed to the drafting team which met for two months. The agenda included the correction of past and present injustices and discriminations, a policy of full employment and the replacement of the word 'localisation' with 'Africanisation.' Regarding the last, Makhan Singh requested a definition of 'African.' The KFL stated that its policy of 'Africanisation' was to be accompanied by 'a total elimination of the policy and results of discrimination operated in the past against the inhabitants of this part of Africa, without any discrimination of race, colour or creed.'

Makhan Singh's personal notes indicate his support for the demand as he felt that 'Africanisation' would lead to 'unity of thinking and practice as citizens and not as racial or communal entities, assure unity of purpose not only in Kenya but also in East Africa and Africa as a whole and help us in our struggle against every form of oppression and exploitation and for raising the standards of living, keeping always in view the African masses.'

The Charter of Industrial Relations was signed on 15th October by Tom Mboya as Minister of Labour, Peter Kibisu on behalf of the KFL and Sir Collin Campbell on behalf of the Federation of Kenya Employers. Makhan Singh had made his own draft in which he quoted from International Labour Organisation documents on similar charters in Venezuela and Belgium. One clause was that the Charter should 'provide for the right to discuss the distribution of the profits of the

James Karebe

undertaking and the duty of the management to submit regular reports . . . particularly on [its] plans for the distribution of profits.' This clause, however, was not included in the final document.

This is hardly surprising given that the real significance of the charter was its non-revolutionary symbolism and the triumph of Mboya's views on industrial relations in Kenya. Makhan Singh was advocating radical, pro-people ideas which were in direct opposition to the capitalistic ambitions of the emergent elite and their imperialist supporters.

On the other hand, in order to undermine the wide-spread popularity of Kubai's Kenya Trades Unions Congress, the KFL did pass a radically left-wing policy statement advocating sweeping nationalisation and collective farming. But at the same time, Kenyatta put pressure on Kubai to relinquish his leadership of the union in return for a KANU nomination for a parliamentary seat.[11]

In August, Makhan Singh had participated in a 'Demarcation Conference' held by the KFL 'to examine and later recommend on the best principles of demarcation of powers and procedures for the purposes of union organising and collective bargaining.' Together with James Karebe and Peter Kibisu, he had been selected to serve on the preparatory committee of, and be responsible for, the forthcoming conference.

At the conference Mak'Anyengo stated:

> political instability has caused economic chaos in Kenya. Government must be made to realise now that the KFL is just as important as the Chambers of Commerce and must be fully consulted in all economic matters . . .

Why did the coalition government not consult the KFL on the land settlement scheme?

Makhan Singh gave a brief history of the trade union movement from the 1920s to the current time. He claimed

A trade unionist is also a politician, and in some respects, a better politician. KANU, KADU and KFL have their positive and negative points . . . imperialist strategy is to divide and rule. The task of a national movement is to defeat imperialist strategy and to do this we need unity. By forming a new party the KFL will divide and weaken itself. It will only play into the hands of reactionary employees and the imperialists . . . trade union pioneers and veterans such as Fred Kubai and other sincere trade unionists should be back in the fold of KFL and its affiliated unions . . . we should play a cementing role and build unity. KANU factional fights should end.

Meanwhile, a KFL report made references to 'organisational rivalries in the trade unions. The Trade Union Congress and the Coast General Workers Union were classified as 'rogue unions' formed by KADU politicians after independence. The Trade Union Congress was later deregistered. It was claimed that the secretary of this union had visited communist countries that were pouring a lot of money into Kenya in order to weaken the KFL. It was decided that 'we need ICFTU aid urgently' and in accordance with this the treasurer of the KFL was designated to manage the ICFTU area office.

In a speech given to a KFL annual general meeting on 1st December, the president of the KFL, P J Muinde, referred to 'very detrimental happenings in the trade union movement' and stated that he was against tribal and ideological groupings. (In his copy of the speech Makhan Singh underlined the above sentences.) Muinde continued

Political independence is meaningless and valueless if we do not have economic independence . . . . Kenya appears to be in a turmoil created by over ambitious leaders . . . some people have claimed that the KFL appears to be pro-West and against the East. May I repeat here again that the KFL has never nor ever will it support any power bloc, be it western or eastern, but will always support those who adhere to democratic principles which grant the right to free expression of opinions and deeds . . . . We are in the ICFTU through mutual consent - considerable amount of money has been received by individuals from Eastern countries . . . for organising trade unions on tribal or political basis. Unity is our only hope, the other alternative is 'divide and die'.

Morris Mulema, the KFL national general secretary and official of the Kenya Electrical Trade Workers Union, gave statistics of workers as 529,386 Africans, 37,821 Asians and 22,184 Europeans; of the total of 589,391 workers employed in Kenya, 49% were organised in 30 unions. He said vehemently,

In the last few months the KFL has been faced with a complete total war from all corners.

MAKHAN SINGH EXPELLED FROM PRINTERS & KINDRED TRADES WORKERS UNION

On 2nd June, the employees of the *East African Standard* and Boyds Ltd (a printing firm) had gone on strike. Their negotiations for a wage increase since the year before had

Wilson Mukuna being welcomed

deadlocked. The Printers & Kindred Trades Workers Union had then called a general strike in which Makhan Singh, its assistant general secretary, had participated. The demands had been an increase in wages, reinstatement of sacked workers and recognition of the union. A notice had been sent to all newspaper vendors and Asian shopkeepers who sold newspapers to stop doing so. In the *Daily Nation* of 6th June, P&KTWU's general secretary was quoted as saying, 'the strike in the printing and kindred trades in Nairobi is continuing with full force. No negotiations between the union and the Federation of Master Printers of East Africa have taken place . . . we are in 1962 but the employers' attitude is of 1922.' On 6th July it was announced that union demands had been met and an agreement had been reached between the union and the employers. Incidentally, the newspaper strike had caused the shutting down of *Mfanyi Kazi*, KFL's newly-launched weekly paper. It also meant that Makhan Singh and his workmates went on strike at Sudh Singh's press. On the 7th, as a gesture of regional trade union solidarity, the president of the Mauritius Confederation of Free Trade Unions addressed the Nairobi branch of P&KTWU.

The central committee of P&KTWU then met in Mombasa from 5th to 8th August. It consisted of Joel Omoka (president),

Makhan Singh (assistant general secretary), Mafime (treasurer) and members J D Patel, Akbar Hussein, Joseph Nyaga, and Mama Annie. (Wilson Mukuna, the general secretary, was out of the country.) The programme included speeches by J D Akumu, general secretary of the Dockworkers Union, and Makhan Singh who recorded the minutes and drafted the memoranda, reports and agreements.

Makhan Singh also conducted a training workshop for P&KTWU. Speaking in both English and Kiswahili he stressed the importance of unity and how it could be achieved and maintained. He stressed the need for a proper understanding of the tasks ahead and the absolutely essential raising of educational and literacy standards. He laid plans for classes to give theoretical and practical training in teaching the fundamentals of union organising and how to cope with the new ways of negotiation, conciliation, voluntary arbitration and, as a last resort, strike action. He described in detail the ambivalent attitudes and policies of the government and the

Printers & Kindred Trades Workers Union

Addressing a public meeting in Mombasa

employers towards workers and how the workers could counter these.

As part of the training workshop, he drafted a ten-point code of conduct for all P&KTWU officials, committee members, shop stewards and union members. It was a demanding code which included observing discipline, efficient performance of duties, brotherly and comradely attitudes, courageous and patient behaviour, refusal to accept gifts and 'a blotless character'. In case of infringement of the code, disciplinary action was to be taken.

A week later, on 15th August, the president of the Federation of Master Printers of East Africa, Captain C D Anderson, met with the top officials of P&KTWU including Makhan Singh and signed an agreement recognising the union.

The Joint Consultative Committee meeting of P&KTWU's Nairobi branch on 9th September had two unusual items on its agenda, to discuss. 'Activities of certain members such as copying documents, colluding with the Criminal Investigation Committee (CID), collection of funds in order to bring action against the general secretary,' and 'Visit by the CID.'

At this time, scholarships for general and trade unionist education in Yugoslavia and Israel were being offered but Makhan Singh 'declined to apply.' On 8th November, he was again in Mombasa, this time addressing a public meeting organised by the coast branch of the KFL.

Suddenly a bombshell exploded. On 26th November, 1962, the *Daily Nation* ran an article headlined 'Row over anti-Red report.' It read: 'Self-avowed Communist Makhan Singh is in hot water with the executive of the Kenya Printing and Kindred Trades Workers' Union, of which he is deputy general secretary, following a public row with general secretary Wilson Mukuna, who has just returned from a visit to East and West Germany.

'Reporting on his visit at a social evening attended by union officials and members on Saturday night, Mr. Mukuna lashed out at conditions in Communist East Germany. And Mr. Singh walked out in protest, describing Mr. Mukuna's views as 'imperialistic' and claiming that Communism was the answer to Kenya's problems.' Mukuna confided that, 'Last night, union president Joel Ochieng told me: 'We are to hold a special conference of delegates to consider Mr. Singh's future position in the union.' At Saturday night's social evening, held at Solidarity House, Mukuna said:

Communists should go on with their politics without interfering with our affairs. I am not opposing anybody, but I am telling you what I saw with my eyes. East German workers are watched by soldiers who are armed with pistols. They are not allowed either to speak among themselves or to anyone else.' He added: 'President Sekou Toure of Guinea, whom I accompanied and who liked Communism before he made the visit to East Germany, has now decided to have nothing to do with it.'

Mr. Mukuna said that unlike in East Germany, West German workers were very progressive. He reported that he had obtained a number of scholarships from West Germany for Kenya trade unionists to 'see for themselves; and for others to take further academic studies.'

On 3ʳᵈ December, the president and general secretary of P&KTWU wrote to Makhan Singh informing him that he (Makhan Singh) had been removed from the membership of the union. The reason given was that he was a 'works manager' in the printing press where he was employed and that this category of employees was excluded by the recognition agreement existing between the union and the Federation of Master Printers.

Makhan Singh wrote back the same day, refuting the allegations made in the letter. He pointed out that membership was regulated only by the union's constitution but that even the recognition agreement did not exclude anyone from membership. 'I have been an organiser of printing workers in

Captain C D Andersen, J B D O Ochieng, W C E Mukuna, M V Patel, Makhan Singh

Copy to K.J.—

FROM:- MAKHAN SINGH,

P.O. Box 1183,

NAIROBI,

10/12/1962.

The President and General Secretary,
The Printing and Kindred Trades Workers Union,
Simla House, Victoria Street,
P.O. Box 12356, NAIROBI.

Dear Brothers,

I am in receipt of your letter of the 3rd December, 1962, in which you have informed me that as from that date my name "has ceased from membership of the Union." The reason given by you is that I am a "works manager" in the printing press where I am employed and that this category of employees is excluded by the Recognition agreement existing between our Union and the Federation of Master Printers.

I consider that according to the Union's constitution my membership has not ceased as it is regulated by Rule No. 1 (c) of our constitution which states :—

"Membership shall be open to all employees in the printing, publishing, stationeries, advertising, box-making (card board), paper making, envelope and paper-bag manufacturing, photographic and engraving industries.

My membership, as of every other member, is regulated only by Union's constitution and not by any clause of the Recognition Agreement. If you read it carefully, even that agreement does not exclude any one from membership of the Union, but, in certain cases, only from "representation" by the Union in case of difficulties with an employer.

I have been an organiser of printing workers in Kenya since 1936, and have been a member of the Union since 1949 (then called the Typographical Union of Kenya) and after my release from restriction my membership was renewed (RENEWED) on the 6th January, 1962, by a meeting of Head Office and Nairobi Branch officials of the Union held on the same date.

Before, on and since that date you and other officials and most of the members of the Union have been well-aware about my being employed as a compositor-cum-works manager in the Punjab Printing Press solely owned by my father. (In this press

(2)

there are only two employees, one myself and the other who works as a treadle machineman-cum-binder.)

While working in the printing press I have been active in Kenya's trade union movement since 1935 and twice went on strike in the press — once in May 1950 (under the directions of our Union then called the Typographical Union of Kenya) when I was arrested and remained restricted for 11½ years mainly for my trade union activities, and the second time I went on strike in the press was in June 1962, when the Union (under the present management) declared a strike in the printing industry.

In conclusion I would say that according to Union's constitution my membership c'nnot cease and has not ceased and that I continue in my elected office as the Assistant General Secretary of the Union and in other positions in the Union and in the K.F.L to which I am elected, appointed or entitled, because membership is governed only by the constitution and not by any other document. I may further add that the unity and strength of our union as well as of K.F.L. should be maintained and further strengthened in the interest of workers, and we should all contribute and work towards this end, and should not allow different political views and ideas (which we all are entitled to hold) to stand in our way.

Yours fraternally,

Makhan Singh.

Copy to:
(1) Kenya Federation of Labour
(2) The Minister of Labour
(3) Registrar of Trade Unions
(4) Federation of Master Printers
(5) Federation of Kenya Employers
(6) All PKTWU Branches.
(7) All KFL affiliates.
(8) The Press.

Kenya since 1936, and have been a member of the Union since 1949 (then called Typographical Union of Kenya) and after my release from restriction my membership was renewed on 6th January, 1962, by a meeting of Head Office and Nairobi Branch officials of the Union on the same date.

'You have been well aware about my being employed as a compositor-cum-works manager in the Punjab Printing Press solely owned by my father . . . the other [employee] works as a treadle machinist-cum-binder.' He insisted on continuing in his position as elected assistant general secretary and urged all not to allow 'different political views and creeds (which we all are entitled to hold) to stand in our way.' He sent copies of his letter to all the relevant organisations and branches.

Makhan Singh's protest letter of 10th December was replied in a *Daily Nation* report published two days later and headed 'Printers firm: Singh must go'. Two days later, *Baraza* published a similar report in Kiswahili. The dismissal was confirmed again in the *Daily Nation* and other newspapers a week later.

The letter from the president of P&KTWU stated that 'the union is satisfied that you are a manager in your father's printing press,' and added 'We make it clear to you that the union will not be in the position of wasting its time to spare even one minute for discussing this matter with you or anybody.' Elections to find a successor to him were scheduled to be held in Thika on 15th and 16th December.

It is ironic that Makhan Singh was expelled from the union in which he held the post of assistant general secretary and which he had been part of since his return from India in 1947. G V Patel had founded the Typographical Union in 1943 and registered it in 1946, the sixth union to be so registered. Its president was Mohamed Hussein Paracha; at that time it had only Asian members. It was only after Makhan Singh became a member in 1947 that African workers joined the union which then took the name P&KTWU as its membership increased. Wilson Mukuna revived the union in 1958 following the clampdown in the years of the Emergency. There were very few

Jaramogi Oginga Odinga arriving for the World Congress in Moscow

workers in the printing trade, about 4000 nationally, as the presses were family firms. Makhan Singh had specifically joined the union in order to distance himself from the family connection. His life-long involvement with workers and trade unionism was well known. The *East African Standard* sent Makhan Singh copies of letters he had written a very long time ago, as secretary of the Labour Trade Union of Kenya. Addressed to the secretary of the Press Workers Union, they were dated 13th January, 1937, and 3rd March, 1938, and concerned recognition of the union and wage demands.

The central committee of the P&KTWU held a meeting on 18th December in Thika in which it endorsed the action taken by the executive committee in expelling Makhan Singh both from his post as assistant general secretary and as a member of the union. Peter Carvalho, also an assistant general secretary, was elected to replace him. On 27th April, 1963, the committee members of the P&KTWU's Nairobi branch were all replaced in hastily held elections. No doubt now assured of support from the conservative majority in the KFL and KANU, Wilson Mukuna announced his intention to contest a parliamentary seat in the Lower House. The fact that, soon after, several students left to study at the Karl Marx University in East Germany shows that it was not Makhan Singh's communist leanings, but rather his unrelenting support of workers and their rights, which was the bone of contention. In July 1962, Odinga had led a delegation to Moscow for the World Conference for General Disarmament and Peace. At that time, he was accompanied by Fred Kubai, Juma Boy, Bildad Kaggia, Odhiambo Okello, Maalim Juma, Othiyo Othieno, Endusa Litwa and James Nyamweya. Later, on 4ᵗʰ November, 1963, a delegation, led by Burudi Nabwera of the Central Legislative Assembly, left for a two-week visit to Moscow to discuss trade matters.

AFRO-ASIAN SOLIDARITY CONFERENCE

At the beginning of 1963, Makhan Singh received a telegram from Diwan Chaman Lal in India, the lawyer who, together with Pritt and Kapila, had defended the Kapenguria Six. 'Reaching Nairobi with Indian delegation 31ˢᵗ en route to Moshi for Afro-Asian Solidarity Conference.' The Kenyan delegation was led by Oginga Odinga and included Pio Gama Pinto. KANU appointed Makhan Singh together with C Kiprotich, K P Shah, S Patel and Fitz de Souza, as observer to the conference. However, Makhan Singh was unable to travel out of Kenya, as he still did not have a residence permit.

The Indian delegation to the conference was comprised of members of the ruling Congress Party and the Indian Communist Party, together with independents. They stressed

Meeting union delegates at the Nairobi Airport

that they were not attending as party representatives but as members of the Afro-Asian Solidarity Committee of India. Delegates from India, Japan, Indonesia, Ceylon and Nepal arrived in Nairobi en route to the conference and were met at the airport by K P Shah, Fitz de Souza, KANU official Joe Murumbi, Makhan Singh and others.

KADU's president, Ronald Ngala, made a scathing attack on the conference claiming that it was a smokescreen to propagate communist ideology in Africa and Asia. 'Communist colonialism would enslave Africans economically . . . KADU had not been invited to the Conference,' he said, and stressed KADU's determination to resist communism in Kenya. Tom Mboya, KANU's secretary-general, declared that 'politically, KADU was well known for their tribalism and their agency for imperialism.' The Indonesian delegate said they had come to the conference to attack 'imperialism, colonialism and neo-colonialism.' The Sino-Indian border dispute and the Kashmir

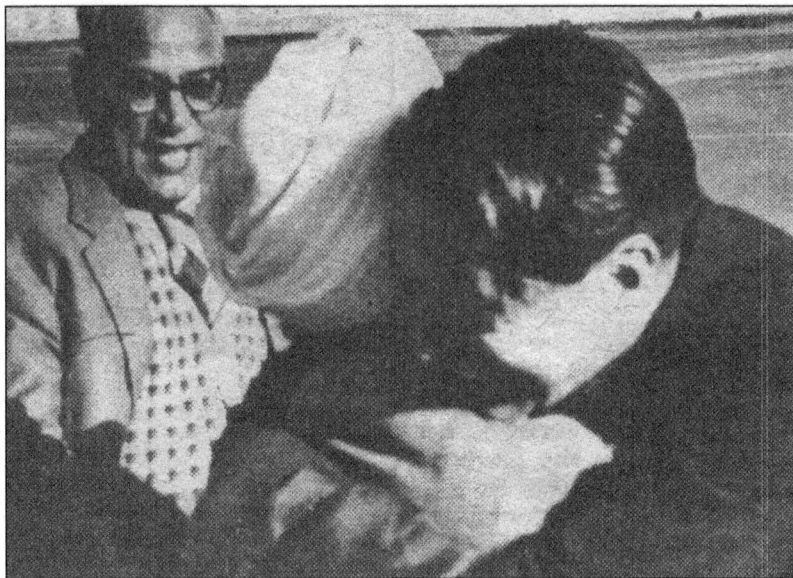

Embracing Indian Communist Party delegate Chandra Ramesh, Nairobi Airport, 1963

issue, being specially sensitive topics, were side-stepped.

Oginga Odinga persuaded the conference to condemn Kenya's new constitution. There were several disagreements and the delegates from India held differing views on the final outcome of the conference. While Chaman Lal considered it to have been 'immensely successful,' another delegate, Dr Gopal Singh, disparaged it as 'a complete flop.' The ruling Congress Party of India condemned it as being 'communist inspired and dominated.'

On 25th March, 1963, 'Kenya's most controversial trade union leader – ex-restrictee, communist sympathiser Makhan Singh – jubilantly waved his passport . . . and announced to the press, "I've got it. After 28 years of struggling, I've got it." So wrote the *People* reporter.

He had submitted his application for a certificate of permanent residence for the umpteenth time a month earlier. Now he called a press conference at his Park Road home to

exhibit his passport, newly stamped
with a certificate dated 'March 18' and
'valid for the lifetime of the holder.'
The *Daily Nation* and the *Taifa Leo* also
covered the story. Dennis Akumu, the
trade unionist, remembers Makhan
Singh as 'having tears of joy in his
eyes.'[12]

Asked to hazard a guess as to the
reason for the turn-around Makhan
Singh said,

> I can only attribute the change of
> heart to the changed political
> situation in the country. Now I am
> looking forward to taking a
> holiday in the firm knowledge that
> I cannot be prevented from
> returning to Kenya. Because of this
> trouble I could not even get to the
> Afro-Asian Peoples' Solidarity Conference at Moshi
> earlier this year . . . . This means that I can no longer be
> declared a prohibited immigrant – a fate that has
> threatened me several times over the years . . . . I can't but
> help think that I have earned it. After all, my eleven years
> in restriction was more than two normal residency
> qualifying periods.

*After 28 years of struggle,
Makhan Singh finally gets his
passport*

Early in April, came the news of the death of Arjun Singh in
India, a well-known journalist and communist. Between 1945
and 1947, Makhan Singh worked with him on the *Jang-e-Azadi*
and was much impressed by his revolutionary spirit, his
dedication and his good-heartedness. Makhan Singh
immediately wrote to comrade Avtar Singh Malhotra, secretary
of the Punjab State Council of the Communist Party in
Jalhandar. He sent his condolences, writing that he had been

Bruce MacKenzie and Joseph Murumbi, with Makhan Singh in the background (extreme left)

greatly influenced by Arjun Singh's writings. He particularly remembered reading a poem of his in the *Kirti* in 1928, which still inspired him. The translation was 'We will not stop at anything; we will make them stop what they are doing.'

The *Nawan Zamana* of Jalhandar published his letter in full. It also published a full page article on 'The Struggle in East Africa for Freedom' by Gopal Singh Chandan. The article stated that to date 34 countries had got their freedom after India won hers. It named Kenya as 'the rising sun of Africa' and narrated the contribution of the Punjabi workers and artisans in building the Uganda Railway. It criticised the EAINC as having 'passed many resolutions with no tangible results' and covered the anti-colonial struggle mentioning the Mau Mau, Jomo Kenyatta and the Kapenguria Six.

At the same time, one of the leaders of the Namdari sect in India, Jaswant Singh, wrote to Makhan Singh to congratulate him on Kenya's achievements towards the forthcoming

With Jomo Kenyatta, Tom Mboya and others celebrating KANU victory

independence. KANU had commenced its election campaign and Makhan Singh spoke at many of its public meetings.

His main points were that only those who had struggled for independence and known its value could win it and maintain it. The fundamental need was to ensure that Kenya became a truly independent and sovereign state and not one dependent on the colonialists in new and indirect ways. Only KANU which had worked with political and trade union organisations could assure this, whereas KADU had been a stumbling block and a divider of the national movement. Asians had been actively fighting for democratic rights and independence and should now be fully involved in the reconstruction of the economy and building the new nation.

Fitz de Souza appointed Makhan Singh his election agent to supervise the City Primary School polling station in his campaign for the Senate or Upper House. He was also the authorised election agent at a polling station in Charter Hall.

YOUR KANU CANDIDATE FOR NAIROBI NORTH-WEST

DR. F. R. S. DE SOUZA.
ELECTION MESSAGE FROM YOUR KANU CANDIDATE FOR
NAIROBI NORTH-WEST

A few weeks ago I was unanimously adopted by all KANU sub-
branches in the Ngara—Desai Road—Parklands—High Ridge—Westlands
area as the KANU candidate for the Nairobi North-West Lower House
constituency. Next Saturday and Sunday you will be voting to select the
member for Nairobi North-West. During the past weeks I have tried to
put over to you in scores of public and private meetings, over the radio
and pamphlets, the policies I stand for. I have tried to publicize as widely
as possible the policy on which my party, KANU, is fighting these most
crucial elections in the history of our country. In this, my final appeal,
I invite you to vote for me and my party for the following TEN reasons:—

1. Without any doubt KANU will form the new government of Kenya
in a few days. Mr. Kenyatta will be the first Prime Minister of Kenya.
It is in your interest to have an Asian in the government party rather
than in the opposition. A vote for the opposition candidate will be a
wasted vote. I INVITE YOU TO DECLARE YOUR SUPPORT FOR
THE NEXT GOVERNMENT BY VOTING FOR ME AS THE KANU
CANDIDATE.

2. KANU is the nationalist party of Kenya. It holds here the same posi-
tion as Congress held in India during the struggle for independence.
I INVITE YOU TO WALK IN STEP WITH THE NATIONALIST
MOVEMENT OF KENYA BY VOTING FOR ME AS THE KANU
CANDIDATE.

3. KANU is determined to exclude all racial ideas from politics. It
values ALL who have made their homes in Kenya as individuals equal
in the eyes of the law, irrespective of race, tribe or religion. I INVITE
YOU TO SUPPORT NON-RACIALISM BY VOTING FOR ME AS
YOUR CANDIDATE OF A NON-RACIAL PARTY.

4. KANU is not a tribal party. It has the support of all the major tribes
and most of the small ones. KANU completely rejects tribalism. The
Asian population in Kenya is too small to risk alignment with a small
tribalist party like KADU. Its interests lie with those of the majority
of the people of Kenya, i.e. with KANU. I INVITE YOU TO JOIN
WITH THE MAJORITY IN THE CHALLENGING TASK OF NATION-
BUILDING BY VOTING FOR ME AS THE CANDIDATE OF THE
MAJORITY PARTY.

5. KANU is the party of progress. It is dynamic and forward-looking
whereas KADU is tribalistic and backward-looking. I INVITE YOU
TO VOTE FOR THE FORCES OF PROGRESS IN KENYA BY

F. R. S. DE SOUZA

Born in 1929. Called to the Bar at Lincoln's Inn in 1948. Took degree
of B.Sc. (Economics) in 1951, from London University. Returned to
Kenya and practised law until 1957. Then went back to England for
further studies. Took degree of Doctor of Philosophy in Economics in

Fitz de Souza's campaign poster

However, Makhan Singh wanted to play a much more active
role. On 29th May he once again wrote to Kenyatta: 'Dear
President, this is to request you that I should be selected as a
KANU nominee to contest one of the (specially elected)
National seats of the House of Representatives . . . the main task
before us is to build a democratic, socialist Kenya.'

Makhan Singh was either not aware of the shift in
Kenyatta's ideology and practice or was choosing to ignore it.

CHAPTER TWELVE

A MAN IN
THE SHADOWS

'A Man in the Shadows' was the title of an article by N S Toofan in the June 22nd, 1963, edition of the *Daily Nation*. 'Why are they not making any use of Makhan Singh?' he asked. 'This is a question which has occurred to many people of all races in Kenya during the past few weeks, and even earlier . . . Singh was an outright firebrand with a great capacity for creating enthusiasm and personal popularity, particularly among the African masses. He was the first Asian to instil the idea of complete independence among them. He had such a way with him that many Africans came to style him *"Mungu"* . . . God.

'The besetting weakness of his campaign was that he openly proclaimed himself as an avowed communist. It was very natural that the authorities should feel that his real aim was to introduce this repulsive creed into this country on a big scale . . . be it noted however that his Communist beliefs formed no part of the [detention] charges against him . . . in detention . . . he was not even released on parole to attend his mother's funeral in 1956 under fears of a general African uprising. During his long absence the new African leaders of all shades of opinion came to regard him as one who had done sterling service for the awakening of their people. Even the Asian leadership, which had originally kept aloof from him, began to press for his release.

'Although Singh has not shed his faith in Communism . . . he has not made the slightest effort to disseminate this creed among the people . . . He accepts the Kanu manifesto without the least reservation. Nevertheless, neither the Kenya Federation of Labour nor Kanu whose very faithful, very ardent supporter he is, have given him any position of major responsibility. The fault lies partly with him because I think he made a great mistake, he actually cheapened himself when after his return he accepted a very junior assignment in the KFL where, however he did not last long. He created for himself the image of a person who could easily be overlooked . . . .

'Singh, however, is not a typical politician who can exert himself for his own personal advancement. I personally have very vital differences with him, but I admire him for the very calm and the philosophical way in which he has accepted his supercession. This, however, is not a trait which has any value these days. From what has been made known to me, Singh has no intention of retiring from public life. The mystery therefore, is: "Why are they not making any use of him?" '

Makhan Singh seemed to be resigning himself to attending functions for other people. The staff of the Kenya Distributive and Commercial Workers' Union held a party to honour their president, Senator Clement K Lubembe; Makhan Singh was a guest. The following month, Judge Thurgood Marshall, America's famed 'Mr. Civil Rights' gave a lecture on the progress being made in race relations in the USA, speaking in Gloucester Hall at the Royal College. Makhan Singh attended. Cultural shows were presented by the Artists' Welfare Guild in honour of the High Commissioner for India, H E Mr Khilnani. Makhan Singh attended this also as he did a sports day of the Technical High School.

However, he kept on writing, expounding his views. A hand-written piece by him addressed the civil servants who had resigned or were about to resign. It is not clear if it was the Asian civil servants and if the writing was ever forwarded. His view was that 'you are giving us a challenge and we accept it. In the old colonial days what was needed by a civil servant was servility to colonialists and know-how. In the new Africa what is needed by him is patriotism and know-how. When a civil servant has no patriotism his know how becomes blind and lame and he drops out in any case. To the EACSO [East Africa Common Services Organisation] and Governments my appeal is this: Accept the resignations without exception, and organise the civil service on the basis of patriotism and know-how in the socialist spirit of harambee.'

A collection of press cuttings from the *Taifa Leo* in his files at this time are evidence that he was reading much more in Kiswahili. It was probably to continue to improve his fluency in the national language but more so to keep informed of the day-to-day concerns of the *wananchi* (rank and file).

And he was not giving up hope. On 30th July, Makhan Singh once again wrote to Kenyatta. 'Dear President, this is to request you that I should be selected as a KANU nominee to contest one of the seats of the Central Legislative Assembly in the forthcoming elections of nine seats. I shall be under the discipline of KANU and would loyally adhere to its policies and decisions.' This last assurance was made in every letter he wrote to the President.

'I DON'T WANT TO ASK FOR A JOB'

Fitz de Souza, who was then the deputy speaker of the National Assembly or Lower House, took Makhan Singh to a lunch at Parliament Buildings. Achieng Oneko, Chanan Singh, Pio Gama Pinto and others were there. President Kenyatta came in with Mbiyu Koinange and greeted all who were present. Fitz told Makhan Singh that in politics 'you don't wait to be asked, you have to push'. He rose to speak to Kenyatta about securing a post for Makhan Singh in government but Makhan Singh became very agitated. 'Fitz, my friend!' he remonstrated, 'I will continue to serve Kenya, but I don't want to ask for a job. I have never asked for anything for myself and I am not going to start now.' According to Fitz, Makhan Singh was 'a totally unadulterated idealist. He would not compromise his principles on anything – Gama Pinto did not agree with Makhan Singh's strident support of communism as he felt that it gave their enemies a chance to malign them.'[1]

Despite being shunned by Kenyatta, KANU and the KFL, Makhan Singh continued to be remembered. In August, he was present at the speech day at the Duchess of Gloucester School where his daughter, Inderjeet, was given a prize for achieving a first class certificate. He was invited to a prize-giving function at the Khalsa Boys and Girls School but sent his regrets. Next month, he went to a fund-raising event in Gichugu Division organised to buy an artificial leg for General Kassam, an ex-freedom fighter.

A typed statement by him referred to the three hunger strikes he had undertaken while in detention and emphasised his loyalty to, and support for, Kenyatta. It also reiterated the messages he had sent out before and after the last hunger strike, none of which had been forwarded by the colonial authorities.

On 20th October, Makhan Singh attended the annual celebrations in honour of the birth of the founder of the Sikh religion, Guru Nanak, organised by the Kenya Punjabi Literary Society. Speeches, poems and items by radio artists were on the programme but Makhan Singh was not invited to recite.

In his notes of that time, there were two trade union entries. The first was about a strike by workers of the Tailors and Textiles Workers Union at Nakuru Industries Ltd. In August

SPEECHES:

xcellency Mr. K. K. Panni, Commissioner for Pakistan.
atish Chander Gautam, Advocate.
ine Sayyed Amir Hussain Najafi.
Iwant Singh Giani,
President, Kenya Punjabi Literary Society.

POEMS:

t. A. "Haidri"
ohan Singh "Josh"
l. H. "Agha"
Jalbir "Walia"
'. L. "Chanan"
lje Kumar "Arun"
yara Singh "Dard"
I. S. "Sukhoo"

RADIO ARTISTS:

khar Singh "Pardesi"
aghubir Singh "Rahi"
Udham Singh & Party
e of the City Art Society.

REFRESHMENTS WILL BE SERVED AT 6 P.M.
arrangements by: M/s. Werret & Co., Stewart ! reet.
lection by: M/s Puran Singh Electrician & Sons.
Hardat Road.

The President and Members of the
Managing Committee of
THE KENYA PUNJABI LITERARY SOCIETY
request the pleasure of the company of

Mr. & Mrs. .... Makhan Singh ....
AT
BIRTHDAY CELEBRATION
OF
SIRI GURU NANAK DEV JI
ON
Saturday, the 26th October, 1963 at 5.30 p.m.
in the
Mauladad Nursery School Hall, Park Road, Nairobi
HIS EXCELLENCY MR. K. K. TANDON,
(Comm. defor to India)
has very kindly consented to preside.

R.S.V.P.
Nairobi Baxh "Thandaa".
H. G. Germany.
Kas 6891, Tel: 27394,
NAIROBI.

Invite from the Kenya Punjabi Literary Society

two Sikh employees, members of the union, were threatened and told to get out of the African trade union, presumably by the employers. When they refused they were sacked. Makhan Singh accused the management of acting on a racial basis which was against the laid-down rules.

The second entry was a dispute between the Domestic and Hotel Workers Union and the Aga Khan Hospital Association. A tribunal was set up to arbitrate the dispute. Makhan Singh was appointed as the assessor for the union. (He pointed out that his name was 'Makhan', not 'Markan'). Other members of the tribunal were H L Renwick (chairman), Sir Charles Mortimer (assessor for the Aga Khan Hospital) and James C Odaya (secretary) from the Ministry of Labour. Much of the dispute centred on the complaints of discrimination by the female employees especially to do with wages, maternity leave and night transport. He made a detailed study of the conditions and wages and presented his findings to a tribunal on 16th December.

The meeting of the tribunal was scheduled for the 23rd at 10.00 a. m. Makhan Singh was informed of this at 11.30 a. m. He phoned the secretary and was told that the chairman had left and would be contacting him. There was no further news on the 23rd or 24th. After the Christmas holidays, he phoned the secretary who said: 'I have not been able to contact you but the chairman has submitted the award.' Makhan Singh objected: 'The award should have been discussed in a meeting attended by me.' The secretary's response was curt: 'Nothing further can be done.' Makhan Singh tried to contact the chairman but his calls were not returned.

On 15th January, 1964, the secretary phoned him to tell him that the award had been approved by the minister and requested him to come and sign it. 'Payment for your services will be made as soon as possible,' he added. Makhan Singh reminded him of the necessity of his presence when the award was discussed and was advised to raise it at the meeting. He gave him his phone contact and reminded him that he, Makhan

Singh, was unemployed and therefore in need of remuneration.

On the 21ˢᵗ he sent a letter to the secretary. 'Regarding this morning's meeting with the Chief Industrial Officer, R A J Damerell, in the presence of Sir Charles Mortimer and Mr. Chege Kibachia . . . kindly attach the enclosed note to the Arbitration Award.' The note stated that 'the maximum amounts should not have been fixed for the increments because this will prejudice the case for higher minimum scales in negotiations for a new agreement. Much higher minimum scales are an economic as well as political necessity of our free Kenya so that the necessities of life of a worker and his family are reasonably satisfied.'

When Makhan Singh received a copy of the award, his note was not included or even mentioned and the maximum scales for increments were stipulated. On further enquiry the secretary informed him that his letter had arrived after the award had been made and distributed to the various stakeholders. He was paid KShs 180 for sitting for 9 hours and being ignored.

FREEDOM FIGHTERS FORGOTTEN

Kenya's Independence date was set for 12ᵗʰ December, 1963, and preparations for the celebration were in full swing. The press published the new national anthem in Kiswahili and English. Makhan Singh received an envelope from Fred Kubai[2] who had won the Nakuru East parliamentary seat and was appointed assistant minister for Labour. It was dated 7ᵗʰ December with the following note: 'Dear Comrade, here are two UHURU invitation cards for you from me. Things had been going wrong way that some of the freedom fighters find themselves forgotten. But we have played our part – history

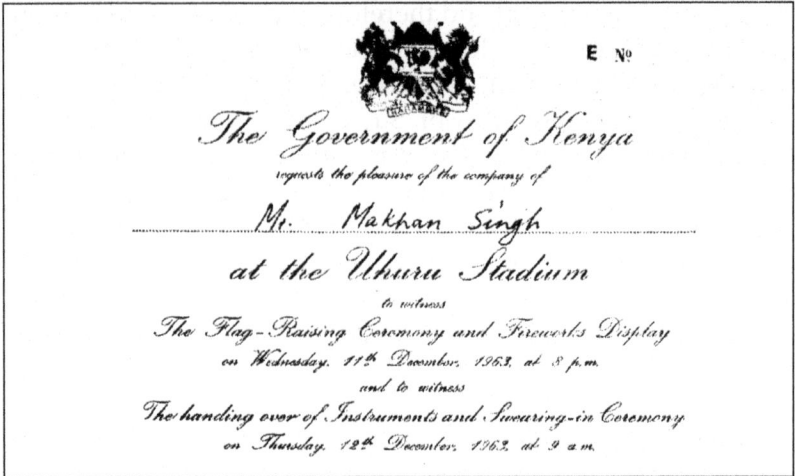

E №

The Government of Kenya

requests the pleasure of the company of

Mr. Makhan Singh

at the Uhuru Stadium

to witness

The Flag-Raising Ceremony and Fireworks Display

on Wednesday, 11ᵗʰ December, 1963, at 8 p.m.

and to witness

The handing over of Instruments and Swearing-in Ceremony

on Thursday, 12ᵗʰ December, 1963, at 9 a.m.

Invite to Makhan Singh, delivered by Fred Kubai on the occasion of the swearing in ceremony of the new Government of Kenya on 11ᵗʰ December 1963.

will always tell who is who. So do not be downhearted I am trying my best. And so Uhuru greetings.'

Kenya's independent government had failed to invite Makhan Singh to the celebration of the momentous historical change-over that he, Makhan Singh, had publicly demanded thirteen years earlier. On 23ʳᵈ April, 1950, in Kaloleni Hall, Nairobi at a joint meeting of the EATUC, KAU and EAINC, he was the first Kenyan leader to call for an end to colonialism. He made this bold and visionary statement at a time when nationalist Kenyans were still busy negotiating for redress in the economic and political fields. In doing so, he radically changed the direction of the anti-colonial struggle, a factor which so alarmed the colonialists that they arrested, detained and harassed him for eleven and a half years. Earlier, he had been imprisoned and restricted in India from 1940 to 1945 and thus became the longest serving detainee in Kenya's anti-colonial history. And this rank injustice did not diminish with time. The following year, on 11ᵗʰ December, almost at the last moment, Makhan Singh received an invitation for himself and

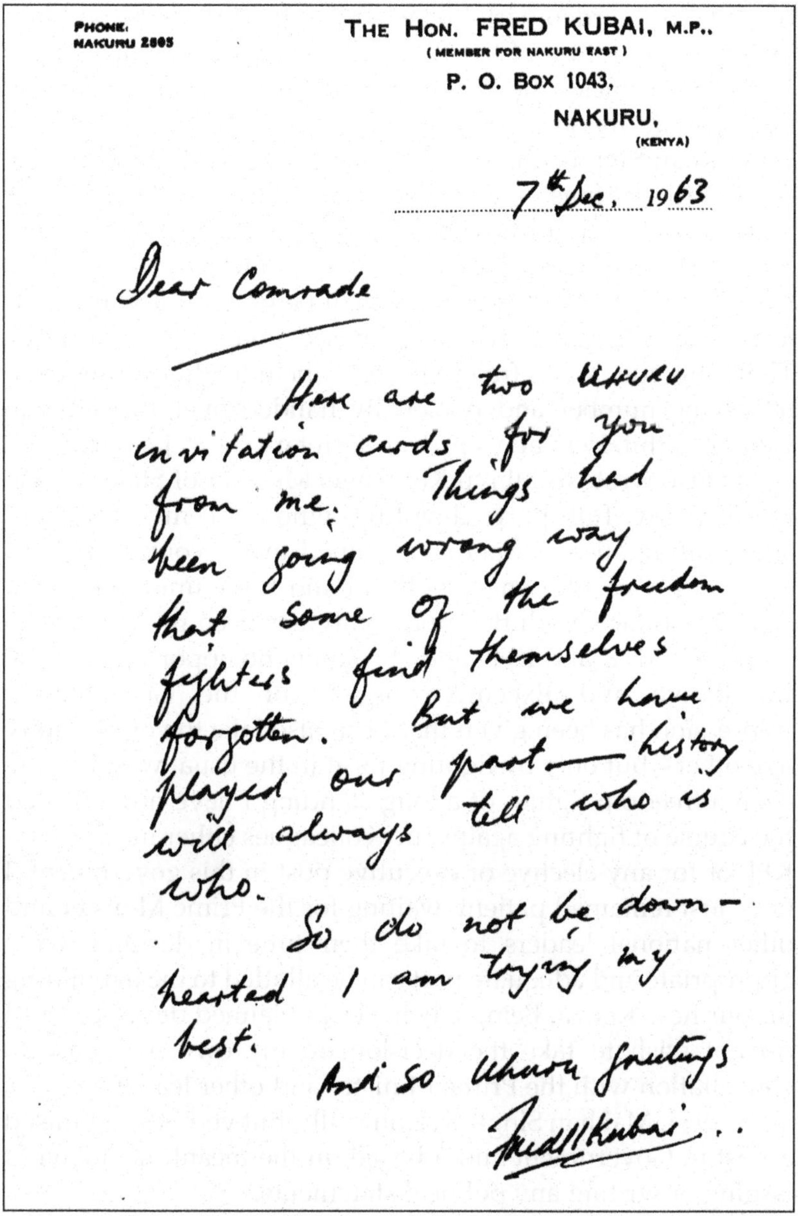

PHONE:
NAKURU 2865

THE HON. FRED KUBAI, M.P.,
(MEMBER FOR NAKURU EAST)

P. O. BOX 1043,
NAKURU,
(KENYA)

7ᵗʰ Dec, 1963

Dear Comrade

Here are two UHURU invitation cards for you from me. Things had been going wrong way that some of the freedom fighters find themselves forgotten. But we have played our part — history will always tell who is who.

So do not be down-hearted I am trying my best.

And so Uhuru greetings

Fred Kubai...

Fred Kubai's note to Makhan Singh

his wife to a garden party to be held on the 14th on the occasion of the inauguration of the Republic of Kenya. The hosts were 'Their Excellencies the President and Mrs Kenyatta' – but K P Shah had addressed the card.

Makhan Singh still did not give up. He wrote to Kenyatta, 'Dear Prime Minister I wish to consult you and have your reliable advice as to how best and in what appropriate and adequate way I could play my part in building up our new Kenya under your leadership. I shall be grateful if you would kindly let me know when I can see you for the purpose. Thanking you, Yours fraternally.' He included his address and telephone number and personally handed over the letter to George Githii, Kenyatta's private secretary on 2nd January 1964.

He also wrote to Mbiyu Koinange, Minister of State. 'I wish to play my full part, devoting whole of my time and contributing all my experience gained in the course of thirty years of my revolutionary political and trade union life. I am now 50. So far very little opportunity has been given to me to work in KANU and KFL, and absolutely no opportunity in the Legislative and Executive organs of the Government. Impression has been given that I can also take the opportunity like others, but only by fighting for it in the usual way. Having been a freedom fighter of a long standing I have not followed the course of fighting against my colleagues either in KANU or KFL or for any elective or executive post in this government. I have just remained patient, waiting for the Prime Minister and other national leaders to take their time in deciding what appropriate and adequate part can be allotted to me in building up our new Kenya. Being a believer in planned development I do not wish to take the decision on my own, but only in consultation with the Prime Minister and other leaders.'

In 1964, Makhan Singh was officially, but verbally, promised a post in Government and advised, in the meantime, to avoid issuing or writing any political statements.

Ambu Patel's New Kenya Publishers announced its forthcoming publication titled *'Struggle for Release of Jomo*

Margaret Kenyatta and Sudh Singh at a banquet in India

Kenyatta and his Colleagues'. The manuscript was compiled by himself and a letter from him thanked Makhan Singh for his message and the photograph which were to be included. Makhan Singh's message was dedicated to 'the imprisonment and detention of our great leader Jomo Kenyatta, the heroic resistance of our people, the Hola massacre and his own hunger strikes in detention . . . . The struggle for independence was great and the struggle for the release of Jomo needed much tact, courage and persistence. The above publication records this courageous effort for others to know and for the coming generations to be inspired. Thanking you for your valuable co-operation and assuring you that we too are interested in the course of events taking place in our country as well as in your personal progress.' He ended his message with 'Now forward to building up of a strong democratic African Socialist Kenya.' The photograph was of the three rondavals he occupied in Maralal when he was in detention.

Kenyatta's daughter, Margaret, who had been cared for by Ambu Patel and his wife Lila during her father's detention,

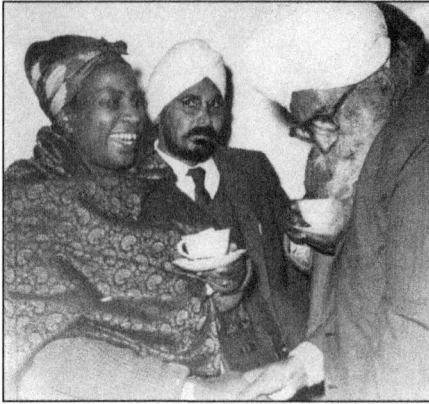

Margaret Kenyatta meets Sudh Singh

visited India in January 1964. In an interview with the *Indian Express* she said:

'People of all nationalities were welcomed to the new Kenya so long as they were prepared to accept its policies.' She recalled how two brave Punjabis, Chanan Singh and Makhan Singh, along with many other Indians had helped the Kenyans fight their freedom battles.

India was helping Africa in the sphere of education. They must go on helping each other. On meeting you all, I feel I belong to India. I have felt very happy during my stay here. We have many things in common and we have so much to give and to take from each other.

The *Daily Nation* of 7th January quoted Margaret Kenyatta: 'Kenya's problems were similar to India's and it would be of interest to the people of her country to know how the Indian people were tackling them . . . a lot of inspiration came from India to the leaders of Kenya during their independence struggle.'

In Chandigarh, she met a group of Kenyans which included Sudh Singh, Makhan Singh's father, who was on holiday there. He welcomed her and said: 'Heartiest congratulations for the freedom of Kenya . . . we are confident that our destiny is safe in your father's hand.'

At the Bagpat community development block near Delhi, she tried her hand at a spinning wheel and mentioned the friendly ties between India and Kenya and the help India was giving Africa especially in the matter of training students. When India's high commission in Nairobi held its annual celebration of India's Republic Day on 26th January, H E the Governor General, Malcolm MacDonald, was the guest of honour, Makhan Singh an invitee.

The next day, he consulted Tom Mboya regarding a statement he

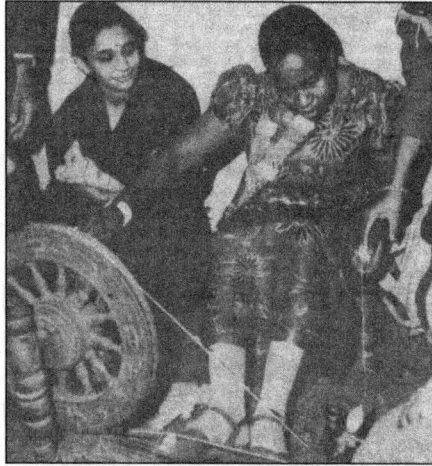

Margaret Kenyatta trying her hand at the spinning wheel on her visit to India

[Makhan Singh] had drafted for the press. It concerned the early January mutinies in the armed forces of Kenya and Tanzania and the revolution in Zanzibar.[3] The British prime minister had reported that he suspected a communist hand while the Soviet Union had warned the British against any intervention in Zanzibar. Makhan Singh maintained that the events were neither communist nor anti-communist. The peoples' Republic of Zanzibar, he claimed, was fully supported by all the East African governments and they would not tolerate any foreign intervention. The mutinies were directed against these same governments, were rightfully crushed and the foundation for really national armies was being laid. Mboya, however, advised him not to issue the statement as 'the issues were too involved.'

However, Jomo Kenyatta, Oginga Odinga, (Kenya's Minister of Home Affairs), Achieng Oneko (Kenya's Minister of Information), Julius Nyerere and Oscar Kambona (Tanganyika's Minister for External Affairs and Defence) had all discounted the British government's allegation of a

```
LABOUR
MONTHLY
Founded 1921   Editor : R. Palme Dutt
─────────────────────────────────
REQUIEM FOR THE HERALD
The Editor

★

GEORGE ELVIN          FIDEL CASTRO
Films: The Lion's Tale    Five years of Progress

★

REFLECTIONS ON EAST AFRICA
Jack Woddis

                    Neither Socialist Nor Democratic, J. R. Campbell
ELECTION    The Press in Election Year, Allen Hutt
YEAR        The Courts and the Trade Unions, D. N, Pritt, Q.C.

MARCH 1964
─────────────────
Two Shillings
```

Labour Monthly

'communist plot'. Odinga castigated the 'imperialist press' and said they were trying to find scapegoats for their unjust policy in Zanzibar where they had intended to support minority rule over a majority. He blamed the mutinies to the failure of the British to adequately train African army officers to take over from them.

Jack Woddis, a reporter with the *Daily Worker* of the British Communist Party, wrote to Makhan Singh that he was on a visit to East Africa and wanted to meet him but did not have his physical address. He had posted to him his three books: *Africa, the Way Ahead; Africa, the Roots of Revolt* and *Africa, the Lion Awakes*, the last having a detailed account of the struggles waged by the early trade union pioneers in Kenya and of the part played by Makhan Singh in these developments. He also arranged to send him copies of the *Labour Monthly* and the *Daily Worker* in which he had written articles on Zanzibar; and said he would be sending him regular supplies of literature that he was sure would be put to good use.

Woddis in his article of 9th March, 'Wind of Change over the Spice Islands' published in the *Labour Monthly*, asserted that the revolution in Zanzibar had mass support. To judge by Makhan Singh's underlining, of particular interest to him was Woddis' account of the very great influence of the workers and the trade unions in the new Zanzibar. The Federation of Revolutionary Trade Unions had 13,000 members and six of the 31 members of the Revolutionary Council were trade unionists, as were many of the officers in the new army and police. In fact, throughout the new state working class cadres, organised and trained by the trade union movement, were playing an important role. Makhan Singh also underlined Woddis' remarks on Zanzibar's foreign policy, which declared that it wanted to be 'friends of all' and planned to build a socialist state.

The same issue of the *Labour Monthly*, which had been founded in 1921 by Palme Dutt with whom Makhan Singh had communicated in the thirties, had 'The Courts and the Trade Unions' by D N Pritt, QC. This article analysed the class war in the long struggle between labour and capital in the courts and parliament.

In May, the *Sunday Nation* printed Mandela's 'Why I Am Ready To Die' speech at his trial in Pretoria on charges of attempting a revolution by using violence. Makhan Singh underlined the part where Mandela denies that he was a communist but had been influenced by Marxist thought. Mandela went on to claim that this was true of such widely different world leaders such as Gandhi, Nehru, Nkrumah and Nasser. 'We all accept the need for some form of socialism to enable our people to catch up with the advanced countries of the world and to overcome their legacy of extreme poverty.' Mandela wanted to be free to borrow from east or west what was best for his people.

The main article in the *New Age*, a Communist Party weekly in India, was 'History Will Not Forgive Them' and related the resolutions of the 6-day meeting held in New Delhi. Peter Kioni, a medical student, brought a copy of it to Makhan Singh together with *Yugantar*, a Marathi weekly from Bombay. Kioni had been interviewed by G Adhikari, the editor of *Yugantar*, about Makhan Singh. 'Who in Nairobi or Kenya does not know him . . . I heard his speeches, he speaks fluently in Swahili and he speaks like an African patriot,' said Kioni.

In a personal note, Adhikari reminded Makhan Singh that they had met when they were in the underground in

Ahmedabad and worked together on *Jang-e-Azadi*. When he had travelled to Britain in 1947 he had carried a letter from him to comrade Gallacher, the British member of parliament regarding the permit to allow him to return to Kenya. He (Adhikari) had followed Makhan Singh's career from those early days up to his release from detention. Whenever he wrote about Kenya's liberation struggle, he referred to the shameful role some Indians had played in Kenya by supporting the British in their repressive measures against the Mau Mau. He continued, 'Then we referred to the other type of Indians typified by you who fought shoulder to shoulder with the Africans against colonialism and imperialism. We told our readers that it was men like Makhan Singh in Kenya and Yusuf Dadoo in South Africa who represented the spirit of our national movement and of Mahatma Gandhi, the spirit of international solidarity of the workers and oppressed peoples of all countries in the common struggle against imperialism.'

Adhikari then requested Makhan Singh to write articles for the *New Age* on the difficulties facing Kenya's people 'because of the neo-colonial conspiracies of the imperialists, how the government headed by Kenyatta was proposing to solve them and what progressive forces in the country have to say about the problems.'

On 26th May, 1964, India's first prime minister, Jawaharlal Nehru, passed away. Makhan Singh sent a telegram to President Sarvepalli Radhakrishnan calling Nehru 'the apostle of freedom and peace.' He went with K P Shah to convey his condolences to the Indian High Commissioner for India, R K Tandon, and attended a memorial service at the Patel Club.

Makhan Singh's role as a trade unionist was not entirely forgotten. On 16th September, when Motion No 5 was debated in the House of Representatives, Makhan Singh was invited by the Speaker, Hon. Humphrey Slade, through Dr Njoroge and Mbiyu Koinange, to attend. The subject was 'The Trade Unions (Amendment) Bill (Bill No. 11)' under the Ministry of Justice and Constitutional Affairs and Makhan Singh heard the debate from the Speakers' Box.

The *East African Standard* of 9th December quoted Mboya as criticising the *Sunday Telegraph* of London for its allegations about disunity in the Kenyan government and in Kenya as a whole. Speaking at the annual prize-giving of the Khalsa Boys and Girls School, Mboya referred to the negative comments he had made earlier about the Asian community and said they were justified. He played down the Asian contribution to the struggle for freedom and never once mentioned Makhan Singh. In fact he was known to have once remarked that 'Jaramogi's weakness is that he is heavily dependent on his Asian advisers.'[4]

Although invited, Makhan Singh did not attend the poetry symposium organised by the Kenya Punjabi Literary Society to which the high commissioners of both India and Pakistan had been invited. He did, however, go to the Republic Day cocktail party held by the Nairobi City councillors where Mboya was the guest of honour.

WHY HAS HE FALLEN FROM POWER?

❋

A reporter from *Drum* magazine conducted a brief interview with Makhan Singh at his home but the latter was reluctant to tell his story or have his picture taken. 'Why has he fallen from power?' was the *Drum's* headline. 'Today, however, Makhan Singh is Kenya's 'forgotten' man. The fruits of Uhuru have passed him by. He has no bank balance, no job, no friends. He has even made enemies in his old trade union circles. But he makes no approaches for help. He turns away journalists and rarely talks – but when he does, it is without any trace of bitterness.

Makhan Singh told *Drum* that he was a believer in Marxist

Makhan Singh seated in the front rows, listening to Kenyatta's speech at Kamukunji in 1964

philosophy. But, questioned further, he admitted that he did not support Lenin's or Stalin's practical application of that philosophy. The charges under which he was jailed in India and Kenya had nothing to do with his being a communist but related to his struggle for India and Kenya's independence. When he was thrown in jail in India, the communists there were looked upon with a favourable eye by the British because Russia had been drawn into the war. The Communist Party of India had pledged its full support to the British war effort. Not so Makhan Singh. But on the other hand, he had never taken any trips to Russia or China.

'When Makhan was released, the old man [his father] asked him to look after his printing works and went to India for retirement. But Makhan was not cut out to be a businessman. Mr. Sudh Singh had to return to take charge of the press.' The reporter lamented, 'he does not seem to be interested in his future. He is a frustrated man. I feel the time has come for him to settle down, to look after his family and lead a happy life. He has sacrificed enough.' Being a Marxist at heart, Makhan Singh did not believe in owning property. 'I am willing to work even for Shs.100/- for you; I would rather be your employee, than an owner,' he told his father. Sudh Singh ultimately sold the press for a pittance and retired to India in 1964.

'Makhan strongly refutes that Kenya has "forgotten" him. "They have not forgotten me, I assure you." Makhan is indeed a controversial figure, but above all, he is a man of principles, a man of integrity of purpose, a man of courage who gave one third of his life in the struggle against colonialism. History will record that the African had no greater champion among the Kenya Asians.'

The *Daily Nation* of the 18th reported that senator Clement Lubembe, general secretary of the KFL, announced that the KFL had passed a resolution on 14th November recommending that Mr Gama Pinto should vacate his seat to allow the election of Mr Mathu. Ochola O Mak'Anyengo, general secretary of the Kenya Petroleum and Oil Workers Union and Vicky Macharia, general secretary of the E A Building and Construction Workers Union, opposed this and said they wanted to give due credit to the only two Asians who suffered as much as African nationalists in the struggle against imperialists and colonialism, Mr Gama Pinto and Mr Makhan Singh.

The *Sunday Nation* of 20th December published a letter from one Ajit Singh Bahaua. 'Mr. Makhan Singh is anti-publicity yet is known to all Kenyans. He is the only unselfish *muhindi* [Indian] who has sacrificed all that was his for the cause of Kenya and now is virtually penniless. He begs none, but Almighty, to give him nothing but a chance to serve humanity as and when and where he pleases. While reminding him of the saying, "Though there is delay, there is no injustice at the door of the Lord," let us pay him a warm tribute.' Referring to this letter, Ahmed Ali from Malindi wrote, under the heading 'He Suffered For An Ideal.' 'All fair-minded persons should support the idea that Mr. Makhan Singh must be given a fitting position in life. I think he has suffered more than anyone else.

He suffered because he had the courage to put an ideal in practice. It is not a joke to be restricted for ten years. After all, he only wanted to improve the condition of the workers.'

Makhan Singh's 1964 file collection contains an *East African Standard* photograph of a symbolic 'burial of Verwoed' on 22nd June, a 15th July editorial on the discord between Odinga and Mboya, a request from the Social Service League for him to volunteer to sell flags and a photograph of a mammoth rally he attended on 27th July at Kamakunji. Sitting in the front rows, he listened to Kenyatta addressing it.

In a pamphlet dated 21st August and titled *Toward a One Party System*, Jomo Kenyatta advocated 'constructive opposition from within.' He made a scathing attack on KADU and its leader, Ronald Ngala and said: 'All 2-party states are not necessarily democratic and all one-party states are not necessarily authoritarian.' Makhan Singh also filed a copy of the *Daily Nation* of 28th August which carried a statement by

'Burial of Verwoed', with Jomo Kenyatta, Tom Mboya and Makhan Singh

Odinga concerning the mischief of the British press and its reaction to the recent deportation of Ian Henderson who was a special branch officer who had organised pseudo gangs to expose the Mau Mau. He was deported to the UK in 1964 by the Kenyatta government.

THE ASSASSINATION OF PIO GAMA PINTO

Pio Gama Pinto was gunned down in his car on Wednesday 24th February, 1965, at the gate of his house, his 18-month old daughter was with him. Two mornings later Makhan Singh made a broadcast, a half-hour report in Hindustani on the Voice of Kenya, recorded by Haroon Ahmed and C L Chaman.

The first time Mr P G Pinto met me was in 1949, after completing his education. He had recently come back from India and was at that time working in Magadi as a clerk. He had come to Nairobi on an outing. During those days our national freedom and trade union movements were going on vigorously. Mr. Pinto told me that he was interested in the movement and was already doing whatever was possible for him under the circumstances. The impression he gave me was that of a good freedom-loving young man. At that time he was in a hurry; so he left after a few minutes.

The second time he met me was a few days before my arrest in 1950. He said he was now ready to take an active part in the freedom struggle and, if necessary, he was prepared to leave his service. I advised him that before doing so he should obtain his certificate of permanent residence so that when he became active the colonial government should not be able to deport him from the country. He agreed, and went away after leaving a few political magazines with me.

After a few days (along with Mr. Fred Kubai) I was arrested on the 15th May, 1950, on account of my political and trade union activities. The arrest was followed by a general strike and a long political case, and I was sent into restriction at a small village, Lokitaung, near the boundary of Kenya and Ethiopia.

By this action the colonial government on the one hand wanted to punish me and keep me in complete isolation from the outside world, and on the other it wanted to frighten the other freedom loving Africans and Asians in order to prevent them from taking part in the freedom struggle. But Pinto was not a man who could be frightened. Even after seeing what had happened to me he entered the arena of struggle. Soon after my restriction Mr. Pinto left his service at Magadi, came to Nairobi, obtained his certificate of permanent residence and took the plunge in the freedom struggle – so much so that since that day he never thought of retreating from the struggle and always moved forward and forward.

During my restriction while I was still at Lokitaung Mr. Pinto sent me a book by H. G. Wells – *An Outline of the World*. He did so fully knowing that in the eyes of the colonial government even the mention of my name was a big crime. On the book he mentioned that it was a present from my Nairobi friends, and also wrote two lines in English to the effect that only that is the man who not only shows the way to others but also himself walks over the same. The lines not only gave me encouragement but also depicted the way in which Mr. Pinto was himself thinking and acting. Until his last breath he walked over the same path which he had shown to others in course of our national struggle for freedom, human dignity and prosperity for all.

After my release in October, 1961, I had the

opportunity of working with Mr. Pinto in Kenya Freedom Party and Kenya African National Union (KANU) and I found him politically very sound and very correct, and day and night he worked as hard and so conscientiously that in the course of my own political life I have seen very few persons of that calibre.

Today P. G. Pinto is not with us, he has been taken away from us by the bullets of ghastly assassins, but his wish is alive and we can keep alive his memory for ever by actively and whole-heartedly devoting ourselves to the cause Mr. Pinto fought for all his life – the cause of freedom, peace, human dignity and prosperity for all in Kenya, East Africa, All Africa and the world.

Pio Gama Pinto's earliest foray into journalism in Kenya had been in 1950 when he was still working as a civil servant and wrote reports on hockey matches for the *Daily Chronicle*. When it was sold the following year he briefly became its editor.[5] He also had grand plans to publish papers in different dialects. The *Nawa Zamana* of 17th May published an article on Gama Pinto's assassination and called it 'part of an imperialist plot.' It stated that Gama Pinto was in charge of the KANU press and that he wanted to break the British monopoly of press coverage. On 19th June, 1966, the Executive Committee of the International Organisation of Journalists awarded the late Pio Gama Pinto a posthumous prize.

Pinto was one of the directors of the Lumumba Institute where Makhan Singh was briefly employed as a lecturer and it is possible that the *Nawan Zamana* article was based on information given by Makhan Singh. Later, in October, the *Nawan Zamana* published an article no doubt written by Makhan Singh, describing how the Communist Party came into being in Africa. It traced its beginnings to the National Socialist League established in South Africa in 1915 up to the banning of the Communist Party with mass arrests and killings in 1950 and mentioned the *African Communist* which spread the ideas all over Africa.

In its May edition, *Drum* magazine called Gama Pinto's murder 'a human tragedy' and 'an outrage to all Kenya and a terrible precedent.' 'Africa had another martyr,' it said. External Affairs Minister Joseph Murumbi said '. . . it was through Pinto that I became interested in politics . . . if ever the country and the party had a friend, it was Pio.' According to *Drum*, 'his forthright views on trade unionism made him unpopular in some quarters. He openly supported the splinter trade union group, led by Mak'Anyengo, which broke away from KFL in 1964. Senator Lubembe, KFL's secretary general, frequently advocated that Pinto should be forced to resign from Parliament to make way for an African member though neither Lubembe nor the African substitute had ever set foot in a detention camp during the days of the struggle . . . . The great men of the land mourned one they looked on as a brother . . . a grief-filled statement from the President was followed by countless tributes from ministers, members of Parliament and nationalist leaders.' Makhan Singh contributed fifty-one shillings to the Mrs Gama Pinto and Children Fund organised by Fitz de Souza and others.

In early 1966, Ambu Patel was in the process of publishing a booklet on Gama Pinto and requested Makhan Singh to write about his personal contact with him. Ambu Patel died in December 1977 and the work was never published. The assassination made international news. Makhan Singh's brother-in-law, H S Mahal in India must have read about it. He wrote to Makhan Singh advising him not to go into government service. Makhan Singh responded by saying, 'In the course of serving the country and the nation all sorts of things, good and bad, do take place and we have to face them in the same good spirit as we show in the service to the country and to humanity at large. If one considers his cause as good he should never relent or go back, whatever the consequences.'

On 9th May, 1966, Makhan Singh and Satwant Kaur attended a reception at the USSR Embassy at a celebration to mark the

20th anniversary of the victory of the Soviet people over the Nazi invaders.

Two researchers, one Richard T McCormack, working on a thesis on 'Duplicity of British policy towards Indians in Kenya,' wrote to him for information on his detention and the assassination of Isher Dass on 6th November, 1942. Another researcher, Chhotu Karadia from the E A Institute of Social and Cultural Affairs, was interested in Makhan Singh's role in the 1947 to 1950 period of Kenya's history. Makhan Singh however declined to grant the interviews.

G Adhikari, member of the Communist Party of India and editor of its paper, *New Age*, wrote to him: 'No reply to my last message – therefore writing again. Comrade Makhan Singh, we have a claim on you as you worked for 10 years in the period of the Second World War and after with our Party as its outstanding member and leader. I am personally happy that I had an opportunity to be in contact with you since 1939-40 to 1947-8 both underground in Bombay and Ahmedabad and later open in Lahore . . . we always cite your shining example of struggle and suffering in the cause of Africa.' He again requested Makhan Singh to write for *New Age*. 'Kenya's stand on the problems of African unity and African Socialism will be particularly important.' He sent this note with comrade Sheila Didi, granddaughter of Lalchand Sharma who had been imprisoned by the British in Kenya in 1914, together with proceedings of the Party's congress, resolutions of the national council and copies of the latest issue of *New Age*.

In June, the World Congress for Peace, National Independence and General Disarmament wrote to Makhan Singh requesting him to sign their appeal. 'Your signature will be of great help in ensuring that the Congress will attract people of an exceptionally wide range of beliefs and viewpoints,' it said. Among other signatories were luminaries such as Picasso, Jean Paul Satre, Pablo Neruda, Simone de Beauvoir and Bertrand Russell. Makhan Singh consulted KANU headquarters and was told he could sign the appeal.

The next day, he phoned the headquarters. 'Since I saw you yesterday I have given further consideration to the matter. About a year and a half ago a decision about me was conveyed to me. [He was referring to the promise made by the Kenyan government in early 1964 regarding his appointment to a government post.] In the light of that decision I have avoided issuing any statements. The decision has so far not been implemented and I don't know when it will be implemented, but I believe it will be implemented. Under the circumstances I have decided to continue the policy of issuing no statements, and therefore I am not signing that appeal.' KANU concurred with his decision.

TRADE UNION MATTERS IN 1965

Makhan Singh must have considered 1965 to have been an important year in independent Kenya's trade union history as he compiled a file of press cuttings on the subject. Almost all were taken from the *East African Standard,* a few from the *Nation* newspapers and *Baraza.*

The clippings dealt with matters as diverse as the American Embassy's refusal to allow its workers to join the Kenya Diplomatic Employees Union; the Industrial Court's recommendation for a pay rise to the railway workers; KFL's protest regarding the Uganda Government's decision to bar Kenyans in Uganda from leadership positions in the trade unions and Senator C K Lubembe's admonition to Asians to 'come off the fence and become Kenya citizens' in a dispute between Barclays Bank employees and the Kenya Distributive and Commercial Workers Union (of which he was president).

Makhan Singh kept track of some of the employment and wage statistics. Figures released in July, 1965, showed 589,600 employed, a drop from 615,100 ten years earlier. The wage bill had however risen to KPounds103,100,000 from KPounds67,100,000 in 1955. Asians in employment numbered 36,700 (34,600 in 1955) and earned KPounds21,100,000 (20,600,000 in 1955). European employment had fallen from 22,400 to 16,000 and their earnings from KPounds25,700,000 to 24,100,000.

There was mounting unrest and confusion in the labour sector with strikes, actual and threatened. Strikes in 1964 had resulted in the loss of 167,767 working days and an epidemic of stoppages had involved 67,155 workers. There were strikes in the EASCO (East Africa Common Services Organisation), the municipal councils, posts and telecommunications, and customs. The meteorology, agriculture, electrical, engineering, petroleum oil and brewery trades were also affected. Teachers and tailors, domestic, hotel, chemical and cinema workers were agitating for an improvement in their living standards. Racial imbalance in the banks with too many non-African employees was leading to undesirable repercussions. The Dennis Akumu group had demonstrated against Lubembe in a Dockworker's Union meeting and Akumu, the general secretary, had been suspended from the union. Akumu, with Pio Gama Pinto, then formed the Kenya African Workers Congress. In 1965, in Mombasa, violence erupted between rival factions and five workers were killed.

THE FORMATION OF COTU

In September 1965, the government decided to reorganise the trade union movement. The reasons given were 'to put an end to the bitter rivalries' and 'to foster economic development and to strengthen the existing trade unions.' The KFL, the African

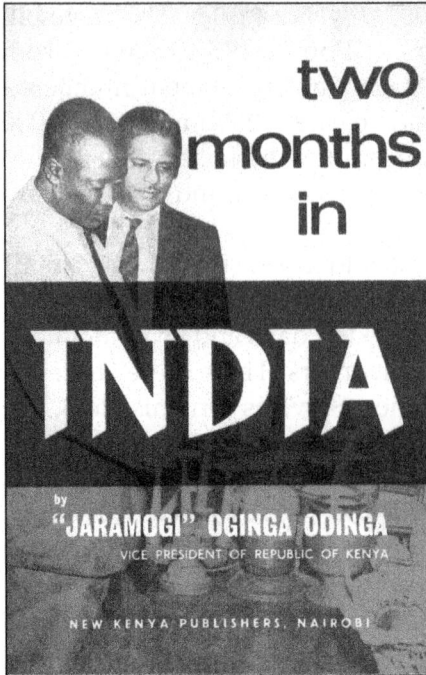

A record of Jaramogi Oginga Odinga's visit to India

Workers Congress and other similar bodies were deregistered, all existing external affiliations were cancelled and fresh elections were held for selecting officials of the new organisation, the Central Organisation of Trade Unions (COTU). The COTU constitution gave the government the right to appoint the secretary general from a panel of three elected officials. This statute ensured government control of the trade union movement in independent Kenya and was a reversal of the freedoms that Makhan Singh and his fellow trade unionists had consistently defended in the colonial era.

In the COTU elections held on 11th October, 1965, Lubembe garnered 38 votes and won by one vote against Akumu. Kenyatta appointed him the secretary general and Akumu as his deputy. Before the year was out, Akumu and others were complaining of being ignored by Lubembe. In 1966, Akumu joined Oginga Odinga in the newly formed Kenya Peoples Union and was later detained for a year by the Kenya government. He emerged to become the secretary general of COTU in 1969 – 'an uneasy victory in a divided leadership' as *Drum* magazine described it in 1972.

THE LUMUMBA INSTITUTE
❋

The Lumumba Institute had been set up in December 1964, in the Kasarani suburb of Nairobi to train cadres of local party officials and to instruct them in both African and scientific socialism. Excluded from parliamentary influence, the left had hoped to use a party platform to gain power. Gama Pinto and Odinga had been prime movers, two Russian and nine African lecturers, including Makhan Singh, taught the first (and last) class of 85 students who graduated in June 1965.[6]

The Institute's ideological orientation was self evident from its commemorative plaque. It read: 'THIS INSTITUTE IS DEDICATED TO LUMUMBA THE PATRIOT WHO DIED AT THE HANDS OF IMPERIALISTS AND THEIR AGENTS FOR HIS FIRM CHAMPIONSHIP OF GENUINE AFRICAN POLITICAL AND ECONOMIC INDEPENDENCE AND SOCIALISM IN AFRICA.'[7] It ran short of funds and Kenyatta's increasingly right wing government ensured that it closed down.

Makhan Singh's employment at the Lumumba Institute at a monthly salary of five hundred shillings was terminated at the end of June. He then applied for a bursary for his daughter Inderjeet to the City Education Department to enable her to study at the University of East Africa. 'I have no other source of income and request for a full bursary to cover all the tuition fees and the fees of residence at the hostel and other expenses,' he wrote. The bursary was granted.[8] On completion of her university course in bio-chemistry, she left for post-graduate studies in Canada for which she was able to secure a grant. She was married in 1977 and settled in the UK where she completed her doctoral degree.

August saw a debate on the need to revitalise KANU. President Mwai Kibaki, then Assistant Minister for Economic Planning and National Executive Officer of KANU, was its prime mover. He attributed the current disagreement among

Kenya leaders to 'the lack of an effective party machinery which could have explained African Socialism to the masses.' 'There must be agreement of ideology, if leadership discipline was to be maintained,' he said and suggested that the country could no longer afford to exclude civil servants from belonging to a 'revitalised' KANU in the new and important role that the party should play. But there was still no role for Makhan Singh.

Makhan Singh was present at the weddings of Fitz de Souza, Sammy Maina and Krishan Gautama. From *Nawa Zamana* he received an obituary of Hira Singh Dard who had passed away in June. Dard was a respected revolutionary Marxist and writer who was the editor of the *Phulwari* magazine of the Punjab. His photograph shows him as a fatherly figure; he had been a source of inspiration to Makhan Singh and probably was a friend of Sudh Singh.

AFRICANISATION

The *East African Standard* of 25th September, 1966, published the speech given by Tom Mboya, Minister of Economic Planning and Development, at the start of the new University College year. He spoke of 'tremendous complexity of development and replied to critics of the Sessional Paper on African Socialism.' Makhan Singh underlined Mboya's comments on income distribution where he said the emphasis was being given to 'levelling upwards' instead of 'levelling downwards.' 'We are told from some quarters that there is no such thing as African Socialism, there is only Scientific Socialism which is valid the world over. We on the other hand reject the suggestion that Scientific Socialism is the proper system for our country.' On 'Africanisation' he maintained it should be a means of providing Africans with new assets instead of just transferring assets from non-Africans to Africans. Makhan Singh also highlighted Mboya's statement that: 'Political power is not to be related to material possessions' and 'Government and Parliament must have control and direction of the economy on behalf of the people.'

In the *Daily Nation* of 16th November, the MP Luke Obok responded to a letter by his colleague, S M Amin MP for Mandera, published on the 11th and titled 'Future of Indians here'. It claimed ' . . . most Africans in this country do not feel very happy with the idea of sharing their future with Indians . . . . The Indian attitude towards life is in itself a barrier to integration and a threat to national unity.' Writing under the heading 'Irresponsible and Misplaced Comments', Obok affirmed that 'Asians have in the past supported our freedom movement and many of them suffered with us and went to prison. One can cite several examples like Pio Pinto and Makhan Singh. They collected money for our leaders visiting London and helped in the defence of our national leaders in court. Likewise in business and commerce the contribution of Asians has been considerable . . . a businessman knows no colour when it comes to profit. But to condemn the whole community for the mistakes of a few is wrong and immoral.'

In June 1966, Obok was to write a lengthy obituary of Sat Bali-Sharma, a patriotic Asian lawyer who had died at a young age. 'Because of his belief in the rule of law, Sat spared no effort to see that the necessary defence was arranged for everyone who appeared to have fallen victim to misfortune; or anyone who was likely to suffer because he had no defence counsel. It is in this role that a great number of Africans, as well members of the other races, will remember him because he appeared in many cases without fear of intimidation or victimisation.' The *Daily Nation* and the *East African Standard* both reported that it was a poignant moment when during the last rites, Jaramogi Odinga exclaimed 'Who can replace Bali-Sharma?'

On 10th June, Makhan Singh saw the world premiere of the film 'Harambee – The Story of the Republic of Kenya'. The invitation card was from Hon. R Achieng Oneko, Minister of

Information and Broadcasting. The film was shown at the Twentieth Century Cinema and there he was given a programme for the second anniversary of Kenya's republic day celebrations.

The snubbing of Makhan Singh by officialdom became more and more explicit. On 19th January, 1966, the *East African Standard* reported that the Central Organisation of Trade Unions (COTU) had appointed directors of various departments but that the post of Director of Economics had not been filled as no application from a suitable person had been received in time. Did the fact that Makhan Singh did not even apply signify his disapproval of the new organisation, or a growing realisation that the odds were stacked against him? He was an obvious candidate but there was no indication that he was even consulted.

TEACHING HISTORY

In the first week of March, president Kenyatta established the eponymous Jomo Kenyatta Foundation. Of special interest to Makhan Singh was the directive to the Ministry of Education to ensure that schoolbooks prepared through the Ministry were channelled through the foundation. 'It was hoped,' the directive stated, 'that the University College, the East African Academy and the East African Institute of Social and Cultural Affairs would stimulate interest among their members to become writers of schoolbooks.'

The irony was that at the same time Makhan Singh was being refused permission to do just that. Earlier in the year Makhan Singh had met with John Gitau, Chief Inspector of Schools in the Ministry of Education. Stressing the importance of teaching such history, he requested for a licence to lecture on Mzee Jomo Kenyatta's biography and the history of Kenya's national movement. He had prepared a series of 25 lectures for the course he had been giving at the Lumumba Institute but had delivered only thirteen before his course had been terminated in June 1966. Now he gave Gitau a copy of his notes and asked if he could be given the opportunity to complete them at some school or college or even write them down.

The chief education officer wrote a confidential note to Makhan Singh on 16th March. 'I regret that it is not customary for this Ministry to issue such a licence to a person until he has been employed as a teacher. It is, however, important that you should not take up an appointment as a teacher until you have received a licence or an authority to teach.' His lecture notes were returned to him.

But there was a flicker of interest from another government department. On 16th March the Ministry of Labour and Social Services wrote the following to him, 'This is a note to confirm to you that my Minister is aware of your present difficulties and that anything we can do to utilise your good services will be done.' Makhan Singh promptly replied, 'Dear Meshak, I sincerely thank you for the efforts the Minister, the Assistant Minister and yourself are making to utilise my services . . .' The secretary of the Ministry's Labour Advisory Board invited Makhan Singh to serve as an independent member of the Board which was a statutory body set up under the provisions of Section 4 of the Employment Act, Cap 226. Its function was to advise the minister upon such matters connected with employment and labour. The normal term for holding office was three years and the board met approximately twice a year. He accepted the appointment.

A condolence meeting on the death of Lal Bahadur Shastri, India's prime minister, and an exhibition on the life of Jawaharlal Nehru were events that he attended at this time. As he waited, his other activities included going to the inauguration of the First South West Asian and African Convention organised by Lions District 411 (where Dr Njoroge Mungai, Minister for Defence, was the guest of honour), a function at the Kenya Punjabi Literary Society, and a meeting with John Nottingham, the director of the E A Publishing House. The meeting was most probably in connection with the publication of the history of Kenya's trade union movement which Makhan Singh was then researching.

On 14th July, 1966, J G Kiano, the Minister for Labour and Social Services, wrote to Makhan Singh. 'Since we last met I have given considerable thought to the most suitable employment of your particular talents in connection with the Ministry of Labour. I now feel that you could best help as an independent member of a Wages Council, and I intend, with your agreement, to appoint you to the Motor Engineering Trades Wages Council in this capacity, instead of an advisory Board as such.' On 20th July, Makhan Singh informed the minister of his acceptance. Nine weeks later he telephoned Mr Lindsay, secretary to the Labour Advisory Board at the Ministry, to enquire and was told that no appointment had yet been made on the Wages Council. As for the Labour Advisory Board, Lindsay replied that he did not know what was in the minister's mind.

THE VOICE OF KENYA SAGA

The taunting and harassment of Makhan Singh did not emanate from some personal vendetta; it was official government policy. The saga of Makhan Singh's mistreatment at the VOK is even further evidence of this. Soon after his release Makhan Singh had worked in the VOK news room in 1962 for a period of seven or eight months. He probably worked in the Hindustani Service when it was headed by his old comrade, Haroon Ahmed.[9]

Chaman Lal Chaman, an ex-Kenyan who now lives in

London, worked for the VOK at the same time and had this to say about Makhan Singh:

'I met Makhan Singh for the first time when he was released from detention. Prior to this, I had heard a great deal about him from a number of people, who talked very highly of him. I also had an opportunity to meet his father, Sudh Singh who ran the only printing press in Punjabi in the country. He used to produce leaflets and simple brochures catering for the linguistic and cultural needs of the community at that time.

'I always had a keen interest in the cultural aspect of the Asian community, in particular in music, dance, poetry and plays at the National Theatre. It was at one of these events, most probably a poetry reading session at Siri Guru Singh Sabha, where I met Gopal Singh Chandan, who owned a photo studio in Grogan Road. It was Gopal Singh Chandan who first told me about Makhan Singh and his trade union activities and his commitment to Communism but my first glimpse of Makhan Singh was at their family residence in Park Road on his release.

'I had gone there from Broadcasting House to cover his release for a broadcast on the Hindustani Service of the Voice of Kenya. Jomo Kenyatta, then the president of KANU, was there to greet Makhan Singh. This was most probably the first and last encounter of Jomo Kenyatta with Makhan Singh. This became evident when Makhan Singh joined VOK as a translator, preparing news bulletins for Asian Programmes. Along with a team of full-time staff, Makhan Singh used to translate news in the Urdu language. There was a full-time staff of fourteen, headed by Haroon Ahmed, an experienced journalist, who had worked for papers like *Africa Samaachar*, *Colonial Times* and *Daily Chronicle*. Haroon had no broadcasting experience and his writings often reflected a bias for African Socialism. He passionately shared the aspirations of the Wananchi. Perhaps this was the commonality of ideology that Haroon shared with Makhan Singh.

'I have a very vivid memory of this dignified gentleman of medium build, wearing a white turban and glasses, summer jacket and trousers. He was always neatly dressed. A quiet serious man, hardly talking to anyone when translating the news bulletin into Urdu. I always wanted to talk to him about his experiences and the hardships he suffered during detention. But he always avoided the topic, just saying briefly in Punjabi: *Kilena ehna beetian galan to!* (What is the use of repeating the past!)

'I found him to be a 'reserved' person. I thought he deserved some prominent position in independent Kenya. Achieng Oneko had been appointed Minister for Information and Broadcasting in the new Government. Makhan Singh had been in detention at the same time as him and participated in the same struggle but it seemed as if Makhan Singh was isolated because of his commitment to Communism. Even then I felt that he deserved a position of some prominence. One day I suggested to him that he should see Mzee [Jomo Kenyatta].When I repeated this and insisted, his response was just a faint satirical smile as if he intended to say:

Chala jata hoon hansta khelta mauj-e-hawadas mein
Agar asanian hon zindagi dushwar ho jaaye.
(In a playful laughing mood, I am facing the waves of adversity
For without these life would be so difficult to lead.)

Makhan Singh gave me a rock-like look that knew no compromises in life.'

Now, four years later, the *Sunday Post* on 8th May, 1966, announced that VOK's Hindustani Service, headed by Makhan Singh's old colleague Haroon Ahmed, had started a new series of talks – the life of Jomo Kenyatta by Makhan Singh to be broadcast every Monday. 'The subject is of great interest of course, but it is something of a scoop on the part of the service to have persuaded Makhan Singh to deal with it,' it said. 'It has always been a mystery how a man like Makhan Singh, who had been so prominent in public life for so long, could withdraw from it as completely as he has done. He created more lively interest when he was in detention than he has done since his release!'

Referring to him as 'An undoubted expert' on the subject it informed its readers that the first of the series dealt with the president's childhood and the tribal customs of the Kikuyus. 'The language he used was the simple, colloquial Hindustani which we need on the Hindustani Service . . .' and went on to decry the type of language used by some VOK staff. The *Post's* 22nd May issue reported on Makhan Singh's third instalment in which he recalled the days in the early '20s when the Indians of Kenya entered the political arena. 'I understand these talks are being translated for the national and the general services and will eventually appear in book form. An excellent idea,' wrote the *Post's* editor, Narain Singh.

On 25th March, 1966, Makhan Singh gave his English script on the life of Kenyatta to the VOK. The broadcast was to consist of 15 talks of 15 minutes each and VOK said they planned to translate them into Kiswahili. The main actors in this drama were James Kangwana, deputy director of the VOK, Hassan Mazoa, head of the General Service, Daniel Gatuga, head of the National Service, Stephen Kikumu, controller of programmes, J J Wanzala, M Kari and Harun Anzia.

Haroon Ahmed, as head of the Hindustani Service, arranged a meeting with Gatuga and Anzia and the script was handed over to Wanzala. Wanzala approved the script and praised it but said the final approval had to be made by Kangwana. On the 29th Kangwana accepted the script for broadcasting and asked Makhan Singh to rearrange the content of the 15 lectures into 12 talks. Ahmed meanwhile asked Makhan Singh to write down the 12 talks in Hindustani and subsequently they were reproduced and broadcast on the VOK.

On 2nd June, Wanzala told Makhan Singh to reduce the first two talks to 15 minutes for a recording session. However, the script had not been typed and a studio was not available. On the 16th, Makhan Singh gave Wanzala a re-written script of the first 7 talks together with a statement with details for payment. Regarding the Kiswahili translation Wanzala told him 'We will let you know later.' And about payment, no decision had been made about the rate of payment.

Starting from 27th June, VOK would call Makhan Singh, by phone or previous arrangement, to meetings but these never took place. Either the person concerned was too busy, or was in the studio, in a meeting or simply not available. Makhan Singh complained to Haroon Ahmed, who suggested that he meet Mazoa. The meeting took place on 28th August and Mazoa offered to look into the problem. On the 6th Makhan Singh was informed that VOK had overspent its budget for the time being and could not do the broadcasts. A month later, they said the delay was temporary and the talks would be broadcast just before Kenyatta Day in October. Makhan Singh gave them the remaining scripts, of talks 8 to 12.

Kenyatta Day came and went. On the 27th Wanzala informed Makhan Singh of the rate of payment. On 8th November VOK informed Makhan Singh that the manuscript was being typed and was with Wanzala but the latter was unwell. Then silence – for three months.

On 1st March, 1967, Wanzala told Makhan Singh that 'the decision to broadcast your talks has been taken and Hassan will write to you officially in a few days' time. Three weeks later he was asked to speak with Kari because 'Wanzala is no longer with us and he is out of Kenya.' On 3rd April, Mazoa told Makhan Singh 'I never got the script. I don't know where Wanzala is after his resignation.' On 17th April, 1967, Makhan Singh made a final phone call to Kari. Boaz Omari and Wanzala had both left the VOK. Kari had enquired from Omari who had said he knew nothing about the script. He offered to set up another meeting with the director of VOK.

Makhan Singh had, over this period from 25th March, 1966, to 17th April, 1967, made 62 phone calls and 31 visits to VOK. He noted each call and visit and has left a detailed account of this long and miserable story. His family was much disturbed and saddened by this deliberate and merciless tormenting of an elderly man, quite apart from the fact that he was a great patriot and leader. His son, Hindpal, repeatedly begged him to 'stop running after these people. You don't need to, we can support you.'

THE END OF DEMOCRACY

These were dark days in Kenya's history as the ideals of the nationalists were being trampled into the dust. But despite the looming storm, Ambu Patel went ahead with the launch of a booklet called *Two Months in India* by Jaramogi Oginga Odinga in January 1965.

It was Odinga's account of a visit he made to India in 1953. By April 1966, Odinga had resigned from KANU to form the Kenya Peoples Union (KPU). The government proscribed the party in 1969 and arrested and detained its leading members. The major bone of contention was the KPU demand for a more militant foreign policy, nationalisation and substantial changes in the working of industrial relations in Kenya.

In August 1966 the government deported a group of Asians from Kenya, amongst them Pranlal Sheth, a Kenyan patriot and close associate of Makhan Singh and Odinga. The *East African Standard* of 23rd December, 1966, termed the detention of KPU members, the deportation of Asians and radio attacks on the Asian community as outrageous assaults upon political liberty and the rights of the citizen. The anti-Asian hysteria had swept Makhan Singh along in its torrent of racial odium but this was only one current amongst the many other adverse currents of neo-colonialism that the country's people were trying to swim against. Had Makhan Singh seen this and opted to stand as a steadfast beacon or was he still stagnating in the pre-independence mind-set? With his older colleagues, Pio Gama Pinto (assassinated), Pranlal Sheth (deported) and D K Sharda (who had returned to India), no longer near him, he was increasingly isolated. Asians generally had moved up the class ladder so he had even fewer friends in the community. In the trade union arena the new incumbents were unwilling to accommodate the old guard and generally there was a jockeying for power in a confused and uncertain situation.

His files of that period contained articles on Odinga and the KPU from *Africa and the World*, a magazine that was once banned in Kenya. He attended COTU's 1967 May Day rally and listened to the speech by the secretary-general. Meshak Ndisi, Permanent Secretary in the Ministry of Labour and Social Services, apologised to him for missing an appointment with him and offered to visit him. Makhan Singh invited him to his house. Some papers are missing from the Makhan Singh collection so it was not possible to ascertain if the visit took place but there was a note signed by Ndisi with instructions that Makhan Singh should be allowed to visit him at any time. Meshak Ndisi became the ILO Regional Director for Africa in 1969.

He received an invitation from All India Revolutionaries' Conference to a meeting on the 13th, the day of the first mass sentences passed on the Ghadr Party leaders and workers. It was to be held at the Desh Bhagat Yaadgar Hall in Jalhandar and specified that 'it was a unique opportunity to old revolutionaries from all over India to get together and exchange their views on the present situation. Also, to rectify the situation, because the Congress Government was a bourgeois government, worse than the colonialists. It had worsened the condition of the working class and was promoting communalism and religious strife.' Makhan Singh thanked them and sent his regrets and greetings to the Ghadrees (Ghadr elders). The invitation included an article by

Arjun Singh Ghargaj on 'Communist Martyrs in the Freedom Struggle' published in *Nawa Zamana*.

In December 1966, Makhan Singh attended the premiere of 'The Nation Kenyans Build – Kenya 1967.' The invitation was from Hon. J C N Osogo, Minister of Information and Broadcasting. But from then on Makhan Singh's social life appears to have shrunk considerably. Apart from a lunch at Fitz de Souza's and visits from the research scholar Jagdish Gundara from Edinburgh University, from T Sisburn, secretary general of the Mauritius Peoples' Progressive Party and from Chiman Bhatt of the United Africa Press Ltd there are no records of any other activities. Makhan Singh was shifting his attention to recording history rather than making it.

THE HISTORICAL ASSOCIATION OF KENYA

The Historical Association of Kenya was formed in 1966 by a group of history teachers, university lecturers and interested persons. Its first chairman was Prof Bethwell Ogot. It was mostly inactive during the Moi years but was revived in 2004. On 19th January, 1968, Makhan Singh read a paper on 'Problems of writing the history of Kenya's national movement' to a meeting of the Nairobi branch of the Historical Association of Kenya. 'The task before the writers of our national history is to unearth and fully present the material about the national resistance, protest campaigns and the final national assault on the citadel of British imperialism in Kenya,' he said and bemoaned the 'lack of historical material especially concerning those who resisted, protested or organised resistance against British rule. Most of the available material is in connection with those who helped or collaborated with the British rulers. For example, in the pre-British period some material is about the activities of the Arab rulers but very little about African slaves and their resistance. The colonial writers laid more stress on divisions and quarrels of the tribal territories so as to facilitate the implementation of the policy of 'divide and rule' but the responsibility of a nationalist historian is to see that, while not ignoring the divisions, differences, quarrels and fights, he writes in greater detail about the things that united the people and the different tribes. He should also try to find out and reveal the stories of those heroes who fought against oppression and injustice.'

He described the first workers' organisations of the 1890s, gave a detailed list of them and the protest movements from 1920 to 1963, and the events which led up to Uhuru. He stressed that foreign intrusion was resisted from the very beginning and that the East African Association was both a political organisation as well as a general workers' union. He included the return of thousands of demobilised soldiers and the experience gained by them, the labour trade union movements, the independent schools movement, religio-political organisations, the struggles put up by the squatters, the Land and Freedom Army, the Kenya African Union, oathing and the development of a secret mass organisation. Throughout he emphasised that Kenya's trade union movement was part and parcel of the national struggle against colonialism.

He spoke of the 'successful accomplishment by Mzee Jomo Kenyatta, as Father of the Nation and as President of KANU, of the difficult task of keeping the moderates and the militants united in the national movement before, during and after the Emergency, and on the whole, his keeping the national movement united up to the present period.

'The task of writing the history of our national movement is both important and urgent. If left only to individual historians of Kenya and foreign countries the task will never be accomplished and will create confusion and serious problems for our national movement. On the other hand, if our task is undertaken as a crash programme, organised by our Government and supported by our national organisations and institutions, with unconditional foreign friendly help not excluded, it would be accomplished in the shortest possible time. The accomplishment of the task will be one of the most suitable memorials to those who gave their sweat, blood and lives for the national cause, It will also provide correct guidance to our present and future generations.'

In May, he sent in a request for the *Panorama* magazine published by the International Labour Organisation explaining that, 'As a veteran trade unionist . . . to keep myself informed about the activities of the organisation and then to use this information in the interests of the trade union movement wherever possible . . . at present I use the information in personal talks whenever opportunity arises.'

His other activities in 1968 included a dinner with Fitz de Souza and an invitation from him to the opening ceremony of a harambee dispensary in Muranga (which Makhan Singh was unable to attend due to lack of transport), a visit by Cherry Gertzel of the Department of Government, University College and an invitation to the 6th Kenya Homes Exhibition officially sponsored by Tom Mboya MP, EGH, Minister for Economic Planning and Development. He received his annual membership card from KANU and was a regular blood donor every year during Kenyatta week held around 20th October, the date Kenyatta was arrested by the colonialists.

On Kenyatta Day Makhan Singh recorded a 20 minute talk in Hindustani for the VOK. It was broadcast the next day at 8.40 p. m. but, to his surprise, it had been edited by the VOK. In keeping with the increasing suppression and distortion of Kenya's history and Kenyatta's 'selective amnesia', the names of Kenyatta's fellow detainees, Fred Kubai, Kungu Karumba, Bildad Kaggia, Paul Ngei and Achieng Oneko had all been deleted. The talk was preceded by a song – *Sandesh Dunia ke Jawano Ko* (Message to the youth of the world).

On 1st February, 1969, he attended the Requiem Mass for

Makhan Singh's 20 minute talk in Urdu that he recorded for the VOK for Kenyatta Day.

Hon. C M G Arwings-Kodhek, the Minister of State in charge of foreign affairs, who died in a questionable road accident.

By 1969, COTU had become quite dynamic. Dennis Akumu, the veteran trade unionist, had himself come out of detention in 1967 having been arrested for being a member of the KPU and was now its secretary general. He offered to arrange for Makhan Singh to work with COTU, (Chege Kibachia had earlier been given an administrative job). But Makhan Singh no longer wanted a role in the trade union movement; he had already commenced writing the history of the movement in pre-independence times. Akumu now mobilised the unions to organise a group to research the history of each union. It was at this time, in a rare moment of confidentiality, that Makhan Singh said to Akumu, 'Kenyatta promised me a post but now I cannot even meet him.'[10] Perhaps the only time that he is known to have voiced a complaint against his one-time colleague and fellow freedom fighter. His old reporter friend of the *Daily Chronicle* days, Piyo Rattansi, met Makhan Singh some years after his release and found him rather withdrawn. He would not talk very frankly. 'What do you do these days?' Piyo asked. With a glint in his eye Makhan Singh replied, 'I am an expert on the life of our President. I give lectures about him and courses on him.'[11] Fitz de Souza says,

> though Makhan Singh never changed his ideology and his feelings about Kenya and the working class, he lost some of his fire. Detention seemed to have softened him.[12]

Having decided to retire from public life, Makhan Singh became an active member of the Historical Association of Kenya, often chairing the presentation of papers and serving for a year as its secretary. Initially the Association dons were sceptical of Makhan Singh's scholarly abilities as he had no academic qualifications but he soon proved them wrong.[13] Makhan Singh's real-life struggles had given him an understanding and clarity that was as good as, if not better than, any university course could render. In 1968 he had presented a paper on 'Problems of writing the history of Kenya's national movement' (See above).

THE HISTORY OF KENYA'S TRADE UNION MOVEMENT

But his real interest was trade unionism and he devoted his remaining years to writing about it. Fred Kubai encouraged him and helped him to contact a great many of the trade unionists and freedom fighters still living from that period and with the assistance of the Historical Association of Kenya, Prof Bethwell Ogot and others, he researched and wrote a detailed history of the trade union movement in Kenya. The

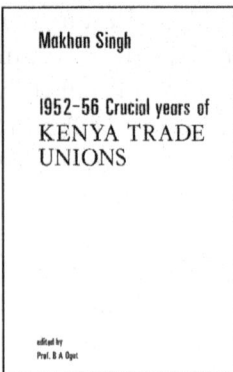

Covers of two books on trade unions authored by
Makhan Singh

first volume, entitled *History of Kenya's Trade Movement to 1952*, covered the period between 1900 and 1952 and was completed and published by the East African Publishing House in 1969. He dedicated it to 'To all those who struggled, suffered and sacrificed for the cause of Kenya's national and trade union movements.'

In his introduction Makhan Singh wrote, 'The history of the past 80 years has been the history of this great struggle, in which the African people of Kenya have been completely victorious. Kenya's trade union movement has been a part and parcel of this struggle, and its history has a place of great pride in the history of our great national revolutionary movement.'

Fred Kubai, in his foreword written on 19th April, 1969, bemoaned the fact that there were very few books on Kenya which exposed the colonialists' minds at work. 'No stone has been left unturned,' he said, 'in the compilation of this history that throws light on the conditions prevailing during the days of colonialism and the selfless sacrifices made by trade union leaders and other freedom fighters during those days.' He explained the close association in those days between trade unionism and politics thus: 'Where the people were in a situation such as the one Kenya was in under colonial rule, surely the only language the colonial rulers could understand was the language of unrest and economic instability brought about by civil strife, strikes and bloodshed.'

Fred Kubai, who had known Makhan Singh for years, had nothing but praise for him: 'He suffered honestly for our

Kenya's working class and independence. He became much feared because of his political beliefs and activism though I have not at any time ever seen him cross the border from Kenya's national struggle to a pure Marxist-communist struggle. He opposed vehemently any suggestion of getting financial aid from any organisation abroad. He also opposed any move to affiliate our trade unions with foreign world organisations but said that we should just ask for their moral support. He strived to identify himself and his activities with the indigenous people and the Kenya African Union's policies. He did not at any time advocate violence or unconstitutional methods. He believed and acted in the foremost task of educating and organising workers in all matters affecting them politically, economically and socially, leaving it to them to decide themselves in a democratic way.

'Mr. Makhan Singh was known, as they said or wrote, as "a controversial figure", "a very dangerous man", "a communist", "a born agitator" and by many other names. But to me I know him as a fighter, every inch a fighter, a Kenya nationalist of the highest order and a brother in trade unionism and in our national struggle for independence.'

He concluded his foreword stating that 'surely, the biggest war that was waged between the nationalists and the colonialists was on unity. The colonialists were not blind. They realised what our unity would bring to them. So they had to use all the destructive machinery in their hands to confuse, whatever they did. In the end the colonialists totally failed in their attempts to destroy our unity and resorted to guns, which also miserably failed.'

Makhan Singh donated all the proceeds of this monumental study equally to the Historical Association and COTU.

The second volume was entitled *1952-56 Crucial years of Kenya's Trade Unions*. It was edited by Prof Bethwell Ogot and published posthumously in 1980 by the Uzima Press. It was launched by Jeremiah Nyagah and Makhan Singh's elder son. Hindpal, as was done with the first volume, donated the royalties. The book provides valuable data for understanding how the process of class formation in Kenya began and shows that the workers' solidarity was based on both a racial and class consciousness. With the outbreak of Mau Mau, new local trade union leaders had emerged and their organisation became the lone voice in the colonial wilderness challenging white supremacy, demanding independence and defending the interests of the workers against the government. Therefore, it could be truly said that the workers also fought for independence.[14]

The last known photograph of Makhan Singh attending a public function was taken on 17th November, 1969. The occasion was the inauguration of the Ramgharia Dispensary in Nairobi, under the auspices of the East Africa Ramgharia Board. Its president, Bakshish Singh Sian presented J Singh Matharu with a gold key to perform the opening ceremony; the project celebrated the anniversary of the birth of Guru Nanak, the founder of Sikhism.

In 1970, on 2nd June, Makhan Singh delivered a lecture on 'The History of Kenya's Trade Union Movement' at the Trade Union Officials' course at the Management Training and Advisory Centre.[15] The lecture appears to have been his last public function. He gave a detailed account of Kenya's trade union movement starting with the worker organisations in the 1890s. He emphasised that the people had resisted colonialism from the time of its inception; the concept that pervaded the entire talk was that of the linkage between the trade union movement and the national liberation struggle.

Makhan Singh's father, Sudh Singh, who had returned to India, passed away there in September 1971. Makhan Singh said his condition (which he did not specify) did not allow him to travel, so Hindpal attended the cremation in India. Makhan Singh's refusal to travel to India could not have been due to any ill health as he was quite well at the time – did he still fear that he might not be allowed to return to the country he had adopted? Or was he reluctant to accept financial help from his

The last known photograph of Makhan Singh attending a public function, taken on 17th November 1969 at the inauguration of the Ramgarhia Dispensary in Nairobi.

sons? Why did he not travel to India where so many comrades and relatives were anxious to see him?

He did, however, participate in the ceremony that was held at the Park Road residence to mark the death of Sudh Singh. As was the custom, friends and relatives visited the house to pay their respects, and the entire *Guru Granth Sahib* (Sikh Holy Book) was recited. Though Makhan Singh never attended the weekly readings of the *Guru Granth Sahib* performed regularly in the gurdwaras, he did observe some symbolic Sikh traditions such as wearing a turban and keeping a beard. Upon his father's death he accepted, according to Sikh custom, to don his father's turban, thus becoming the titular head of the household.

DEATH AND CREMATION

But less than two years later on 15th May, 1973, Makhan Singh was admitted to the Aga Khan Hospital in Nairobi with a cardiac complaint. This was the second time he was being hospitalised for the same complaint. His bed was in the general ward and he was treated by Drs B P Arya and A N Dhanji who, as always, did not charge him any fees. It was the last time he ever entered a hospital as a patient. There he died peacefully in his sleep three days later at the age of 60. His body was brought home and it was cremated two days later to allow for the arrival of his daughter, Inderjeet, from Canada. His fellow workers and trade unionists helped to carry the bier. A red carpet was draped over the body, just as he had requested. Fitz de Souza remembers the cremation well.

The crematorium was overflowing, 75% of the crowd consisted of Sikhs, there were very few African leaders, only Fred Kubai and some trade unionists.

There was no official government representative. Though there were speeches after the cremation, the funeral was more like a private function. It was very disappointing. Once a person is out of politics he is out of the limelight and is forgotten.[16]

Makhan Singh's younger son, Swarajpal, says,

My father struggled up to the last moment, he did everything for the country but never received the recognition that should have been his. My father died of frustration.

Hindpal says,

Though he was never bitter, he was deeply disappointed and attributed his side-lining to differences of opinion. His loyalty to the nation never wavered to the extent that when the national anthem was played on the radio, he would invariably stand to attention. He would do this even if he was at the table having a meal or resting. My young children used to be amused by this.

Makhan Singh's ashes were immersed in the River Chania at Thika as was the Sikh and Hindu practice in those days.

E U L O G I E S [18]

In spite of the official silence, press editorials eulogised him and individuals sent messages. Perhaps the most incisive one was that sent by his long-time comrade, Haroon Ahmed, who wrote that Makhan Singh was 'at heart, a humanitarian and ardently advocated equality for all human beings whatever the pigmentation of their skin . . . . Religious intolerance was inconceivable to him for the simple reason that he was a confirmed Communist . . . . Makhan Singh's pity for the poor was not a mere passing commiseration and hollow sympathy devoid of concrete action. His sympathy was meaningful and practical. He worked during most of his life for the welfare of the labourers. Labour Trade Unionism was for almost his entire life his arena of activity . . . . Makhan Singh had no personal enemies. Friends he had many and they all had to be either connected directly with the labour movement or with the struggle for freedom. He hated British imperialism, but not the British. He abhorred capitalism, but had no trace of venom against capitalist individuals. He despised the system of exploitation and not the human cogs that formed the wheels of juggernaut or oppression.

'In his heart there smouldered an inextinguishable flame of desire to fight for freedom from imperialist subjugation. But freedom from foreign domination was not enough for him. He struggled all throughout his life for equality of opportunity for everyone – the black, brown and white, for the peasant, worker and the poorest of the poor . . . . He was not one to wallow in the glory of self-righteousness and past performances. He did not hanker after luxury or high positions. He was not the one to stagnate in inertia of authority or wealth . . . . The ambition, the idealism to strive to improve the conditions of the working class kept on burning incessantly in him till it finally consumed his frail body into cinders.'

His concluding remarks were to remind us of Makhan Singh's words: 'Now, forward, to build up a strong democratic African socialist Kenya, East Africa and ultimately Africa.'

Justice Chuni Madan, Q C wrote, 'Both Makhan Singh and his father have died. Makhan Singh was steadfast and staunch. His father was a loving parent. Makhan Singh has left behind memories of individual sacrifice for a principle which others may well emulate . . . . Appropriately enough the street facing the entrance to Jamhuri school has been renamed by the city council as Makhan Singh Road, no doubt to preserve the memory of his name as a tribute to services rendered by him to the peoples of Kenya.'

Duncan Mugo, general secretary of the Domestic and Hotel Workers Union described Makhan Singh as 'a practical socialist who had no racial discrimination since he had been believing in human equality.' Clement Lubembe, general secretary of the former Printing and Kindred Trades Workers Union, said that 'The foundation that he laid for the trade union movement will always be remembered.' (This was the union which had evicted Makhan Singh from its membership a decade earlier!) The Kenya Game Hunting and Safari Workers Union remembered 'comrade Makhan Singh as a heroic freedom fighter'. James Karebe, general secretary of the Kenya Local Government Workers Union, said the 'late Makhan Singh was a great son and a pioneer to the trade union movement. Makhan Singh was the only outstanding non-African figure who could speak against exploitation of workers, hence the colonial government imprisoned him without trial.' Fred Omido, chairman of the Central Organisation of Trade Unions, 'those who have had the opportunity of reading his book will conclude that the man was a genius in his time. He faced the British colonialists with unbelievable courage . . . . He believed in the ultimate victory of the African masses.'

What moved J D Kali, a trade unionist and assistant general secretary of KANU, most about Makhan Singh was 'his courage and fearless way of doing and saying what he wanted . . . . I remember at one public meeting he confessed that he was a communist. To say such a thing during those colonial days was not an easy thing. I also remember another occasion when he and Fred Kubai were the first people to mention the word "Uhuru" . . . . Before that time our slogans were, equality, abolition of all forms of discrimination and more representation in Legislative Council. From then on the demand for Uhuru grew, and spread . . . Mr Singh identified himself with wananchi and consequently suffered with and for them. He spent eleven years in detention without trials in the arid areas of Northern Kenya. Together with the late Pio Gama they had assisted the young and up-coming Trade Unionists in Kenya . . . . Makhan Singh was more interested in workers' welfare than anything else. Though a self-confessed communist, wananchi at that time did not care at all about communism. In fact we had no idea as to what communism was. All that we knew that we had an enemy to fight and whoever helped us in that fight was regarded as one of us . . . . I even remember about two whites – British – who were with us in our advisory committee during 1950-52 . . . . With all his eleven years in suffering in colonialist detention Makhan Singh was not lucky enough to enjoy the fruits of Uhuru.'

Writing in the early edition of the *Sunday Post* of 19th May, 1973, Bildad Kaggia recalled that he first met the late Singh in 1947 when the latter was president of the East African Trade Union Movement and worked with him until he was detained in 1950 when he [Kaggia] took over from him to lead the movement. He remembered him as 'the first non-African to train Africans in the trade union movement. Without him, there could be no trade union movements in Kenya.'

J Dencer-Brown, a correspondent with the *Daily Nation*, wrote, 'Since the authorities have thought it necessary to change the name of Gurdwara Road (a completely non-colonial title meaning "temple" and referring to the large Sikh Temple and Hindu Temple which comprise the major proportion of the buildings on that road), would it not be fitting to name one of our new streets after the late Makhan Singh? Or, are the peoples of other races who fought in the struggle for Uhuru alongside the wananchi to be forgotten?'

Narain Singh, also known as N S Toofan, in his editorial in the *Sunday Post* of 20th May, drew attention to the first volume of Makhan Singh's books on the history of Kenya's trade union movement. 'In it he [the author] set out in great detail the opposition, the trials and the determination by the then rulers to prevent working people from organising themselves for the purpose of their collective betterment. Makhan Singh provided the main inspiration, his was the driving force, his was most of the thinking, the planning and the working. But right through the volume he has taken no credit for himself. He has been more than generous in acknowledging the contribution of his colleagues and others.'

An obituary by Rasik Shah in the *Sunday Post* of 3rd June, stated that Makhan Singh 'believed in an ideal of equality for all men but instead of bandying about such abstract clichés, he quietly set about taking practical action towards reducing the existing inequalities among people . . . . In his published work, there is not a trace of self-consciousness in the writing of events in which the author played such a major role. References to himself are in the third person and there is no attempt to highlight his own contribution – the book is objective to the point of complete self effacement.

'He was not a man, however, whom anyone could know intimately. All his life he maintained an exterior of total control, a man steady in his beliefs and consistent in action. He never revealed his private feelings – not even to members of his own family. One gets the impression that here was a man animated by some inner spring of action of such strength, that he did not need counsel or comfort from 'friends' . . . . All his life the man owned nothing – at all, no business, no car, no property – all that on principle – a man who married conviction with action and remained uncorrupted in a world which tends to turn hostile to so much integrity! If Makhan Singh was a communist, his was not the communism of subversion and party line, but a pristine communism such as that preached by Jesus Christ.'

Karim Hudani, a reporter with the *Daily Nation*, characterised Makhan Singh as 'truly an unknown legend . . . . When he died two years ago, I was at his funeral. So were many other once prominent Indian Congress and Kenya Freedom Party Leaders. There was Mr. Fred Kubai and a few African trade unionists. The funeral scene was overwhelmingly pathetic. And yet there was tense atmosphere in the air. Kenya's historical monument was being laid to the ashes in a typical Sikh funeral ceremony with the monotonous chanting of the religious rites . . . . There was natural sympathy for Makhan Singh from the majority of the Asians who had gathered around. These were the very same Asians whose business interests had isolated Makhan Singh, more or less as a black sheep of African Asians . . . . There were hardly any messages of even condolences from leaders of this country. The death of Makhan Singh signified dramatically the frightfully lowered status of the Asian in this country . . . . Probably more than anybody else, Makhan Singh personified that selfless spirit of service to humanity at large that only Asians – and Indians in particular – are capable of endowing and imparting to mankind. If only an effort is made that Africans would have a different outlook when they chastise wholesale the international tendencies of traders as particularly that of a *muhindi* type of East African origin . . . . But lack of information from himself personally is the main reason why posterity will ponder aimlessly about his career as a political activist . . . . If this is true, then his almost ten years in jails and all the glory and newspaper articles about him will present to future historians of Kenya an enigma of unprecedented proportions. Why did Makhan Singh chicken out when he was in the position to make an impact because his sincerity in his advocacy of legitimate African inspirations was never in any doubt – even now?'

I myself remember an incident in 1984 when I visited Makhan Singh's widow, Satwant Kaur, then still living in their Park Road home. The elderly lady was bemoaning the lack of recognition of her husband's sacrifices for the country when there was a knock on the door, and she went to attend to the caller. And who was the visitor, I enquired? 'Oh, they come all the time and bring chickens and eggs and vegetables, just workers who knew my husband,' she explained. It became clear to me that though the Government had ignored him and sidelined him, just as it had ignored most of its heroes, ordinary Kenyans would not let his memory die.

Makhan Singh's daughter, Inderjeet, has written, 'Everyone was absolutely ecstatic when the news about papaji's release came through – it was the happiest moment of my life that my father was finally going to be united with the family at their own home and be able to actively participate in their lives. By this time I was a young girl just starting A levels and pretty much engrossed in studies. Papaji was a very private person and never revealed much about his feelings, emotions or thoughts and I was not mature enough at the time to sit down with him, talk to him and find out more about him as a person – I still have regrets about this. One thing is for sure that he was a very forward looking and not a traditionalist Indian father – he was all for me to do further studies and very much wanted me to carry on with a PhD (for which I was not ready at the time) – he used to say to my biji not to worry about my marriage, that I have got the capabilities and should carry on studying. When I wrote the PhD thesis, it was a hard slog as both my children were only toddlers – that is when I used to draw inspiration from his thoughts and often used to say – papaji you are not here now but I'll somehow complete this for you! When I left for Canada his parting advice to me was that with perseverance and determination one can accomplish anything – this advice has seen me through all the upheavals in my life right up to this day.

The short period that I spent in Nairobi after his release, not once did I hear him complain or even mention anything about not being given the recognition by the current ruling government. Whenever anyone raised this issue, his answer was "I did the work not for receiving any rewards" – a totally selfless, un-materialistic person. However he did become very quiet and withdrawn, I am not sure whether he revealed his feelings to anyone at all or not. All I remember is that in his later years he worked feverishly at his typewriter trying to finish his books. His passing away devastated me as that is when it dawned upon me that my communication with my father will always stay unfinished.[19]

Makhan Singh's sister, Kulwant Kaur, passed away in 1987 in Canada. His daughter, Dr Inderjeet Gill, is settled in the UK working as a biochemist with a research organisation. Her husband, Sardul Gill, now retired, was an art lecturer at Nottingham University. Makhan Singh's daughter and two sons are all happily married with children. In 1970 Hindpal and his family moved out of the home on Park Road; in 1985 it was sold and Satwant Kaur moved to Loresho to live with Hindpal, his wife, Joginder, and two sons. She often stayed too with her younger son, Swarajpal, his wife, Amarjeet Kaur and their three children in their maisonette on Arwings Kodhek Road in Nairobi. Satwant Kaur continued to live with her sons until she passed away on 14th April, 2000. The elder son, Hindpal, had become a leading power engineering consultant in Kenya and has just retired as technical adviser to the Ministry of Energy under a World Bank programme. The second son, Swarajpal, runs a mechanical workshop in Nairobi and now spends some of his time with his wife and children who have emigrated to Australia.

Makhan Singh did not leave any material wealth for his family but for them, and for the people of Kenya, he left a legacy and a history that will inspire and guide us for generations to come.

CHAPTER THIRTEEN

CONCLUSION

Makhan Singh's role as the founder of the trade union movement in Kenya and his reputation as an exemplary Kenyan patriot are undeniable. There are many facets to the struggle that he waged; the lessons that can be drawn from his experiences are both as relevant and instructive today as they were then.

Though, in 1963, colonialism was officially ended it was, correctly speaking, a 'flag independence.' Many of the colonial structures and attitudes, even forty-five years later, have yet to be dismantled, Hence the phrase 'neo-colonialism'. Makhan Singh mobilised the workers to build the trade unions not as an end in itself, but as part of the national struggle for freedom. Shiraz Durrani in his book, *Never Be Silent*,[1] states:

The working class in Kenya has brought about fundamental change in the political and economic fields. While every progressive social class has been struggling for change, it was the working class that ensured major qualitative changes and influenced other classes in the process.

Kenyan workers began struggling for their economic and political rights as soon as foreign capital came to Kenyan for its resources and labour. The first mass campaigns against colonialism were organised by peasants and were nationality-based. Although they scored valuable victories, they were defeated by a better armed colonial force. The lessons of these struggles were not lost on the growing working class who soon took leadership in the anti-colonial movements. The working class began to set up their own organisations - trade unions – and used the strike weapon to achieve their goals.

Not only was Makhan Singh a good organiser and trade unionist but he was an excellent communicator who understood well the needs of ensuring effective communications between trade unions and workers.

Shiraz Durrani's portrayal of Makhan Singh as an 'effective communicator' helps us to understand how the EATUC was built and why workers, Asian and African gave it, in spite of very difficult economic and societal obstacles, such immense support.

It is very evident from the research that the colonial government went to great lengths to try and deflect attention from Makhan Singh's leadership role. Unable to drive a wedge between him and the people, it resorted to removing him from the national arena. Ngugi wa Thion'go in his book, *Detained: A Writer's Prison Diary,*[2] sums up the part played by Makhan Singh in the anti-colonial struggle thus:

> The positive contribution of Kenyan workers of Asian origin to the struggle for independence has been deliberately played down by European colonialists and their Kenyan intellectual sympathisers and chauvinists of all shades. From 1893, the Indian workers, Indian labour leaders and progressive newspaper editors, have contributed a lot to Kenya's anti-imperialist struggle.
>
> But the name of Makhan Singh, a remarkable Kenyan of Asian origin, is synonymous with the growth of a modern workers' movement and progressive trade unionism. We see him in successive stages as the able and dedicated general secretary of the Indian Trade Union, the Labour Trade Union of Kenya, and the East African Trade Unions Congress. Like Thuku in the 20s, he correctly saw the economic emancipation of workers in political terms.
>
> When arrested on 15th May 1950, and tried before R S Thacker under the prosecution of A G Somorough, in the colonial court; Makhan Singh carried himself with calm dignity, answering all the racist provocation of the prosecution with a progressive political line that further maddened Thacker and Somorough. When, for instance,

he told the kangaroo court that the British government had no right to rule Kenya, that the country should have a workers' government with a parliament freely elected by the people and only answerable to the country's workers and peasants through their organisations, the settler magistrate was so outraged that he took over the role of prosecution.

Makhan Singh was detained in Lokitaung, Maralal and Dol Dol for eleven and a half years from 5th June 1950 to 22nd October 1961. During that time, he was constantly visited by the demons in the physical form of prison officers, district commissioners, and other colonial agents, who tried to pressure him into agreeing to leave and be awarded for it, or to recant and start working against the Kenya workers' movement and progressive nationalism, with rewards of course, but he refused. After his release, he resumed his patriotic activities in the workers' movement. His book *Kenya's Trade Union Movement to 1951*, is up to now, the only patriotic treatment of the emergence of modern Kenya.

It is clear that even Makhan Singh, of Asian origin, derived his strength to say NO from his roots in the progressive aspects of Kenyan peoples' culture. In an article he wrote for the *Daily Chronicle* of 12th February 1949, he urged Kenyans of Asian origin to forge common links with native Kenyans. "The main task before us," he wrote, is "to forge a strong unity among ourselves and with Africans for the common cause of democratic advance in this country." He advocated the establishment of common schools for all Kenyans. "Learn the language of the people – Swahili. Teach the best of your culture, learn the best from African culture. This way lies our salvation and this is the way out."

Dr Fitz de Souza, a close friend and admirer of Makhan Singh, deeply regrets the post uhuru neglect and humiliation of this great patriot. He regards Makhan Singh as 'a very very great leader,' and describes him as, 'affectionate, charming, loving and humble.'

> He was very honest – too honest and too humble in today's world – it doesn't pay. He was mild and self effacing and hated praise and flattery. He did not want self glory. He believed in sacrificing everything for his principles. He had a massive following which perhaps he himself was not aware of.[3]

Ideologically Makhan Singh adopted those theories and philosophies which helped him to fulfil his objectives   the ultimate goal was achievement of sovereignty of the Kenyan people. The Kenyan Communists[4] give pride of place to one of their own and, while bemoaning the failure of the Kenyan 'left' to become an established entity, they recognise Makhan Singh's contribution to socialist thought and practice in Kenya. Their organ *ITIKADI*, states that

> Makhan Singh was one of the most courageous and visionary leaders produced by the Kenyan anti-imperialist struggle. At a time when Kenyatta and other reformist minded constitutionalists were busy beseeching the British with petitions and deputations, Makhan Singh articulated the demands of Kenya's working people by calling for the immediate and unconditional independence of Kenya, Uganda and Tanganyika by any means necessary.
> Because of his working class base, his Indian racial origins and most significantly, his ideological outlook (he was the first Kenyan leader to state publicly that he was a Communist), the British colonial authorities did their utmost to remove Makhan Singh from the frontline of the struggle for Kenyan independence. His working class and revolutionary politics threatened the colonial agenda

of grooming petty bourgeois nationalists like Kenyatta and Mboya to evolve into acceptable "moderate statesmen" who could work with the imperialists under a revamped neo-colonial arrangement.

The very fact that he worked hard to continue and deepen the tradition of the multi-ethnic, non-racial alliances of the Kenyan national liberation movement represented a grave danger to the well known tactics of divide and rule tribal politics which Kenyans are so familiar and weary of.

Makhan Singh served a much longer term of imprisonment than Kenyatta and the famous Kapenguria Six. This was because the British feared him more than the other nationalist leaders.

Makhan Singh who dared to call himself a communist, was effectively cut off from the mass movement – first by the British who jailed him for ten years and then by the Kenyatta regime which killed him with neglect after 1963.

From the 1950s right up to the 1990s there has been one consistent trend in the Kenyan Left. Those patriots who consider themselves anti-imperialists and/or socialist have preferred to work within broader fronts rather than set themselves up as belonging to separate and ideologically distinct parties. Part of this had to do with the historical demands of the day. In the 1950s, even though Makhan Singh and other progressives had a solid base and commanded respect as leaders of powerful working class organisations, they threw their weight behind the progressive nationalist leadership of the Mau Mau.'

In the single-minded pursuit of his patriotic goal, Makhan Singh made enormous sacrifices which impacted on himself personally as well as on his family. Dr Vishva Sharma in an unpublished thesis[5] asserts that Makhan Singh could have amassed a fortune had he put his mind to it, but instead he chose to 'ride buses'.

Makhan Singh will remain a legend. He will be remembered for his untold sacrifices during the freedom struggle, when he could provide his family with little but pride and values. As father of the labour movement in Kenya, he takes a prominent position in Kenyan history; for, as many people know, with political parties banned, unionism for long remained the only avenue for political advancement. The Labour government in Britain saw in the fledgling Kenyan trade union movement a new fulcrum of influence; the Soviet bloc nations also vied for inroads. It is a measure of Makhan Singh's integrity and vision that he steered the movement between the shoals with a steady hand. He became no one's stooge; he kept riding buses as a result. Some of us should keep reminding everyone that, as he was being taken to the Kenyan outback for long years of incarceration, it was Sardar Makhan Singh who first declared: "Uhuru Sasa!"'

Fred Kubai , in 1969, wrote that Makhan Singh was known as 'a controversial figure', 'a very dangerous man', 'a communist', 'a born agitator' and by many other names. But this fellow trade unionist had a very different opinion.

To me I know him as a fighter, every inch a fighter, a Kenyan nationalist of the highest order and a brother in trade unionism and in our national struggle for independence.

Makhan Singh was a highly disciplined worker who had a network of contacts in the rural areas. Arthur Ochwada, a member of the East African Federation of Building & Construction Workers Union, worked with Makhan Singh in 1947. In an interview in 2005 at COTU headquarters, he related to me that

Makhan Singh helped to organise the workers, including farm workers. He went into the rural areas and also convinced some Asian leaders to support his campaign. When the KAU leaders were detained, workers were the voice of the people. They had freedom of movement but were restricted in action. Makhan Singh was a staunch adherent of quiet politics. He did a lot of quiet trade union work even after his release in 1961.

Makhan Singh's life and times epitomises the very crucial and central role that the South Asians have played in the political development of Kenya. The community, nevertheless, is generally recognised solely for the significant contribution it has made, and continues to make, in the economic sphere.

Writing in *The Sorcerer's Apprentice*,[6] Elspeth Huxley, the ardent white settler, drew attention to the fact that,

African newspapers are printed on terms of easy credit on Indian presses; Indians give money to such bodies as the K.A.U.; African political leaders are made welcome in Indian houses; one of the K.A.U. officials . . . is now touring India as a guest. The latest move which has aroused great African enthusiasm, is the award of five scholarships to take Kenya Africans to Indian universities.

In her writing Huxley captures the close bond which existed between Africans and Asians, a bond which the colonialists strove constantly to sever. The policy of dividing Africans and Asians (as well as other ethnic communities) was inherited by Kenya's leaders after independence and continues to undermine the drive towards nationhood, even today.

This deliberate down-grading of the Asian role in Kenya's history was very graphically revealed to me in a photograph taken in the courtroom at Nyeri; the picture shows General China flanked by four armed askaris. General China is dressed in a hospital gown. The photograph is available in the Kenya National Archives and other libraries, and has been widely used by publishers. The feature of the photograph that interested me was the questioning look in General China's eyes as he stood there with his head turned to his left. I have only recently discovered that the photograph has been cropped. The original one shows General China conversing with his lawyer who is none other than Achhroo Kapila[7]. This deliberate attempt to obliterate the positive role of the South Asians in the struggle for independence, first by the colonialists and later by the Kenyan government, is what personifies the injustices perpetrated against Makhan Singh. In 1923, the concerted struggle of the EAINC, under the leadership of Manilal Desai and Alibhai Mulla Jeevanjee, compelled the British Government to formulate the Devonshire Declaration which, while giving nominal 'paramountcy' to Kenya's Africans, nullified the settlers' hopes of achieving dominion status in their drive to white supremacy.

Twenty-five years later, Makhan Singh supported the EAINC when it played a significant role in opposing the plans of the white settlers to form a federation of the British East African territories. An article in *Awaaz*[8] reads

If successful, the settler drive to capture power within a forced East African Federation would have posed a powerful barrier to African advance . . . Historians now acknowledge the importance of the Kenyan Asian opposition, in the absence of an organised African one, in thwarting it. Pranlal [Sheth] was particularly active in alerting the public to its grave dangers and inspiring Congress resistance to it through his news reports and commentaries in the [*Daily*] *Chronicle*.

Makhan Singh and his many compatriots brought from

India an experience and strategic knowledge of building a mass movement geared towards ousting the colonialists. He was in constant contact with Indian political leaders who in turn, gave Kenya significant support and solidarity on the road to independence. The economists and planners of present day Kenya are increasingly turning their attention eastwards to countries such as India, Malaysia and China to learn from, and emulate, the policies which helped to launch the tiger economies. Kenyan South Asians continue to involve themselves in the economic sphere. But in the field of social interaction and in the political realm, the community remains largely isolationist. It has yet to fully incorporate the approach that Makhan Singh so ardently advocated and merge itself into the national context.

On the other hand, the South Asian community has a wealth of skills, know-how, cultural and philanthropic traditions as well as close contacts with its counterpart in the Indian sub-continent – it is a resource that has greatly benefited the countries where many of its members have settled. The Kenyan government could, and should, harness and make greater use of this resource which exists within its borders.

Makhan Singh was very aware of the vital importance of unity and preached it constantly. He made strenuous efforts to bring together differing South Asian religious groups, 'tribal' political leaders and vested class interests, and to bridge the generation gap. He taught us that only when the vast human and material capital of the country is mobilised by the nationals of the country, pulling together in a common direction, can they pull themselves out of the circle of poverty and rise to a higher platform. To do so, the government must institute policies which enhance the concept of nationhood and steer its citizens away from the divisive and self-defeating confines of ethnic chauvinism and racial bigotry. No foreign donor can provide this impetus.

The colonialists and neo-colonialists, with their Kenyan collaborators, have constantly schemed to turn the African and

South Asian communities against each other and more often than not, the unsuspecting populace has fallen prey to these tactics. The labelling and ostracism of Makhan Singh as a 'communist' was spurious and fraudulent; as Rasik Shah stated in his obituary,

> If Makhan Singh was a communist, his was not the communism of subversion and party line, but a pristine communism such as that preached by Jesus Christ.[9]

Makhan Singh, in 1950, was the first leader to demand independence for Kenya. At that time KAU, EAINC and other leaders were negotiating for equality and justice and did not envisage uhuru for another 30 – 40 years. In 1961, at an encounter at Nairobi airport, Sir Ernest Vasey, Kenya's then Minister of Finance, predicted the event to occur 'after 75 years', Fitz de Souza differed, his estimation was '15 – 20 years'.[10] Clearly Makhan Singh's involvement in India's freedom struggle, his knowledge of imperialism and his firm base in the masses of Kenya, gave him the confidence and foresight to demand independence sooner rather than later.

Makhan Singh was in fact closer to, and in tune with, the masses than he was to the political leaders. His years in detention sequestered him from the developing and differing political trends; he embraced uhuru with the slogan, 'Now, forward, to build up a strong democratic African socialist Kenya, East Africa and ultimately Africa' and had an abiding conviction in the doctrine, 'to each according to his need, based on the requirements of the family'. When after his release his brother-in-law, H S Mahal, advised him to stay out of politics, he wrote:

> In the course of serving the country and the nation all sorts of things, good and bad, do take place and we have to face them in the same good spirit as we show in the service to the country and to humanity at large. If one

considers his cause as good he should never relent or go back, whatever the consequences.

Makhan Singh shunned power politics; he preferred to put his theories into practice by being the facilitator, the organiser, the arbitrator. It is highly unlikely however, that, with his know-how and understanding, he did not soon become aware of the volte-face of many of his erstwhile comrades in the Kenyan ruling class. In later years historians have debated if Kenyatta should be described as a nationalist or an opportunist.

Unlike his close compatriot, Pio Gama Pinto, Makhan Singh chose to focus his entire attention to building a workers' state – a dictatorship of the proletariat. Pinto, though he shared Makhan Singh's ideology, took a more pragmatic line. While he strove to expand the trade unions and cement their alliance with the All Africa Trade Union Federation, he conceded the overall role of parliamentary politics and a mixed economy at that particular juncture in Kenya's history.

As it so happened, neither men lived to see their cherished dreams realised. Pinto was assassinated in 1965; Makhan Singh was effectively side-lined and disempowered until his death in 1973. Jaramogi Oginga Odinga, Bildad Kaggia, Joseph Murumbi, Achieng Oneko and others, with the same convictions, were similarly isolated. The divide between the Kanu ruling class and this band of people-oriented leaders was a clash between two visions of independent Kenya – a clash which came to be caricatured in terms of the 'Cold War' discourse of that period and there was no room for debate or a creative interplay between those two visions. It deprived Kenya of the services of a true patriot and signalled a new authoritarianism and intolerance of dissent, whose legacy Kenyans still have to dismantle.

The government must do much more than just pay lip service to the concept of 'nationhood' if they are to mould the various races and ethnic communities of Kenya into a cohesive citizenry. As part of this process, the South Asian community must also venture out more boldly into the political and social life of the country for history has proven beyond doubt that economic growth cannot be generated without political involvement. The withdrawal, in 1962, from the political arena by the Kenya Indian Congress, continues to influence the South Asian mind set. It is vitally important that role models be resurrected to guide and inspire Kenyans to a better future. Makhan Singh has amply demonstrated to us by his actions and his deeds and the life he led, a way forward.

However, at the time of writing, the only recognition of Makhan Singh is a lane named after him, in the Ngara area of Nairobi. It leads to Jamhuri High School, his alma mater, and at the time of going to print, even that road sign is missing. His home has been sold and the major road it stands on bears the inconsequential name of 'Park Road'. At the Central Organisation of Trade Unions' (COTU) offices in Solidarity Building, there is no reference to him. In 1987, a zealous office manager, lit a bonfire and burnt all the files dating back to the organisation's inception. Makhan Singh must have had some premonition of this travesty as he meticulously copied COTU's minutes, correspondence, press releases and statements, up to the time of his death. These records are now preserved in his private papers in the University of Nairobi archives.

South Asians, many from the Sikh community, and a few Africans have said to me that, while they admired Makhan Singh greatly, they felt he should have compromised and adapted to the changing times. Comments have ranged from, 'there was no need for him to remain in detention in Kenya, he should have accepted the conditions set by the government for his early release,' to 'after his release he should have got himself an office and car and forgone some of his ascetic habits,' and 'he should have got into politics and manoeuvred for, rather than just waited to be given, a post in government.' The most widely held view was that Makhan Singh erred most seriously when he refused to denounce his communist ideology. His uncompromising insistence on upholding his principles and observing the rule of law must have, without doubt, generated much tension among his family members.

However, it is precisely because he remained steadfast and unwavering in his beliefs and his practice that Makhan Singh towers, even today, head and shoulders above the crowd. From this unsullied pulpit he continues to guide and inspire us, and will do so for generations to come. Were it not for this incredible commitment and sacrifice, this biography would have been written very differently, if at all. As it is, I would encourage another generation of historians to revisit and reinterpret the fascinating material which I have encountered in my own researches.

NOTES

CHAPTER ONE
❀

1. Ghadr-di-Gunj, Vol 1 No. 4.
2. Ibid.
3. Gregory, Robert G, 1971, p 153.
4. Puri, Harish K, 1983, pp 178 & 288.
5. Ibid.
6. In Kenya, the term 'Indian' referring to people from the sub-continent changed to 'Asian' after the partition of India and Pakistan. The more geographically correct term being currently used is 'South Asian'.
7. Chandan Amarjit, p43.

CHAPTER TWO
❀

1. In East Africa, Sikhs are commonly known as 'Kalasinga' named after a Sikh called Kala Singh who was a trader in Maasailand at the turn of the twentieth century and was well known both because of his flowing beard and turban as well as his camaraderie.
2. Hindpal Singh Jabbal, interview Nairobi, 2004.
3. Singh, Sudh – autobiography.
4. Makhan Singh's teachers were: Lakhmi Dass and Fazal Karim Aroop (primary school), Mohan Singh, Shanker Dass and Giani Balwant Singh (Class V); Lal Singh, Sunder Dass, Giani Balwant Singh and Kartar Singh (Class VI); Inder Singh, Sohna Mal, Giani Tulsiram Singh, Daulat Ram, and Kartar Singh (Class VII); Ramdass, Brijlal, Daulat Ram, Giani Inder Singh and Sunder Singh (Class VIII).
5. Clayton, Anthony and Donald Savage, 1974, p210.

CHAPTER THREE
❀

1. Pan Africa p49.
2. Pan Africa p59.

CHAPTER FOUR
❀

1. See Appendix II.
2. They were: Roshan Lal, Pandya, R C Patel, Rugnath Sahi and Magan Lal taught him in Std. VI. Abdul Aziz, K. D. Punjani, Mohan Singh and Rugnath Sahai at the preliminary Cambridge level, David Somen, Amar Nath, Mohan Singh, S. M. U. Shah and Maganlal at Junior Cambridge level. Except for Maganlal, the other four teachers continued to teach the London Matriculation class from January 1930 to June 1931.
3. Kalu was the father of Guru Nanak.
4. Chandan, Amarjit pp12, 26.
5. Singh, Sudh – autobiography.
6. Lal Singh had gone to Kenya and on landing was followed by the police and ultimately imprisoned. His wife died in India while he was in jail. In India he led a march of 101 Sikhs to court arrest and formed a committee for the settlement of all matters privately without having recourse to public authorities. The colonial police there labeled him as 'a dangerous character requiring careful watching' and noted that he came from a family 'notorious for holding political views.'
7. Chandan, Amarjit, p49.
8. Chandan, Amarjit, p51.
9. Puri, Harish K, 1983, pp 178 & 288.
10. Ibid.; and correspondence from Amarjit Chandan, UK 2004.
11. Chandan, Amarjit, p43.
12. Sharma, Dr Vishva Bandhu Lalchand.
13. Gregory, Robert G, 1971, pp153-4.
14. Correspondence from Amarjit Chandan, UK, November, 2004.
15. Makhan Singh was versatile linguistically. At an Arya Samaj function he recited a poem in the Persian language and he wrote a play in Urdu on the theme of workers' rights and the caste system.
16. Bhagat Singh was hanged by the British in Delhi in 1931 at the age of 24. Kartar Singh Sarabha was a prominent activist.
17. Nawan Yug was a nationalist weekly paper published in Punjabi in Lahore, India
18. Correspondence from Amarjit Chandan, UK, 2004.
19. The Mangat case refers to an incident when N S Mangat, a radical turned conservative, was alleged to have set fire to one of his properties on River Road and then made an insurance claim.
20. Singh, Makhan, 1969, Chapters 6-8.
21. Durrani, Shiraz, NAMASKAR-AFRICANA-L, 20th

Notes

March, 1999.
22. Durrani, Shiraz, 2005.
23. Singh, Makhan, 1969, Chapters 6-8.
24. Durrani, Shiraz, NAMASKAR-AFRICANA-L, 20th March, 1999.
25. Clayton, Anthony and Donald Savage, 1974, p212.
26. Singh, Makhan, 1969, Chapter 8.
27. Salvadori, Cynthia, 1983, p283.
28. Singh, Makhan, 1969, Chapter 8.
29. Ambu Patel Private Collection.
30. On 27th December, seven Asians calling themselves 'Plot Owners in Eastleigh Township' met and Makhan Singh took notes. They planned to get the services of an advocate and quantity surveyor. The objective of this group is not clear and there is no record of any further meetings.
31. Gregory, Robert G, 1971, Chap XII, p440.
32. Clayton, Anthony and Donald Savage, 1974, p214.
33. Gregory, Robert G, 1971 p440.
34. Singh, Makhan, 1969, Chapter 9. Gregory, Robert G, 1971, p454.
35. Singh, Makhan, 1969, Chapter 9. Gregory, Robert G, 1971, p454.
36. Singh, Makhan, 1980, Introduction.
37. Clayton, Anthony and Donald Savage, 1974, pp210-14.
38. Chandan, Amarjit, p43.
39. Singh, Makhan, 1980, Introduction.
40. Singh, Makhan, 1969, Chapter 10.
41. Singh, Makhan, 1969, Chapter 11.
42. Patel, Zarina, 1997, pp144-5.
43. Chandan Amarjit, p43.
44. Patel, Zarina, 1997, pp144-5.
45. Ibid.

CHAPTER FIVE

1. Singh, Makhan, 1980, Introduction.
2. EAS 7th March, 1941.
3. Correspondence from Bhagat Singh Bilga, Desh Bhagat Yadgaar, Jalhandar, India. In 1948, Mota Singh was again imprisoned during the anti-communist wave in India. After his release he worked on his farm and as a building contractor and was on the executive committee of the Punjab Freedom Fighters Association. He died in India in 2002 aged 98.
4. Hindpal Singh Jabbal, interview Nairobi, 2002.
5. Ibid.
6. Rattansi, P, interview Nairobi, December, 2003.
7. Hindpal Singh Jabbal, interview Nairobi, 2005.
8. Ambu Patel, Private Collection.
9. Sing, Sudh, autobiography.
10. Beauttah, James, 1983, p83.

CHAPTER SIX

1. Singh, Makhan, 1969, Chapters 13 & 14.

2. Singh, Makhan, 1969, Chapters 13 & 14.
3. Singh, Makhan, 1969, Chapters 13 & 14.
4. Singh, Makhan, 1980, Introduction.
5. Singh, Chanan, Makhan Singh Cases,1976.
6. Ibid.
7. Ibid.
8. Ibid.
9. Ibid.
10. Clayton, Anthony and Donald Savage, 1974, p327.
11. Nanalal Sheth, interview Nairobi, July 2004.
12. Durrani, Shiraz, 2005.
13. Awaaz, Issue 1, 2004, 'The Patriot Kenya Lost –Pranlal Sheth'.
14. Rattansi, P, interview Nairobi, December 2003.
15. Rattansi, H, interview Nairobi, January 2003.
16. T P O'Brien was a committee member in the Kenya League, formed in 1951. The officers were Haroon Ahmed (president), Arwings Kodhek (vice-president) and F R S de Souza (secretary). Its main aim was to work for a democratic government elected on a common roll. It was proscribed in 1953. O'Brien, an archaeologist by profession, was an anti-colonialist and most probably, a communist. Later, he opened a photography shop in Nyeri from where he helped the Mau Mau. The group used to meet in his house until once, while driving together, they were stopped by the police and thoroughly checked out. A woman bank clerk from England joined the group and ultimately, after O'Brien divorced his first wife, the two got married.
17. Rattansi, P, interview Nairobi, December, 2003. He narrated the story of the Marxist study group and gave the insight into Makhan Singh's ideology and personality. Indu Desai was a journalist who later edited a fortnightly magazine called Nav Yug (New Youth). 'Humanity is my religion, Freedom is my goal,' Desai wrote on 28th August, 1970.
18. Ambu Patel Private Collection.
19. Singh, Makhan, 1969, Chapter 15.
20. File No L/PJ/12/663.
21. Ibid.
22. Rattansi, P, interview Nairobi, December, 2003.
23. Ibid.
24. File No L/PJ/12/663.
25. Ibid.
26. Ibid.
27. Ibid.
28. Kenya Intelligence Review No 18/48, para 264.

CHAPTER SEVEN

1. Chandan, Amarjit, p43.
2. Singh, Chanan, Makhan Singh Cases,1976.
3. Kenya Intelligence Review No. 18/48, para 267.
4. Ibid., para 266.
5. File No L/PJ/12/663.
6. Singh, Makhan, 1969, Chapter 15.
7. File No L/PJ/12/663.
8. File No L/PJ/12/663.
9. Singh, Makhan, 1969, Chapter 15.
10. File No L/PJ/12/663.

11. Singh, Makhan, 1969, Chapter 15.
12. *Kenya Intelligence Review* No 18/48, para 265.
13. Singh, Chanan, *Makhan Singh Cases*,1976.
14. Anderson, David, 2005, p65.
15. Clayton, Anthony and Donald Savage, 1974, pp334-5.
16. Singh, Makhan, 1969, Chapter 17.
17. *Awaaz*, Issue 1, 2004, 'The Patriot Kenya Lost –Pranlal Sheth'. P????? Rattansi, interview Nairobi, December 2003.
18. Clayton, Anthony and Donald Savage, 1974, p329.
19. Singh, Makhan, 1969, Chapter 16.
20. Clayton, Anthony and Donald Savage, 1974, p32.
21. Clayton, Anthony and Donald Savage, 1974, p329.
22. When Meshak Ndisi returned, after completing his studies at Ruskin College, Oxford, and with the ILO in Geneva he resumed his duties as general secretary of his union. After independence he served as the permanent secretary in the Ministry of Labour and Social Services and in 1969 became the ILO Regional Director for Africa.
23. *EAS* 12 September 1947
24. *EAS* 12 June 1957.
25. Singh, Makhan, 1980, Introduction.
26. Kaggia, Bildad, 1975, p78.
27. Singh, Makhan, 1969, Chapter 17.
28. Ibid.
29. EAS 6 March 1950.
30. EAS 25 April 1950.
31. Clayton, Anthony and Donald Savage, 1974, p330.
32. Singh, Makhan, 1969, Chapter 17.
33. Ambu Patel Private Collection.
34. Rattansi, P, interview December, 2003.
35. Ibid.

CHAPTER EIGHT
❉

1. Singh, Makhan, 1980, Introduction.
2. After his release, Kenya-born Jarnail Singh Liddar went to India where he was declared a prohibited immigrant. He returned to Kenya in 1953 and was sent back to India from the airport. He was finally allowed back into Kenya in 1963, after the colony had become independent.
3. Clayton, Anthony and Donald Savage, 1974, p331.
4. Ngugi, James, *A Grain of Wheat*, p205.
5. Singh, Makhan, 1969, Chapter 17.
6. *The Times*, London, 10 May 1950.
7. Singh, Makhan, 1969, Chapter 18.
8. Ibid.
9. Ibid.
10. Makhan Singh denied this, saying he did not work with communist organizations in 1935-6.
11. Singh, Makhan, 1969, chapter 18.
12. Clayton, Anthony and Donald Savage, 1974, 9 330fn.
13. Salvadori, Cynthia, 1996 vol III, p181.
14. EAS, 25.5.50.
15. Salim, A I, p212. Tom Mbotela, vice-president of KAU, disassociated KAU from the boycott call in a communiqué and had to be given police protection. He

was appointed vice president of KAU in 1951 but was assassinated in 1952.
16. Singh, Chanan, *Makhan Singh Cases*, 1976.
17. See Appendix II.
18. Singh, Chanan, *Makhan Singh Cases*,1976
19. Ibid.
20. Singh, Makhan, 1969, chapter 18.
21. Gill, Inderjeet, 2003 'Father's dearest memories'.

CHAPTER NINE
❉

1. Kyle, Keith, 1999, pp156-7.
2. Maciel, Mervyn, 1985, p 47.
3. Hindpal Singh Jabbal, interview Nairobi, 2004.
4. Maciel, Mervyn, 1985, pp50, 68.
5. Elkins, Caroline, 2005, p196.
6. Correspondence from Mervyn Maciel, UK, February 2005.
7. Maciel, Mervyn, 1985, p61
8. This followed a costly sedition trial, police raids and an organised boycott by advertisers. The last was instigated by the government and supported by employers who were opposed to the paper's pro-trade union stand. Interestingly after A B Patel's takeover, the government ban was lifted. Haroon Ahmed then rejoined the *Colonial Times* while D K Sharda started the *Tribune* which was banned a year later in 1952.
9. Some of the titles were Development Committee Report Volume 1 and 11, Economics, Handbook of Labour Laws, Indian Constitution and magazines of the International Labour Organisation.
10. See Appendix II.
11. Anderson, David, 2005, p65.
12. Kyle, Keith, 1999, p62. Pan Africa, 12 December 1963, p32.
13. *The Lawyer*, October 2003, p16.
14. Maciel, Mervyn, 1985, p148.
15. *EAS*, 17 October, 2004, p15.
16. Elkins, Caroline, 2005, p321.
17. Gavaghan, Terence, 1999, pp205-6. Salvadori, Cynthia, 1996 vol III, p181.
18. Hindpal Singh Jabbal, interview Nairobi, 2004. Hindpal Singh Jabbal, however, maintains that there were no restrictions and that he was able to visit his father at least three times before his departure for India in 1955.
19. Gill, Inderjeet, 2003 'Father's dearest memories'.
20. Swarajpal Singh Jabbal, interview Nairobi, 2001.
21. Singh, Sudh – autobiography.
22. *Sunday Post*, Harambee, May 20, 1973 by Narain Singh.
23. The Constituency Elected Members Organisation and the New Kenya Group claimed to have a non-racial approach to the country's problems. In the latter he urged them to demand an end to the Emergency, unconditional release of all detainees and restrictees, an amnesty for all political prisoners and the introduction of civil liberties. He especially stressed the importance of the formation of a national, African political organisation.
24. The fortress in London where well-known persons

Notes

had been imprisoned or executed.
25. Achieng Oneko interview, 22 October 2005
26. Edgerton, Robert B, p 228
27. Hindpal Singh Jabbal, interview Nairobi, 2004.
28. Ibid.

CHAPTER TEN

1. *Pan Africa* p45. The first Kikuyu independent school was started by Musa Ndirangu in Githunguri in 1922. He paid all the expenses of the school from his own pocket.
2. Singh, Makhan, 1969, Chapter 19.
3. Clayton, Anthony and Donald Savage, 1974, p332.
4. Between 1966-7 Aggrey Minya served as the area secretary for the Central Organisation of Trade Unions (COTU) which was set up post-independence.
5. Durrani, Shiraz, 2005.
6. Kyle, Keith, 1999, pp 47-51.
7. *Pan Africa* p59.
8. Singh, Makhan, 1969, chapter 19.
9. Singh, Makhan, 1980, p 3.
Willie George: President, Nightwatchmen, Clerks and Shopworkers Union (NCSU); Chege Kiburu: Vice-President, Domestic and Hotel Workers Union (D&HWU); Peter Mutabi Simba: Chairman, Nairobi Branch, D&HWU; John Mungai: Ex-president, Transport and Allied Workers Union (TAWU); Gachangi Gikaru: Member, Executive Committee, TAWU; Paul Kariuki Karanja: Ex-President and Member, Executive Committee TAWU; Said Mohamed: Secretary, Mombasa Branch, TAWU; Matano Omari: Treasurer, Mombasa Branch, TAWU; Mwangi Waweru: Member, Executive Committee, TAWU; Karuru Marefu: Member Executive Committee, TAWU; Ngare Kagecha: Member, Executive Committee, TAWU; Ndiboi Waweru: Member, Executive Committee, TAWU; Dishon Kahiato: Chairman, Shop Workers Section, Labour Trade Union of E. A.; J. D. Kali: Member, Executive Committee, Labour Trade Union of E. A.
10. Singh, Makhan, 1980, p 24.
11. Ibid., p 43.
12. Ibid., p 46.
13. Ibid., p 86.
14. Ibid., pp 100-101.
15. Ibid., chapter 12.
16. Ibid., chapter 19.
17. Ibid., chapter 21.
18. Ibid., chapter 24.
19. Kyle, Keith, 1999, Chapter 3.
20. Elkins, 2005, p366.
21. Kyle, Keith, 1999, Chapter 5.
22. Ibid., Chapter 6.
23. Ibid., Chapter 7.
24. Ibid., Chapter 10
25. Durrani, Shiraz, 2005.
26. *Transition*, 1966, 'The changing face of Kenya politics'.
27. Bailey, Jim, 1993.
28. *Transition*, 1966, 'The changing face of Kenya

politics'.
29. Kihoro, Wanyiri, 2005, pp 120-121
30. Barkan, Joel D, 1994.

CHAPTER ELEVEN

1. Correspondence from Amarjit Chandan, UK, November 2003.
2. The Namdari Sikhs are followers of a religious cum political movement. Their followers were killed in their thousands by British forces in India.
3. The request appears to be about a person called Swaran and getting him remarried.
4. Mehraam Yaar, interview Nairobi, November 2003.
5. Fitz de Souza, interview Nairobi, 2003.
6. Fitz de Souza, intverview Nairobi, 2004.
7. Fitz de Souza, interview Nairobi, 2004: Ambu Patel's regard for Kenyatta was such that he would bow down and touch his feet, an Indian custom denoting respect to an elder. I tried to dissuade him from doing this . . . Relations between Kenyatta and Ambu did deteriorate . . . later he was deeply hurt when Kenyatta refused to return, in spite of Patel's several entreaties, the large collection of photos and articles he had lent him at his request.
8. Tarlok Singh Nandhra, interview Nairobi, January 2004.
9. Durrani, Shiraz, 2005.
10. *Daily Nation* 20 November 1962.
11. Clayton, Anthony and Donald Savage, 1974, p 443.
12. Dennis Akumu, interview Nairobi, January 2004.

CHAPTER TWELVE

1. Fitz de Souza, interview Nairobi, 2004.
2. Fred Kubai retired from politics in 1988 and passed away in 1996 at the age of 74, neglected and having suffered a stroke.
3. Wilson, Amrit, 1989, Introduction. Soldiers in the Kenyan and Tanganyikan armies had mutinied over their terms of service. A revolution in January 1964 had led to US intervention and the creation of "Tanzania" aimed at defusing socialist influences in Africa.
4. Correspondence from Rattansi, P, UK, August 2003.
5. Ibid.
6. Transition, 1966, 'The changing face of Kenya politics'.
7. Ambu Patel, Private Collection
8. Neither Hindpal nor Inderjeet have any recollection of this bursary.
9. Correspondence from Chaman Lal Chaman, UK, May 2004.
10. Dennis Akumu, interview Nairobi, January 2004.
11. Rattansi, P, interview Nairobi, December 2003.
12. Fitz de Souza, interview Nairobi, 2002.
13. Dennis Akumu, interview Nairobi, January 2004.
14. Singh, Makhan, 1980, Introduction.

15. See Appendix I.
16. Fitz de Souza, interview Nairobi, 2002.
17. Swarajpal Singh Jabbal, interview Nairobi, 2001.
18. See Appendix II.
19. Gill, Inderjeet, 2003 'Father's dearest memories'.

CHAPTER THIRTEEN
❀

1 Durrani Shiraz, 2005.
2 Thiong'o, Ngugi wa, 1981.
3 Fitz de Souza, interview Nairobi, 2003.
4 Itikadi, 1995.
5 Sharma, Dr Vishva Bandhu Lalchand.
6 Huxley, Elspeth, 1951.
7 This information was given to me by David Anderson, author of *Histories of the Hanged*, in April 2005.
8 *Awaaz*, Issue No 1 2004.
9 *Sunday Post* , 3 June 1973.
10 Fitz de Souza, interview Nairobi, 2005.
11 George Gona Dr., interview 2005.

BIBLIOGRAPHY

Anderson, David, *Histories of the Hanged, Britain's Dirty War in Kenya and the End of Empire* (London: Weidenfeld & Nicholson, 2005).

Bailey, Jim, *Kenya: The National Epic* (Kenya: Kenway Publications Ltd, 1993).

Barkan, Joel D, *Beyond Capitalism vs. Socialism in Kenya & Tanzania* (USA & UK: Lynne Rienner Publishers Inc, 1994).

Chandan, Amarjit, *Gopal Singh Chandan* (India: Punjab Centre for Migration Studies, 2004).

Chandra, Bipan, *The Epic Struggle* (India: Orient Longman Limited, 1992).

Clayton, Anthony and Donald Savage, *Government and Labour in Kenya, 1895-1963*. (London: Frank Cass, 1974).

Elkins, Caroline, *Britain's Gulag: The Brutal End of Empire in Kenya*, (London: Jonathan Cape, 2005).

Edgerton, Robert B, *Mau Mau, An African Cruicble*, (New York, Ballantine Books, 1989)

Gavaghan, Terence, *Of Lions and Dung Beetles: "A Man in the Middle" of Colonial Administration in Kenya*, (Devon: Arthur H Stockwell, 1999).

Gregory, Robert G, *India and East Africa: A History of Race Relations within the* British Empire 1890-1939, (Oxford: Clarendon Press, 1971).

Huxley, Elspeth, *The Sorcerer's Apprentice: A journey through East Africa*, (London: Chatto & Windus, 1951).

Independent Kenya. (1982). Sponsored by the Journal of African Marxists in solidarity with the authors. London: Zed Press. ("Independent Kenya was the underground work of the December Twelve Movement" – Kinyatti wa Maina, (in forthcoming book).

James, Lawrence, *RAJ The Making and Unmaking of BRITISH INDIA*, (UK: Little, Brown and Company, 1997)

Kaggia, Bildad, *Roots of Freedom 1921-1963: The autobiography of Bildad Kaggia* (Kenya: East African Publishing House, 1975).

Kenyan Communists, Voice of, ed Zinduka U Pambane, *Itikadi*, (Number 1, First Quarter 1995, an underground publication).

Kihoro, Wanyiri, *The Price of Freedom, The Story of Political Resistance in Kenya* (Nairobi: Mvule Africa Publishers, 2005)

Kinyatti, Maina wa, (forthcoming): *History of Resistance in Kenya, 1885-2002: Kenyatta and Kanu betrayed Mau Mau*

Kyle, Keith, *The Politics of the Independence of Kenya* (UK: Macmillan Press Ltd, 1999, USA: St Martin's Press,

Inc 1999).

Low, D A, & Alison Smith, ed, *History of East Africa*, vol III (Oxford: Clarendon Press, 1976).

Maciel, Mervyn, *Bwana Karani*, (UK: Merlin Books Ltd, 1985).

Mangat, J S, *A History of the Asians in East Africa* c. 1886 to 1945 (Oxford: Clarendon Press, 1969).

Maxon, Robert M, *Struggle for Kenya: The Loss and Reassertion of Imperial Initiative 1912-1923* (UK, USA, Canada: Associated University Presses 1993).

Patel, Zarina, *Challenge to Colonialism: The Struggle of Alibhai Mulla Jeevanjee for Equal Rights in Kenya*, (Nairobi: Self-published, 1997).

Puri, Harish K, *Ghadar Movement – Ideology, Organisation, Strategy* (India: Guru Nank Dev University, Amritsar, 1983).

Rosberg Jnr, Carl G and Nottingham, John, *The myth of 'mau mau' Nationalism in Kenya* (USA: Frederick A Praeger Inc, 1966).

Salim, Ahmed Idha, *The Swahili-Speaking Peoples of Kenya's Coast 1895-1965*, (Nairobi: East Africa Publishing House, 1973)

Salvadori, Cynthia, *Through Open Doors: A view of ASIAN CULTURES in Kenya* (Kenya: Kenway Publications Ltd, 1983).

Salvadori, Cynthia, *We Came in Dhows*, vol III (Kenya: Paperchase Kenya Ltd, 1996).

Seidenberg, Dana April, *Uhuru and the Kenya Indians: The Role of a Minority Community in Kenya Politics* (India: Vikas

Publishing House, Kenya: Heritage Bookshop Ltd, 1983).

Seidenberg, Dana April, *Mercantile Adventurers: The World of East African Asians 1750-1985* (India: New Age International (P) Ltd Publishers, 1996).

Singh, Dr Gopal, *A History of the Sikh People 1469-1978* (India: Oxford University Press, 1966).

Singh, Kushwant, *A History of the Sikhs*, vols I, II (India: Oxford University Press, 1966).

Singh, Makhan, *History of Kenya's Trade Union Movement to 1952* (Kenya: East African Publishing House, 1969).

Singh, Makhan, *1952-56 Crucial years of KENYA TRADE UNIIONS*, ed Prof B A Ogot, (Kenya: Uzima Press Limited, 1980).

Spencer, John, *James Beauttah: Freedom Fighter* (Kenya: Stellascope Publishing Company Ltd, 1983).

Thiong'o, Ngugi wa, *Detained: A Writer's Prison Diary* (Kenya, USA: Heinemann Educational Books, 1981).

Wilson, Amrit, *US Foreign Policy and Revolution* (UK: Pluto Press, 1989).

ARCHIVE COLLECTIONS

Makhan Singh Papers, University of Nairobi Archives, Nairobi, Kenya.

File No L/PJ/12/663, "Indians in East Africa", India Office Records, British Library.

Kenya Intelligence Review No 18/48, para 264. British Library, London.

Ambu Patel Private Collection, Nairobi, 2004.

UNPUBLISHED MANUSCRIPTS

Chandan, Gopal Singh, "Mera Jivan-My Life - Memoirs of Gopal Singh Chandan", (India: Desh Bhagat Yadgar Archives, Jalandhar, India.).

Ambu Patel Private Collection, seen in Nairobi, 2004.

Gill, Inder, "Father's dearest memories" by Makhan Singh's daughter, Written for this biography of her father in November 2003, UK.

Sharma, Dr Vishva Bandhu Lalchand, "The Nationalist Movement in Punjab: A Kenya Connection", (USA: Western Michigan University).

Singh, Chanan, "Makhan Singh Cases", (Ambu Patel Private Collection, Nairobi 2004).

Singh, Sudh – autobiography; written with Makhan Singh during his detention in Kenya, (From Hindpal Singh Jabbal).

NEWSPAPERS

Baraza
Blitz
Colonial Times
Daily Chronicle
Daily Nation
Daily Worker
East African Standard
Hindustan Times
Kenya Daily Mail
Kenya Weekly News
London Times
Milap
National Guardian
Navyug
Naya Zamana
New Age
Partap
People's Age
Radio Posta
Sunday Nation
Sunday Post
Sunday Standard
Taifa Leo
Tribune

JOURNALS

Awaaz, The Patriot Kenya Lost – Pranlal Sheth, Issue 1, 2004
Guardian (SA)
Jang-e-Azadi
Labour Monthly
New Africa
The Lawyer, (Kenya).
Transition, "The changing face of Kenya politics", (Uganda: No 25 1966)
Yugantar

ABBREVIATIONS

BBC	British Broadcasting Corporation
CEMO	Constituency Elected Members Organisation
CID	Criminal Investigation Department
COTU	Central Organisation of Trade Unions
DC	District Commissioner
DO	District Officer
EACSO	East Africa Common Services Organisation
EAINC	East Africa Indian National Congress
EATUC	East Africa Trade Union Congress
EGH	Elder of the Golden Heart
HE	His Excellency
IBEAC	Imperial British East Africa Company
ICFTU	International Confederation of Free Trade Unions
ILO	International Labour Organisation
KADU	Kenya African Democratic Union
KANU	Kenya African National Union
KAU	Kenya African Union
KCA	Kikuyu Central Association
KFL	Kenya Federation of Labour
KFP	Kenya Freedom Party
KFRTU	Kenya Federation of Registered Trade Unions
KPU	Kenya Peoples Union
KShs	Kenya Shillings
LEGCO	Legislative Council
LTU	Labour Trade Union
LTUEA	Labour Trade union of East Africa
MLC	Member of the Legislative Council
MP	Member of Parliament
NFD	Northern Frontier District
NKG	New Kenya Group
QC	Queens Counsel
P&KTWU	Print and Kindred Trades Workers Union
PC	Provincial Commissioner
TUC	Trade Union Congress
UK	United Kingdom
USA	United States of America
UNO	United Nations Organisation
USSR	United Soviet Socialist Republics
VOK	Voice of Kenya
WFTU	World Federation of Trade Unions

GLOSSARY

baraat	bridegroom's procession
bazm-i-adab	poetry session
bhai	brother
bhangra	spirited dance performed by Sikh males
certiorari	to quash an illegal decision
churidar	tight pyjama
deg	kitchen
duka	small shop
dukhia	wretched, miserable
diwali	festival of lights
guli-danda	game using a stick and piece of wood
gurdwara	sikh temple
habeas corpus	a writ commanding a person who detained another to produce him/her before a court
hartal	suspension of business
haya	shame
Hind	India
inquilab	revolution
jaggery	coarse, dark sugar
jats	farmers
kaccha	knee-length drawers
kameez	long loose shirt
kangha	comb
kara	steel bracelet
kavi darbar	gathering of poets
kavi sammalan	poetry session
kesh	beard
kipande	registration for African males
kirpan	dagger
khadi	homespun cloth
khalsa	pure
kshatriyas	warriors
kurta	loose shirt
majimbo	federalism
maharao	prince
mandamus	a writ issued by a superior court to a subordinate court
moto	fire
muhindi	Indian
mungu	god
order nisi	interim order
pagri	turban
pal	protector of
persona non grata	unwelcome person
ramgharias	skilled workers
sardar	chief
sat sri akal	sikh greeting
sathiji	comrade
satyagraha	a form of passive resistance based on truth and non-violence
shamba	garden
shikar	hunting
sikh	disciple
singh	lion
swaraj	independence
talao	pond
teg	sword
tehmet	sarong
uhuru	freedom
ultra vires	beyond the lawful powers
vaisakhi	Sikh New Year festival
vande mataram	national anthem of India
volte-face	turn around
wafanyakazi	workers
zemindars	landowners

APPENDIX I

HISTORY OF KENYA'S TRADE UNION MOVEMENT BY MAKHAN SINGH

(Delivered at the Trade Union Officials' course at the Management training and Advisory Centre on 2nd June, 1970)

HISTORY OF KENYA'S TRADE UNION MOVEMENT is a part and parcel of the history of Kenya's national struggle for resisting the imperialist colonial rule, for winning it national independence, for consolidating the independence after winning it, and for bringing prosperity to the workers and peoples of Kenya.

In spite of bitter, continuous and heroic resistance by the African people of the territories now comprising Kenya, the British imperialists and colonialists were able to enslave its people with their overwhelming military and administrative force. The British declared the territories to be under their protection and colonial rule. They called the country British East Africa and declared the African land as "Crown land". They built the Railway to effectively occupy the country and completely subdue its African people, much of the good land was given by the British rulers to their kith and kin, the white settlers. Previously all this land used to be occupied and utilized by Africans, who were now turned out of that land and compelled to become wage labourers or squatters to work for white masters or other employers.

From the very beginning the African people began resisting and struggling against the foreign rule and its consequences – land robbery, forced labour, long working hours, compulsory registration (Kipande) system, racial segregation, colour bar, oppressive laws and such other practices.

In order to resist and struggle, the African people, whenever and wherever possible, resorted to armed struggle, harassing of the authorities, attacks upon those building the Railway, and boycott of work for settlers and other employers. All this struggle was secretly organized. At times the people who struggled used the tribal organization with the sanction or tacit consent of a patriotic chief. At other times the struggle was organized by secret tribal groups or combination of groups in face of opposition from stooge chiefs. On settlers' farms there came into existence workers' organizations to struggle for removal of their grievances and for improvement of their wages and other conditions of employment. In most cases these organizations were secret to avoid victimization. Only on rare occasions they came into the open, such workers' organizations also came into existence in towns and at other places of employment. Their struggles were continuous and took many forms, such as slow working, defiant language, leaving the work without permission for which they were occasionally prosecuted and sentenced, refusing to obey orders and going on strikes. The news of their struggles seldom appeared in the press, but these are the struggles from which the workers' organizations or trade unions in Kenya originated and which are the foundations of our trade union movement.

The first trade union or workers' organization which came into existence in Kenya (or British East Africa as it was then called) and which according to written records functioned openly was the African Workers Council. This was formed in the late 1890's by the Africans working for the C.M.S. Mission at Frere Town near Mombasa for protecting and promoting their interests as employees of the mission. With continuous struggles, including petitions to the C.M.S. headquarters in Great Britain, the African Workers Council was able to win improvements in the conditions of employment for the African workers of the mission. The Council drew its members from the freed slaves, both young and old. Its leader was James Deiler, who was an African and ex-slave. With the efforts of the African Workers Council all African priests began receiving sixty rupees per month, deacons fifty rupees, village pastors between forty rupees, senior catechists thirty, junior catechists twenty five and evangelists between eighteen and twenty rupees. The C. M.S. thought that its authority was being threatened. The colonial regime also got frightened when the District Commissioner, Mombasa, came to know about the activities of the African Workers Council. They all thought the activities and influence of the workers council would spread to other workers at the Coast and in the country. The result was that by means of gradual dismissals or transfers of the active leaders and members of the Council this organization of African workers was brought to an end soon after 1900.

In that year there was a strike of Railway workers on the Railway. The strike was for the restoration of privileges which the authorities had withdrawn and was initiated by the European subordinate staff. It was probably later joined by some Asian and African workers. The strike started in Mombasa and then spread to other centers along the line. The railway authorities dismissed the strike leaders, who were then departed or sent away from East Africa. However, the authorities were compelled to settle the dispute by restoring most of the privileges. The strike greatly frightened the authorities.

Two years later, in December 1902, fifty police constables went on strike at Mombasa for removal of their grievances. In October 1906, there was a strike of policemen in Zanzibar. More than 500 askaris were involved. The result of their militant action was that their wages were increased from ten to fourteen rupees per month.

The Zanzibar police strike took place when Maji Maji uprising against German rule was continuing in Tanganyika, then called German East Africa. The uprising has been organized by the African people under their own leaders. It had arisen from the resentment against foreign rule, alienation of African land to settlers and the conditions of forced labour under which the workers were recruited and had to work on settlers' farms and other places of employment under very horrible conditions.

In the same period the unrest amongst the Africans of Kenya or British East Africa was also very intense. It had been and was being expressed both in armed and unarmed struggles by such people as the Kikuyu, the Maasai, the Nandi, the Wakamba, the Somalis, the Luo, the Baluhya, the Kisii, the Elegeyo and Marakwet, the Lumbwa, the Girima, the Taita, the Turkana and the Africans of many other tribes in Kenya. A similar situation was prevailing in Uganda.

In this situation in East Africa the workers were more and more resorting to the peaceful and effective weapon of strikes, especially in Kenya.

In March 1908, there were strikes of African workers employed at a Government farm at Mazeras near Mombasa and of those engaged on loading railway engines with wood at fuel-stations along the line. Two months later there was a strike of railway

Asian workers employed at Kilindini harbour works. During that year there was an African rickshaw-pullers' strike in Nairobi, which lasted for several days. It was against stringent rickshaw regulations of the Nairobi Municipal Committee.

In May 1912, the African boat-workers in Mombasa went on strike in protest against police beatings and very hard Government regulations concerning boatmen. A few months later the African employees of the railway goods-shed in Nairobi had to go on strike against increase of working hours from 8 to 9 hours a day.

During that year there was a persistent refusal by thousands of African workers to work on settlers' farms due to unbearable working conditions prevailing there. In face of this growing resistance of African workers the Government appointed the Native Labour Commission in September 1912, consisting of only officials, settlers and a missionary, all of who were Europeans.

In March 1914, there existed in Mombasa an organization called Indian Union. Probably a similar workers' organization existed in Nairobi, especially among the railway workers.

In July 1914, most of the Asian railway and P.W.D. workers, later joined by some African workers, went on strike to oppose the introduction of Poll Tax and for the removal of other grievances regarding housing, rations, medical facilities and wages. The strike lasted for more than a week. It ended on the assurance of the authorities that the demands of the workers would be given consideration. Later some of the grievances were removed or eased, but the workers' leaders including Mr. Meharchard Puri, Mr. L.W. Ritch, a European colleague of Mahatma Gandhi, and Mr. Tirath Ram were deported from the country. Soon after the strike the First World War started on the 4th August 1914.

During the war about a hundred thousand Africans working as carriers in the Carrier Corps lost their lives. This was in addition to thousands of Africans killed as members of the armed forces. The dependants of the carriers were not given any pension or compensation. The Hut and Poll Tax was increased from 3 to 5 rupees during the war, and from 5 rupees (6 shillings 67 cents) to 16 shilling after the war, which ended in November 1918. The abolition of all passes and removal of restrictions on movements had been demanded by Africans, but instead of granting the demand the Kipande (registration of Africans) law was passed during the war and brought into force from 1st November 1919. This was further to tighten the forced labour system and to bring the African land would be taken, but no sooner had the war ended than hundreds of thousands of acres of African land was given to European soldiers-settlers or reserved for them. All this incensed the African people. They now openly began to organize themselves on modern lines.

In 1919, an organization called the Kikuyu Association was formed. Its President was Chief Koinange and other leaders included Chief Josiah Njojo, Philip Karanja, Mathew Njeroge and Waweru wa Mahoi.

In 1919 there also came into existence a European workers' organization called The Workers Federation of B.E.A. and an Indian. President of the former was Lee Mellor and of the latter Hassanali Amershi. Both organizations lasted for a few years.

In 1921, the burning issues facing the Africans of Kenya were the danger of further alienation of African land, high taxes, low wages, forced labour, registration certificates (Kipande), the changed status of Kenya from "Protectorate" to "Colony" (in July 1920), segregation, Executive, Legislative and Municipal Councils. To these issues were added the demands of the European settlers that the wages of all African workers and employees should be reduced by one third from 1st June 1921. This further intensified the anger of the African people and workers.

The Kikuyu Association which had so far concerned itself mainly with the land issue, now protested against the threatened reduction of wages and against the Kipande. It made the protest by holding a meeting.

From 1st June 1921, when the one-third reduction in wages was to come into force, there was a General Strike of African workers in Nairobi. It lasted for a few days.

The strike action induced a new thinking amongst Africans. This was that a strong organization of Africans was needed. At that time there was an organization in Nairobi of Africans from Uganda. It was called Nairobi Baganda Union. On the 4th June 1921, it held a meeting and passed resolutions protesting against the reduction in wages. Three days later another meeting of Africans was held in Nairobi. It formed an organization called the Young Kikuyu Association, which later sent a memorandum to the Governor demanding the removal of African grievances, including the reduction of African wages. Its leader was Harry Thuku. The issues raised in the memorandum were discussed at a huge meeting of Africans, held at Dagoretti near Nairobi on the 24th June 1921. The meeting was attended by the Chief Nairobi Commissioner and other Government officials, the leaders of the Kikuyu Association headed by Chief Koinange and the leaders of the Young Kikuyu Association headed by Harry Thuku.

Meanwhile, serious thinking was continuing amongst leaders and members of the Young Kikuyu Association as well as amongst those of Nairobi Baganda Union and other African groups that African Associations confined to members of particular tribes were not the best form of African organization to solve problems which were common to all Africans and were not confined to members of one tribe. They held mutual discussions and came to the conclusion that the need of the hour was an African organization which would be open to all Africans. Not only that, they also decided amongst themselves that the African organization so formed should co-operate with people of other races on issues which concerned all the people in the country irrespective of race, colour or creed. The result of these discussions was that on the 1st July 1921, when the Committee of the Young Kikuyu Association met, it decided that the name of the Association be changed to East African Association.

On the 10th July 1921, a huge meeting attended by thousands of Africans was held in Nairobi under the auspices of the East African Association. The meeting passed resolutions against forced labour, against the reduction of wages and against the Registration Ordinance and demanded their repeal. It also asked Government to make suitable provision for the education of children of the soil and that schools be started at all important centers, and that the revenue derived from the Africans be applied for their education. The meeting of the East African Association further asked the Government to give franchise to all educated British subjects in the country. On the above lines the East African Association made representations to the British Government as well as to the colonial regime in Kenya.

The East African Association was both a political organization and general workers union. Its leaders included the following: Chairman: Harry Thuku; Vice Chairman: Daniel Kamau; Hon. Secretary- Paulo Njuguna; Hon. Treasurer I.M. Ishmael: Hon. Auditor – Douglas Mwangi; Members - Abdulla bin Assuman. Kibwana Kombo, James Peter, Haron Matono, Norman Mboya, Moses Mucai, Kinyanjui wa Wathingo, Job Chrispen, James Njoroge, Kunywa Nyamu, Jesse Kariuki, JosephKangethe, Johnstone (now Jomo) Kenyatta, James Beattah, Waiganjo Ndotono, Udingoe, Lawi Mwangi, Njoroge Kangacha, George Mugekenyi, David Njuguna and F. Dracott. The leaders of the Association began organizing if in Nairobi and other parts of Kenya, and its activities had their effect all over the country.

The formation, policies and activities of the East African Association as a national organization and as a general workers union were an important milestone not only in the history of Kenya but also of Uganda, Tanganyika and Zanzibar, because it could be joined by Africans and other people of all the East African territories and its activities could spread from Kenya to Uganda, Tanganyika and Zanzibar.

On the 23rd December 1921, an important development took place when the people in the Nyanza held a huge meeting at Lundha, Gem Location. The meeting which was called by Jonathan Okwiri and was attended by about 8,000 people, formed an organization called the Kavirondo Association. The meeting demanded "for Africans education and schools, representation on the Legislative and other Councils and replacement of hut tax by poll tax". It opposed the Registration Ordinance, forced labour and the status of 'colony' for Kenya. Its leaders included Jonathan Okwiri, Ezekiel Apindi, Simeon Nyende, Benjamin Owour and Joel Omino. It sent to the Government a memorandum based on the resolutions of the meeting.

Meanwhile, the activities of the East African Association were spreading to all parts of Kenya. The colonial authorities got frightened that before long the East African Association and the Kavirondo Association would join hands and become a very strong force. They struck the blow.

On the 14th March 1922, the Government arrested Harry Thuku, the chief leader of the East African Association, to deport and restrict him to a remote part of Kenya.

Following the arrest of Hurry Thuku there was a Genaral Strike in Nairobi and many other parts of Kenya. On the 16th March 1922, there was a huge demonstration at the police Lines in Nairobi, where Harry Thuku was detained. Thousands of Africans were in the demonstration. They demanded his release. In order to break the demonstration and the general strike the government brought troops of the K.A.R., armoured cars and machine guns. The troops fired on the unarmed peaceful demonstrators, who were praying, carrying flags and demanding their leader's release. According to the daily newspapers, *The Leader*, 27 were killed and 24 wounded, but according to a letter published in the *Manchester Guardian* of 20th March 1929, one hundred and fifty Africans lost their lives on that day and much larger number were wounded. Thus on that historic day the tree of Uhuru was watered with the blood of our martyrs. They were martyrs of Kenya's national movement as well as of the trade union movement. The fight for Kenya's independence and for workers' rights began in the right earnest with modern methods.

A tremendous African upsurge was created during the period. The upsurge was such that it was able to compel the British Government to make in July 1923, the famous declaration of "paramountcy of African interests".

The Government, however, did not like the African upsurge. Therefore it took steps to weaken it.

In 1922, after Harry Thuku's deportation, the Kavirondo Association was replaced by an organization called the Kavirondo Taxpayers Welfare Association. Its membership was open to all taxpayers in the Nyanza (then called the Kavirondo) Province. Archdeacon Owen was its President and Senior Commissioner and District Commissioners in the Province were its Vice-Presidents. The other officials and members of its Executive Committee were elected by the main body of the members. All the old leaders of the Kavirondo Association began taking part in the new Association, which concerned itself with general and labour matters.

The formation of the Kavirondo Taxpayers Welfare Association was a part of the

Government's new policy of allowing formation of African association only on provincial or tribal basis with the aim of weakening the national and trade union movements.

The East African Association continued its activities under very difficult circumstances, but in 1925 under the compulsion of the Government's new policy it had to change its name to Kikuyu Central Association so that political activity and workers' activities in the interests of all Africans could be continued and conducted openly. The policies and fighting spirit of the Kikuyu Central Association remained and those of the East African Association and the change was only in name.

From the beginning of 1928, Mzee Jomo Kenyatta became the General Secretary of the Kikuyu Central Association and also the editor of its monthly paper Muigwithania. In February 1929, he was sent to England by the Association to make direct representations to the Secretary of state for the colonies and to create public support for the demands of Kenya's African people as a whole. Kenyatta returned from there in September 1930.

Kenyatta's persistent work in England supported by intense activity of the Kikuyu central Association (K.C.A.) in Kenya compelled the British Government to change its policies concerning Kenya. It began considering the question of Harry Thuku's release who was released at the end of 1930. It issued instructions to the Governor that boundaries of African reserves be fixed after consultations with the people concerned. It gave a pledge that no more African land would be taken for alienation to non-Africans. It issued instructions to ease forced labour regulations. It began to give importance to African education and issued instructions that permission for independent schools should be given, which previously used to be refused. It issued instructions to ease the Hut Tax for women, which was later totally abolished. It asked the Governor that the attack against tribal customs, such as circumcision, should not be pressed. It declared in favour of common roll, but to be implemented in the distant future. It stated that the ultimate goal in Kenya was a democratically elected responsible government.

After Kenyatta's return the constitution of the Kikuyu Central Association (K.C.A.) was amended to enable it to act as a trade union and to co-operate with other bodies and associations of African or mixed membership if it would seem that general interests in social, political or industrial direction would thereby be advanced. At that time K.C.A. had about 10,000 members. It was acting as a national political organization as well as a workers' trade union.

Mzee Jomo Kenyatta, after a stay of about six months in Kenya, again left for England as a leader of K.C.A.'s delegation for giving evidence to the Joint Parliamentary Committee on Closer Union of East African territories and to make representations to the British Government and the people on the national problems facing Kenya. This time he was to remain abroad for more then 15 years.

By this time several direct attempts to establish trade unions or employees' associations had been successfully made. There were then in existence Kenya African Civil Service Association, whose Secretary was Newland Gibson; Kenya European Civil Servants Association and Kenya Indian Civil Servants Association. There were also in existence Associations of European and Indian employees of the Railways.

During this period there was a great national upsurge amongst Africans in all parts of Kenya on the question of land, when African and other organizations were submitting memoranda and evidence to the Kenya Land Commission. This Commission was appointed in April 1932, through the efforts of African people,

African organizations and African leaders including Jomo Kenyatta, Harry Thuku, Joseph Kangethe, Jesse Kariuki, Parminas G. Mockirie, Chief Koinage of Kiambu, Ezekiel Apindi of Nyanza and James Mutua of Machakos.

In 1934, while the upsurge amongst the Africans was continuing, there was a great strike of African workers who were employed at Mombasa by Kenya and Uganda Railways and Harbours and by Kenya Land and Shipping Company. The strike was to prevent a proposed reduction in wages by the stevedoring companies from Shs. 2/- to Shs. 1/50 per day. The strike succeeded in preventing the reduction.

In the year the Kenya African Teachers Union was formed. Two of its chief leaders were Eliud Mathu and James Gichuru.

In February 1935, the African fishermen at Kisumu went on strike for better conditions of employment. They were able to win an increase in their wages.

Two months later, on April 1935, a non-racial union called the Labour Trade Union of Kenya came into existence. This was the culmination of several attempts to form a properly constituted trade union. The membership of the union was open to all workers irrespective of race, religion, caste creed, colour or tribe. Its President was Gulam Mohamed (Railway) and Makhan Singh was its Secretary. Later, when its membership extended to Uganda and Tanganyika, its name was changed to the Labour Trade Union of East Africa. Its other leaders included Mota Singh, Damodardas V. Sachania, M.J. Deman, Shah Mohamed, Gulam Mohamed Luhar, Taj Din, Govird Okeda, Ujagar Singh, Mohan Singh, Jesse Kariuki, and George K. Ndegwa, Amar Singh Jullunduri, Gopal Singh, Hazara Singh and Singh Cheema.

In 1936, the Labour Trade Union successfully conducted a campaign for achieving eight-hour-day, and was able to achieve it from 1st October of that year.

In April-May 1937, there was a series of strikes organized by the Labour Trade Union of East Africa for increase in wages. The Union was able to achieve an increment in wages from 15 to 25 percent. In May, while the strike was continuing the African quarry workers in Nairobi also went on strike and were able to win an increase in their wages or piece-rates.

It was during these strikes of Asian and African workers in 1937 that the colonial regime in Kenya, after obtaining urgent approval from the Secretary of state for the colonies, published the Trade Unions Bill, which was passed by Kenya's Legislative Council in August. It was in this way that the Trade Unions Ordinance 1937, came into existence. It provided for compulsory registration of trade unions.

The Labour Trade Union of East Africa was registered under the Trade Unions Ordinance on the 30th September 1937. Three days earlier on the 27th a sectional union called the East African Ramgarhias Artisan Union, which was formed during the April-May strike, had also been registered. Subsequently the Labour Trade Union of East Africa was registered in Tanganyika. The number of its registration certificate was 1. No other trade union was then registered there. The Union also applied for registration in Uganda, but due to the Second World War having begun it did not press its application.

In 1938, the Labour Trade Union of East Africa established fraternal relations with the British Trade Union Congress, South African Trades and Labour Council and the International Labour Office, Geneva. The Union also began making serious efforts to bring in African workers in large numbers.

In the same year, a new African organization called the Ukamba Members Association was formed in Kenya with Samuel Muindi as President. In September 1938, Muindi was deported to Lamu after he had led a huge demonstration in Nairobi lasting several days against the forcible seizure of Kamba cattle and against the restocking policy of the Government. In December, the Government had to indefinitely postpone its policy and return to their owners all the 2,500 head of the seized cattle. It was a great victory for the Kamba people.

In this period the North Kavirondo Central Association was formed to struggle for the land rights of the Nyanza Africans especially in the Kakamega area. Another organization which was formed at about this time was the Taita Hills Association. Its aims included the return of the Taita lands which had been alienated to European settlers. Both these organizations and the Ukamba Members Association fully co-operated with the Kikuyu Central Association. This unity of the African nationalist organizations was further strengthened by an important and historic event, when, in April 1939, after the promulgation in the previous year of the Highlands Order-in Council, which confirmed the reservation of the Kenya Highlands for the white settlers, a joint memorandum was signed and sent to the Secretary of State for the Colonies by the Kikuyu Central Association and the Kavirondo and the Kavirondo Taxpayers Welfare Association, the two organizations which previously had not co-operated with each other. The memorandum demanded the rescindment of the Highlands Order-in-Council and the related ordinance.

The unity between the African organizations was further strengthened and the basis for a new national upsurge and unity was laid when at that time some of the leaders of the African associations, and especially those of the K.C.A., began co-operating with the Labour Trade of East Africa, and the African workers began joining the Union in large numbers.

The May-Day meeting in 1939, which was held by the Labour Trade Union in Desai Memorial Hall, Nairobi, was the first meeting that was attended by African workers in large numbers and addressed also by the African leaders – Jesse Kariuki and George K. Ndegwa. The third annual conference of the Labour Trade Union held on the 23rd July 1939. on the open ground behind Desai Memorial Hall, was also attended by a large number of African workers and addressed by the above-mentioned leaders, both of whom were elected, the first as a Vice-President of the Union and the second as a member of the Central Bureau of the Union. The significance of the Conference lay in the fact that there were joint deliberations by African and Asian workers for the first time in East Africa. The workers' unity demonstrated at the Conference had an immediate effect upon the Kenya workers' struggle, especially in the railways where the Railway African Staff Association came into existence. The Conference also intensified the workers' struggle in Mombasa.

In July and August 1939, there was a series of African workers' strikes in Mombasa, popularly called the Mombasa African Workers General Strike of 1939. The strike was the manifestation of trade unionism amongst African workers as it had begun developing during that period. More than 6,000 workers took part in the strikes which lasted for several days. The Government appointed an Inquiry Commission to go into the demands of the Mombasa workers. The Labour Trade union of East Africa submitted a comprehensive memorandum and its General Secretary, Makhan Singh, gave oral evidence to the Mombasa Labour Inquiry Commission. The Union demanded Shs. 50/- as minimum wage so as to also satisfy the family needs of the African workers. The prevailing wage at that time was 12 to 15 shillings. As a result of the strike, representations of the Union and recommendations of the Commission all the workers in Mombasa began receiving a housing allowance of three shillings and some of their other grievances were removed.

Soon after the Mombasa General Strike the Labour Trade Union of East Africa established relations with Mzee Jomo Kenyatta, who was then in London. The Union requested him to attend on its behalf the International Conference on problems of the Defence of Democracy, Peace and Humanity, which was to be held in Brussels on September 30th and October 1st 1939. He agreed to the request and sent to the Union his cordial good wishes for the success of its work. Due to the Second World War, which commenced on the 3rd September 1939, the Conference with Mzee Jomo Kenyatta could not continue.

During the Second World War the strikes were banned under the Denfence Regulations, which were unjustly promulgated by the Colonial regime. In May 1940, the Government banned the three most active African organizations – the Kikuyu Central Association, Ukamba Members Association and Taita Hills Association – and detained 23 of their Leaders. The General Secretary of the Labour Trade Union of East Africa was detained at about the same time, while he was in India on a short visit.

As the war situation developed the stringent anti-strike regulations could not prevent strikes in Kenya. In 1941 and 1942 in spite of the ban, there were strikes of African worker in Mombasa, Nairobi and many other places in Kenya for increase in wages to meet the increased cost of living. The Government, the Railway and other employers were forced to grant increases in wages. Another result of the strikes was that the Government was obliged to replace the Trade Unions Ordinance, of 1937 by a slightly improved trade union law called the Trade Unions and Trade Disputes Ordinance, 1943. During 1943 and in the following year there were more strikes of African workers. All the strikes were participated in by workers as workers and not as members of tribes. The leaders who led and conducted the strikes were generally of non-tribal thinking. The upsurge that was created by the strikes was a great national upsurge, which the Government could no more ignore. Moreover, by the second half of 1944 all the nationalist leaders who had been in detention under the Defence Regulations had been released and they were again active. A new situation had now arisen in the country.

The result was that the Government was compelled to appoint an African Member on the Legislative Council and also allow the formation of a country – wide political organization of Africans Study Union and then Kenya African Union (KAU). The African Member was appointed in the beginning of October 1944, and he was Mr. Eliud Mathu. He began representing in the Legislatives Council the view- point of African workers. The African national organization came into existence at the same time. Another result of the African workers' strikes was that the committees which organized the strikes gradually began coming into the open and began forming themselves into permanent associations of workers or trade unions. The process went on not only during the war, which ended on 8th May 1945, but also after it had ended.

During the war and immediately after the war there came into existence the East African Standard, Asian Staff Union, which was formed in 1941 and registered on the 5th April during the same year. The printing workers had begun organising as a union in a 1936, first as Press Workers Union and then as a Section of the Labour Trade Union of East Africa. In 1943 the printing workers formed the Typographical Union of Kenya (now the Printing and Kindred Trades Workers Union), which was registered on 5.9.46. Its President at that time was Mohamed Husein Paracha. At first its membership was confined to Asian workers but in 1948 it was made open to all workers irrespective of race. When the African Printing Workers Association under the leadership of William amalgamated with it. During 1945 there came into existence two unions of Nairobi domestic workers. One was Nairobi Houseboys Association of Employees of Indian and Goans. Its President was Chege Kiburu. Later both the associations amalgamated to form the Kenya Houseboys Association, the name of which was later changed to the Domestic and Hotel Workers Union. In the same period there came into existence an organisation of night watchmen, called the Nightwatchmen Association. Its President was Willie George and Secretary Mushegi Karanja. On the 21st March, 1946, was formed the Nairobi Taxi Drivers Union. Its President was John Mungai. It was resistered on 30.7.46. This was the first trade union with the African Leadership to be registered in Kenya. Later its name was changed to Kenya African road Transport and Mechanics Union and then in December, 1948, to its present name, the Transport and allied Workers Union. At that time its other leaders included Fred Kubai and M.A.O. Ndisi. Another union called the Thika Motor Drivers Association, whose President was Douglas Mbugwa, was registered on 9th October , 1946 but it did not last long. In Mombasa the East African Seamen's Union was formed. Its General Secretary was Mohamed Saleh. In Nairobi, in 1946, the Tailoring workers began holding meetings with intention of the forming their union. The tailors and Garment workers Union was registered on 10.7.48. Its leaders then included Melikisadek Anyanje, Gichure Gatama and S. Osore. Kenya African Civil Service Association was very active in 1946 in the struggle for its demands. And so was the Railway African Staff Association, which was formed in 1939 on the eve of the Second World War since then had been very active. One of its leaders was Phillip Muinde. The Kenya and Uganda Railway Asian Union and Kenya Asian Civil Service Association, both of which were registered on 21.4.47, were also active in the struggle for better conditions of employment.

Kenya's trade unions and the national organization, Kenya African Union, were working hand in hand. The ideas of nationalism and trade unionism had begun reaching the far corners of the country. It was during this period that Jomo Kenyatta, who had been Kenya's national emissary to England and other countries of the world, returned to his motherland on the 24th September 1946. For more than 17 years he had represented Kenya's national union movements to the best of his capacity. With his return there was a new enthusiasm and awakening in Kenya. His call for unity, struggle and sacrifice for the cause of freedom gave great encouragement.

Meanwhile, seeing the growth strength of Kenya's trade union movement and workers' struggles the Government introduced in Legislative Council and got passed Legislation on Minimum and Workmen's Compensation.

At about the end of 1946, the struggle of agricultural workers and squatters was gathering strength. It was for better conditions of employment. There were squatters' demonstrations in January 1947, on the laws of Government House, Nairobi. The struggle of other workers in Kenya was also growing, and it expressed itself in the historic General Strike of Mombasa workers during that month.

Mombasa General Strike of more than 15,000 workers took place from 13th to 24th January 1947.Its leaders included Chege Kibachia, Mwangi Macharia and Mabaruk Kenze. The strike was for increase in wages and for "equal work". It ended through the intervention of Eliud Mathu, who negotiated with the Government, which appointed a Tribunal under the chairmanship of Justice Thacker to investigate into the causes of the strike and make recommendations. Wages were increased, a result of the General Strike was that there was a tremendous growth of national awakening and a very strong urge for trade unionism.

On the first day of the General Strike, African Workers Federation was formed. It was later registered as a trade union, when its president was Chege Kibachia.

Following the Mombasa General Strike there were strikes in April 1947, at Kisumu, Kisii, Maseno and Asembo Bay. As a result of the recommendations of the Tribunal, wages were also increased in Nairobi, Nakuru, Kisumu, Eldoret and various other places in Kenya. There was now a great national upsurge in the country.

It was during this great upsurge that on 1st June 1947, was held the Annual Conference of Kenya African Union. The Conference gave a clarion call for a United Front to win the fight for Freedom and Conference demanded the abolition of Kipande and made other demands. It also supported the demands of the workers for better conditions of employment. The Government got frightened of the growing unity of the national movement and the trade union movement. It was especially afraid of workers' struggles. It began striking blows to crush or at least weaken the movements.

In August 1947, Chege Kibachia, the President of the African Workers Federation, was arrested and later deported and restricted at Kabarnet in the Baringo District, far away from Mombasa and Nairobi. In the same month, at about the same time, Makhan Singh the General Secretary of the Labour Trade Union of East Africa was served with an order to quit Kenya. He defied the order. He was prosecuted, but was acquitted. The Government could not succeed in deporting him. Several leaders of the African Workers Federation at Mombasa were prosecuted and imprisoned. But all these actions could not repress the movement.

Organization of trade unions continued, their activities intensified. In 1948, Government got passed Trade Unions and Trade Disputes (Amendment) Ordinance, which gave more powers to the Registrar of Trade Unions.

During 1948, a new union, the Shoemaker Workmen's Union, came into existence. Its President was Manchhubhai Lala, Secretary Chaganlal and Assistant Secretary Walter. It was registered on the 17th December 1948.

In August 1948 there was a meeting of the representatives of the registered Trade Unions in the office of Mr. James Patrick, the Trade Union Labour Officer to discuss a draft bill to make provision for the fixing of wages and general conditions of employment. In the following month was held a Cost of Living and Wages Conference attended by several trade union representatives. These occasions brought the trade union leaders of that period nearer to each other.

During 1948, Mr. Patrick issued trade union pamphlets both in English and Swahili. He also conducted trade union courses. Meshak Ndisi, the General Secretary of the Transport and Allied Workers Union was granted a scholarship by the British T.U.C. and he went to study trade unionism at the Ruskin College, Oxford.

Seeing the growing activities of trade unions the European settlers in Kenya got upset. On the 10th January 1949, the European settlers' meeting held at Thika passed a resolution opposing the furtherance of trade unionism. The bill provided for the institution of wages councils, joint industrial councils, works or staff councils and registered agreements, the purpose of all of which was to avoid, bypass or weaken trade unions.

The same draft bill was discussed by the representatives of trade unions in a meeting convened by Mr. Patrick and held in his office on the 28th and 30th January, 1949. After the joint meeting the representatives decided to initiate discussions amongst themselves with the aim of forming a central organization of trade unions. As a result of those discussions, on the 1st May 19 49, was formed the East African Trade Unions Congress (EATUC). It was formed by the representatives of the Labour Trade Union of East Africa, the transport and Allied Workers Union, the Tailors and Garment Workers Union, the Typographical Union of Kenya and the Shoemaker Worker's

Union. Later the EATUC was also joined by the Domestic and Hotel Workers Union, the East African Federation, the East African Seamen's Union and the East African Painters and Decorators Union. The East African Trade Unions Congress was affiliated neither to the World Federation or Trade Unions nor to the International Confederation of Free Trade Unions.

The main activities of the EATUC and its affiliated unions during 1949 and in the first half of 1950 were the strikes and struggles organized for the achievement of workers' demands: increase in wages; reduction of working hours where they were more than 8 hours a day, such as in the cases of shoe-workers and sweetmeat-workers; 45 hours a week and overtime for extra work; pay during sickness; pay for gazetted holidays; local leave with pay; one month's notice for the termination of employment or a month's pay in lieu of notice; housing allowance; and a provident fund scheme for all workers with six months' service. Other activities included campaign against the repressive labour laws and other such ordinances brought by the colonial regime, campaign against the repressive taxi-cab bye-laws of the Nairobi Municipal Council, campaign for the release of Chege Kibachia who was still in deportation living under strict restrictions, and boycott of the City Celebrations in March, 1950.

On the 23rd April 1950, a decision of very great importance was made in a huge mass meeting held under the joint auspices of the Kenya African Union and E.A. Indian National Congress. A resolution demanding complete independence for East African territories was passed unanimously. The resolution was moved by Makhan Singh and Fred Kubai, the General Secretary and President of the East African Trade Unions Congress. Later the EATUC formally supported and adopted the resolution.

The colonial regime got frightened by the growing unity in the national and trade union movements and by the close cooperation between the two. The Government struck the blow.

On the 15th May 1950, Fred Kubai, the President and Makhan Singh the General Secretary of the EATUC were arrested. A General Strike against the arrests and for the demands of workers took place all over the country. Demands were: release of leaders, a minimum wage of Shs.100/-, abolition of the repressive Municipal bye-laws regrarding taxi drivers, no arrests of workers at night in their houses, and freedom for all workers and freedom of East African territories. Chege Kiburu and Mwangi Macharia were appointed as Acting President and Acting General Secretary of the EATUC after the arrest of its officials. The Acting officials were also arrested. More than a hundred thousand workers took part in the General Strike throughout the country. Its maximum duration was nine days in Nairobi. At other places it lasted for two or three days. A tremendous national awakening was demonstrated during the strike.

A major development in the period following the General Strike was the rapid progress of a secret mass organization called the Mau Mau or Kenya Land Freedom Army. The organization , which previously had been in existence for some time, could be joined by persons of any tribe who took an oath according to their customs, traditions and beliefs, pledging themselves to secrecy, dedication and sacrifice for the cause of land and freedom (uhuru) of Kenya. The aim of the Uhuru-oath-organization was to unite and mobilize the African people of Kenya in the struggle for independence and to resort to armed struggle against the colonialists if and when it became obvious to the organization that there was no other way of achieving independence of Kenya. The Mau Mau came into light in the course of a court case at Naivasha in the beginning of June 1950. On the 12th August in the same year it was banned.

The arrests of the President and General Secretary of the EATUC had been made and they were prosecuted on charges of being officiated of an unregistered trade union. A fine was imposed upon them. Thus the East African Trade Unions Congress became a banned organization. Makhan Singh and Mwangi Macharia were deported and restricted to remote places under the Deportation Ordinance. Chege Kiburu was imprisoned for a year at a far off place. Fred Kubai was prosecuted for attempted murder. He was acquitted and released in February 1951. As a result of the strike, hundreds of workers were arrested and sentenced to imprisonment. One of them was Peter Mungai, a member of Central Council of EATUC and official of the Domestic and Hotel Workers Union.

Soon after Fred Kubai's release a joint committee of All trade Unions was formed to perform the functions of a central organization of trade unions as much as could be legally done. All the constituent unions of the EATUC became the constituents of the Joint Committee. The Joint Committee could only call meetings of trade union representatives for common purposes but could not call public meetings or perform any other function of a central organization. The Joint Committee therefore occasionally asked the Government to allow the formation of a central organization of trade unions of Kenya. The formation of the Joint Committee of all Trade Unions took place at about the end of February 1951. The Committee continued the campaign against the anti-trade-union clauses of the Regulation of Wages and Conditions of Employment Bill which was published in the previous year and passed its third reading in the Legislative Council but had not yet come into force. Due to the campaign of the trade unions in the previous months some of the clauses had modified and the Labour Commissioner. Mr. Carpenter, had clearly stated that "the proposed wages councils were not intended to replace trade unions, they would merely supplement them". The Ordinance came into force on the 7th April 1951.

Two weeks later, the colonial regime banned the importation into Kenya of all the publications of the World Federation of Trade Unions (WFTU) as the authorities were worried not only by the reorganization and increased activity and unity of the trade unions in Kenya established in the form of the Joint Committee of All Unions but also by the active solidarity the World Federation was showing with the cause of the trade union movements and liberation struggles in Kenya and other colonies. The colonial authorities in Kenya were also upset by the fact that WFTU had lodged a formal complaint with the International Labour Organization (ILO) that the Convention on Freedom of Association had been infringed by the U.K. Government and the Government of Kenya. It based its complaint on the forcible dissolution of the East African Trade unions Congress and arrest and detention of trade union leaders in Kenya for their trade union activities. The complaint was later heard as Case No.29 by the ILO's Committee on Freedom of Association. The Committee later decided not to take any further action after the Government of Kenya wrote to it through the British Government that a central organization of trade unions could be formed in Kenya.

Struggles of trade unions intensified with the formation of the Joint Committee. The Shoemaker Workmen's Union, the Tailors and Garment Worker Union and Typographical Union of Kenya were busy in getting proper implementation of the agreements, which they had obtained from the employers after strikes and long struggles. The Domestic and Hotel Workers Union, the Transport and Allied Workers Union and all sections of the Labour Trade Union of East Africa were pressing on their demands. The struggle of the Nairobi City Council African Staff Association was also bringing pressure for the demands of the Municipal workers.

On 10th June 1951, Fred Kubai was elected the Chairman of the Nairobi Branch of Kenya Union (KAU). In a speech he demanded Kenya's Freedom within three years. Close co-operation between KAU and trade unions was continuing. Mau Mau's activities were growing.

On the 4th November 1951, the annual conference of the Kenya African Union was held in Kaloleni Social Hall, Nairobi. In this conference President Jomo Kenyatta made the historic announcement that the Central Committee of KAU had decided upon the national flag of Kenya and he produced it in the meeting. Mzee Kenyatta said "The black in the flag represents Africans, the red the blood of Africans, the green the condition of Africans' land and the shield, the arrow and the spear are weapons to arrest our enemies." The announcement was the sign of the intensification of the national struggle for Kenya's liberation.

It was in this period of rising nationalism and growing trade unionism in Kenya that a delegation of the International Confederation of Free Trade Unions (ICFTU) began arriving in Nairobi on the 5th November 1951. The delegation consisted of Br. George Bagnall (former secretary of the National Union of Dyers, Bleachers and Textile Workers of Great Britain), Br. Guy Rozemont (President of the Mauritius Trade Union Council), Br. Renzo Lomazzi (Editor of the Journal of Italian Confederation of Labour unions), and Br. Charles-Jacques Leurs (who was born in the Belgian Congo and was Board Secretary of the Luxemburg State Railways). They were accompanied by Br. Martin Levinson of the ICFTU's staff, from its headquaters in Brussels. Br. Bagnall was the leader of the delegation. He said: "The aim of the visit is to establish contact with existing trade union organizations and to study the problems which confront them; to make a general survey of the economic and social needs of the people; to ascertain the views of governments and various political parties and to make proposals for the development of the free trade union movement." The delegation stayed in Kenya for a few days. It had talks with trade union leaders, Government officials and others. It later submitted a report to the Executive Board of the ICFTU.

One achievement of the trade union movement at about the end of year 1951 was that after the Domestic and Hotel Workers Union had given strike notice, the union was registered on the 27th of November 1951. Its application for registration was made on May 1949.

In the year, 1952, the colonial regime in Kenya launched a big attack on Kenya's trade union movement. This was in the form of a new trade union bill which, when passed, was to replace the Trade Unions and Trade Disputes Ordinance, 1943, and its amending ordinances.

The bill was published on the 8th January 1952, in the Official Gazette for introduction into Legislative Council. The new features of the bill were: It made a provision in the legislation for staff associations and employees' organizations which were to be under the general supervision of the Labour Commissioner. It introduced a provision for probationary trade unions. It provided that the officers of a union must normally be persons actually employed in the industry or occupation with which the union was concerned. Others could be employed as such only with the permission of the Member for Labour. It provided that registration of a union could be cancelled or suspended not only in cases of infringement of the provisions of the ordinance but also in cases of not complying with the union's own rules. It also provided that the secretary or treasure of a union must be sufficiently literate in English, and that trade union officials must restrict their activities to one trade union.

Kenya's trade unions immediately reacted and opposed the retrograde clauses of the bill. Meetings of the Domestic and Hotel Workers Union and the Transport and Allied Workers Union, held on the 20th January 1952, in Pumwani Memorial Hall, passed resolutions strongly opposing the bill. B.M. Kaggia said in his speech that the new bill was aimed at "finishing the trade unions in Kenya". Some of the speakers also said that the trade union struggle was being hampered by the Government's refusal to allow the formation of the central organization of trade unions in Kenya.

For more than a year the unions had been demanding permission for the formation of a central organization. The ICFTU delegation had supported the demand. The World Federation of Trade Unions had already lodged a complaint with the I.L.O. regarding the suppression of the previous central organization, the East African Trade Unions Congress. Another factor, although small, had added to the pressure for the demand. This was that Makhan Singh, the General Secretary of the banned EATUC, who was now under restriction at Lokitaung had gone on a ten-day hunger-strike, from the 26th January 1952, for the removal of the ban and for the deported and restricted trade union leaders. The result of all the pressures was that two days later on the 28th January 1952, an intimation was sent to the Joint Committee of All Trade Unions that the Government was prepared to allow the formation of a Kenya Federation of Registered Trade Unions. Soon after the receipt of the intimation a central organization of Kenya Trade Unions called the Kenya Federation of Registered Trade Unions was formed in a meeting attended by representatives of seven trade unions which were previously affiliated to the banned East African Trade Unions Congress. The following officials were appointed: President Mushegi Karanja, General Secretary Aggrey Minya and Treasurer S. Osore. The General Council of the Federation (KFRTU) was to consist of five representatives from each affiliated union. A draft constitution sent by Mr. Jas Patrick on behalf of the Labour Department was not approved by the General Council, but a draft constitution prepared by M.A.O. Ndisi in consultation with the officials of K.F.R.T.U. and approved by Mzee Jomo Kenyatta, was later adopted by the KFRTU General Council. Letters about the formation of the Federation were sent to the Governor, the Labour Commissioner, the Colonial office, the International Confederation of Free Trade Union; and the KAU delegation in London (Mbiyu Koinange and Achieng Oneko). They all recognized the KFRTU as the central organization of trade unions of Kenya. The first mass meeting called by KFRTU in which the news about the federation of the new central organization of trade unions was given in detail was held on the 7th June 1952, in the Kaloleni Social Hall, Nairobi.

Meanwhile the Trade Unions Bill had passed its third reading in the Legislative Council on the 1st April 1952. This was done in spite of the strong opposition by the KFRTU and also by the African and some other Members of the Legislative Council.

A few days later, on the 10th April, extracts from the report of the ICFTU delegation, which had recently toured East Africa, appeared in the press. The delegation had strongly recommended to the Executive Board of ICFTU that full support should be given to the trade unions in East Africa, and it stated in the report: "That a powerful employer should negotiate with his workers as equals is nothing short of a revolutionary conception in East Africa. The African has for so long been regarded as a chattel that it will take years of struggle before the concept of trade unionism, implying equality of the workers, is accepted by the bulk of the employers. ...One of the greatest threats to the trade union movement in East Africa is the attitude held by many Government officials that the African is not ready for trade unionism...The delegation is of the opinion that, given the proper advice and guidance, the African is capable of running trade unions...... Unfortunately the 'African is not ready' opinion has became so prevalent in some territories that legislation is being introduced to encourage employees' associations and staff councils as a substitute for bonafide trade unions ....The coming challenge in Africa is the avoidance of a bloody clash between opposing ideologies which regard the African on the one hand as human being and on the other a subordinate or a chattel. In this struggle there can be no question of the side which the ICFTU must take."

It was during this period that, seeing the growing strength of the trade union movement in Kenya, a call was given for the formation of a union of employers, and a resolution was unanimously passed at the annual meeting of the Kenya Sisal Growers Association, held on the 21st April 1952, asking the Sisal Control Board to follow up the matter.

With the formation of the Kenya Federation of Registered Trade Unions important developments were taking place in the trade union movement. Two new trade unions came into existence. The first was the Night watchmen, Clerks and Shop Workers Unions. Its President was Willie George. It was registered on the 11th June 1952. The second was the East African Federation of Building and Construction Workers Union. Its President was Zakaria Mathegethe and General Secretary Saulo Lubayo. It was registered on the 27th June 1952. The officials of the former union had previously been among the leaders of the Labour Trade Union of East Africa, which was continuing its activities as a general workers union. The leaders of KFRTU were able to form trade councils in Nakuru, Kisumu and Thika during this period and later in Eldoret and Mombasa. In September 1952, M.A.O. Ndisi amd Fred Kubai on behalf of KFRTU met the General Secretary, Sir Vincent Tewson and other leaders of TUC and explained to them the problems facing the trade union movement in Kenya. As a result, the T.U.C. later sent to KFRTU books on Trade Unionism to the value of 50 pounds.

The organized and active strength of Kenya's trade union movement compelled the Government to increase the minimum wage from the 1st June 1952 and then again, only two months later, from the 1st August, when in Nairobi it was raised to Shs.56/50. The Trade Unions and workers considered the new minimum wage as totally inadequate.

In June 1952, the appointment was announced of the first statutory wages council to be set up in Kenya under the wages council and conditions of employment ordinance, 1951. The wages council was for the Tailoring Trade. As a result of the decisions of the wages council the wages and conditions of employment in the tailoring and garment making industry were improved.

During 1952 the Government was compelled to accept a joint demand of the three civil service associations that a Whitley council be appointed. The Whitley Council was appointed with 26 members and was now actively functioning.

At that time the total membership of the registered trade unions in Kenya was in the region of 40,000 members, out of which, according to the Labour Department's report for 1952, the paid-up membership was 27,600. According to the same report it was estimated that in addition to the membership of the trade unions about one-third of the 438,702 African employees in the country were associated with some form of consultative machinery, "mainly through employment with Government or local authorities." The associations of civil servants and local Government employees constituted the bulk of the 19 staff and employees' associations "known to the Labour Department."

The tempo of workers' struggles was increasing throughout Kenya. And so was the tempo of the struggles organized by the organization, the Kenya African Union under

Appendix I

the leadership of Mzee Kenyatta.

The signature campaign organized by the KAU for the land rights of the African was continuing, and hundreds of thousands of signatures in Kenya and tens of thousands in England had already been obtained. The petition was later duly submitted to the British Parliament. In all parts of the country KAU meeting were being held and every meeting was attended by tens of thousands. One meeting at Nyeri on the 25th July 1952 was attended by more than 50,000 people. In the course of their speeches at these meetings Mzee Jomo Kenyatta and other leaders emphasized the need for negotiations between the Government and the African Union for the achievement of Kenya's national aim of complete independence. They also stressed that they preferred non-violent methods. However, the colonial regime and the European leadership were not in any mood of listening to the suggestions of the national leadership.

There were at that time about 250,000 students in the independent schools and all such schools under the management of Kikuyu Karinga Education Association and Kikuyu Independent Schools Association had become forts of the struggle for freedom.

The Uhuru-oath-organization, which was called the Kenya Land and Freedom Army as well as Mau mau, was hotting up its struggles, especially the violent struggles. It was becoming abvious to its leadership that armed force against the colonialists was necessary, because no other way was left to achieve the complete independence of Kenya. The majority of the people in the Central Province and Nairobi had taken the uhuru-oath, and there were also such oaths-takers in some other parts of Kenya. Some trade-unionists with some other national leaders were playing an important part in the activities of the uhuru-oath-organization.

The tremendous upsurge of the people for freedom, land and prosperity made the European officials and settlers very panicky. On the 8th August 1952, the European Elected Members Organization made the following proposals to the Government:

1. That Emergency powers should be brought into force immediately in certain areas such as the Kikuyu Reserve and contiguous districts.

2. That the leaders of KAU should be dealt with immediately under the powers.

3. That a Special Commissioner for Security be appointed.

4. That the posts of Attorney-General and Member for Law and Order should be separated.

5. That the Government should make a statement to the effect that African nationalism, on the lines of West Africa, was not H.M. Government's policy for Kenya and once this had been made perfectly clear, any statement which suggested such a thing were possible should be considered seditious.

6. That in the opinion of the European Elected Members there was a real danger that European might take matters into their own hands if the forces of law and order did not deal immediately with the present lawlessness throughout the country.

It is obvious that the real purpose of the European leaders and reactionary colonial officials was to crush African nationalism, which, as in West Africa, demanded complete independence of the country. For them it was not a question of violence or non-violence. To their mind anyone who demanded freedom, whether by violent or non-violent methods, must be arrested and prosecuted on a charge of sedition. Therefore, day in and day out, they continued their pressure, which began to have effect both on the British Government and on the colonial regime in Kenya.

The African Members of Legislative Council seeing what was happening in the country and judging what might happen in the near future issued a statement on the

Appendix I

15th October 1952. The statement was signed by Messrs. E.W. Mathu, F.W. Odede, Muchohi Gikonyo, J.M. Ole Tameno and W.W.W. Awori. The main points of the statement to alleviate the situation in the country were:

1. Government should announce soon the establishment of the consultative body to deal with constitution reforms, as further delay would only cause greater political frustration among the Africans.
2. The terms of reference of the coming Royal Commission should include a re-examination of the distribution of the land among the various racial groups. The Commission would evoke greater confidence if there were Africans on its membership. We attach great importance to this point.
3. Immediate increase in African wages by one-third. The effect would be terrific in alleviating the present situation.
4. Provision of housing, because desperate people, who at the moment could not eat and had
5. Nowhere to sleep would be encouraged to take work and look to the future by an improvement in conditions.
6. Creation of senior posts for Africans. Capable men are available. Creation of the Queen's Commissioned Ranks for Africans in Forces.
7. All–weather roads in the African Reserves.
8. Allow Africans to hold public meetings.
9. End all discriminatory practices and end discrimination in hotels and restaurants.
10. We re-iterate African members' firm stand against violence but feel that restoration of law and order is sure of gaining some permanency if more vigorous steps are taken at the same time to affect the necessary reforms.

The Government ignored the African Members' suggestions and on the 20th October 1952. The Governor Sir Evelyn Baring declared a state of emergency in Kenya. The same night Mzee Jomo Kenyatta and many other national and trade union leaders were arrested and detained under Emergency regulations. British battalions began arriving at Eastleigh Airport and the British cruiser "Kenya" was already at Mombasa.

An imperialist colonial war was now on against the people of Kenya. A new situation had arisen, not only for the national movement, but also for the trade union movement in Kenya.

The most prominent of the arrested leaders were Mzee Jomo Kenyatta, Achieng Oneko, Fred Kubai, Paul Ngei, Bilded Kaggia and Kungu Karumba. Their famous Kapenguria trial not only roused the people of Kenya for the cause of freedom but also roused the people all over the world in support of the complete independence of Kenya and other enslaved countries of Africa. Although the main charge against them was that they were "managers of MAU MAU", to which they pleaded not guilty, their real crime in the eyes of the colonial regime was that they had played and were playing an important part in the struggle for Kenyan's independence. They were later sentenced to seven years' rigorous imprisonment, after which they were to be restricted under the Deportation Ordinance for an indefinite period.

Of the above, Fred Kubai and Bildad Kaggia were also prominent trade union leaders. The other trade union leaders who were arrested and detained immediately on the declaration of the Emergency were Willie George, the President of the Nightwatchman Clerks and shopworkers Union, Chege Kiburu, the Senior Vice-President of the Domestic and Hotel Workers Union, John Mungai and Paul Kariuki, the veteran leaders of the Transport and Allied Workers Union, and Dishon Kahiato and J.D. Kali, prominent officials of the Labour Trade Union of East Africa. Three other trade union leaders – Chege Kibachia since 1947 and and Makhan Singh and Mwangi Macharia since 1950 – were already under restriction. Hundreds of other members of trade unions were then also languishing in prisons on various charges concerning the struggle for land and freedom, which charges were brought against them before the Emergency.

Immediately after the declaration of the Emergency the officials of the Kenya Federation of Registered Trade unions were called by the Labour Commissioner to the Labour Department on the 21st October, 1952. The officials included its president Mushegi Karanja and General Secretary Aggrey Minya, and they were accompanied by Rufus Kinuthia, the General secretary of the Domestic and Hotel Workers Union, and some other members of the General Council of KFRTU.

The meeting was addressed by the Chief Secretary of the Kenya Government, who told them that the Emergency had been declared on account of the activities of Mau Mau. He further said that the Government would not tolerate any strikes but would allow the trade unions to carry on their activities without any hindrance. He added that Government would give consideration to improving wages and other conditions of employment. The purpose of the meeting was to give warning to trade unions.

After the meeting the leaders of the Kenya Federation of Registered Trade Unions decided that in the difficult situation that had arisen with the declaration of the Emergency the unity of the trade union movement must be maintained, the activities of the Trade Unions in the interests of workers must be continued and support for the trade union movement must be mobilized not only nationally but also internationally. The KFRTU and its affiliated trade unions – the Transport and Allied Workers Union, the Tailors Tent sail Makers and Garment Workers Union, the Domestic and Hotel Workers Union, the Night watchman, Clerks and Shopworkers Union, the Typographical Union of Kenya and East African Federation of Building and Construction workers Union – all of which had branches in the main towns of Kenya and were a very strong organized force of about 45,000 workers began carrying on their activities to the best of their capacity. They supported the new officials of Kenya African Union (KAU) – F.W. Odende President, Joseph Murumbi General Secretary, and W.W.W. Awori Treasurer. They strongly opposed the Government's divide and rule moves against the Kikuyu, and supported and advocated only those moves which were based on nationalism. They also gave support to the nationalist policies of the Africans Members of Legislative Council. For the international support they decided the KFRTU should make application for affiliation with the ICFTU, continue contacts with the British T.U.C., and also continue contacts with the British M.P.s, such as Fenner Brochkway and Leslie Hale. They also decided the contacts with the KAU emissary abroad, Mbiyu Koinange, should be maintained and strengthened. They began implementing their policies. The Government and settlers' leaders were anxiously watching the policies and practices of the trade union movement.

By a decision of the General Council of the Kenya Federation of Registered Trade Unions, Ag[g]rey Minya, the General Secretary made on behalf of the Federation an application for its affiliation with the ICFTU. The application was made on the 19th November 1952, and it was considered and approved by the meeting of the Executive Board of ICFTU, which was held in New York from the 1st to 5th December 1952,

Meanwhile on the 3rd December 1952, had begun the trial of Mzee Kenyatta and others at Kapenguria. The rumour for a general strike of workers was very rampant at

Appendix I

this time. The Mau Mau freedom fighters had intensified their activities. Most of them were ordinary workers and peasants and some of them had been members of trade unions and workers' organizations. Thousands of workers and squatters employed at European settlers' farms had been turned out from the farms and sent back to the reserves. They were feeling very bitter. Since the beginning of the Emergency thousands of workers in Kenya had been arrested and were daily being arrested under the Emergency Regulations. The other workers were fully dissatisfied with the unsatisfactory conditions their life. They all were pressing for a general strike. All this had effect upon the Government, which decided that something should be done for workers even though not for all workers. On the day the Kapenguria Trial began the Chief Secretary announced in the Legislative Council that decision had been taken by the three East African Governments with the approval of the Secretary of State for the Colonies that a Civil Services Commission would be set up "to review the salaries and condition of services of the Civil Service of the East African territories". The Commission was soon set up and came to be known as Lidbury Commission on salaries from the name of its chairman Sir David Lidbury. Later the main recommendation of the commission was that salaries of all civil servants should be on a non – racial basis and it recommended increases in salaries.

A week after the announcement about the setting up the Civil Services Salaries commission the Colonial regime announced a very repressive measure, which was to affect workers very seriously. On the 10th December 1952, new Emergency Regulations were announced that all Kikuyu would have to carry special history of employment cards as a means of their identity. These cards came to be known as Green cards. The measure was immediately opposed by the Kenya Federation of Registered Trade Unions, its affiliated unions and other democratic organisations in the country. They all said the measure was aimed at dividing and further controlling all the Africans not only Kikuyus. They added: "Today it is meant for the Kikuyus tomorrow it will be introduced for all Africans". They all began strongly opposing it and made representations to the Government. Some workers later refused to take the card and were sent to prison for refusal.

The trade unions, in addition to opposing the Green Cards, began advancing their demands for improvement in conditions of employment, especially for increase in wages. On or about the 30th of December 1952, the Domestic and Hotel Workers Union sent a memorandum to employers of all races making the following demands:

1. Wages of stewards should start at 250/- (annual increment 20/-); Cooks, 200/ - (increment 15/-); (and so on for all grades. For nurses and ayahs the wages demanded was Shs. 185/- with annual increment of 15/-).
2. Eight-hour working day with a 20% extra for overtime.
3. Shs.39/50 as house rent.
4. 18 days local leave, 72 days' long leave after 3 years' service, and sick leave with full pay.
5. Provision of uniforms.
6. Long service gratuities.
7. Traveling and safari allowances.
8. Fares from late duty employment.
9. Compensation for death or injury.
10. Work-free public holiday(s) or pay in lieu thereof.
11. Month's notice for termination of employment.

12. No dismissal without proper reason.

Other unions also made similar demands and all of them always said that necessary action would be taken if the demands were not met.

In the beginning of January 1953, there were two strikes at Mombasa. One was of the workers of the Kenya Meat Commission in protest against the new arrangement whereby they were not allowed to have any of the offal. The second stoppage involved ayahs at the Pandya Memorial Clinic and concerned new hours of duty. In the following month there were strikes of agricultural workers at settlers farms in the Molo and Elburgon areas.

It was in this situation when the trade unions in Kenya were submitting workers' demands with the threats of necessary action and when strikes were actually taking place in various parts of the country that Mr. Michael Blundell, the leader of the European Elected Members Organization, moved in his individual capacity a motion in the Legislative Council that a Committee be appointed to consider the conditions of African Workers, particularly in the urban areas. The motion was moved on the 20th February 1953, and was passed by 36 votes to 4. It was supported by the Government, by a majority of the European Members and by all the African, Asian and Arabs Members. Supporting the motion Mr. E.W. Mathu, the leader of the African Members Organization, said in the course of his speech.

"The motion is not too early, it is too late. I am surprised that some of the employers who have spoken appear to know nothing about the conditions in which African labourers live. Whatever is said the fact remains that a man has a stomach and a family and wages are not catching with costs. If we do not go ahead of the wishes of the workers and the workers go on strike, whether legally or illegally, it will cost the country more in settling these strikes than if we plan ahead and give them what is their due."

The Committee was later appointed and became known as the Carpenter Committee on African Wages from the name of its Chairman, Mr. F. W. Carpenter, then the Labour Commissioner of the Kenya. Later the main recommendation of the Committee was that African wages should be individual requirements as in the past.

By the time the motion on African wages was moved in the Legislative Council about 25,000 workers employed at the settlers farms in the Rift Valley Province had been compelled to leave their employment and move away from the province. The unrest and dissatisfaction among them were terrific.

The actions of the Mau Mau or Kenya Land and Freedom Army became more intensive. The influence of Mau Mau was spreading to people of other province and areas.

The Transport and Allied Workers Union was now pressing on its demands and had asked the Government for a Wages Order for improving the conditions of employment in the transport industry. The order was made a few months later. The struggles of other registered unions were also continuing.

In addition to the registered trade unions the staff unions and associations were also active. The Nairobi City council African staff Association under the leadership of its Secretary Tom Mboya and other officials was mobilizing the workers of the Council behind the Unions demands, which were for improved conditions of employment. The other staff association, which was becoming more active, was the African Railway staff union. It held a huge mass meeting of Railway workers on the 5th March 1953, in the Muthurwa location. The meeting empowered the Executive Committee of the staff union "to do everything necessary" to place the terms of service and salary grievances of the Railway African workers directly before the Civil services Salaries Commission. The meeting voiced its disapproval at the railway General Manager's intention to set up internal machinery to review salaries and conditions when a Commission had been appointed to deal with the question of Civil Services generally. A similar resolution had been adopted by a mass meeting of the Railway Asian Union. There was at that time co-operation between the two unions.

On the day the meeting of the Railway African Workers was held there took place an important function in the Desai Memorial Hall, Nairobi. In this function Mr. F.W. Odede, the Acting President of Kenya African Union installed Mr. D.N. Pritt, Q.C., in elder's status in honour and recognition of the services he had rendered to Kenya's national cause by very ably and courageously defending during the Kapenguria trial Mzee Jomo Kenyatta and other national leaders. The leaders of the Kenya Federation of Registered Trade Unions and other trade union leaders took a prominent part in the function.

Three days later, on Sunday, the 8th March 1953, in the Pumwani Memorial Hall, Nairobi, was held a huge mass meeting of more than 1,500 workers under the auspices of the Kenya Federation of Registered Trade unions under the chairmanship of Mushegi Karanja, the president of KFRTU. One of the resolutions adopted by the meeting was the following:

"While the federation is opposed to all unconstitutional methods of fighting for any rights it urges the Government to realize that workers in Kenya have got their legitimate demands:

(a) Freedom of speech, assembly, and movement of Trade union officials to any part of the country where there are union branches;

(b) Principles of equal work and equal pay and opportunities,

(c) Compulsory education for workers' children to enable them to take their place in community, etc."

The officials of the KFRTU urged the workers that they should support the Federation and the trade unions in the struggle for the workers' demands.

On the following day the colonial regime struck a blow aimed at weakening the forces of struggle. In the morning F.W. Odede, the Acting President of Kenya African Union was arrested under the Emergency Regulations and was sent for detention to a remote place in Kenya

There also began a period of mass arrests. On or about the 22nd March 1953, 2,345 Africans were held after a police swoop in the Pumwani area of Nairobi. In the following month, on or about the 16th April, 1,800 Railway African workers were screened, a check on taxi drivers was conducted by the authorities and there was again a police swoop on the villages in Nairobi and the Mathari Village was razed by bulldozers. There were swoops and in the Pumwani area of Nairobi. In the following month, on or about the 16th April, 1,800 Railway African workers were screened, a check on taxi drivers was conducted by the authorities and there was again a police swoop on the villages in Nairobi and the Mathari Village was razed by bulldozers. There were swoops and swoops by police all over the country. Most of those arrested and detained were members of trade unions.

On the 18th April 1953, four prominent trade union leaders were arrested along with 11 others who had also been active in the trade unions or in the national movement. The four were: Mushegi Karanja, the President of the Kenya Federation of Registered Trade Unions and Treasurer of the Night watchmen Clerks and Shopworkers Union; Nyamo Marea, the National General Secretary of the Transport and Allied Workers Union; Rufus Kinuthia, the General Secretary of the Domestic and Hotel Workers Union; and James Wainana, the National Treasurer of the Transport and Allied Workers union and Trustee of the Kenya Federation of Registered Trade Unions. All of them were the members of the KFRTU General Council.

Aggrey Minya, the General Secretary of the Kenya Federation of Registered trade Unions, had regularly been keeping informed the ICFTU and the British TUC of the Trade Union situation in Kenya so that if possible they should keep the world informed and so something to alleviate the situation in Kenya. On the 16th April 1953; Aggrey Minya as General Secretary of KFRTU had sent an "S.O.S." letter to Brother Oldenbrook, the General Secretary of ICFTU, requesting him to immediately send ICFTU representatives to visit Kenya and see the situation for themselves and then report to the international organization. He mentioned that there was censorship in Kenya and nothing much could be written. He had sent the S.O.S. under the directions of the General Council. In reply the General Secretary of ICFTU cabled Minya that efforts should be made to send them a detailed report of the trade union situation. Aggrey Minya sent the report to the ICFTU in a letter dated the 1st May 1953. After describing in detail which leaders of the trade union movement in Kenya had been arrested and restricted or detained before and since the beginning of the Emergency he wrote:

" .... And many thousands, members of the Trade Unions are now under the barbed wire languishing without food or water; many of them died. When we went to make a protest of their arrest we met the deputy Labour Commissioner. They told us that these people were arrested because (of) other activities of violence. The general Council (of KFRTU) did not agree to those accusations. It suggested to the Government it was trying to go around the back to kill trade unions in Kenya because the whole Government machinery is contracted by settlers, who have been from the very start of Trade Unions in our country, which was 1946 to 1953, opposed total (ly) to any growth of workers' organizations.

"Many thousands of workers have suffered untold suffering, many thousands have been killed (in) discriminately because of their colour. They have been robbed (of) any properties found in possession. Squatters have been repatriated and robbed of their property and many children have died and are starving. When they arrest you or kill you they must brand you as a member of the Mau Mau organization. We have been destroyed and the toll of death is day by day going on as Germany did in South West Africa during 1914 and 1918 with Oranbo people, etc., all educated and rich people have been killed.

"The local Labour Department, this department is a watchdog of the administration. It has employed a method to disorganize the trade unions. It has started staff councils and staff associating for each factory, which restricts a worker joining the trade unions....

"The Emergency laws have curtailed completely as follows:

(a) Any meeting of a trade Union; (b) No organization into whatever form can be allowed in all branches as is desirable.

"No any member of Kikuyu tribe who is an officer of Trade Union can be allowed to go 10 miles in Total. (No such) officer of the trade Unions can address a General Meeting.

"Collectors. These workers of Trade Unions are not allowed to collect the Union's monthly dues. Female collectors have been refused resident passes to reside in the city .... We are not independent as we should be. Trade Unions are state controlled............ Trade Union memberships have been instantly destroyed wherever they (were) found ...."

This was the situation and such were difficulties through which the trade union movement in Kenya was passing at that time. This was in May 1953.

In the subsequent period of seventeen years, the narration of the history of which I have now to leave due to lack of time, the trade union movement in Kenya was able to overcome its difficulties and problems and rapidly move forward. This it did with its unity, struggles, sacrifices, able leadership, and by fully mobilizing all its local resources and utilizing the aid of solidarity from the international and world trade union movement.

As a part of Kenya's national movement the trade union movement of Kenya played its full part in the struggle which led to Kenya's winning its complete independence on 12th December, 1963, and in the subsequent period of consolidating the independence, nation-building and working for the prosperity of Kenya's workers and people.

During this period there were many changes. On the 6th September 1953, Tom Mboya became the General Secretary of Kenya Federation of Registered Trade Unions. On the 8th May 1955, the name of the Federation was changed to Kenya Federation of Labour (KFL). Tom Mboya continued as General Secretary of KFL until May 1962, when he became Kenya's Minister for Labour. He was succeeded by Peter Kibusu, after whose resignation in 1963 Clement Lubembe became the general Secretary of KFL. In 1965, when for a short period there were in existence two registered central organizations of trade unions in Kenya – the Kenya Federation of Labour and Kenya African Workers Congress – the Government intervened and by the deliberations of a Commission, appointed by His Excellency Mzee Jomo Kenyatta, President of Kenya, the present Central Organization of Trade Unions (COTU) came into existence in the same year. Its first General Secretary was Clement Lubembe, who, in the first quarter of 1969, was succeeded by the Present General Secretary, Dennis Akumu. All the General Secretaries had able Presidents, Assistant Secretaries, Treasurers and other officials and members of General Council, Executive Committee and Governing Council, to assist them. On the whole they all worked as good teams. The result is that today COTU has 28 affiliated unions and there are two unions, which were recently disaffiliated from it by President's order. All of them are very strong workers' organizations with a total membership of about 300,000.

Kenya's trade union movement has made a great progress. It has achieved this progress with unity, struggle and sacrifices of has of workers and by acting as a part and parcel of the national movement. Since Uhuru it has continued in the spirit of unity, struggle and sacrifices and has fully co-operated with KANU and the Government under the able and wise leadership of President Kenyatta for achieving not only its own aims of protecting and advancing the interests of workers but also for implementing the programme of Sessional Paper No.10, the Programme of African Socialism.

The lesson from the history of Kenya's trade union movement is that workers of Kenya should go forward with unity.

APPENDIX II

Makhan Singh: A Communist Fighter for Workers' Rights

HAROON AHMED

It is difficult, if not well-nigh impossible, to come across a person who is totally free from colour prejudice and religious intolerance which bedevil not only the African continent but the entire world. Makhan Singh was such a man. To him colour prejudice was odious not only because whites were, and still are in some parts of Africa, dominating and exploiting the black masses – but because he was, at heart, a humanitarian and ardently advocated equality for all human beings whatever the pigmentation of their skin.

Religious intolerance was inconceivable to him for the simple reason that he was a confirmed Communist. Religion, according to Marxist dialectical materialism, is poison for the masses. How many raging bloody internec[l]ine wars were fought and still are raging in the Middle East, the Indian sub-continent and in the British Isles to name only a few in the hallowed name of religion? One may not so readily agree with Karl Marx in condemning religion so unceremoniously. But we are talking of Makhan Singh.

Makhan Singh was born a Sikh. He wore a turban. He nurtured a beard and looked like a Sikh. But these were mere accidents of birth and heredity. In his heart he was a steadfast humanitarian, and a staunch communist.

All efforts and coercions failed to make him otherwise. The then almighty British colonial powers tried, through protracted imprisonment and detention to cow him down and make him surrender his principles but he remained unyielding to the last.

On 5th June, 1950 the Governor-in-Council made out a Restriction Order against him and he remained restricted for about eleven and a half years at Lokitaung, Maralal and Dol Dol, until October 22nd, 1961, when he was released unconditionally. "During the restriction, pressures were brought upon him either to leave Kenya or change his attitude; Makhan Singh did neither." Makhan Singh wrote this about himself in the book *Struggle for Release of Jomo and His Colleagues*, published by New Kenya Publishers. The present humble tribute to Makhan Singh is based on my knowledge of him, obtained while we worked together.

We all, at some time, pity the poor and shed crocodile tears at their plight but do practically nothing to alleviate their sufferings. However, Makhan Singh's pity for the poor was not a mere passing commiseration and hollow sympathy devoid of concrete action. His sympathy was meaningful and practical. He worked during most of his life for the welfare of the labourers. Labour Trade Unionism was for almost his entire life his arena of activity.

He spent more time for this movement then for himself or his family. Naturally, with his preoccupation with Trade Unionism and politics, he had little time for 'money-making' which, alas is the main goal of the majority of the Asian community in East Africa. Makhan Singh, however, chose to live simply and stoically. His only income was what came his way in the family. He had no extravagant habits; naturally, being born a Sikh, he did not smoke, neither did he drink alcohol in any form. He wore simple clothes and never owned a car. How many times was he seen walking briskly to and from the General Post Office in Nairobi! He had no time for small talk or gossip. He ate simple food at home and was seldom seen lounging idly in public bars and hotels as many of the so-called 'leaders' in our midst do. This simplicity and austerity enabled him to engage in politics and labour movement without selfish motives or hankering after cheap publicity or ill-gained money.

Makhan Singh had no personal enemies. Friends he had many and they all had to be either connected directly with the labour movement or with the struggle for freedom. He hated British imperialism, but not the British. He abhorred capitalism, but had no trace of venom against capitalist individuals. He despised the system of exploitation and not the human cogs that formed the wheels of juggernaut or oppression.

In his reedy, high-pitched voice he used to condemn colonialism and exploitation of the masses whenever and wherever he found the opportunity. He spoke with gusto and exuberance, but in his writings he was quite logical, succinct and explicit. Few may remember his speeches, but his writings, particularly his two books on 'The History of the Labour Movement in Kenya' will remain a lasting memorial to this life-long fighter for freedom, equality and socialism.

In his heart there smouldered an inextinguishable flame of desire to fight for freedom from imperialist subjugation. But freedom from foreign domination was not enough for him. He struggled all throughout his life for equality of opportunity for everyone – the black, brown and white, for the peasant, worker and the poorest of the poor.

He was not one to wallow in the glory of self-righteousness and past performances. He did not hanker after luxury or high positions. He was not the one to stagnate in inertia of authority or wealth.

The ambition, the idealism to strive to improve the conditions of the working class kept on burning incessantly in him till it finally consumed his frail body into cinders – the cinders that will keep on glowing in the heart of many a man devoted to the cause of uplifting the exploited majority and giving equal opportunity to the ones who are under-privileged.

It is not often in these times of utter selfishness, self-aggrandisement and get-rich-quick mentality that one comes across a man of Makhan Singh's unselfish devotion to the cause he espoused so dearly. But there is always a ray of hope in the midst of enshrouding clouds of exploitation, corruption and covetousness for the light of true economic, social and political equality to shine. It might take time. In the meanwhile, time marches on and let us all march with Makhan Singh's words in mind: "Now, forward, to build up a strong democratic African socialist Kenya, East Africa and ultimately Africa."

KARIM HUDANI

Makhan Singh was truly an unknown legend.

That he suffered the most in British colonial prisons as a trade unionist fighting for the rights of the African workers and for Kenya's freedom as a whole is the most unpublished unpublicity of Kenya's otherwise glorious fight for freedom.

When he died two years ago, I was at his funeral. So were many other once prominent Indian Congress and the Kenya Freedom Party Leaders. There was Mr. Fred Kubai and a few African trade unionists.

The funeral scene was overwhelmingly pathetic. And yet there was a tense atmosphere in the air. Kenya's historical monument was being laid to the ashes in a typical Sikh funeral ceremony with the monotonous chanting of the religious rites. There was natural sympathy for Makhan Singh from the majority of the Asians who had gathered around. These were the very same Asians whose business interests had isolated Makhan Singh, more or less as a black sheep of Africans and Asians.

Needless to add, Asians are rather good at showing natural sympathy at a weekend funeral when shops are closed and when they have nothing to lose in their dukas, it can be stated without much fear of contradiction that the African population at large for whom Makhan Singh virtually lived and died did even worse.

There were hardly any messages of even condolences from leaders of this country. The death of Makhan Singh signified dramatically the frightfully lowered status of the Asian in this country – even for a Makhan Singh.

Of course, Makhan Singh was not the type of person who could seek self-pity. He was a man among men and for this reason alone, he was a pain in the neck of the British. Why did he fight the British so hard and suffered so much?

It is not easy to make generalization of ulterior motives for an Indian Sikh gentleman fighting for Black Africans. Probably more than anybody else, Makhan Singh personified that selfless spirit of service to humanity at large that only Asians – and Indians in particular – are capable of endowing and imparting to mankind. If only an effort is made that Africans would have a different outlook when they chastise wholesale the international tendencies of traders as particularly that of a *muhindi* type of East African origin.

Before Makhan Singh came to Africa, he had what the British called a record in India. A confirmed communist, he suffered imprisonment in India fighting the British. Makhan Singh was that romantic freedom fighter and he simply loved doing his thing – that of being a rebel – and that of being in the news. But while it is a great deal of fun and excitement being a freedom fighter, particularly against the British colonialists who I must say left their imperial positions not because the British Army was militarily defeated but because they were shamed out as colonizers, Makhan Singh was not up against the tyranny of a Latin American Dictatorship financed by the infamous CIA. There he would have been killed in no time. But fighting the British was a different piece of cake.

I don't particularly single out as unique the British sense of justice and their tolerance of prisoners. But political prisoners in British jails during the fight against the British Raj enjoyed a higher standard of living and had good medical care. So if going to political prisons was a tireless process of getting bored reading only the Bible and the British Sunday Papers, it was also not particularly a hazardous risk.

If honesty and integrity don't necessarily make good politicians, the British colonialists paved an easy way for many ambitious politicians by imprisoning them and turning them into instant freedom fighters – almost martyrs.

This is not true, of course, of many statesmen like Nehru and Gandhi. But is it also true of Makhan Singh? If it is not true of Makhan Singh, were other African freedom fighters any different?

Now that Makhan Singh is dead, an honest appraisal of his work is not particularly difficult to make. But lack of information from himself personally is the main reason why posterity will ponder aimlessly about his career as a political activist.

When Makhan Singh was released from the jail, he made no effort to assert himself as a national leader which he then surely was. Instead, he wasted his time squabbling in petty trade unionism at branch levels. What I have failed to grasp is: why did Makhan Singh – the giant killer and the father of trade union movement in Kenya – go in for such small petty political power?

There can only be two answers: ONE: being an Asian, he might have felt an outsider on the then raging political struggle for freedom. KANU / KADU political battle fronts. TWO: he must have thought, trade unionism was the best outlet for his political activities.

If this is true, then his almost ten years in jails and all the glory and newspaper articles about him will present to future historians of Kenya an enigma of unprecedented proportions. Why did Makhan Singh chicken out when he was in the position to make an impact because his sincerity in his advocacy of legitimate African inspirations was never in any doubt – even now.

DUNCAN MUGO
Secretary General of the Domestic and Hotel Workers Union

Mr Makhan Singh has been a practical socialist and had no racial discrimination since he had been believing in human equality.

Kenya has not only lost a true trade unionist, but also a political and trade unionism historian.

He is going to be remembered by many people since he was one of the founders of the trade union movement in Kenya and who had not feared the colonialists during the struggle for UHURU.

CLEMENT LUBEMBE
General Secretary of the Printing and Kindred Trades Workers Union

My union has learned with extreme shock of the death of brother Makhan Singh, who was one of the pioneers of the labour movement in this country (Kenya). The foundation that he laid for the trade union movement will always be remembered.

Kenya Game Hunting and Safari Workers Union
Described comrade Makhan Singh as " a heroic freedom fighter".

JAMES KAREBE
General Secretary of the Kenya Local Government Workers Union

Late Makhan Singh was a great son and a pioneer to the trade union movement.

I have learnt of his death with sorrow, and on behalf of my union I send my heartfelt condolences to his family and relatives. I would like here to mention that he and Chege Kibachia started the trade union movement in this country.

He recalled that Makhan Singh had suffered detention for his activities in the trade union movement and struggled for independence. By then, he said, Makhan Singh was the only outstanding non-African figure who could speak against exploitation of workers, hence the colonial government imprisoned him without trial.

I am deeply shocked to hear of this death. Kenya has lost a staunch trade unionist and his activities in his country (Kenya) will not be forgotten for many years to come.

FRED OMIDO
Chairman of the Central Organisation of Trade Unions

He described Makhan Singh as the "one who gallantly marched with the African masses in the freedom struggle and the labour movement"

He said: "those who have had the opportunity of reading his book will conclude that the man was a genius in his time. He faced the British colonialists with unbelievable courage.......He believed in the ultimate victory of the African masses"

J D KALI
Trade Unionist

In this brief account I want to say a few things about the late Makhan Singh.

I knew him around 1950's when he was busy with trade unionism in Nairobi with Fred Kubai. What moved me most about his man was his courage and fearless way of doing and saying what he wanted. I remember at one public meeting he confessed that he was a communist.

To say such a thing during those colonial days was not an easy thing. I also remember another occasion when he and Fred Kubai were the first people to mention the word "Uhuru".

Before that time our slogans were, equality, abolition of all forms of discrimination and more representation in Legislative council. From then on the demand for Uhuru grew, and spread.

Mr Singh identified himself with wananchi and consequently suffered with and for them. He spent eleven years in detention without trials in the arid areas of Northern Kenya. Together with the late Pio Gama Pinto they had assisted the young and up-coming Trade Unionists in Kenya.

Makhan Singh was more interested in workers welfare than anything else. Though a self-confessed communist, wananchi at that time did not care at all about communism. In fact we had no idea as to what communism was. All that we knew was that we had an enemy to fight and whoever helped us in that fight was regarded as one of us.

I even remember about two whites – British – who were with us in our advisory committee during 1950-52. with all his eleven years in suffering in colonialist detention Makhan Singh was not lucky enough to enjoy the fruits of Uhuru. He died a poor man, but with his chin up. I am sure that when the history of our country is being written brother Makhan Singh will have a space somewhere.

Sunday Post 19/5/73, early edition
TRIBUTES TO THE LATE MAKHAN SINGH

MR BILDAD KAGGIA

"The death of Makhan Singh is a great loss to Kenya. He was the first non-African who sided with Africans during the struggle for independence while other non-Africans were away from it because they believed Africans could not gain the upper hand in the struggle. His role was more pronounced in the trade union movement. I remember him because he was the first non-African to train Africans in the trade union movement. Without him, there could be no trade union movements in Kenya . . . It is a great pity that we have lost him and his role in Kenya's struggle for equal rights and for independence will be remembered for many years to come." Mr. Kaggia recalled that he first met the late Singh in 1947 when he was president of the East African Trade Union Movement until he was detained in 1950 when Mr. Kaggia took over from him to lead the movement.

J DENCER-BROWN
Nairobi

Since the authorities have thought it necessary to change the name of Gurdwara Road (a completely non-colonial title meaning "temple" and referring to the large Sikh Temple and Hindu Temple which comprise the major proportion of the buildings on that road), would it not be fitting to name one of our new streets after the late Makhan Singh?

Makhan Singh spent 11 years of his life in detention with our beloved President Kenyatta for no other crime than trying to fight the colonial authorities for better working conditions for the wananchi. Or, are the peoples of other races who fought in the struggle for Uhuru alongside the wananchi to be forgotten?

%

Sunday Post Harambee May 20, 1973
PIONEER TRADE UNIONIST DIES

Editorial by
N A R A I N   S I N G H

A PIONEER of the Trade Union movement in Kenya, Makhan Singh, is no more.

The inevitable end to all mortal beings has brought to an untimely conclusion a saga of courage and vision; exceptional foresight and sincere feelings for the dignity of the working man; long suffering and separations.

Makhan Singh's life was dedicated to the service of the people of Kenya at a period and in a way when such efforts were faced with suppression by force and firmness by the colonial rulers. Makhan Singh remained consistently undaunted. He persisted in the cause he believed to be just. He never expected and he never received any material reward. He earned what very few people of a non-indigenous race have ever earned and that was the sincere respect and the lasting admiration of the masses of Kenyans.

This was demonstrated by a very tragic incident.

His mother died when he had been in detention in the North-Eastern District of Kenya for many years. A large crowd of Africans gathered at his house in Park Road in openly expressed grief.

Her last wish, that she be allowed to see her beloved son, was refused by the Government even though several leading personalities gave their assurances that no untoward incident would take place if he was permitted to come to Nairobi for a short while for such a purpose. Such was his hold on the African mind that the authorities could not overcome their fear. His mother passed away without seeing him.

Makhan Singh was a totally self-effacing man and a man who had the courage of his beliefs.

In 1969 he wrote the first part of the history of the Trade Union Movement (to 1952). In it he set out in great detail the opposition, the trials and the determination by the then rulers to prevent working people from organizing themselves for the purpose of their collective betterment. Makhan Singh provided the main inspiration, his was the driving force, his was most of the thinking, the planning and the working.

But right through the volume he has taken no credit for himself. He has been more than generous in acknowledging the contribution of his colleagues and others.

For 11 long years, from 1950 to 1961, when Kenya reached the threshold of freedom, he was in detention. The "charge" against him was that he was "a communist", "an agitator" and so on. He was certainly a danger to the colonial system of administration which was always based on the policy of "divide and rule".

He brought the Asian and African workers together. He made them think alike. He made them forget the colour of their skins; their distinctions of caste and race. They were all sufferers from racial discrimination and economic policy resting on low wages.

His patent honesty and the force of his personality carried conviction right through. During the visit of H. R. H. the Duke of Gloucester to grant Nairobi the city charter, he organized a successful strike. Other strikes and demonstrations had taken place before and have taken place since.

As General Secretary of the Labour Trade Union of East Africa, Makhan Singh wrote a letter to Mr. Jomo Kenyatta in London requesting him to represent Kenya at the Brussels Conference of the World Committee against War and Fascism.

Mr. Kenyatta wrote back to him accepting the request and said "I am very glad to be in touch with you and offer my cordial good wishes for the success of your work".

When he returned from detention in 1961 he was welcomed by Mzee Kenyatta and many other African leaders and thousands of his fellow countrymen.

Makhan Singh was only 59 years old. Educated in India and Kenya he worked for a while in his father's, (Mr. Sudh Singh), printing press. When he returned after a stay in India in 1947 he was arrested and ordered to be deported as an undesirable immigrant. He won his appeal to stay here because he was a permanent resident of Kenya and could not be sent to another country.

He was hardly 18 years old when he started taking an interest in the problems of workers. When his book on the history of the trade union movement in Kenya came out in 1959, I told him it was a pity he had stopped at 1952, the year in which the emergency was declared. He assured me he had every intention of writing a second volume.

Shortly before his death he had sent his manuscript for printing. I hope the publishers, East African Publishing House, will hasten its advent in the market.

Makhan Singh is survived by his wife and three children. The elder son Hindpal Singh, is a senior engineer with East African Power and Lighting Co. His daughter has taken up a teaching career in the University of Toronto after doing her Ph. D. The younger son, Swarajpal Singh, is employed by the Kenya Breweries as a senior draftsman.

To them all, and to all the other relatives and friends of the late Makhan Singh, I and the *Sunday Post* extend our heartfelt condolences. Kenya has lost an outstanding personality.

Sunday Post June 3, 1973
OBITUARY

RASIK SHAH

. . . . He believed in an ideal of equality for all men but instead of bandying about such abstract clichés, he quietly set about taking practical action towards reducing the existing inequalities among people.

(Left India after it got independence) – He was indeed a lost man when he did not have a cause to fight for.

In his published work : There is not a trace of self-consciousness in the writing of events in which the author played such a major role. Reference to himself are in the third person and there is no attempt to highlight his own contribution – the book is objective to the point of complete self effacement.

He was not a man, however whom anyone could know intimately. All his life he maintained an exterior of total control, a man steady in his beliefs and consistent in action. He never revealed his private feelings – not even to members of his own family. One gets the impression that here was a man animated by some inner spring of action of such strength, that he did not need counsel or comfort from 'friends'.

All his life the man owned nothing – at all, no business, no car, no property – all that on principle – a man who married conviction with action and remained uncorrupted in a world which tends to turn hostile to so much integrity!

If Makhan Singh was a communist, his was not the communism of subversion and party line, but a pristine communism such as that preached by Jesus Christ.

HON. MR. JUSTICE C MADAN, Q.C.

The late Makhan Singh and I grew up together in school. We were pupils in the same class and we completed our secondary education in the Government Indian High school, now Jamhuri School, Ngara Road, Nairobi in the year 1931. In those days we both passed Matriculation examination of University of London. Appropriately enough the street facing the entrance to Jamhuri school has been renamed by the city council as Makhan Singh Road, no doubt to preserve the memory of his name as a tribute to services rendered by him to the peoples of Kenya.

I remember distinctly that while we were in school Makhan Singh had a magic brain and he used to leave most of his class mates behind in the subject of maths - arithmetic, geometry, algebra.

After school hours Makhan Singh used to help in his father's Punjabi printing press and I worked in my father's grocery shop which was run from a wood and iron building in the Bazaar, now Biashara Street. The building has been replaced by the edifice known as India House in Muindi Mbingu Street (old Stewart Street). We used to live as a family in tight and inadequate accommodation at the back of our not too long large duka. My sleeping quarters were a bed improvised every evening among gunny bags of rice and superfine wheat flower imported from India, sugar, maize meal, beans and matoke imported from Uganda, which my father used to sell in his shop. Our school hours were 8.15am to 12.30pm. My lot improved later, I shared the kitchen with a motherless Muslim boy who was more or less adopted and brought up by my mother.

Makhan Singh was exiled out of Nairobi into a remote part of Kenya by the Colonial Government. The non-European elected members of Legislative Council kept up the pressure on the Government for their release. The following is an example of debate which used to take place (Hansard 1st May to 9th July, 1957, Vol.LXX11, Part 11, 166):

The late Mr. Tom Mboya, then African elected member for Nairobi area, asked the Minister for Internal Security and Defense (Mr Cusack) to state the number of persons detained under detention orders issued under Emergency Regulation No 2. Mr Cusack replied that the number of persons detained under orders issued under Emergency Regulations Number 2 was 26181 on 30th April, 1957.

Mr Mboya: Will the Minister state the racial breakdown of detainees?

Mr Cusack: There is one Asian, all the rest are Africans.

Mr Madan: Mr Speaker, Sir, arising out of that reply...

The Speaker: (Sir Ferdinand Cavendish-Bentinck): You cannot ask supplementary questions on replies to supplementary questions, you can only ask supplementaries on the original reply.

Mr Madan: Arising out of all the replies, Sir, would the Hon. Minister consider release of the Asian as the odd man out.

Mr Cusack: No

Mr Harris: The odd man in.

Mr Mboya: Arising out of the reply, Sir, would the Minister tell us, in the case of the Asian detainee, whether it is true that when his father was seriously sick, he or his family asked that he should be allowed to visit his father who was apparently a civil servant in this Government for over 20 years, and that permission was refused.

The Speaker: I cannot allow that, it is going too much into detail. If you wish a reply to that last question, I am sure the Minister will give you a reply in writing.

Sir Charles Markham: Hear, hear Mr. Speaker, arising out of the original reply is it not true that the one Asian detained was also a trade union leader?

Mr Cusack: No, Sir.

The Speaker: We will pass on to the next order.

The Indian elected members and the African elected members had the force of alienable rights and undeniable facts on their side but we were too few to topple the government benches which were packed with civil servants and nominated members whose survival as members of Legislative Council depended upon voting for the Government without thinking. On such subjects the European elected members also voted government.

I came to be appointed Asian minister without portfolio under the Lyttleton constitution, my appellation being purely racial like the derivative of my two counterparts, European and African ministers without portfolio. Makhan Singh's father believed I could perform a miracle and obtain his son's release from detention. How to achieve this end. I decided to adopt an artifice to cajole the Chief Secretary of the day for the release of Makhan Singh. I wrote to him saying among many other things that I believed Makhan Singh was probably misguided. I sent a copy of my supplication on his behalf to Makhan Singh. He promptly wrote back to the chief secretary that I was entirely wrong. He was polite enough not to say that I was the one who was misguided.

Both Makhan Singh and his father have died. Makhan Singh was steadfast and staunch. His father was a loving parent. Makhan Singh has left behind memories of individual sacrifice for a principle which others may well emulate.

APPENDIX III

The following list of press cuttings, articles, books and handwritten collection of papers is extracted from Makhan Singh's own archives to give the reader a sense of his extremely wide reading and his range of interests.

The press cuttings were mainly from the *Kenya Weekly News*, *Colonial Times* and *East African Standard* 1930-1950. Subjects included:

▣ *Kenya Weekly News*
   ✳ Edward Rodwell's articles
   ✳ Safaris along the Nile
   ✳ Thousand years of history
   ✳ The Story of the Masai, Sirikwa, Wanderobo, Zulu Chiefs, the
     Northern Frontier nomads, the Rendille, Turkana, Samburu, Gabra.
   ✳ Background to Mau Mau
   ✳ The Capricorn Contract

▣ *Colonial Times*
   ✳ A brief history of Kenya's Legislative Council

▣ *East African Standard*
   ✳ Mau Mau and the Kikuyu by LSB Leakey
   ✳ Agriculture and Commerce
   ✳ History of the Kenya African Rifles
   ✳ The Slave Trade
   ✳ Miscellaneous items on Congo, Somaliland, Uganda

▣ Published articles on:
   ✳ Indian Immigration
   ✳ Kenya's Land Problems
   ✳ Nakuru – Asians, Municipal Council elections
   ✳ E A High Commission, E A in General
   ✳ West Africa and Nkrumah
   ✳ Tanganyika
   ✳ Uganda
   ✳ Central Africa
   ✳ Slave trade in East Africa
   ✳ Kenya Land Commission reports on Kikuyu, Masai , Ukamba provinces
   ✳ Kenya government structure

* International Declaration of Human Rights
* Legco of Northern Rhodesia
* Peoples and Policies of South Africa
* African Development
* Land Aspects of Labour Problems in Kenya – ILO report
* Notes on Kenyan history – 600 BC to 1950
* List of Orders-in-Council, Ordinances, etc.
* History of British Trade Unionism

Books:
Makhan Singh borrowed books mainly from the Desai Memorial Library and the British Council. From the books which were of special interest to him, he wrote lengthy and detailed summaries and this he did since his arrival in Kenya in 1927 as a 14-year old student. Some of the books (listed as per his notes) were:

* *Eastern Africa Today* by F S Johnson
* *Race and Politics in Kenya* – Correspondence between Elspeth Huxley and Margery Perham
* *The African - Today and Tomorrow* by D Westermann
* *A Last Chance in Kenya* by Norman Leys
* *A Cuckoo in Kenya* by W R Foran
* *The East African Problem* by J W Driberg
* *African Afterthoughts* by Sir Philip Mitchell
* *African Political Systems* by Fortes & Pritchard
* *African Discovery* by M Perham and J Simmons
* *Permanent Way* by M F Hill
* *Slavery and Slave Labour* by Adam Smith
* *The First Rise of Modern Industry* by J L Hammond
* *Zambesi Journal* of James Stewart
* *Black & White in East Africa* by R C Thurnwald
* *Africa Morning* by R O Hennings
* *Demographic Survey* of the British Colonial Empire, Vol III by R R Kuczynski
* *Native Administration* in the British African Territories by Lord Hailey
* *My Tanganyika Service* by Sir Donald Cameron
* *African Survey* by Lord Hailey (lengthy extracts)

Trade Union writings:
Makhan Singh's handwritten notes:

* Manuscript for the book on *History of the Trade Union Movement in Kenya*
* Annual reports of Kenya Native Affairs Department 1923-30 and 1931-1938 including the Independent Schools and a section on Labour for each year
* Notes on 1939 Mombasa Labour Inquiry Committee – Evidence submitted
* Copied from COTU archives:
  File numbers 1965, 1966
  Recorded in 1970 and 1971, notes from December 1961- December 1962, January 1963-December 1964, including:
  KFL correspondence, incoming and outgoing
  Meeting and conference resolutions, matters discussed, reports, minutes,

press releases, programmes, statements and schedules
Trade union seminar reports and articles 1961-1970
Trade union related Legco proceedings and *East African Standard* press
cuttings 1940-1950 (Large and detailed collection)

▨ COTU print-outs 1966-1971

▨ Papers presented by Makhan Singh at the Annual Conference of the Historical
Association of Kenya:
  * East African Association - The National Organisation of Kenya Africans in the
    Early Twenties - August 26-29, 1969, Nairobi
  * Problems in Writing the History of Kenya's National Movement - August
    25-28, 1970
  * East African Trades Union Congress – The First Central Organisation of Trade
    Unions in Kenya - August 24-27, 1971

▨ Marxist theory.
Makhan Singh appears to have attended regular study classes during his work
with *Jang-I-Azadi* in India in early 1940s. Each of his handwritten notebooks dealt with
a specific subject:
  * Imperialism, 139 pages
  * Capital, 161 pages
  * Exploitation, in Punjabi
  * Psychology, 187 pages
  * Importance of Theory, in Punjabi
  * Outline of Political Economy, 188 pages

▨ Miscellaneous handwritten notes included:
  * Essays on evolution, science, chemistry, atomic energy and astronomy
  * Two notebooks of poems in Punjabi, written in Kenya, each of approximately
    87 pages
  * Accounts and minutes of the Social Service League 1969-70. Makhan
    Singh's name, however, did not appear on the membership list
  * 1950-56 correspondence with Patwa News Agency, *East African Standard*, British
    Council, Desai Memorial Hall, *Kenya Weekly News*, CMS Bookshop, *Colonial
    Times* Ltd, *Baraza*. He ordered books and papers and paid subscriptions.

INDEX

280, 281, 287-8, 300, 317-8, 324, 339,
451, 463, 473, 490, 495
Daily Nation 312, 349, 376, 383, 385-6,
392, 394-5, 399, 413, 416, 420, 425,
430, 440, 447-8, 459, 482-3
Daily Worker 167, 442
Daly & Figgis 68
Damerell R A J 435
Das Ganesh 8
Das Sheth Govind 76
Dass, Isher 27, 40, 54, 94
Dass, Mangal 40, 60
David Elijah Odhiambo 339
Daulat Singh 57
Dave 142
Delhi 48, 126, 163-4, 406, 440
Deman M J 154
Dencer-Brown J 482
Desai Indu 143, 225
Desai Memorial Hall 45, 81, 87-9, 135,
144, 209, 215, 242, 295, 338
Desai, Manilal 21-2, 27, 40, 44, 495
Devinder Singh 37, 97
Devonshire Declaration 26-7, 495
Dhanji Dr A N 478
Dhanwant Singh 54
Dhillon Dr S S 322
Didi Sheila 453
Dilbagh Singh & Bros 105
Din, Mehraj 22
Din Taj 154
Durrani Shiraz 488-9
Dutt Palme R 185, 230, 443
Dwivedi, Keshavlal 8
Dyer, General 9-10

◁ E ▷

East African Association 22, 26
East Africa Common Services
Organisation 431, 455
East African Indian National Congress 8,
22, 27, 44, 54, 59, 64-5, 69, 76-83, 86-7,
89-90, 112, 122, 126-7, 133, 135-6, 141,
144-7, 152, 155-62, 165-6, 193, 200-7,
222, 225-6, 228, 311, 318, 348, 426,
436, 495, 497
East African Standard 59, 66, 126-7, 131,
133, 146, 166, 204, 209-10, 234, 254,

261, 292, 322, 348, 376, 412, 421, 445,
448, 454, 458-9, 460, 467
East African Trade Union Congress 76,
110, 204, 207-13, 215, 217-22, 224-5,
232, 236-7, 240-6, 248, 251, 265, 271-3,
280, 291, 332-4, 336, 436, 489
East India Company 2
East African Students Federation 134,
139, 147, 203
Egypt 24, 198
Electors Union 203, 337
English 31, 34, 48, 53, 60, 77, 85, 88, 93,
96, 137, 139, 140, 178, 225, 278-9, 283,
288-9, 290, 305, 323, 336, 338, 414,
435, 450, 465
Errol, Earl of 97
Erskine D Q 322

◁ F ▷

Federation of Progressive Trade Unions,
Zanzibar 350
Federation of Revolutionary Trade
Unions, Zanzibar 442
Finnegan C 281

◁ G ▷

Gahir G S 137, 146
Galeni Gichuri 248
Gallacher W 127, 131, 167, 228, 444
Gandhi Mahatma 3, 8, 10, 36, 46, 54, 93,
96, 105, 141, 147, 148, 159, 213, 214,
220, 383, 443, 444
Garghajj Arjan Singh 378
Gathani Bachulal 146, 152, 206
Gathangu Isaac 329
Gathithi H W 178
Gatuga Daniel 465
Gautama K 396, 458
Gautama M D 77
Gautama R C 136, 152, 155, 206
Gautama S C 318, 322
Gavaghan Terence 303
Germany 7, 25, 54, 63, 77, 86-7, 267, 416-
7, 422
Gertzel Cherry 471
Ghadr 7, 37-9, 42, 95-7, 174
Ghadrites 7-8, 10, 27, 34, 36-8, 40, 42, 52,

◄ N ►

Shastri, Lal Bahadur 461
Shastri, Srinivas 21
Sheikhpura 38
Sheth Dr A U 156
Sheth Nanalal 139, 203
Sheth Pranlal 139142-3, 209, 248, 286,
   333, 343, 345, 467-8, 495
Shivcharan Singh 98
Shri Sanatan Dharma 85
Sikhs 3, 4, 5, 6, 9, 16, 17, 20, 27, 32, 48, 52,
   65, 68, 82, 84, 113, 155, 156, 174, 202,
   348, 377, 478
Sikh Students Federation 392
Simon J J 333
Singapore 7, 299, 392
Siri Gurdwara Bazaar 50, 67-8, 174
Siri Guru Singh Sabha 34, 37, 39, 69, 136,
   463
Sisburn T 469
Skinnard M P 175
Slade Hon Humphrey 385, 444
Smedley, Agnes 8
Smuts Jan 149, 197
Social Service League 51, 156, 448
Somerhough A G 187, 237, 258, 267,
   270, 272
Sohan Singh 45-6, 98
Sohan W L 111
Sousa de A C L 54, 64, 80
South African Communist Party 143
South African Trades and Labour
Council 82
Southall 350
Souza de Fitz 289, 298, 322, 340, 345, 349,
   382, 385, 396, 422-3, 427, 432, 452,
   458, 469, 471, 473, 478, 490, 497
Soviet Union 2, 242, 247, 395, 441
Stalin Joseph 65, 95, 446
Stanley H M 208
Stevens and Kindall 7
Stuart Will 128
Suba Singh 37-8
Sudh Singh Jabbal 17-28, 30, 32-4, 46, 51,
   53, 24, 56-7, 110-12, 118, 138-9, 230,
   236-7, 277, 280, 283, 287-9, 293, 298,
   300, 301, 304-5, 308, 311, 315, 322,
   324, 329, 348, 375, 376, 413, 440, 446-
   7, 458, 463, 476, 477
Sunday Nation 318, 443, 447

Sunday Post 399, 464, 482-3
Suri, Charanjit 55
Sutantra, Teja Singh 8, 10, 40, 52, 69
Swami Dayanand 52-3
Swarajpal Singh Jabbal 163, 274, 287,
   289, 301, 308-9, 324, 329, 479, 486
Swaran Singh 377

◄ T ►

Tagore, Rabindranath 10
Taifa Leo 383, 389, 402, 425, 431
Tandon R K 444
Tarlochan Singh 287
Tarlok Singh 84
Tewson Sir Vincent 313
Thacker, Samuel Ransley Q C 119, 187,
   190-1, 237, 242-3, 245, 248, 252-4, 257,
   259, 265, 280, 292-3, 489
Thakore S T 137
Thion'go wa Ngugi 489
Thuku, Harry 22, 26-7, 383-4, 388, 489
Thuku Mrs 383
Tibet 315
Tilak Lokmanya 3
Toure Sekou 416
Toynbee, Arnold 4
Travadi K D 314, 316
Tribune 167, 292

◄ U ►

Udham Singh 10
Uganda Railway 7, 20-1, 24, 37, 88, 426
Ujagar Singh 21, 38, 96, 176, 215
Unions, trade: African Workers 119;
   Asian Postal (Kenya) 380; Clerks and
   Commercial Workers 212; Coast
   General Workers 411; Dockworkers
   339, 414; Domestic and Hotel
   Workers 217, 240, 335, 339, 408, 434,
   480; E A Building and Construction
   Workers 339; E A Federation of
   Building and Construction Workers
   339, 493; E A Painters 177; E A
   Painters and Decorators 217, 240; E
   A Railways and Harbours Asian
   (Kenya) 380; E A Standard Asian
   Staff 182; Kenya Diplomatic

Employees 454; Kenya Distributive and Commercial Workers 339, 431, 454; Kenya Electrical Trade Workers 412; Kenya Game Hunting and Safari Workers 481; Kenya Government Office Workers 177; Indian Trade 57, 59, 489; Kenya Local Government Workers 339, 481; Kenya Petroleum and Oil Workers 447; Kenya Shoe and Leather Workers 308; Kenya Uganda Railway Asiatic 81; Mill Kamdar, Ahmedabad 239; Muslim Labour 81; National Union of Civil Liberties 127; Plantation and Agricultural Workers 334, 406; Press Workers 60, 81, 421 Printing and Kindred Trades Workers 379, 408, 413-7, 481, 420-1; Railway Artisans 21, 38; Railway African 339, 413-4; Railway African Staff 208; Ramgharia Artisans 67-8; Ramgharia Labour 67-8, 81; Shoemaker Workmen's 240; Shopworkers 177; Stone and Masons Quarry Workers 177; Tailors and Garment Workers 182, 207, 250, 339; Tailors and Textile Workers 411; Tent and Sailmakers 339; Transport and Allied Workers 179, 182, 207, 211, 220, 240, 243, 248, 250, 259, 333, 339, 374-5; Typographical 207, 240, 273, 339, 379, 420
Urdu 34, 46, 60, 63
USA 7, 25, 40, 42, 213, 252, 340, 431

◄ V ►

Vaid S P 403
Varma, B S 21, 78
Vasey Sir Ernest 497
Vasudev Singh 38, 42, 54, 67, 80, 95, 174
Venezuela 409
Verjee, H S 54
Vidyarthi G L 139-40, 295
Vincent Sir Alfred 149, 197, 199
Virdi Mohinder 324, 330
Visram, Allidina 25, 181
VOK 462-6, 471

◄ W ►

Wachira Vicky 344
Wahid, Abdul 34
Wainright R 306
Wanzala J J 465-6
Waryam Singh Gharjakhia 84
Waryamu Singh 37
Watchendu, Bishen 40
Whitehouse Leslie E 278, 293
Willan H C 91
Woddis Jack 442-3
Wokabi V 325
Workers Federation of British East Africa 57
Workers Protective Society of Kenya 58
World Federation of Trade Unions 205, 210, 220, 224, 251, 336
World Trade Union Conference 118
World War I 21, 54

◄ Y ►

Yugoslavia 416
Yugantar 443

◄ Z ►

Zanzibar 24, 37, 40, 78, 87, 323, 350, 441-3

Lightning Source UK Ltd.
Milton Keynes UK
UKOW01f0725101017

310726UK00009B/257/P

9 789966 712301